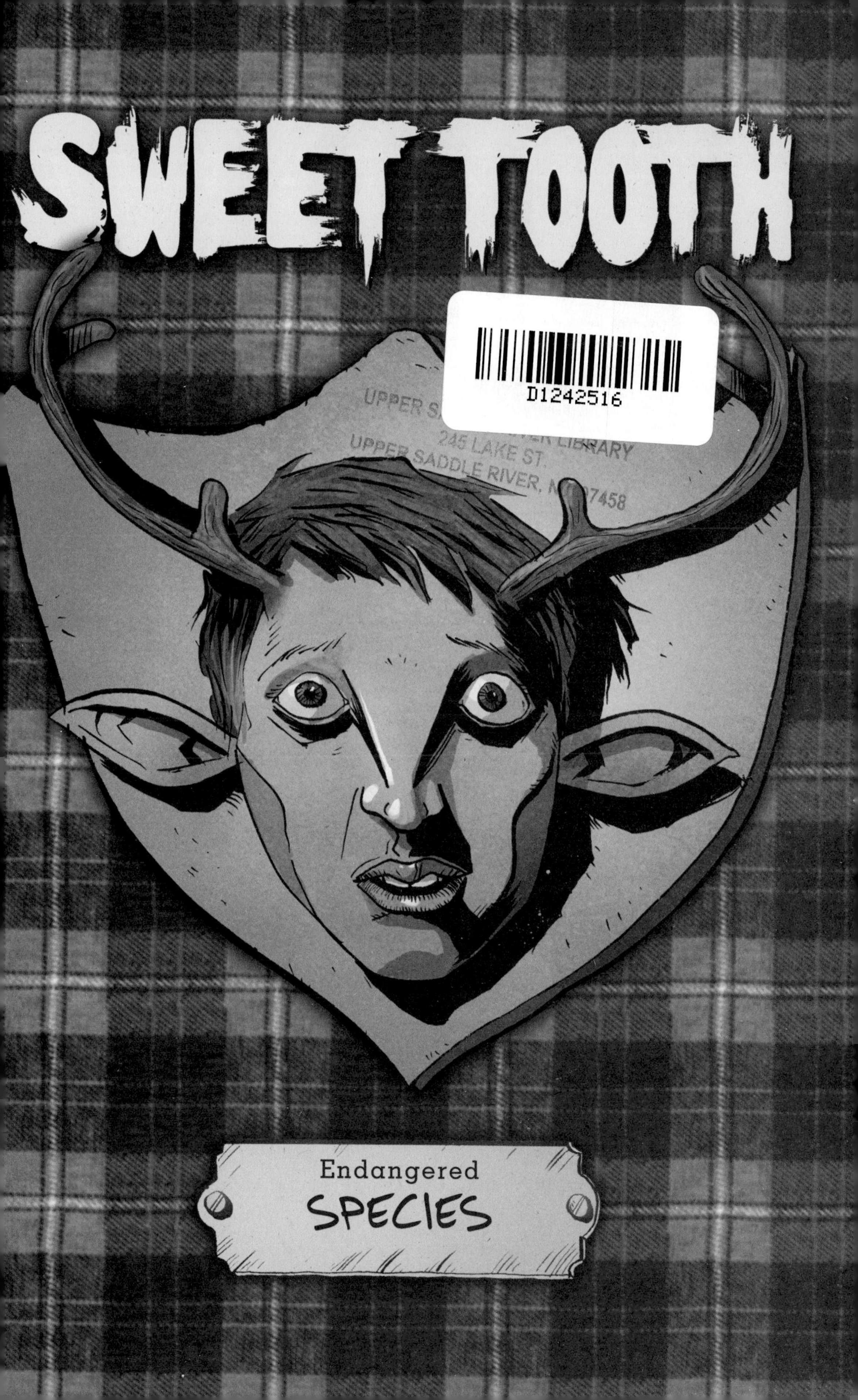
SWEET TOOTH
Endangered
SPECIES

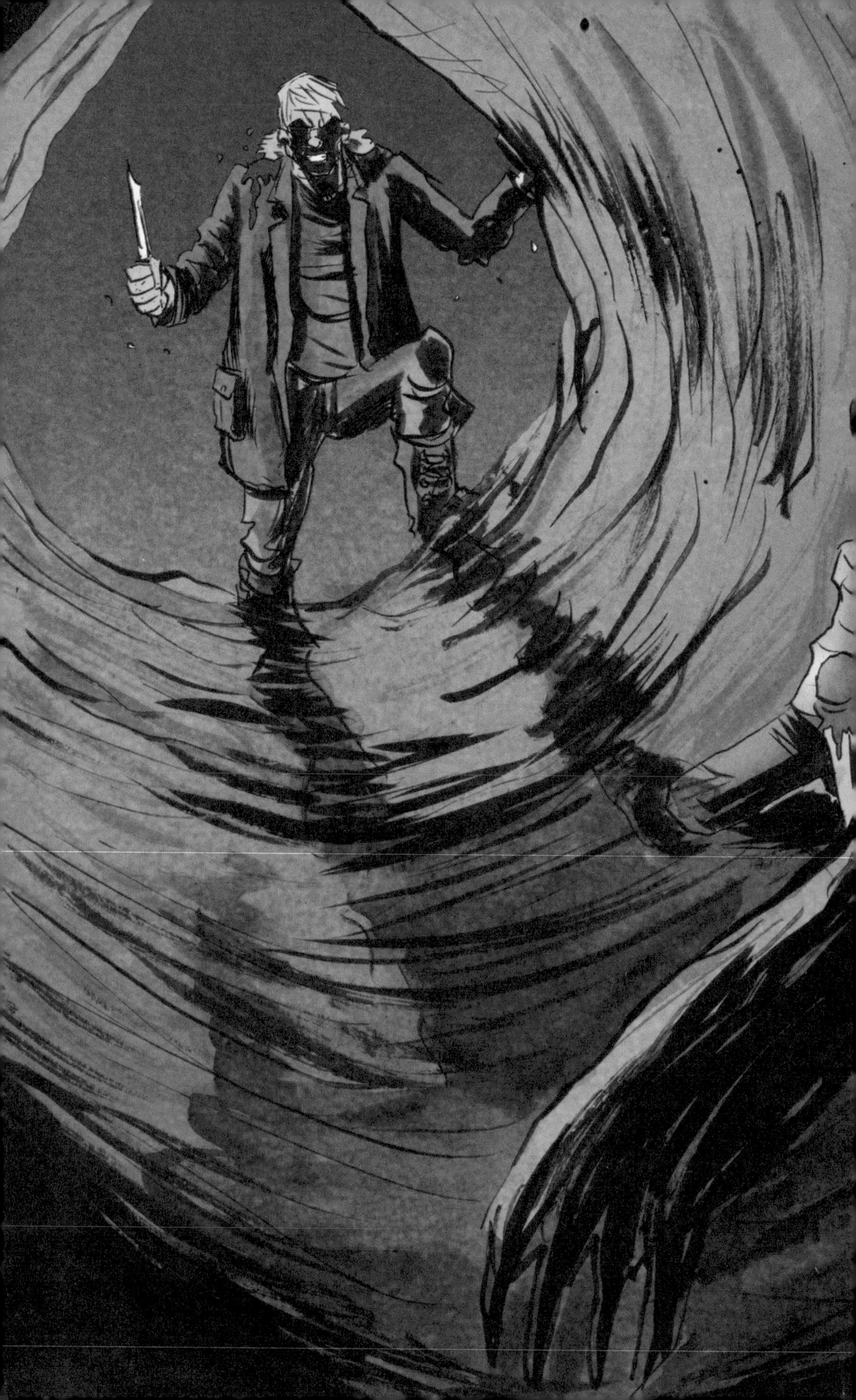

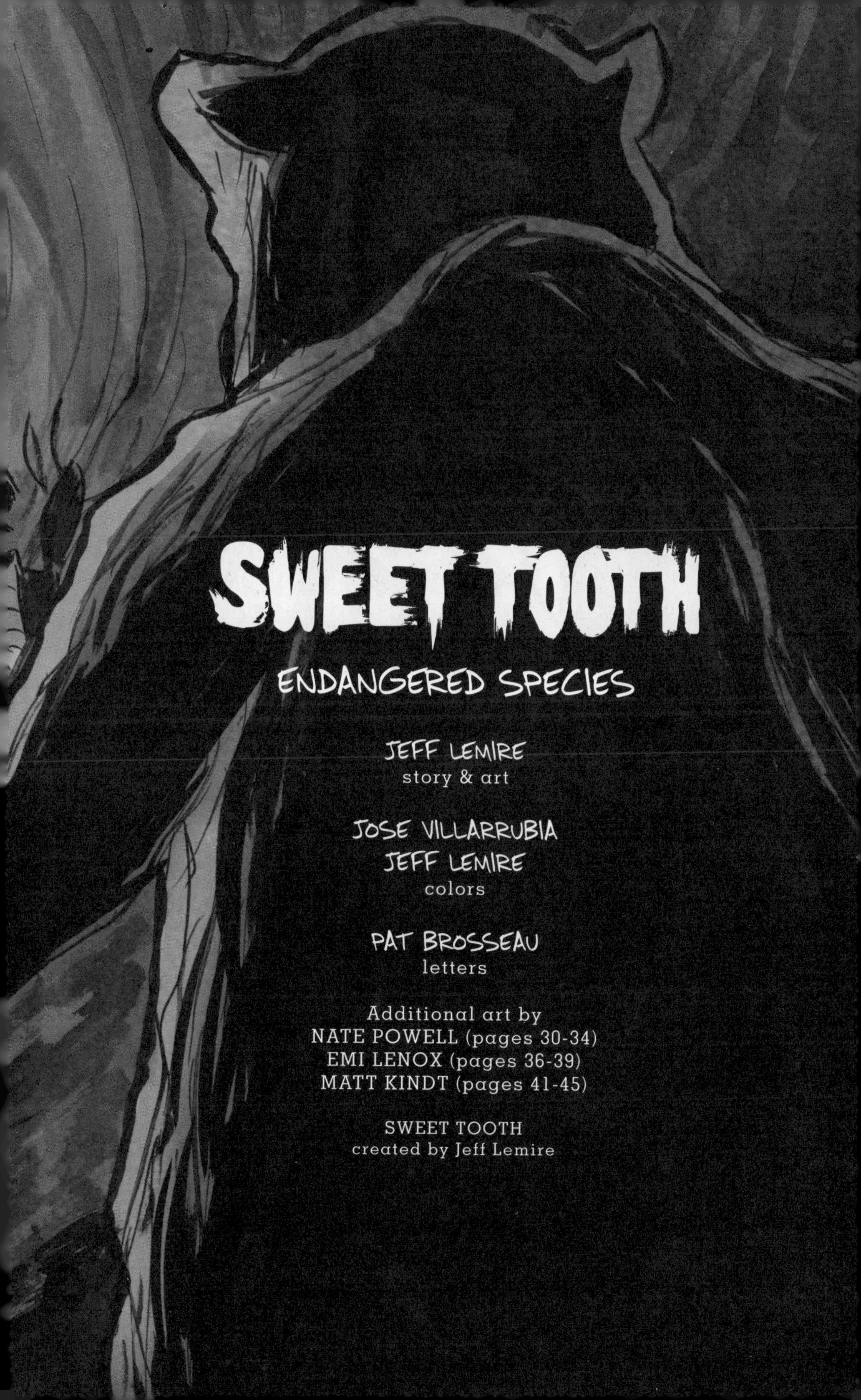

SWEET TOOTH

ENDANGERED SPECIES

JEFF LEMIRE
story & art

JOSE VILLARRUBIA
JEFF LEMIRE
colors

PAT BROSSEAU
letters

Additional art by
NATE POWELL (pages 30-34)
EMI LENOX (pages 36-39)
MATT KINDT (pages 41-45)

SWEET TOOTH
created by Jeff Lemire

MARK DOYLE PORNSAK PICHETSHOTE Editors – Original Series IAN SATTLER – Director Editorial, Special Projects and Archival Editions
ROBBIN BROSTERMAN Design Director – Books ROBBIE BIEDERMAN Publication Design

KAREN BERGER Senior VP – Executive Editor, Vertigo BOB HARRAS VP – Editor-in-Chief

DIANE NELSON President DAN DIDIO and JIM LEE Co-Publishers GEOFF JOHNS Chief Creative Officer
JOHN ROOD Executive VP – Sales, Marketing and Business Development AMY GENKINS Senior VP – Business and Legal Affairs
NAIRI GARDINER Senior VP – Finance JEFF BOISON VP – Publishing Operations MARK CHIARELLO VP – Art Direction and Design
JOHN CUNNINGHAM VP – Marketing TERRI CUNNINGHAM VP – Talent Relations and Services ALISON GILL Senior VP – Manufacturing and Operations
DAVID HYDE VP – Publicity HANK KANALZ Senior VP – Digital JAY KOGAN VP – Business and Legal Affairs, Publishing
JACK MAHAN VP – Business Affairs, Talent NICK NAPOLITANO VP – Manufacturing Administration
SUE POHJA VP – Book Sales COURTNEY SIMMONS Senior VP – Publicity BOB WAYNE Senior VP – Sales

PREVIOUSLY

A decade ago a horrible disease raged across the world killing billions. Afterwards, it spawned a new breed of human/animal hybrid children...the only children born since the plague.

GUS is one such hybrid. A young boy with a sweet soul, a sweeter tooth — and the features of a deer. After his father died and Gus finally left the seclusion of his forest home, Gus hooked up with a hulking and violent drifter named JEPPERD. But Jepperd betrayed Gus, selling him to the vicious Militia in exchange for the remains of his dead wife LOUISE.

In captivity Gus met other hybrid children including the sweet pig-girl named WENDY, the lovable ground-hog boy named BOBBY and the perpetually silent BUDDY. While Gus found solace with these children, the militia leaders—a brutal man named ABBOT and a misguided doctor named SINGH—examined Gus, eventually determining that Gus was born before the plague hit, making him the first of the hybrid children.

After burying his wife on their farm, a guilt-plagued Jepperd returned to the militia camp and rescued Gus and his friends, with the help of LUCY and BECKY, two women he previously saved from a prostitution ring, and Abbot's kinder brother JOHNNY. While escaping, the group was forced to abandon Buddy to a vicious pack of hybrid dog-boys and learned too late that the boy they left behind was actually Jepperd's son.

Once again believing his son to be dead, Jepperd and his companions set out toward Alaska, hoping to uncover Gus's history and with it the source of the plague...

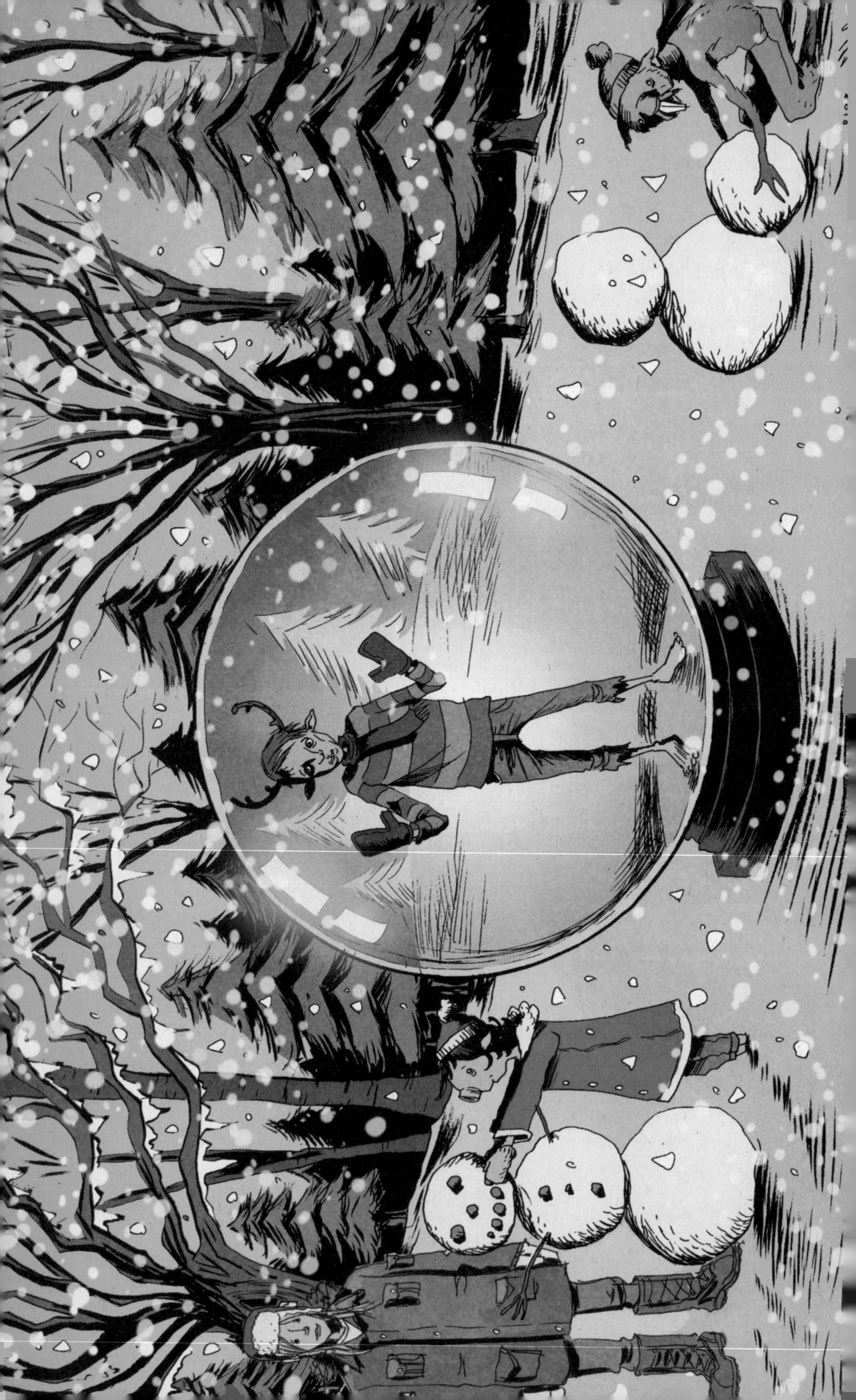

THE FURTHER ADVENTURES OF THE BOY AND THE BIG MAN

They had left the militia camp and the cages behind, and The Big Man and The Boy were together again.

"But things were different now," thought The Boy, "Everything has changed. We may be travelin' together, but we ain't one."

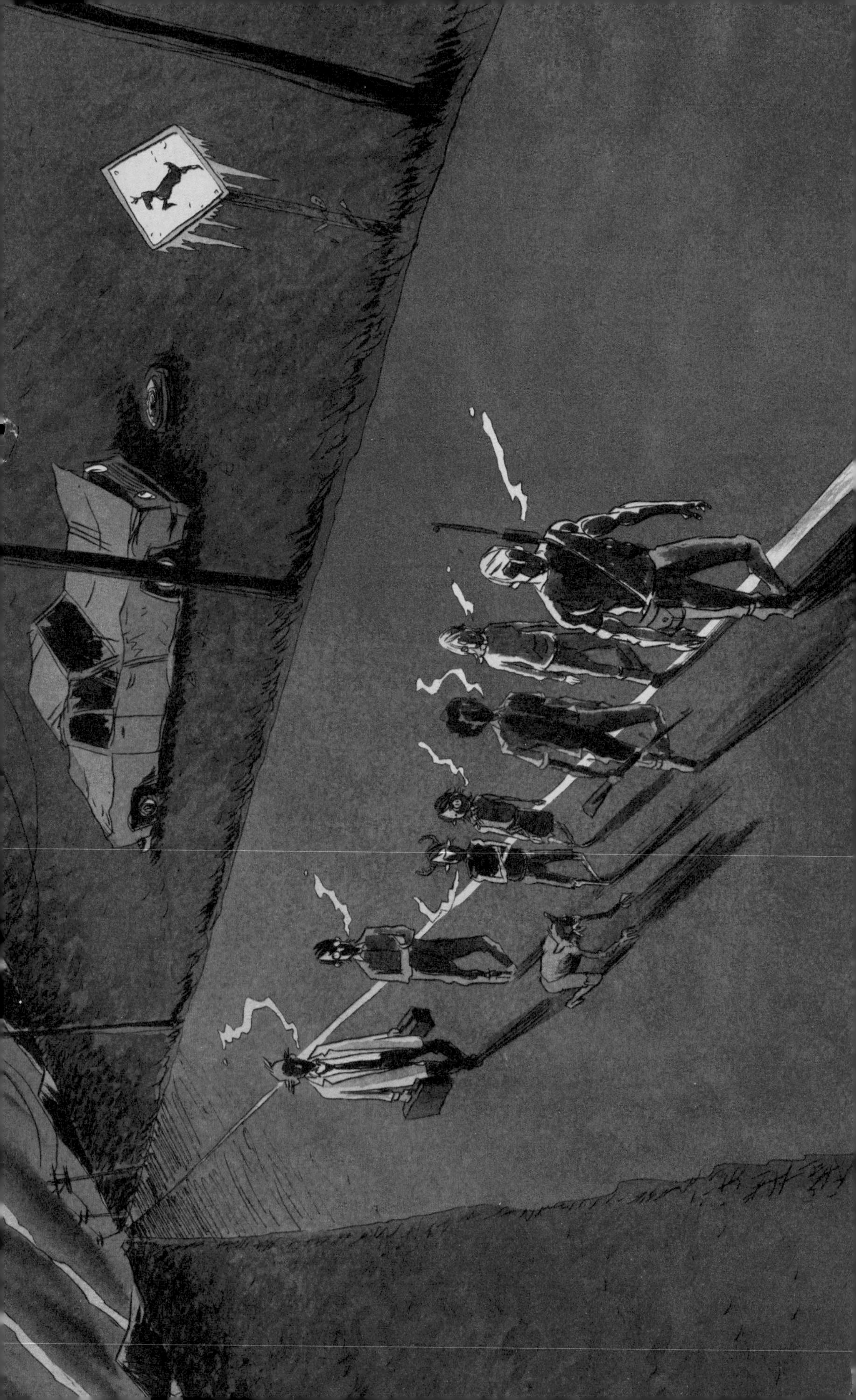

The last time The Boy had seen The Big Man he had betrayed him. He'd promised to take him to The Preserve, where little animal kids like him would be safe, but he had lied and left The Boy with the Bad Men.

Afterwards, The Boy would lie awake in his cage at night thinking about how much he hated The Big Man. But then he met other animal kids like himself. Wendy, Bobby and Buddy. They all became best friends.

Then The Big Man found The Nice Lady and The Pretty Girl, and together they had come back to save The Boy. But then something real bad happened. The Big Man found out that one of the other little animal kids, Buddy, was really his son. Then The Dog-Boys killed Buddy.

This hurt The Big Man worse than anything ever had. Hurt him so much that he wouldn't even speak or cry about it. Then The Boy realized that The Big Man had always been hurt about this. Even before he met The Boy, he must've known about Buddy deep down inside.

And The Boy figured that was why he had betrayed him in the first place. He was just trying to make the hurt stop. This confused The Boy more than ever. He didn't know if he still hated The Big Man or not. Either way, he wasn't ready to talk to him. Not yet, anyway.

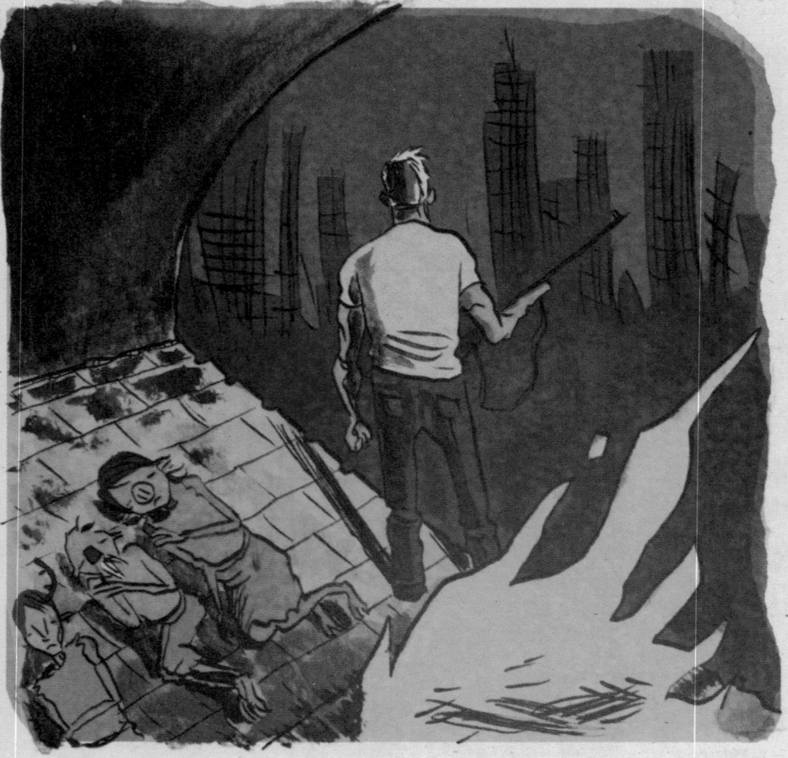

So The Boy never looked at The Big Man, and The Big Man never looked at The Boy, and they all just kept walking north. It had started to get real cold too. The Nice Lady told them they were heading to a place called Alaska, and that it would get even colder.

She said they'd have to find warmer clothes and supplies. She and The Big Man argued, but finally he agreed, and they went into the outskirts of The City. It was real dangerous, and they had to camp under bridges, and The Big Man never slept. He just stayed up all night keeping watch.

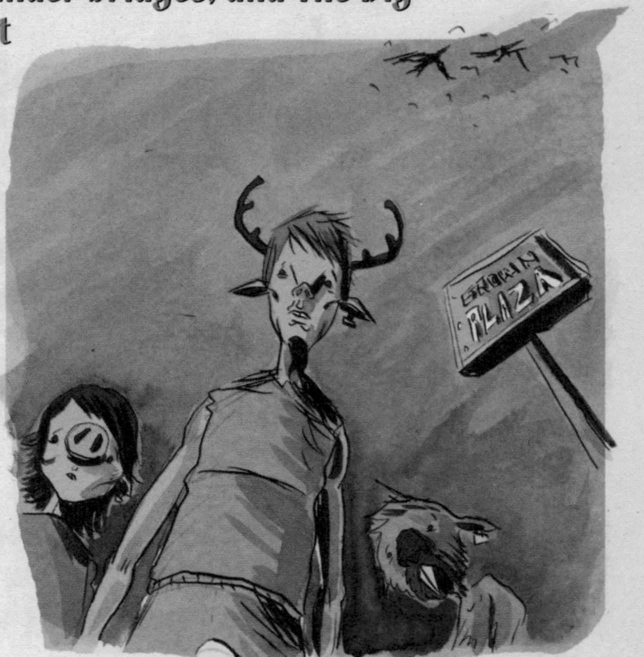
PLAZA

Finally on the third day they found the place they had been looking for. A place called "The Mall."

The Pretty Girl explained to the Boy and his friends that The Mall was a building where "you could buy anything you needed." The Boy and his friends were excited to see what was inside.

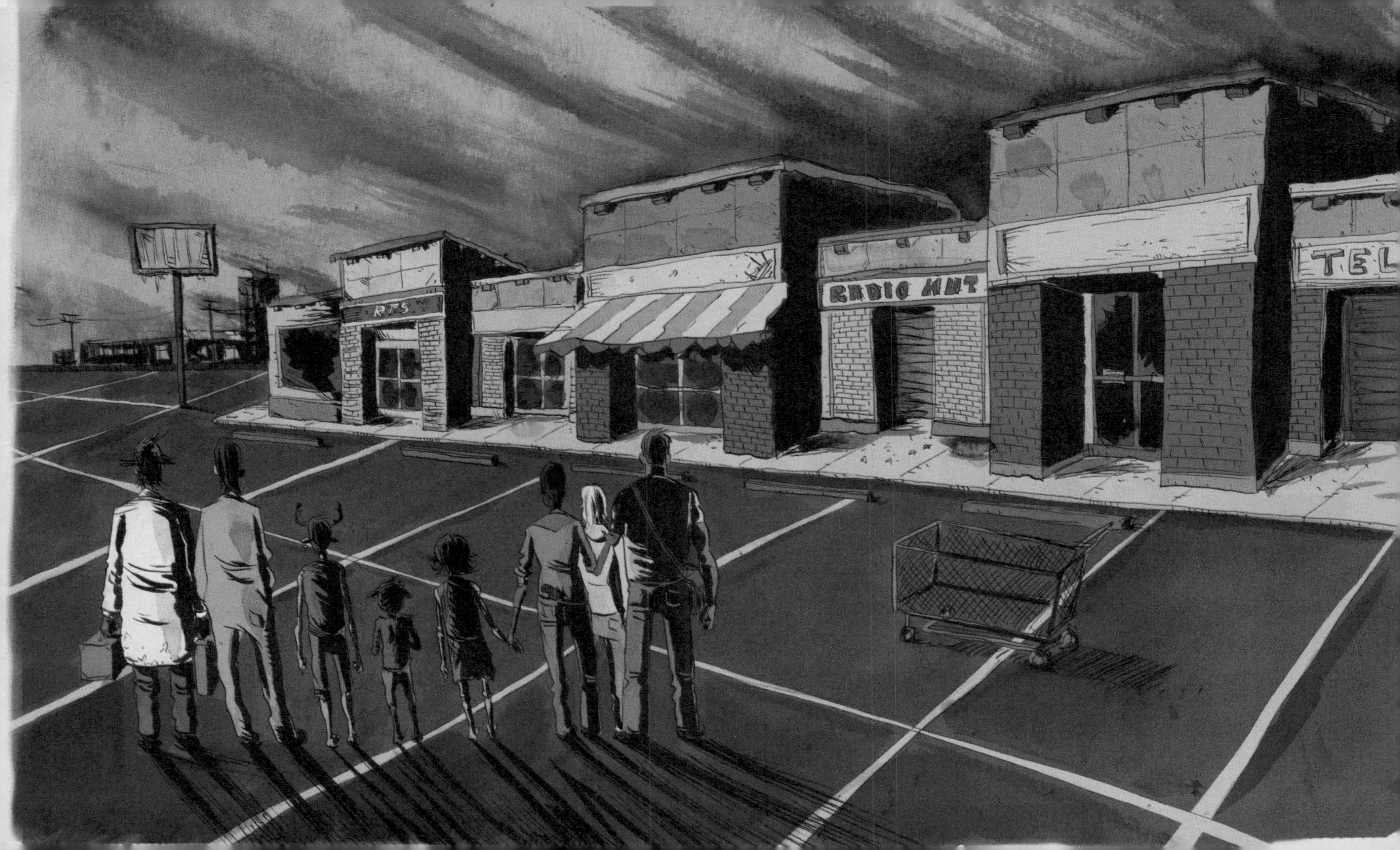
RTS
RADIO HUT
TEL

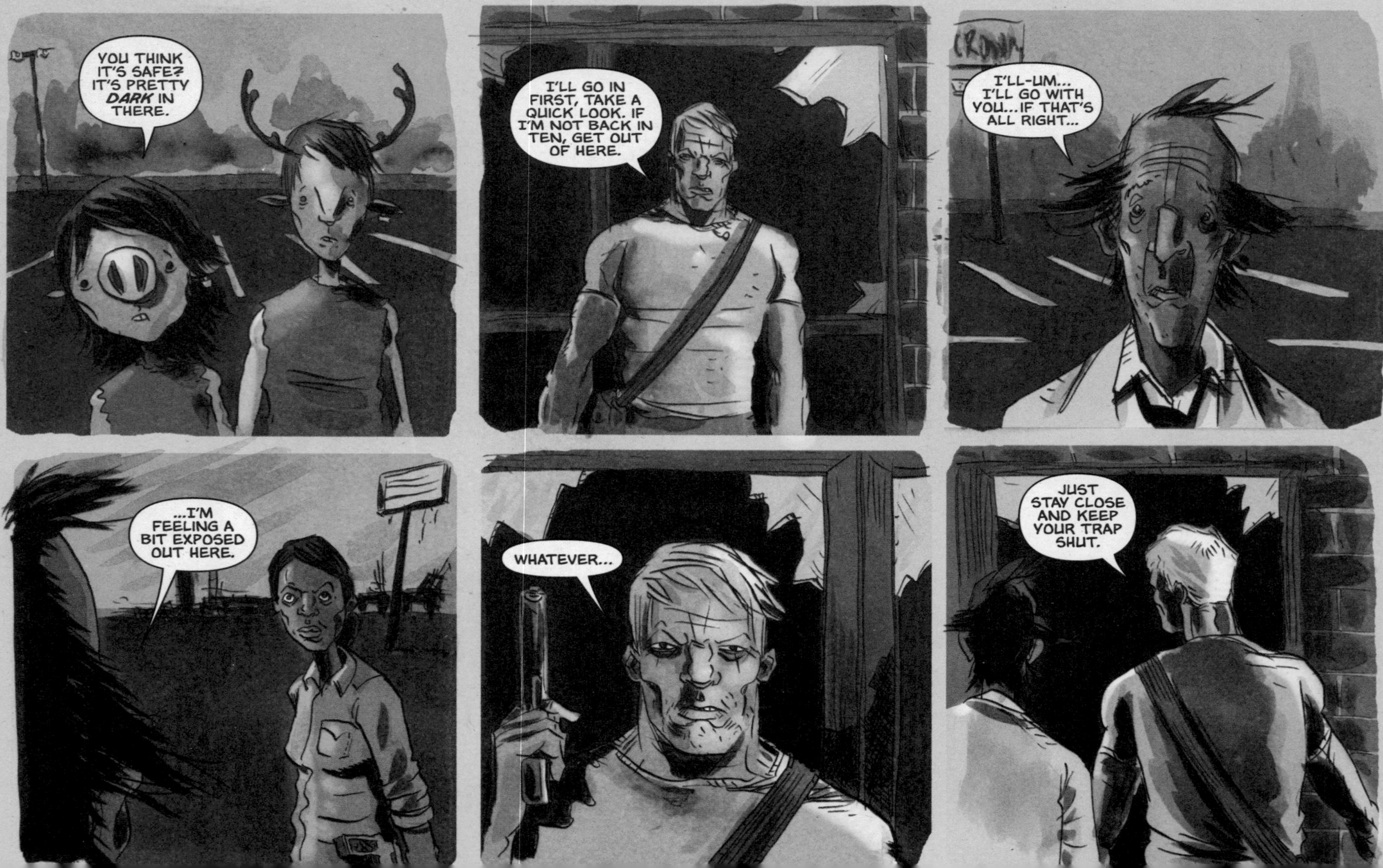
YOU THINK IT'S SAFE? IT'S PRETTY *DARK* IN THERE.
I'LL GO IN FIRST, TAKE A QUICK LOOK. IF I'M NOT BACK IN TEN, GET OUT OF HERE.
I'LL-UM... I'LL GO WITH YOU...IF THAT'S ALL RIGHT...
...I'M FEELING A BIT EXPOSED OUT HERE.
WHATEVER...
JUST STAY CLOSE AND KEEP YOUR TRAP SHUT.

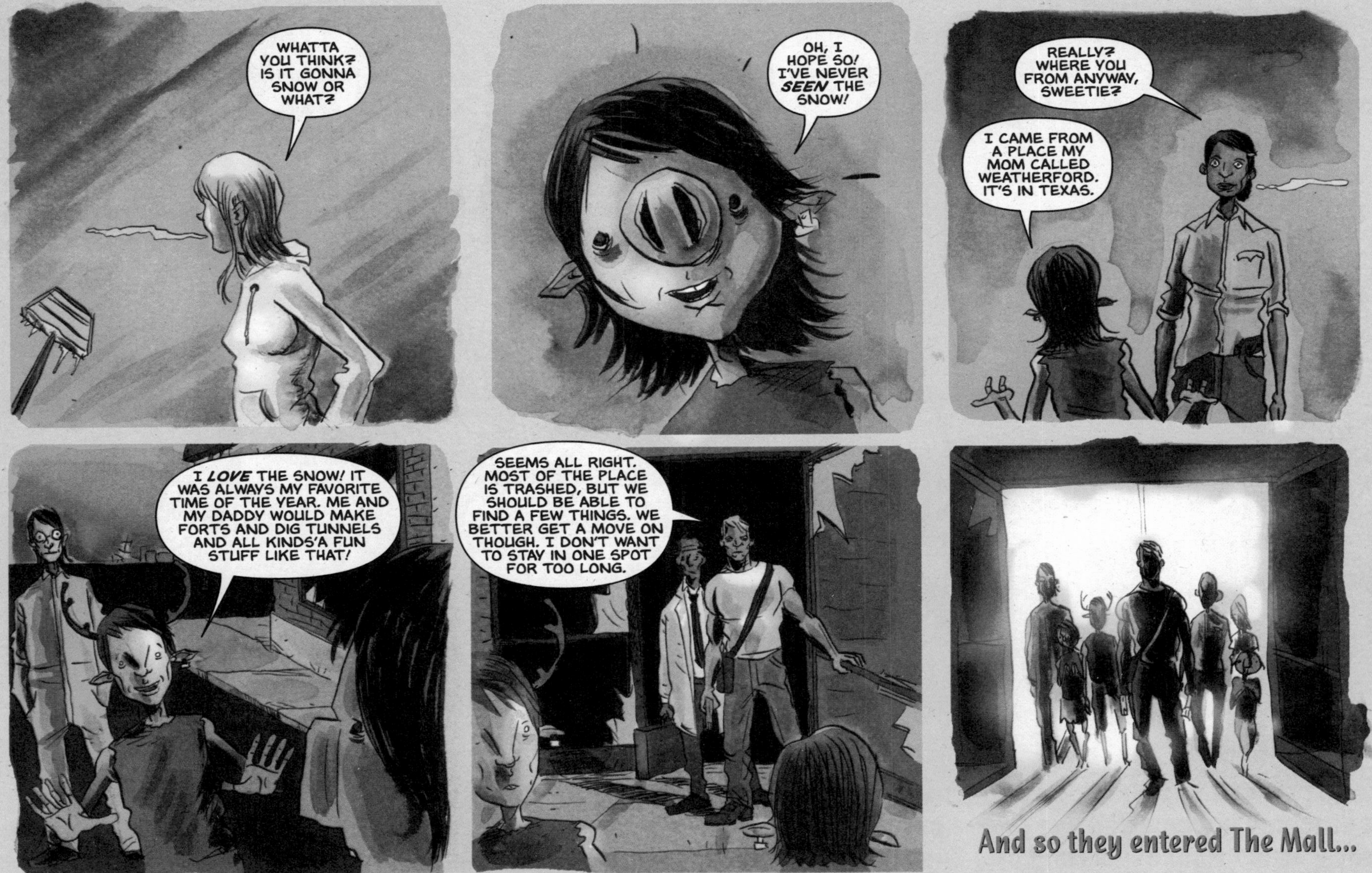
WHATTA YOU THINK? IS IT GONNA SNOW OR WHAT?
OH, I HOPE SO! I'VE NEVER *SEEN* THE SNOW!
REALLY? WHERE YOU FROM ANYWAY, SWEETIE?
I CAME FROM A PLACE MY MOM CALLED WEATHERFORD. IT'S IN TEXAS.
I *LOVE* THE SNOW! IT WAS ALWAYS MY FAVORITE TIME OF THE YEAR. ME AND MY DADDY WOULD MAKE FORTS AND DIG TUNNELS AND ALL KINDS'A FUN STUFF LIKE THAT!
SEEMS ALL RIGHT. MOST OF THE PLACE IS TRASHED, BUT WE SHOULD BE ABLE TO FIND A FEW THINGS. WE BETTER GET A MOVE ON THOUGH. I DON'T WANT TO STAY IN ONE SPOT FOR TOO LONG.
And so they entered The Mall...

It turned out to be just another big building full of junk. The Boy didn't like going into places like this, 'cause it just reminded him of all the people who had once been alive but now were dead. And even if The Boy's Daddy had been right, even if all the people had been sinners and had died 'cause God had wanted them to, The Boy still felt sad for them.

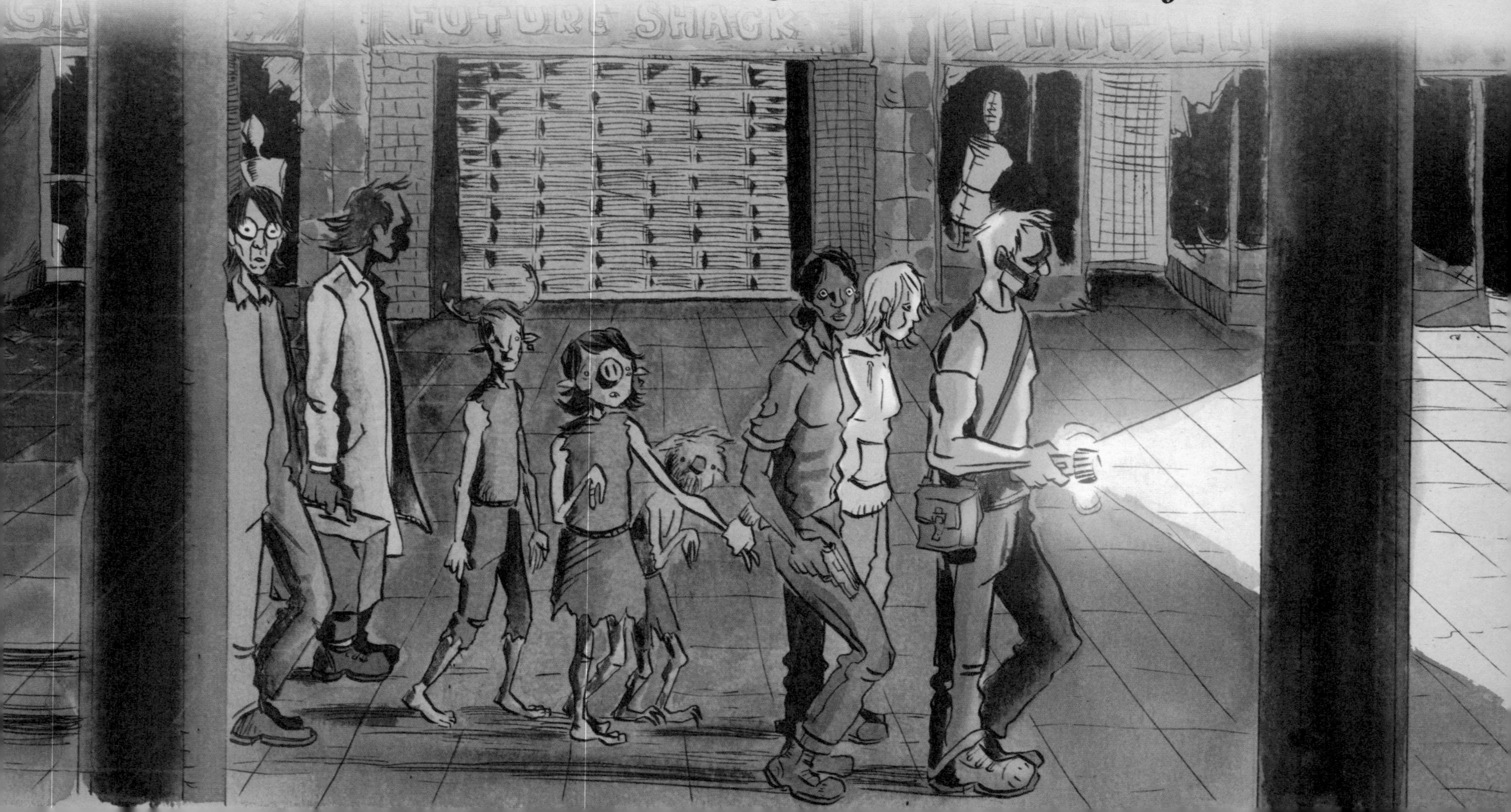

FUTURE SHACK

But soon they found what they were looking for...

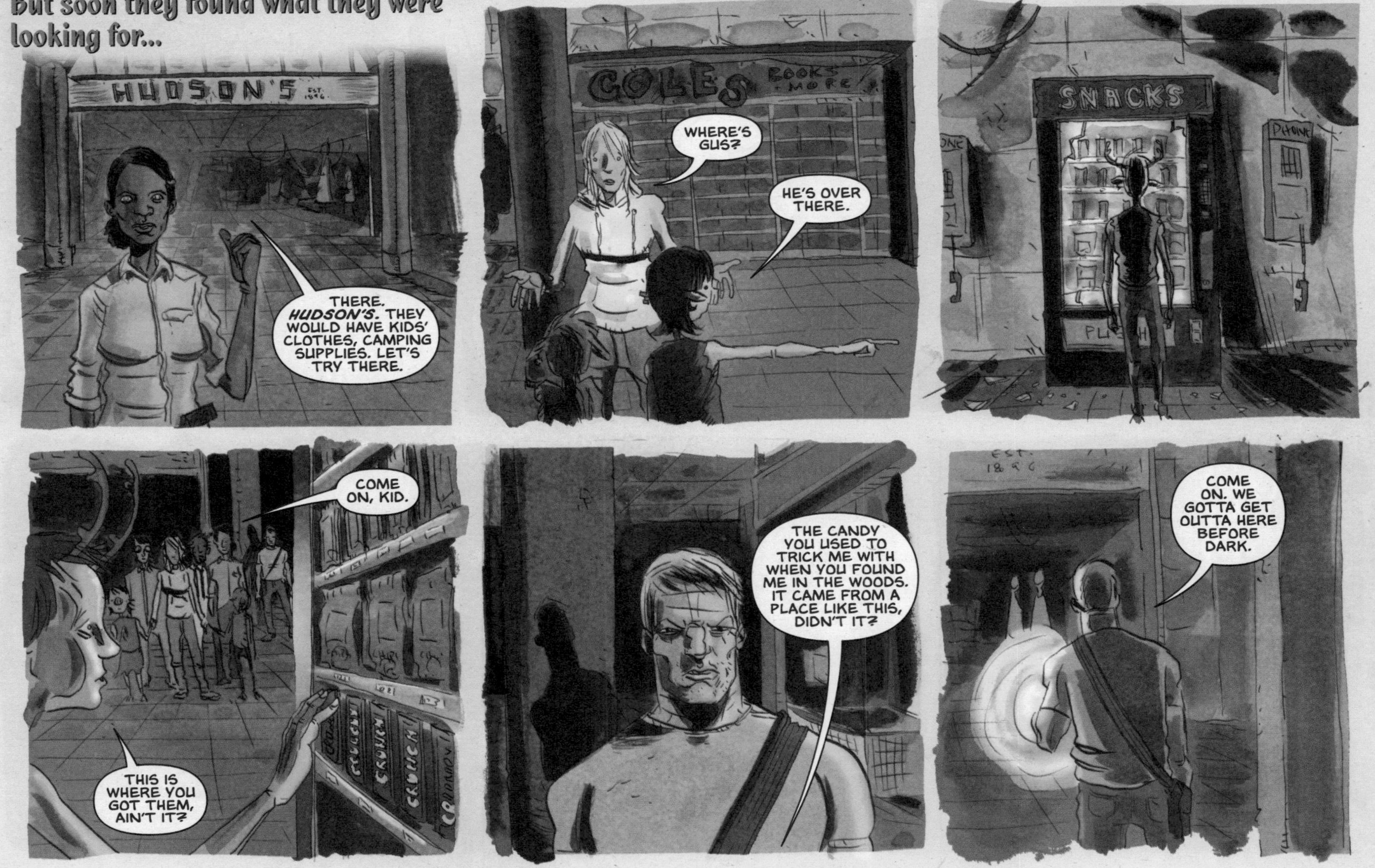
HUDSON'S EST. 1896
COLES BOOKS + MORE
SNACKS
PHONE
THERE. HUDSON'S. THEY WOULD HAVE KIDS' CLOTHES, CAMPING SUPPLIES. LET'S TRY THERE.
WHERE'S GUS?
HE'S OVER THERE.
COME ON, KID.
THIS IS WHERE YOU GOT THEM, AIN'T IT?
CRUNCH
CRUNCH
THE CANDY YOU USED TO TRICK ME WITH WHEN YOU FOUND ME IN THE WOODS. IT CAME FROM A PLACE LIKE THIS, DIDN'T IT?
COME ON. WE GOTTA GET OUTTA HERE BEFORE DARK.

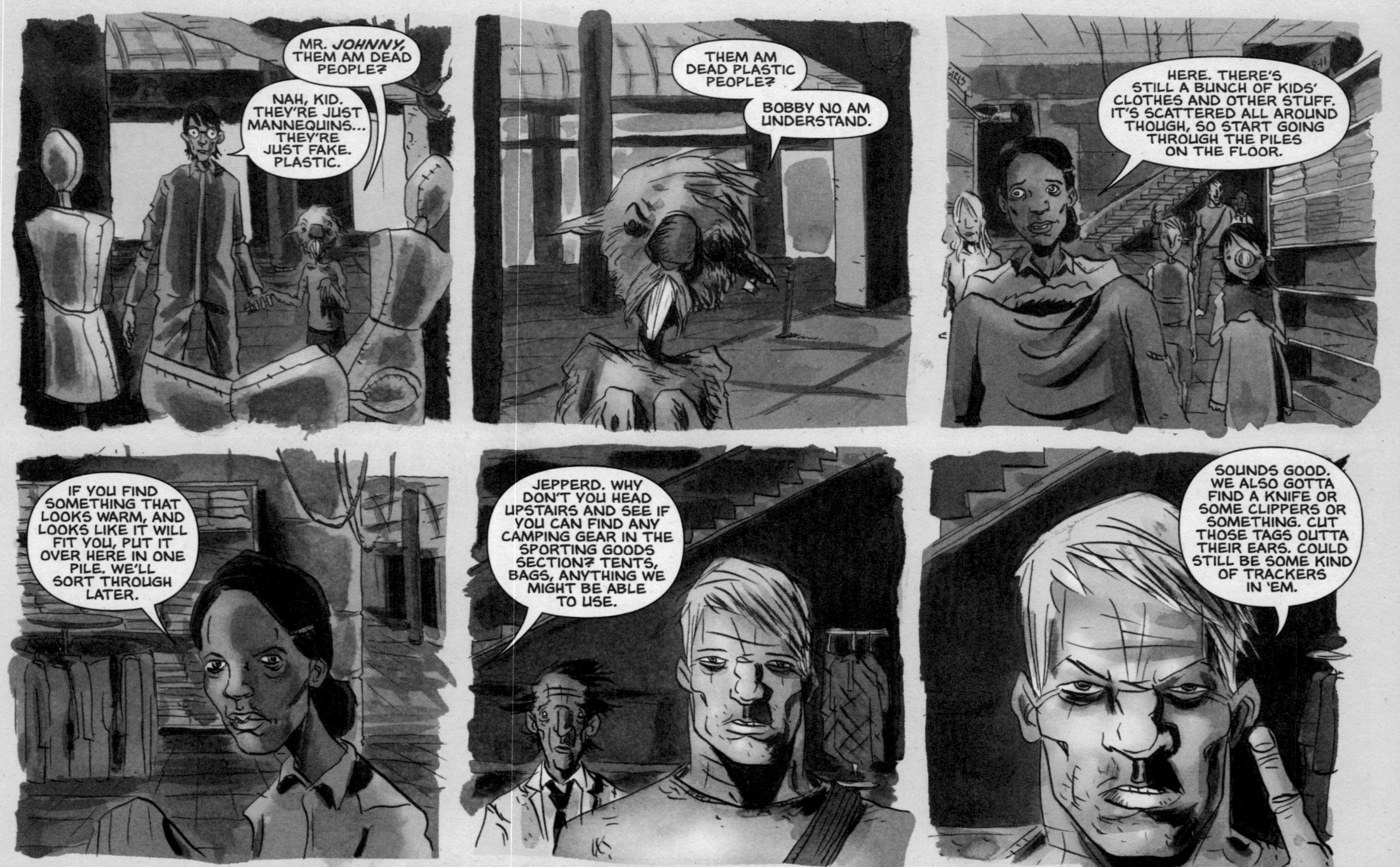
MR. *JOHNNY*, THEM AM DEAD PEOPLE?
NAH, KID. THEY'RE JUST MANNEQUINS... THEY'RE JUST FAKE. PLASTIC.
THEM AM DEAD PLASTIC PEOPLE?
BOBBY NO AM UNDERSTAND.
HERE. THERE'S STILL A BUNCH OF KIDS' CLOTHES AND OTHER STUFF. IT'S SCATTERED ALL AROUND THOUGH, SO START GOING THROUGH THE PILES ON THE FLOOR.
IF YOU FIND SOMETHING THAT LOOKS WARM, AND LOOKS LIKE IT WILL FIT YOU, PUT IT OVER HERE IN ONE PILE. WE'LL SORT THROUGH LATER.
JEPPERD. WHY DON'T YOU HEAD UPSTAIRS AND SEE IF YOU CAN FIND ANY CAMPING GEAR IN THE SPORTING GOODS SECTION? TENTS, BAGS, ANYTHING WE MIGHT BE ABLE TO USE.
SOUNDS GOOD. WE ALSO GOTTA FIND A KNIFE OR SOME CLIPPERS OR SOMETHING. CUT THOSE TAGS OUTTA THEIR EARS. COULD STILL BE SOME KIND OF TRACKERS IN 'EM.

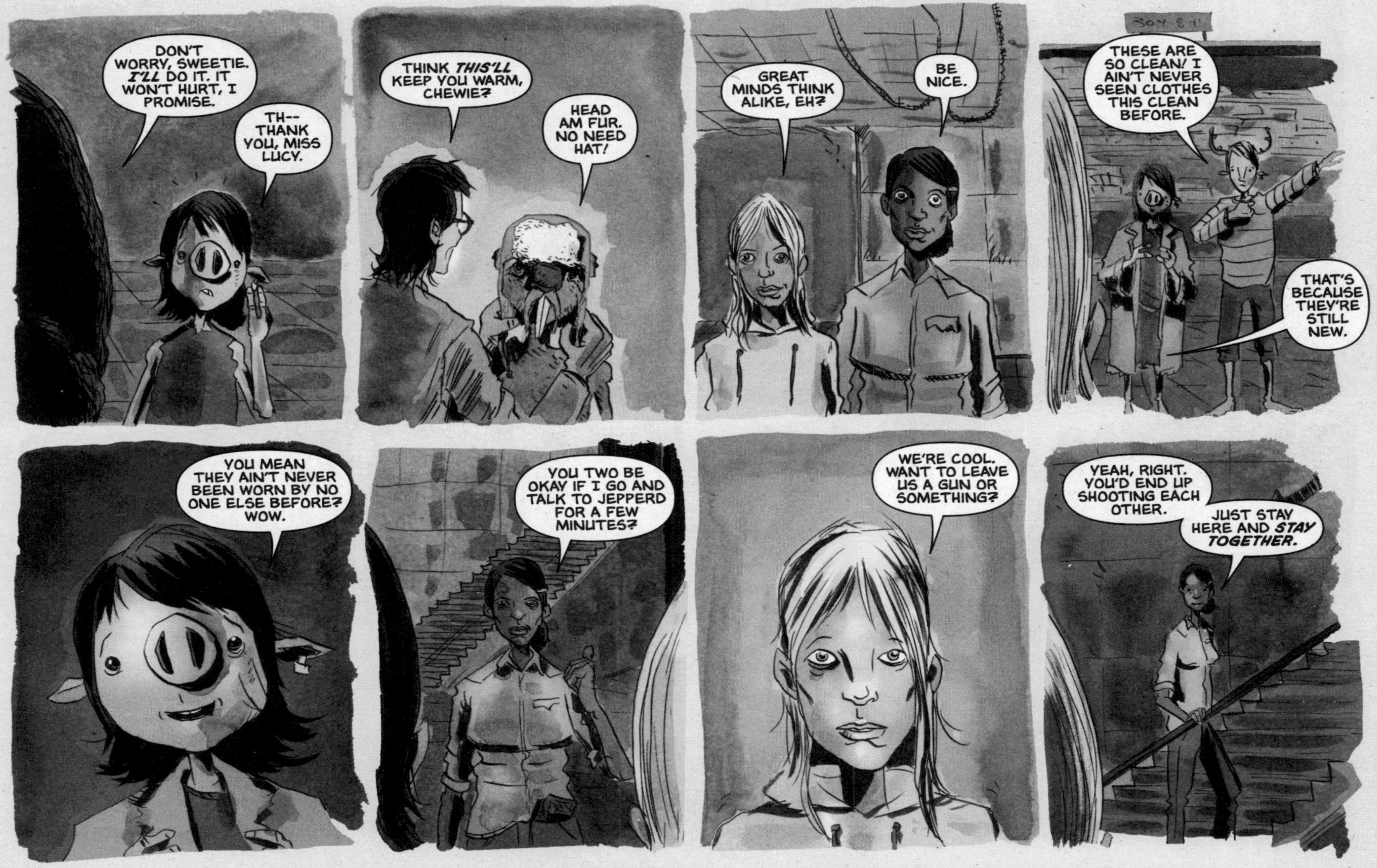
DON'T WORRY, SWEETIE. *I'LL* DO IT. IT WON'T HURT, I PROMISE.
TH-- THANK YOU, MISS LUCY.
THINK *THIS'LL* KEEP YOU WARM, CHEWIE?
HEAD AM FUR. NO NEED HAT!
GREAT MINDS THINK ALIKE, EH?
BE NICE.
THESE ARE SO CLEAN! I AIN'T NEVER SEEN CLOTHES THIS CLEAN BEFORE.
THAT'S BECAUSE THEY'RE STILL NEW.
YOU MEAN THEY AIN'T NEVER BEEN WORN BY NO ONE ELSE BEFORE? WOW.
YOU TWO BE OKAY IF I GO AND TALK TO JEPPERD FOR A FEW MINUTES?
WE'RE COOL. WANT TO LEAVE US A GUN OR SOMETHING?
YEAH, RIGHT. YOU'D END UP SHOOTING EACH OTHER.
JUST STAY HERE AND *STAY TOGETHER.*

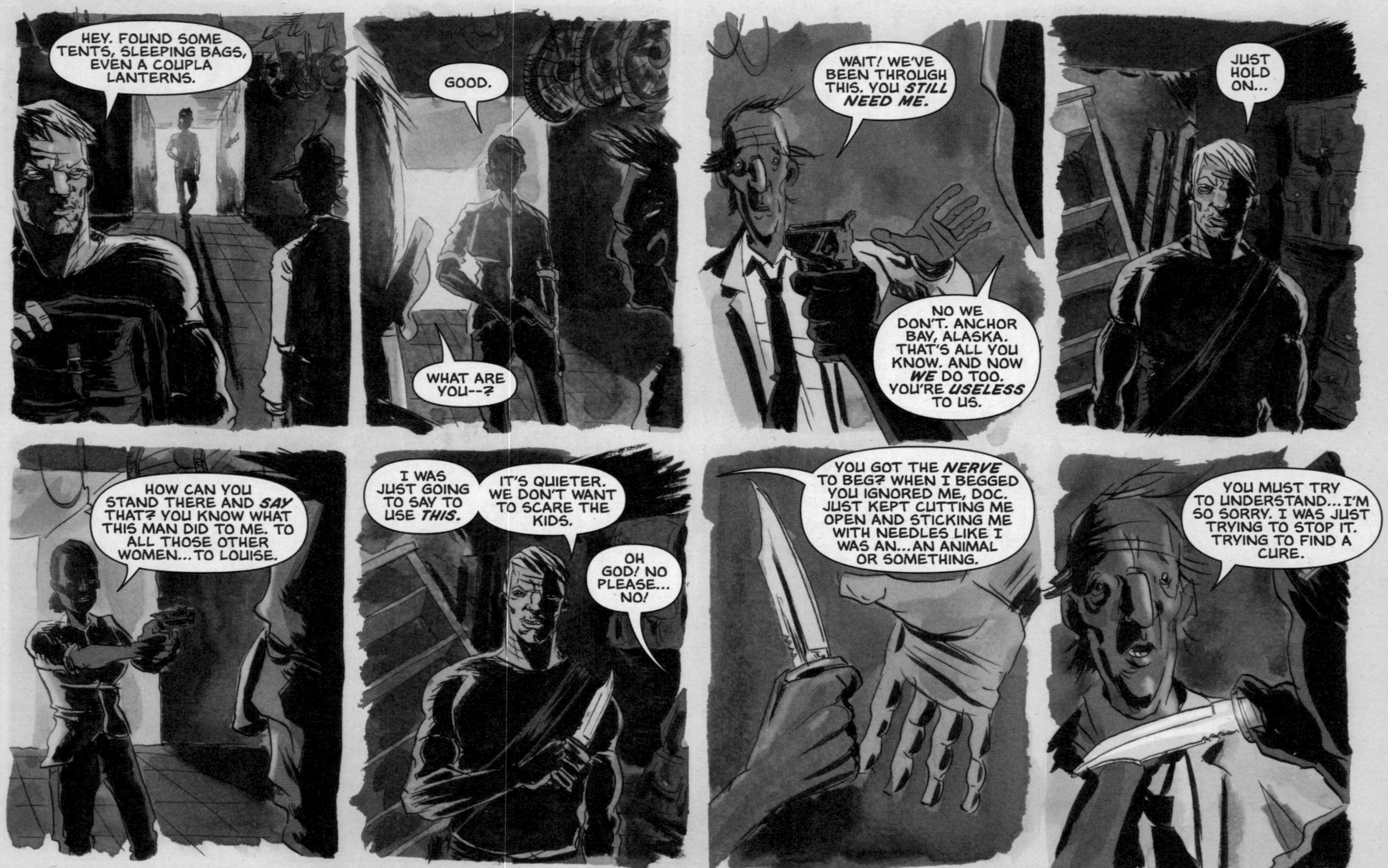
HEY. FOUND SOME TENTS, SLEEPING BAGS, EVEN A COUPLA LANTERNS.
GOOD.
WHAT ARE YOU--?
WAIT! WE'VE BEEN THROUGH THIS. YOU *STILL NEED ME.*
NO WE DON'T. ANCHOR BAY, ALASKA. THAT'S ALL YOU KNOW. AND NOW *WE* DO TOO. YOU'RE *USELESS* TO US.
JUST HOLD ON...
HOW CAN YOU STAND THERE AND *SAY* THAT? YOU KNOW WHAT THIS MAN DID TO ME. TO ALL THOSE OTHER WOMEN... TO LOUISE.
I WAS JUST GOING TO SAY TO USE *THIS.*
IT'S QUIETER. WE DON'T WANT TO SCARE THE KIDS.
OH GOD! NO PLEASE... NO!
YOU GOT THE *NERVE* TO BEG? WHEN I BEGGED YOU IGNORED ME, DOC. JUST KEPT CUTTING ME OPEN AND STICKING ME WITH NEEDLES LIKE I WAS AN... AN ANIMAL OR SOMETHING.
YOU MUST TRY TO UNDERSTAND... I'M SO SORRY. I WAS JUST TRYING TO STOP IT. TRYING TO FIND A CURE.

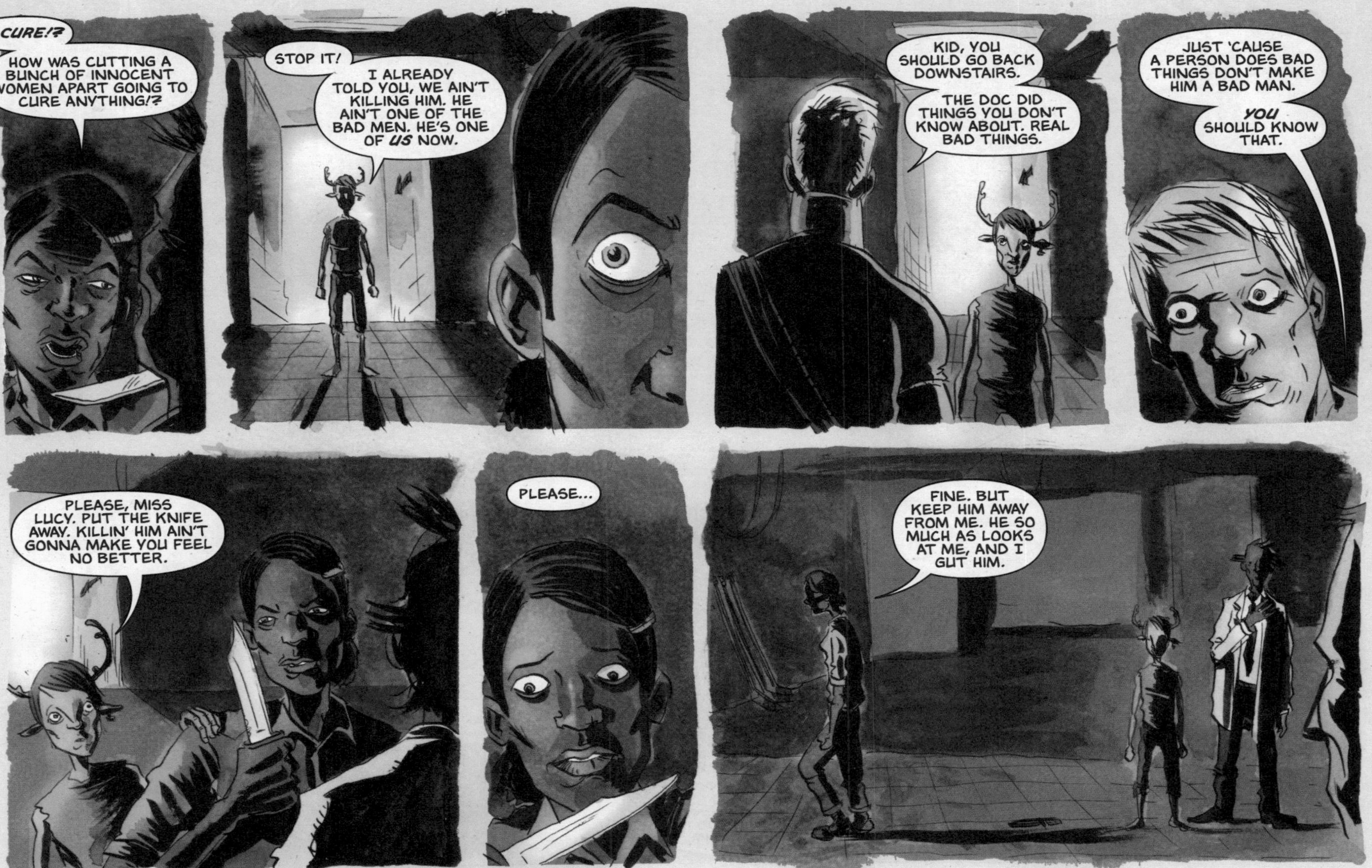
A *CURE!?*
HOW WAS CUTTING A BUNCH OF INNOCENT WOMEN APART GOING TO CURE ANYTHING!?
STOP IT!
I ALREADY TOLD YOU, WE AIN'T KILLING HIM. HE AIN'T ONE OF THE BAD MEN. HE'S ONE OF *US* NOW.
PLEASE, MISS LUCY. PUT THE KNIFE AWAY. KILLIN' HIM AIN'T GONNA MAKE YOU FEEL NO BETTER.
PLEASE...
KID, YOU SHOULD GO BACK DOWNSTAIRS.
THE DOC DID THINGS YOU DON'T KNOW ABOUT. REAL BAD THINGS.
JUST 'CAUSE A PERSON DOES BAD THINGS DON'T MAKE HIM A BAD MAN.
YOU SHOULD KNOW THAT.
FINE. BUT KEEP HIM AWAY FROM ME. HE SO MUCH AS LOOKS AT ME, AND I GUT HIM.

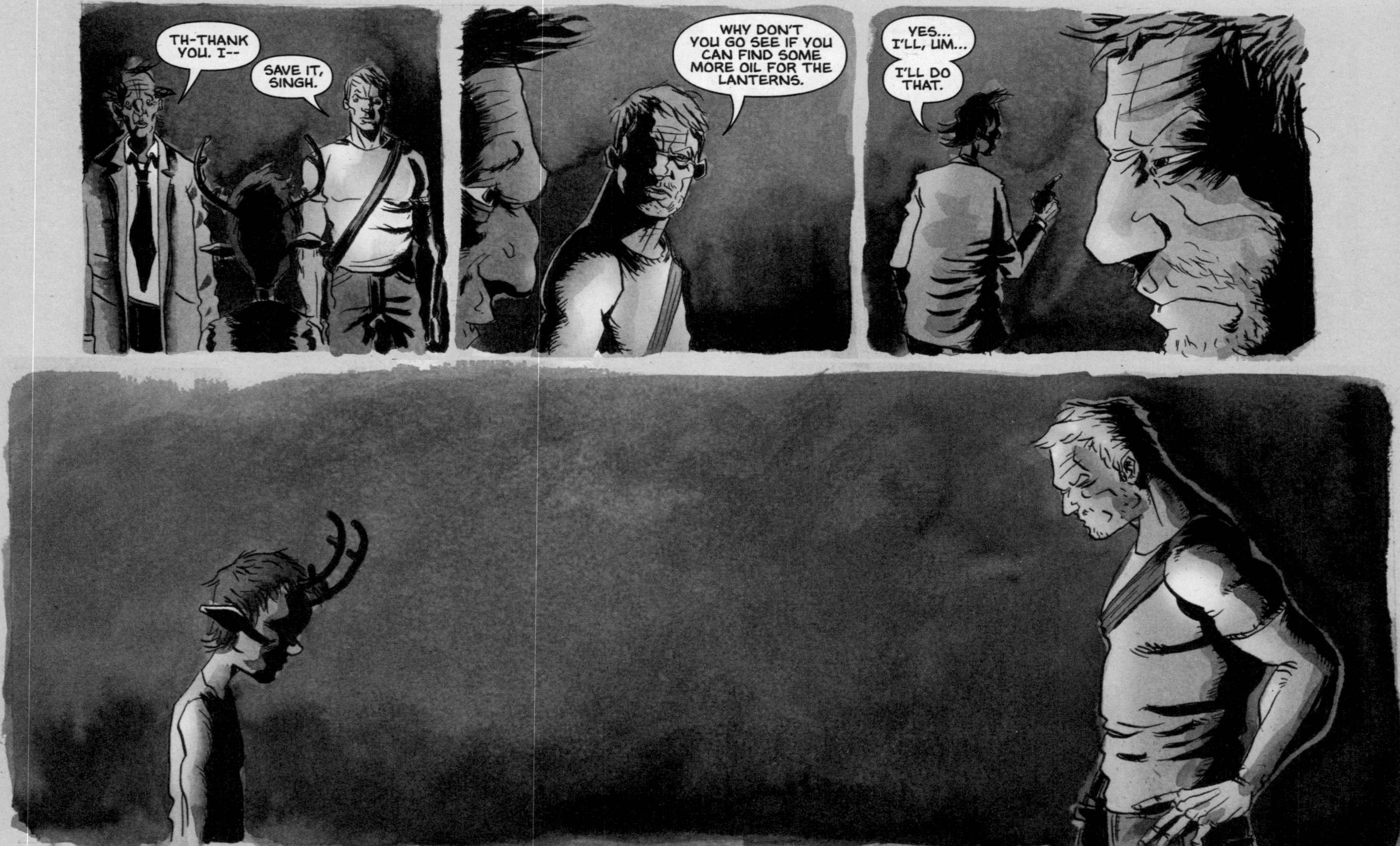
TH-THANK YOU. I--
SAVE IT, SINGH.
WHY DON'T YOU GO SEE IF YOU CAN FIND SOME MORE OIL FOR THE LANTERNS.
YES... I'LL, UM...
I'LL DO THAT.

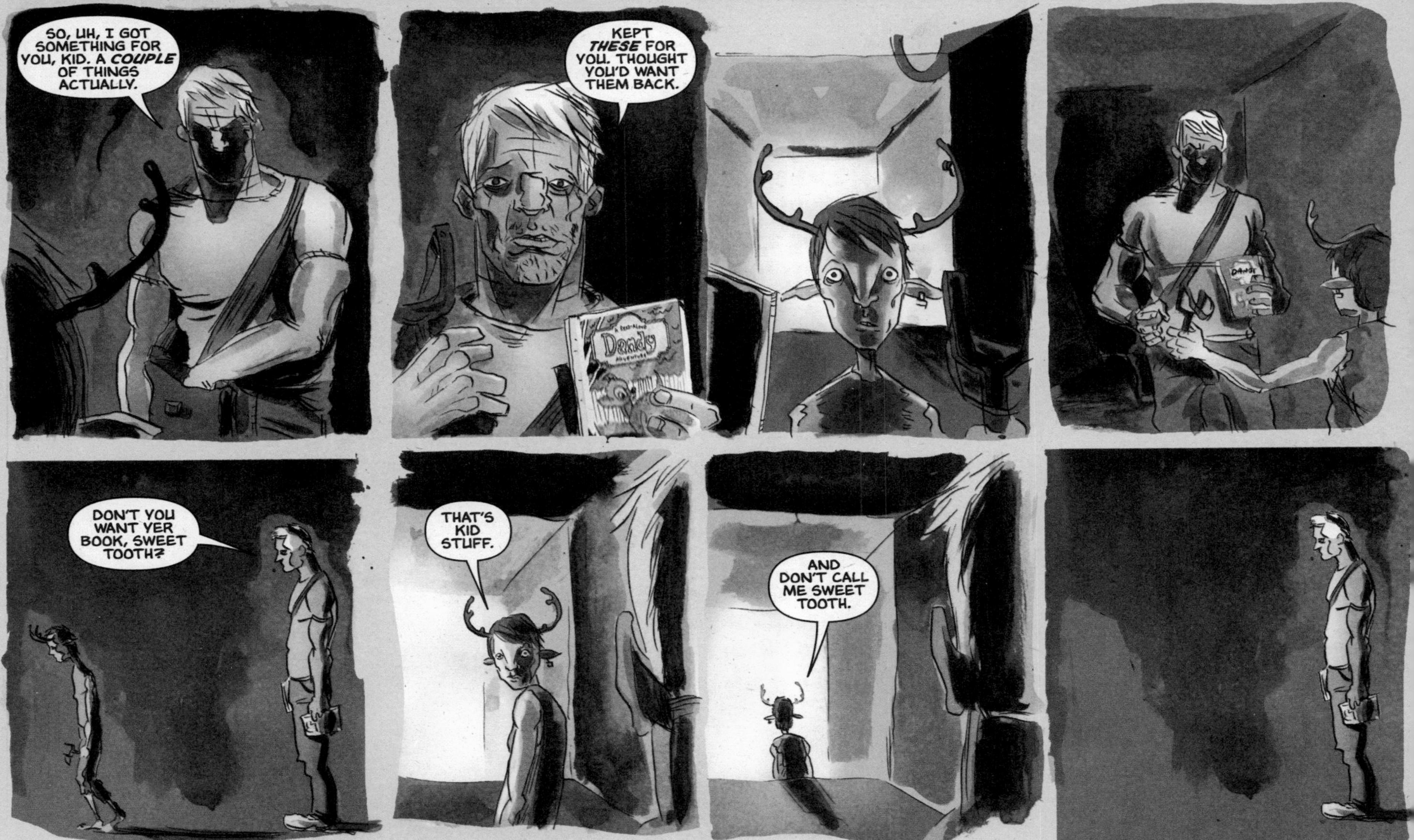
SO, UH, I GOT SOMETHING FOR YOU, KID. A *COUPLE* OF THINGS ACTUALLY.
KEPT *THESE* FOR YOU. THOUGHT YOU'D WANT THEM BACK.
DON'T YOU WANT YER BOOK, SWEET TOOTH?
THAT'S KID STUFF.
AND DON'T CALL ME SWEET TOOTH.

The Big Man decided it was too close to dark to leave, so they would stay the night. The children were excited and wondered why they couldn't just stay there forever. The Big Man said it wasn't safe to stay in one spot, no matter how nice it was. He said the militia was still out there and that sooner or later they'd come looking for them.

Besides, The Boy wanted to keep going to Alaska. He wanted to see where he had come from.

That night they slept in warm tents with lots of blankets and everything. But as comfortable as it was, The Boy couldn't fall asleep. He just lay there staring up at the tent. The Boy thought of everything that had happened since he had left the woods. They had all had so many bad things happen to them, he just couldn't see how he would ever feel truly safe or happy again. Eventually he drifted off, but he didn't dream that night.

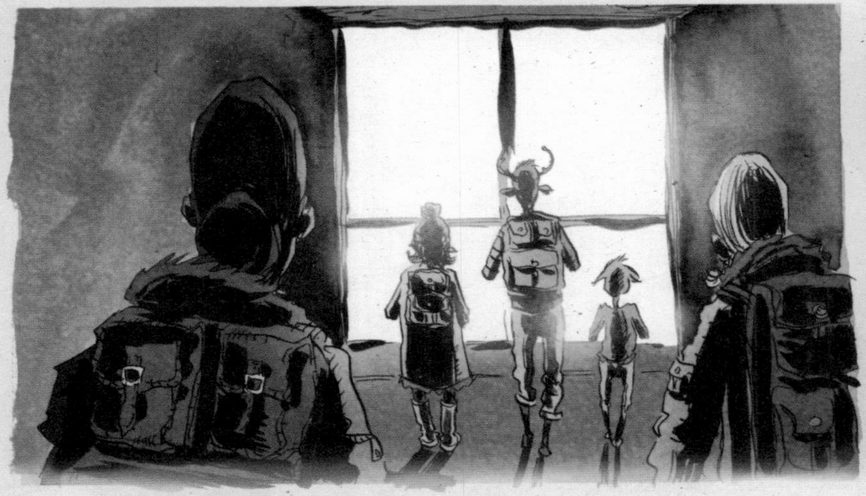

The next morning they packed up what they could carry and moved out.

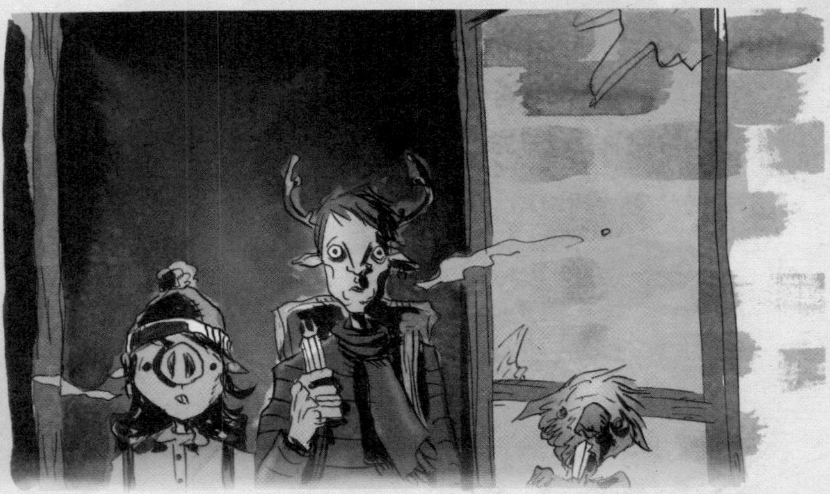

But nothing could prepare them for what they saw when they left the Mall.

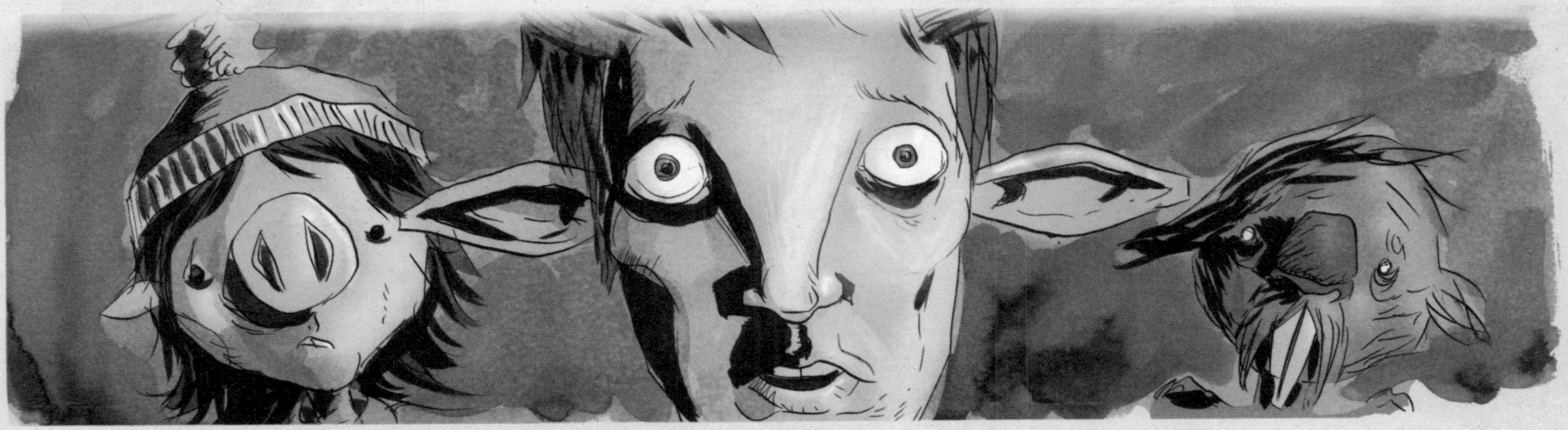

It had come in the night. Silent. And it had changed everything...

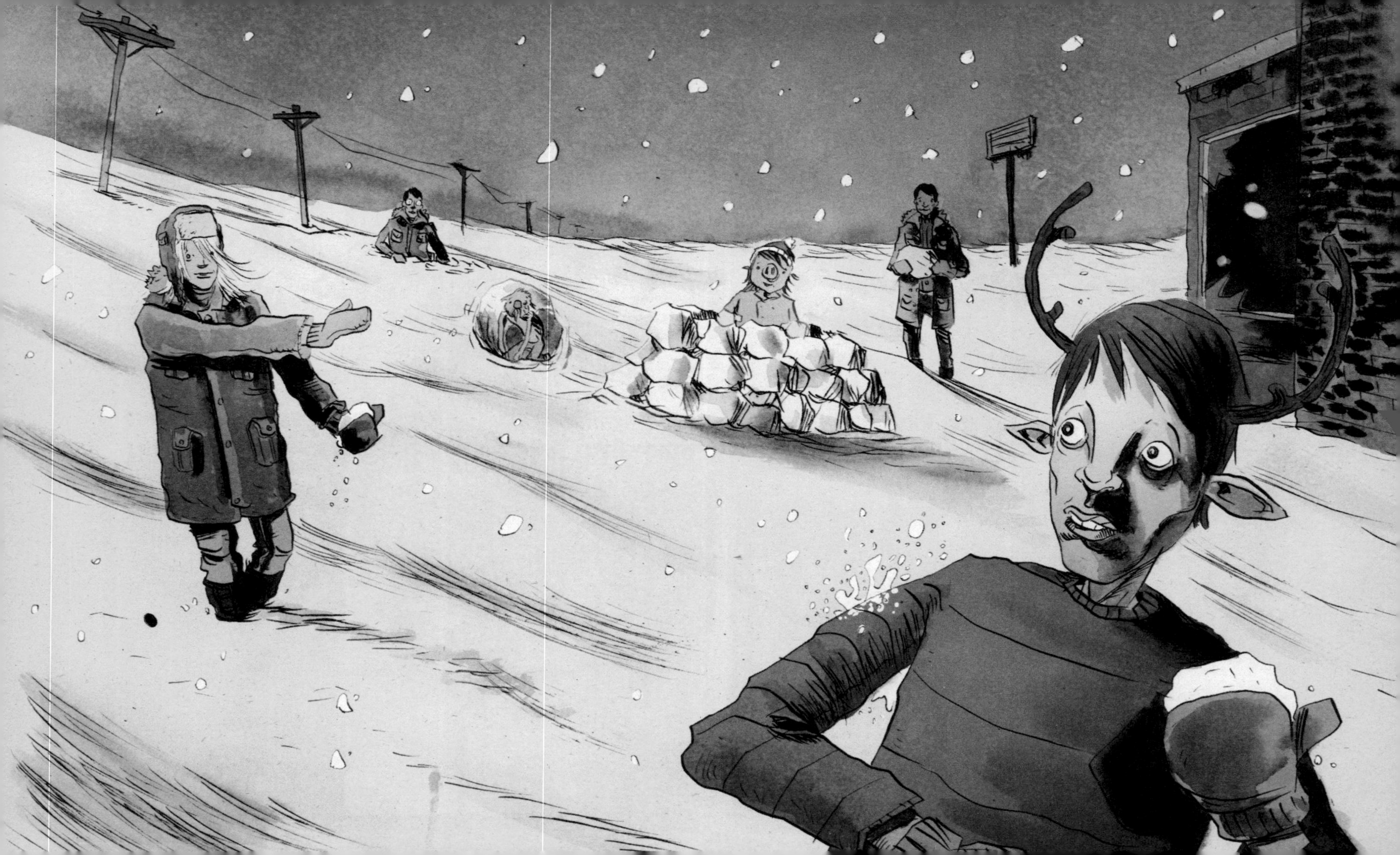

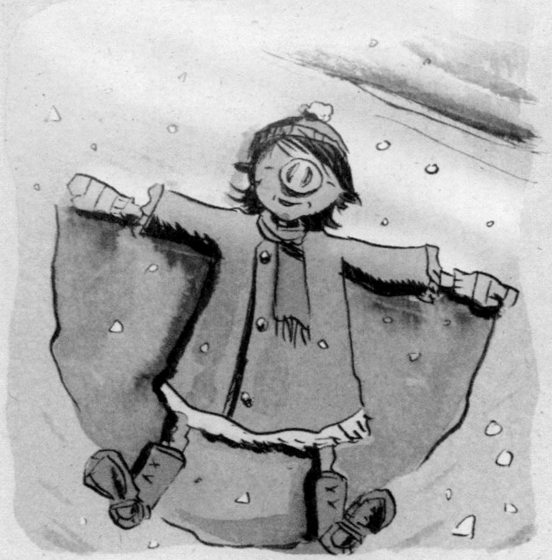

Snow.

It had come while they slept, and it was as deep as their shins and soft and bright and clean! They ran around and jumped in it and ate it and laughed. The Nice Lady showed them how they could all see angels in the snow if they lay on their backs and flapped their arms and legs. The Boy liked seeing angels.

Then The Man With The Funny Eyes and The Pretty Girl started digging big holes in the snow and making walls. They called them "forts." All the girls made one fort, and The Man With The Funny Eyes and Bobby and The Boy made another. They made snowballs and had a war. Not a real war with killing and blood like they had seen at the camp, just a pretend one.

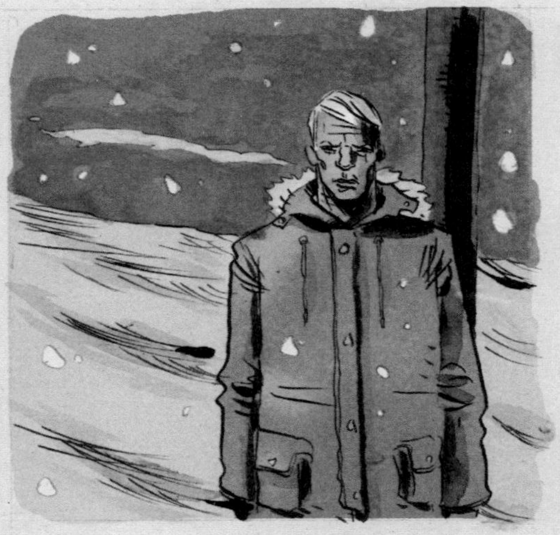

They all laughed and smiled. The Boy looked over and even thought he saw a smile on The Big Man's face. . . but it was so bright out he couldn't be sure.

Finally The Pretty Girl and Wendy started to make a Snowman. The kids had never seen one of those before. They made eyes and a nose and a mouth out of stones.

They liked the Snowman, but Johnny said something was missing...

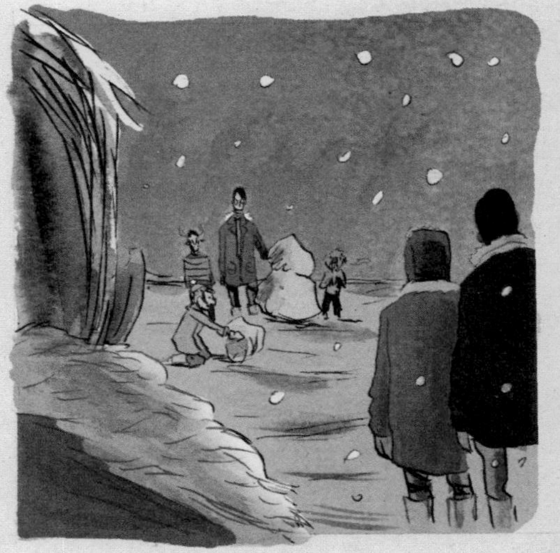

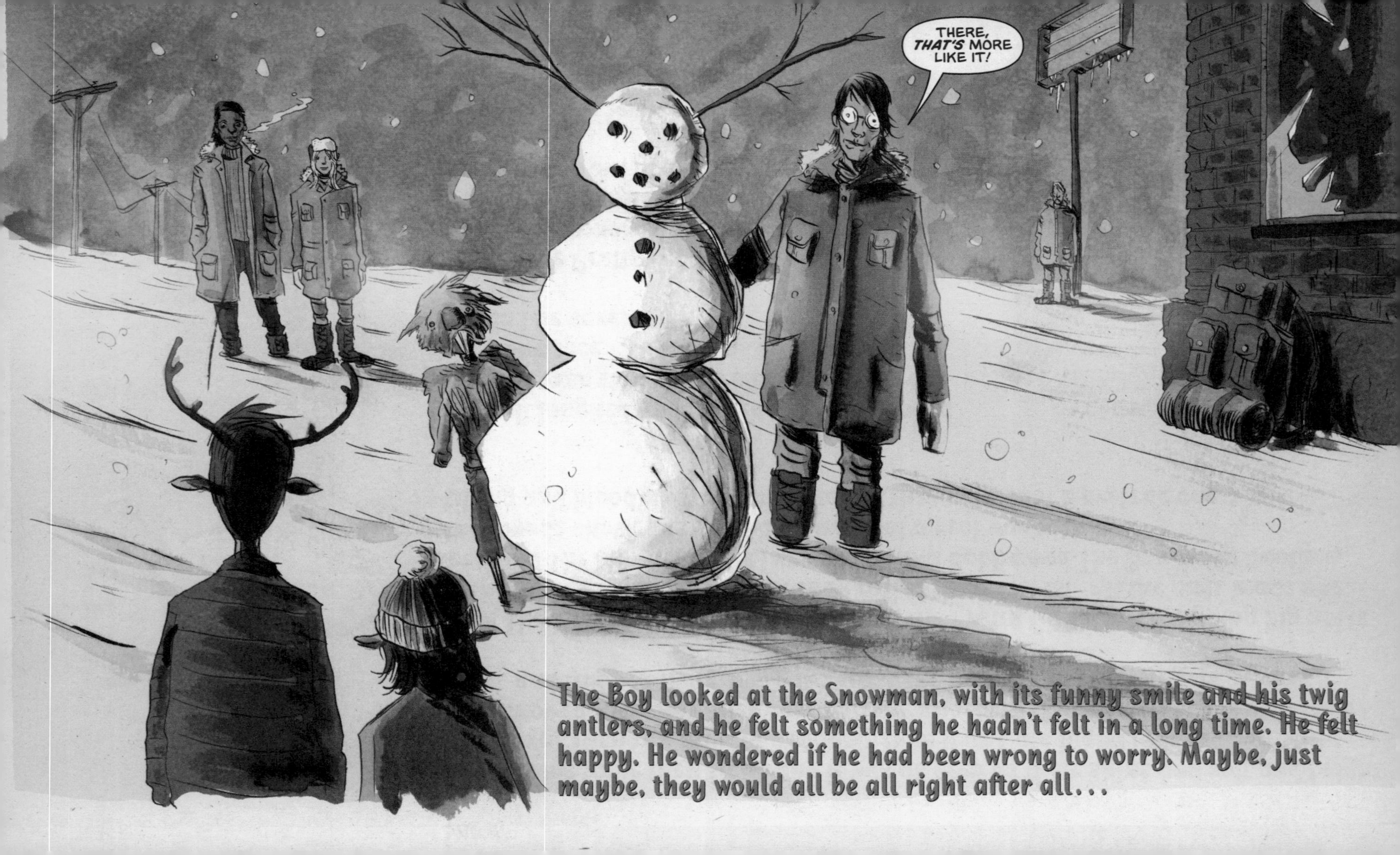
THERE, *THAT'S* MORE LIKE IT!
The Boy looked at the Snowman, with its funny smile and his twig antlers, and he felt something he hadn't felt in a long time. He felt happy. He wondered if he had been wrong to worry. Maybe, just maybe, they would all be all right after all. . .

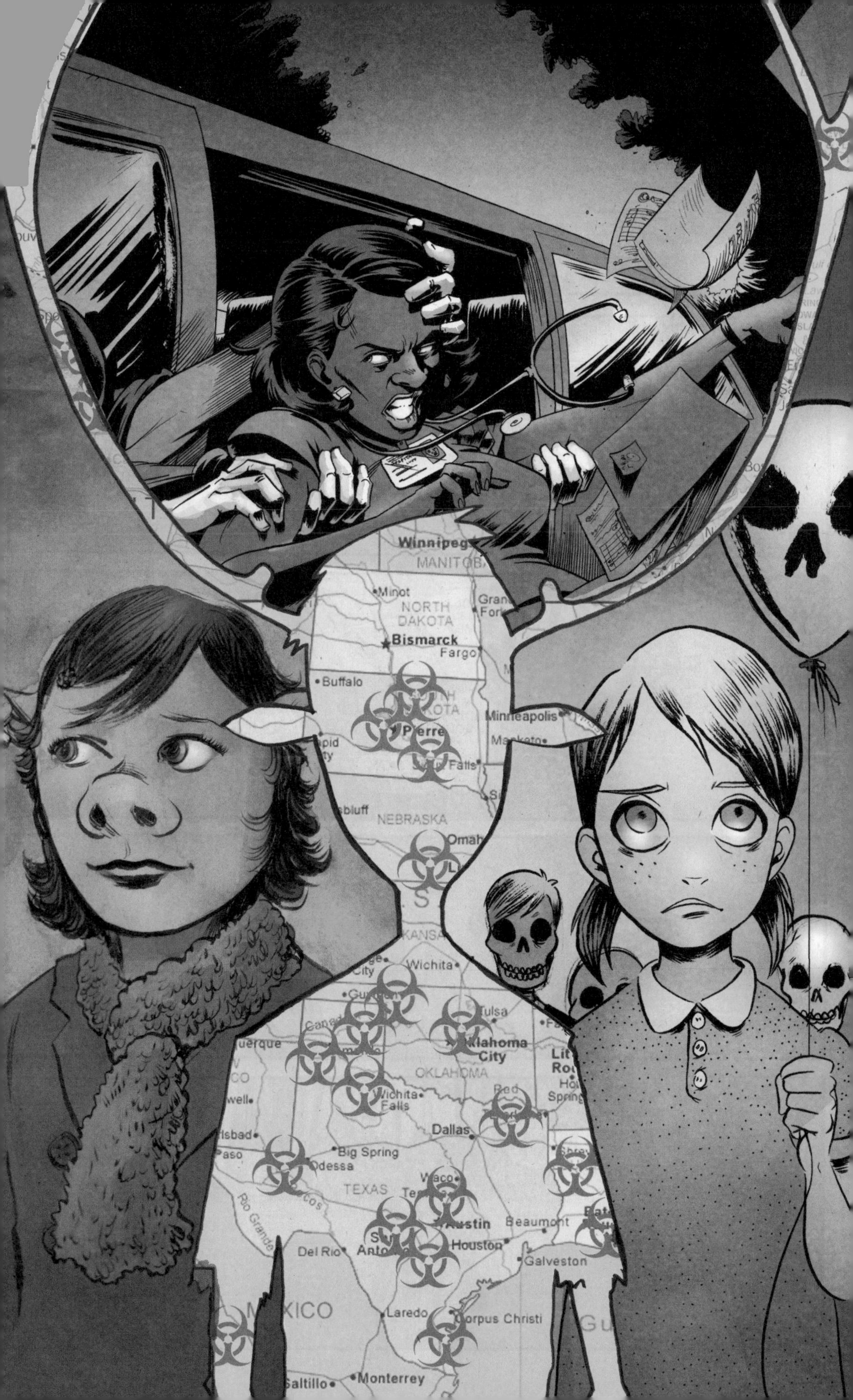

Winnipeg
MANITOBA
Minot
NORTH DAKOTA
Bismarck
Fargo
Buffalo
Pierre
Minneapolis
NEBRASKA
Wichita
Tulsa
Oklahoma City
OKLAHOMA
Wichita Falls
Dallas
Big Spring
Odessa
TEXAS
Waco
Austin
Beaumont
Houston
Galveston
Del Rio
Rio Grande
Laredo
Monterrey

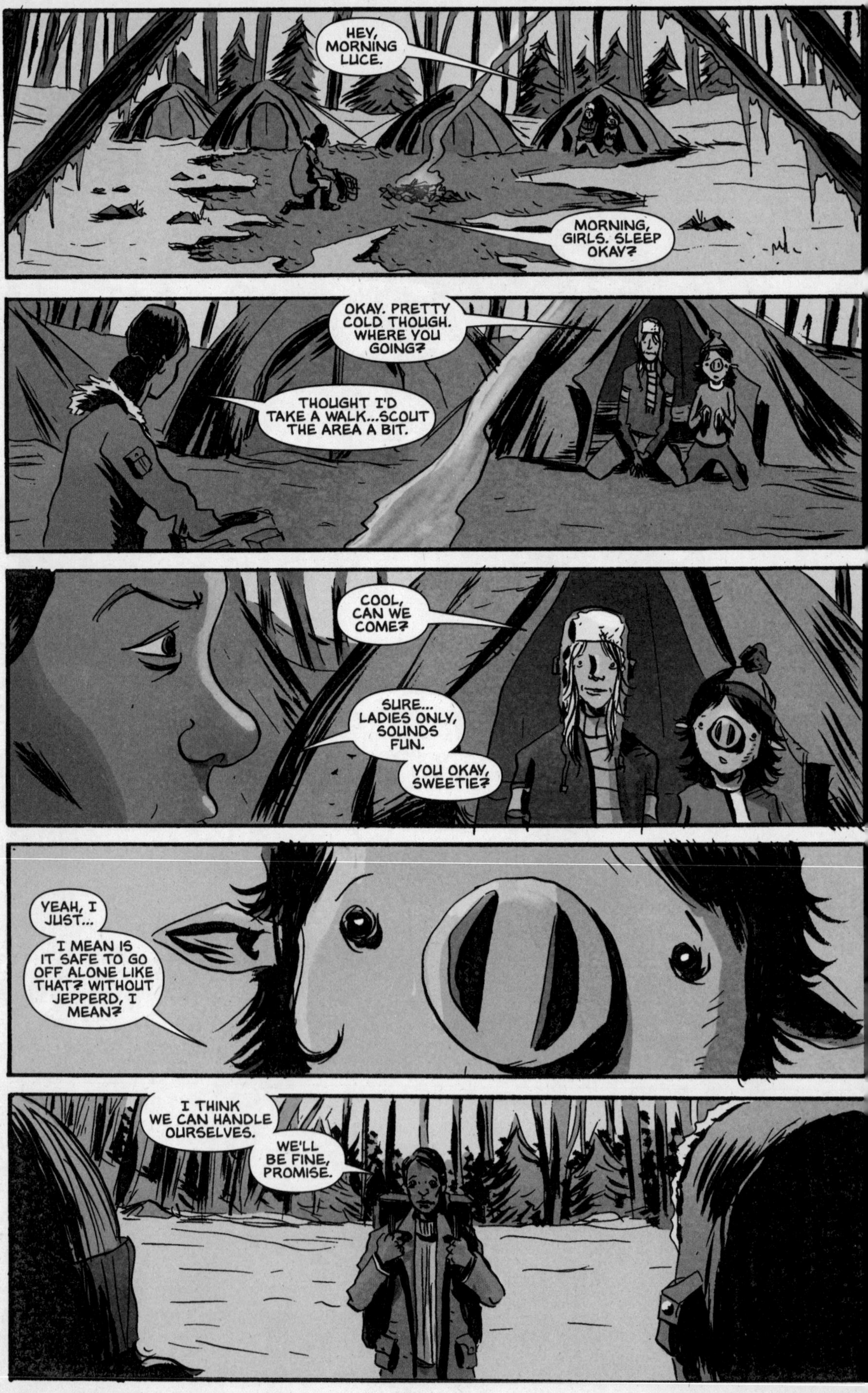
HEY, MORNING LUCE.
MORNING, GIRLS. SLEEP OKAY?
OKAY. PRETTY COLD THOUGH. WHERE YOU GOING?
THOUGHT I'D TAKE A WALK...SCOUT THE AREA A BIT.
COOL, CAN WE COME?
SURE... LADIES ONLY, SOUNDS FUN.
YOU OKAY, SWEETIE?
YEAH, I JUST...
I MEAN IS IT SAFE TO GO OFF ALONE LIKE THAT? WITHOUT JEPPERD, I MEAN?
I THINK WE CAN HANDLE OURSELVES.
WE'LL BE FINE, PROMISE.

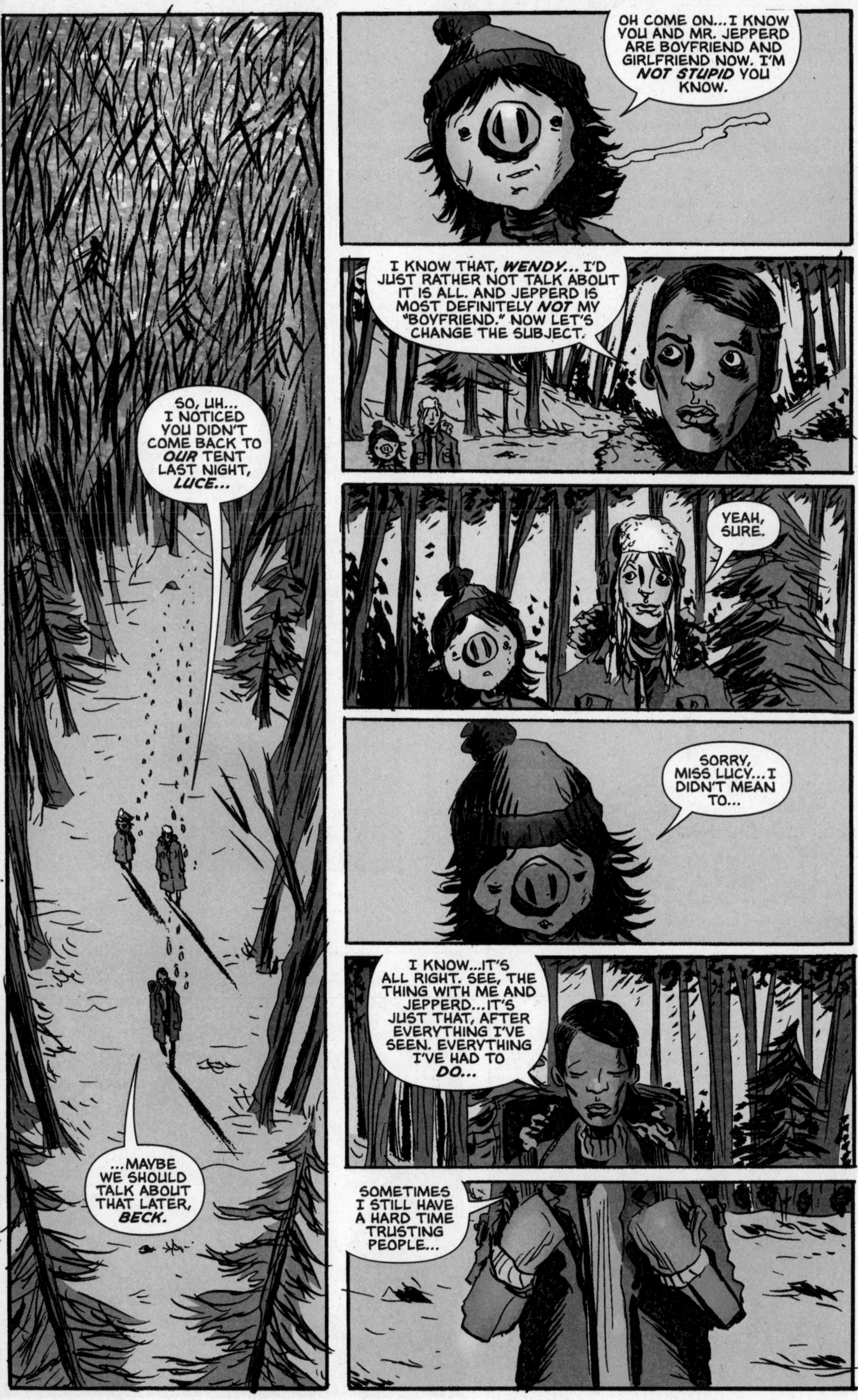
SO, UH... I NOTICED YOU DIDN'T COME BACK TO *OUR* TENT LAST NIGHT, *LUCE...*
...MAYBE WE SHOULD TALK ABOUT THAT LATER, *BECK.*
OH COME ON...I KNOW YOU AND MR. JEPPERD ARE BOYFRIEND AND GIRLFRIEND NOW. I'M *NOT STUPID* YOU KNOW.
I KNOW THAT, *WENDY...* I'D JUST RATHER NOT TALK ABOUT IT IS ALL. AND JEPPERD IS MOST DEFINITELY *NOT* MY "BOYFRIEND." NOW LET'S CHANGE THE SUBJECT.
YEAH, SURE.
SORRY, MISS LUCY...I DIDN'T MEAN TO...
I KNOW...IT'S ALL RIGHT. SEE, THE THING WITH ME AND JEPPERD...IT'S JUST THAT, AFTER EVERYTHING I'VE SEEN. EVERYTHING I'VE HAD TO *DO...*
SOMETIMES I STILL HAVE A HARD TIME TRUSTING PEOPLE...

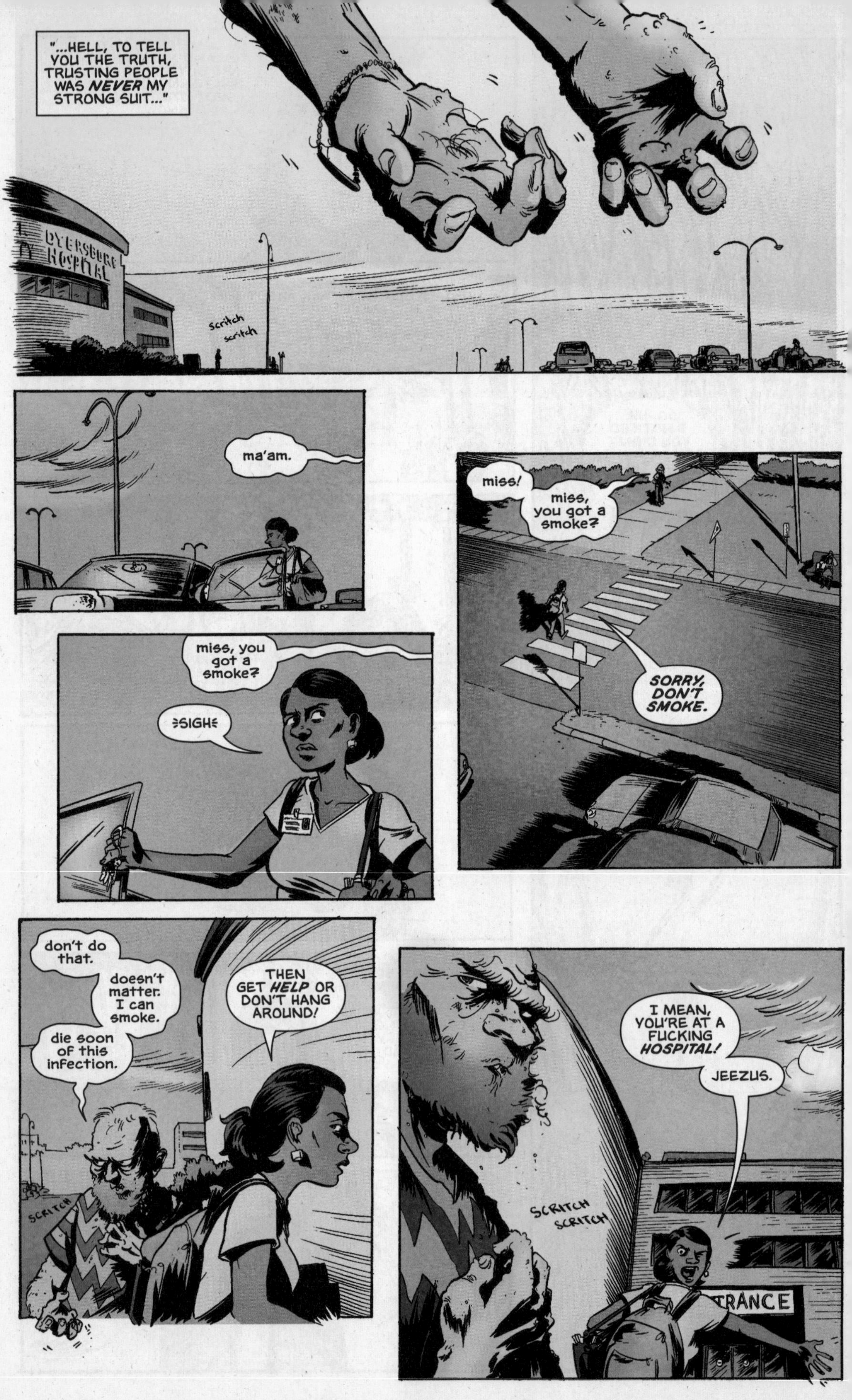
"...HELL, TO TELL YOU THE TRUTH, TRUSTING PEOPLE WAS *NEVER* MY STRONG SUIT..."
DYERSBURG HOSPITAL
scritch scritch
ma'am.
miss!
miss, you got a smoke?
SORRY, DON'T SMOKE.
miss, you got a smoke?
SIGH
don't do that.
doesn't matter. I can smoke.
die soon of this infection.
THEN GET *HELP* OR DON'T HANG AROUND!
SCRITCH
I MEAN, YOU'RE AT A FUCKING *HOSPITAL!*
JEEZUS.
SCRITCH SCRITCH
TRANCE

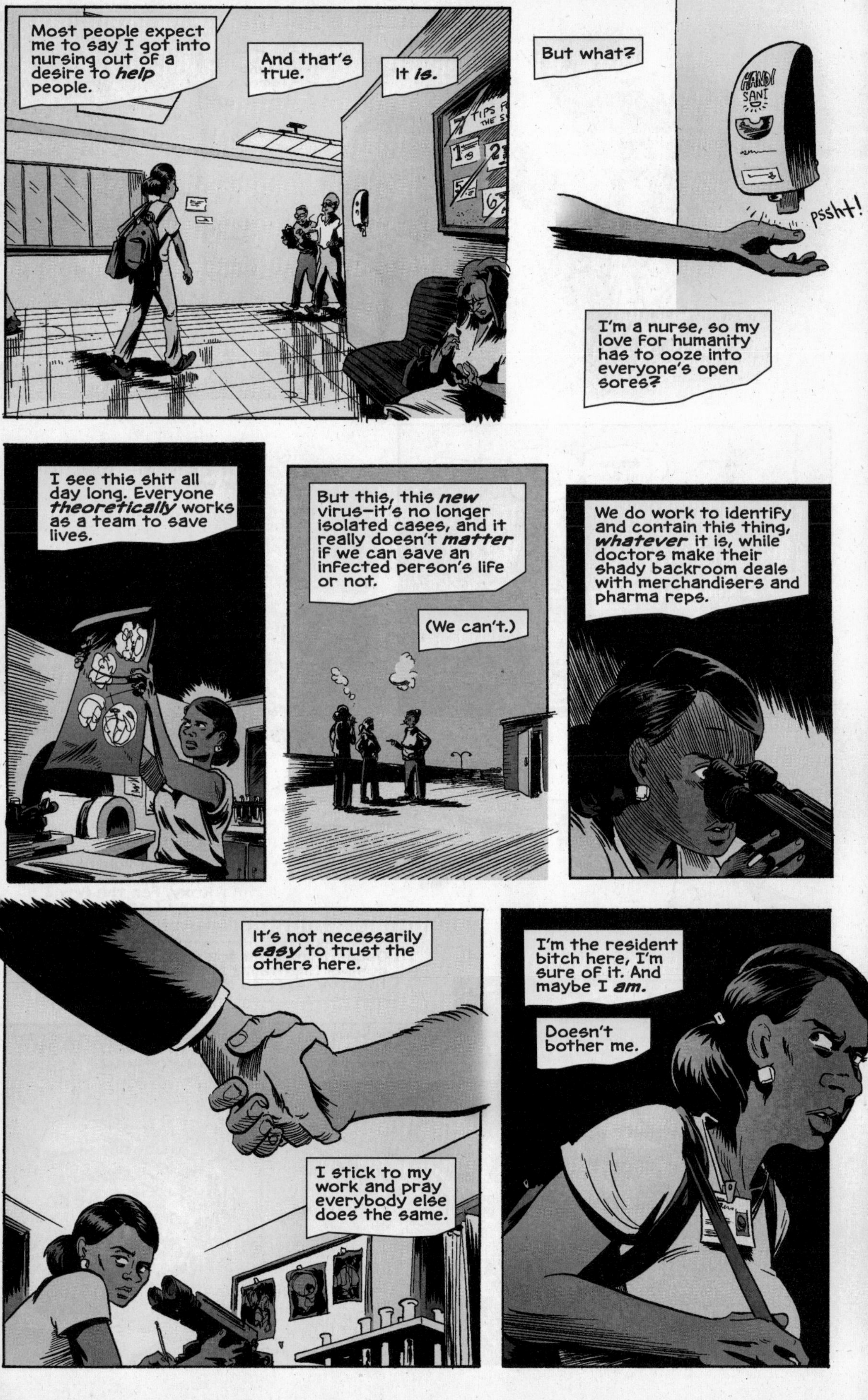
Most people expect me to say I got into nursing out of a desire to *help* people.
And that's true.
It *is.*
But what?
HANDI SANI
pssht!
I'm a nurse, so my love for humanity has to ooze into everyone's open sores?
I see this shit all day long. Everyone *theoretically* works as a team to save lives.
But this, this *new* virus—it's no longer isolated cases, and it really doesn't *matter* if we can save an infected person's life or not.
(We can't.)
We do work to identify and contain this thing, *whatever* it is, while doctors make their shady backroom deals with merchandisers and pharma reps.
It's not necessarily *easy* to trust the others here.
I stick to my work and pray everybody else does the same.
I'm the resident bitch here, I'm sure of it. And maybe I *am.*
Doesn't bother me.

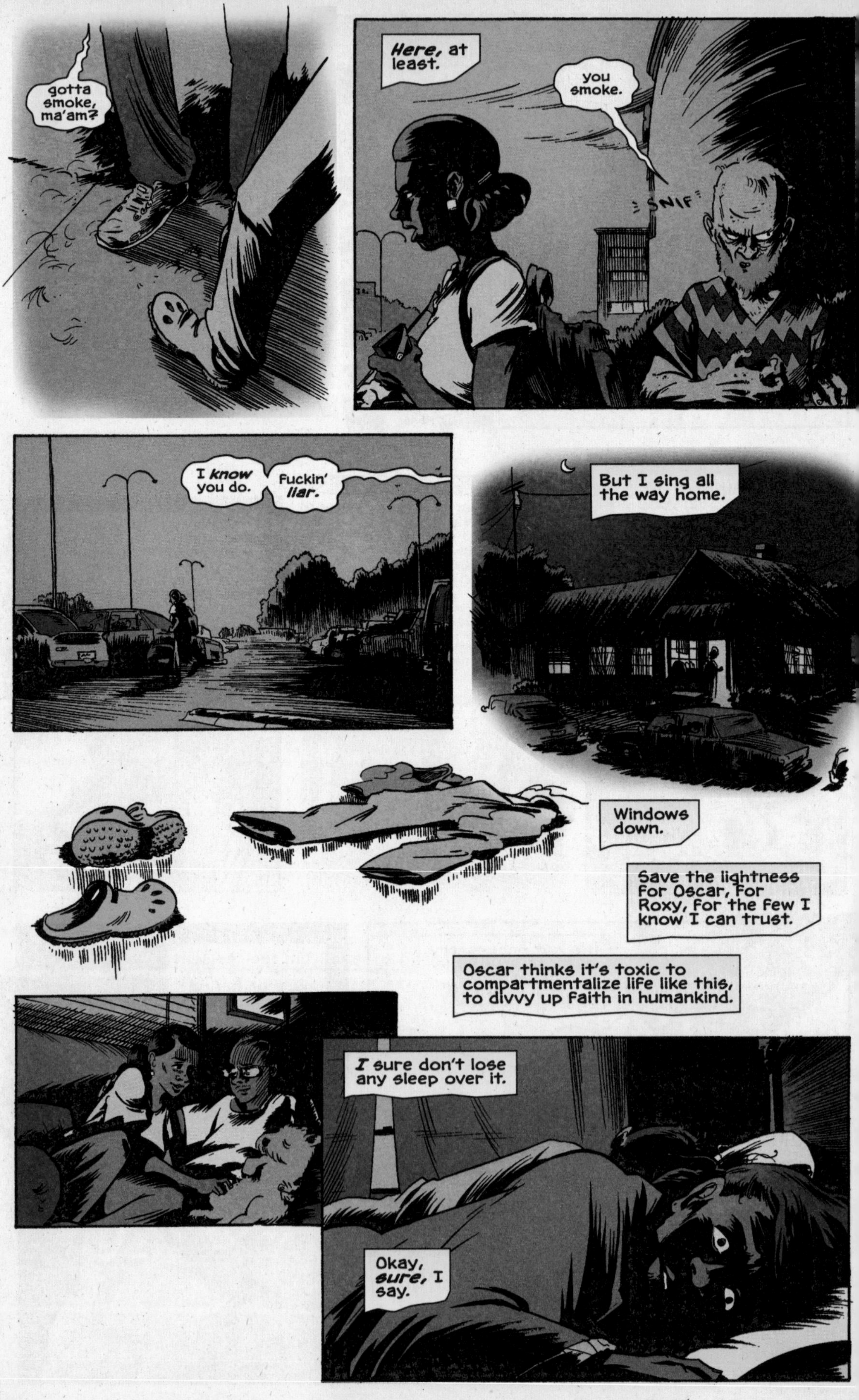
gotta smoke, ma'am?
Here, at least.
you smoke.
SNIF
I know you do.
Fuckin' liar.
But I sing all the way home.
Windows down.
Save the lightness for Oscar, for Roxy, for the few I know I can trust.
Oscar thinks it's toxic to compartmentalize life like this, to divvy up faith in humankind.
I sure don't lose any sleep over it.
Okay, sure, I say.

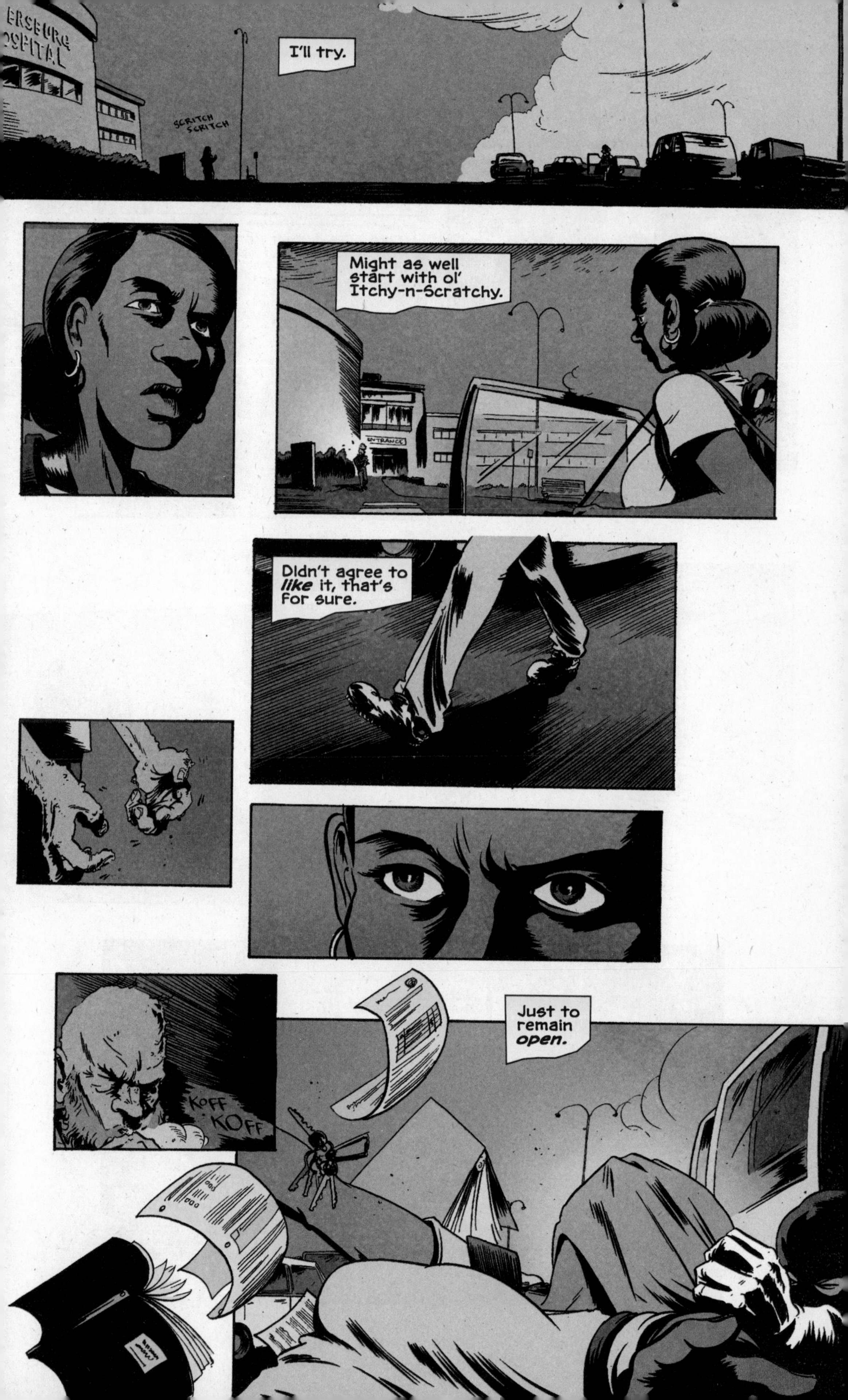
ERSBURG
OSPITAL
I'll try.
SCRITCH
SCRITCH
Might as well start with ol' Itchy-n-Scratchy.
ENTRANCE
Didn't agree to *like* it, that's for sure.
KOFF
KOFF
Just to remain *open*.

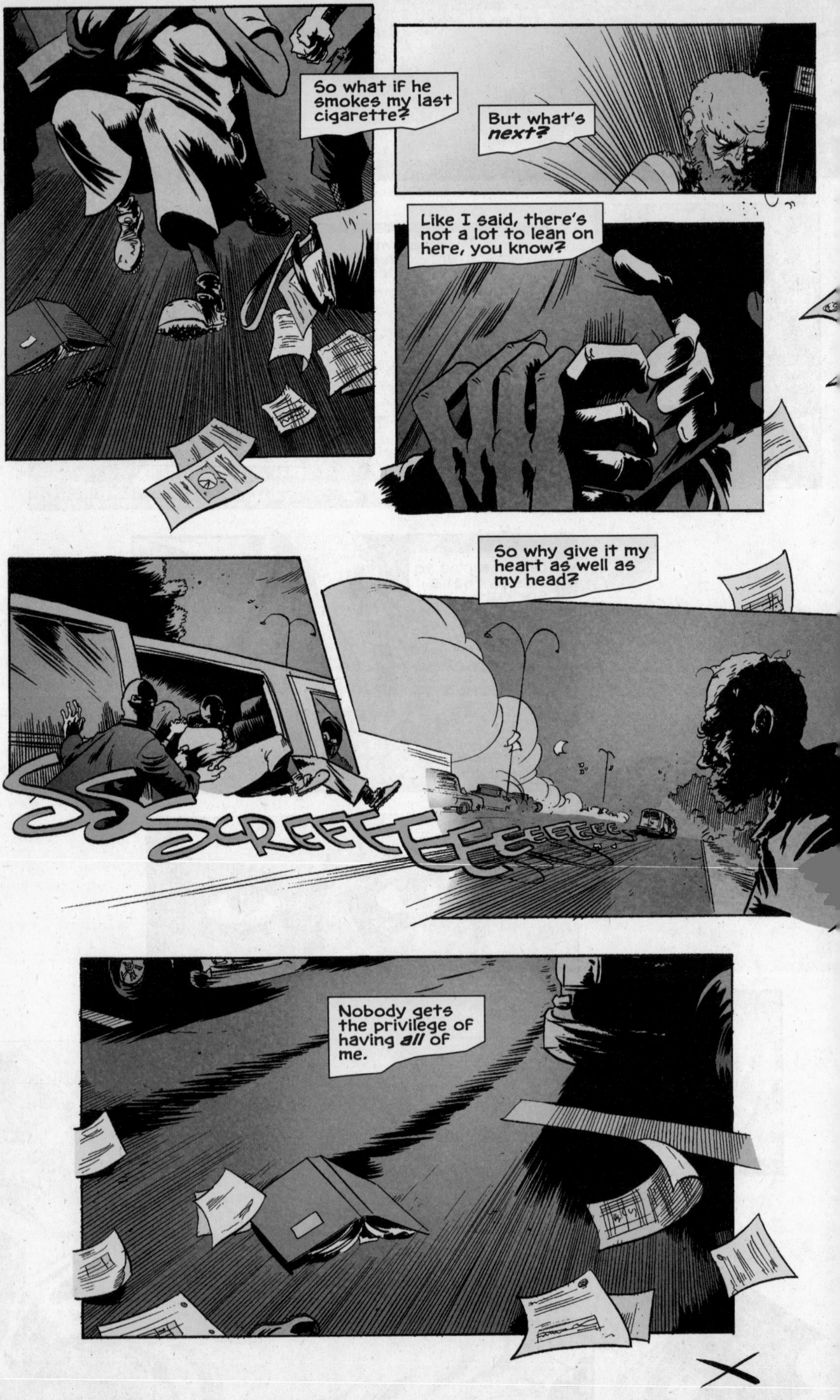
So what if he smokes my last cigarette?
But what's *next?*
Like I said, there's not a lot to lean on here, you know?
So why give it my heart as well as my head?
SSSCREEEEEEEEEEEE
Nobody gets the privilege of having *all* of me.

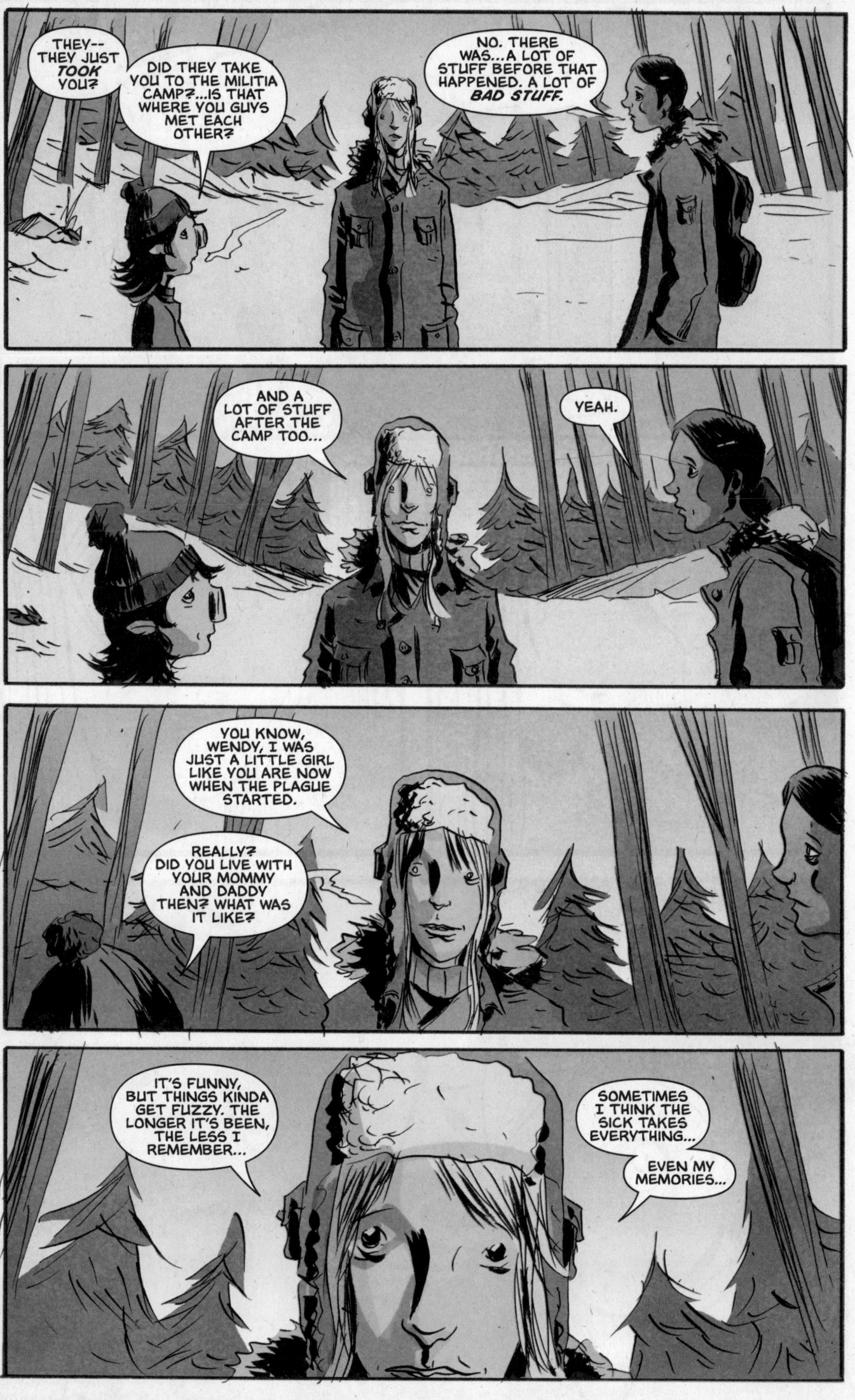
THEY-- THEY JUST TOOK YOU?
DID THEY TAKE YOU TO THE MILITIA CAMP?...IS THAT WHERE YOU GUYS MET EACH OTHER?
NO. THERE WAS...A LOT OF STUFF BEFORE THAT HAPPENED. A LOT OF BAD STUFF.
AND A LOT OF STUFF AFTER THE CAMP TOO...
YEAH.
YOU KNOW, WENDY, I WAS JUST A LITTLE GIRL LIKE YOU ARE NOW WHEN THE PLAGUE STARTED.
REALLY? DID YOU LIVE WITH YOUR MOMMY AND DADDY THEN? WHAT WAS IT LIKE?
IT'S FUNNY, BUT THINGS KINDA GET FUZZY. THE LONGER IT'S BEEN, THE LESS I REMEMBER...
SOMETIMES I THINK THE SICK TAKES EVERYTHING...
EVEN MY MEMORIES...

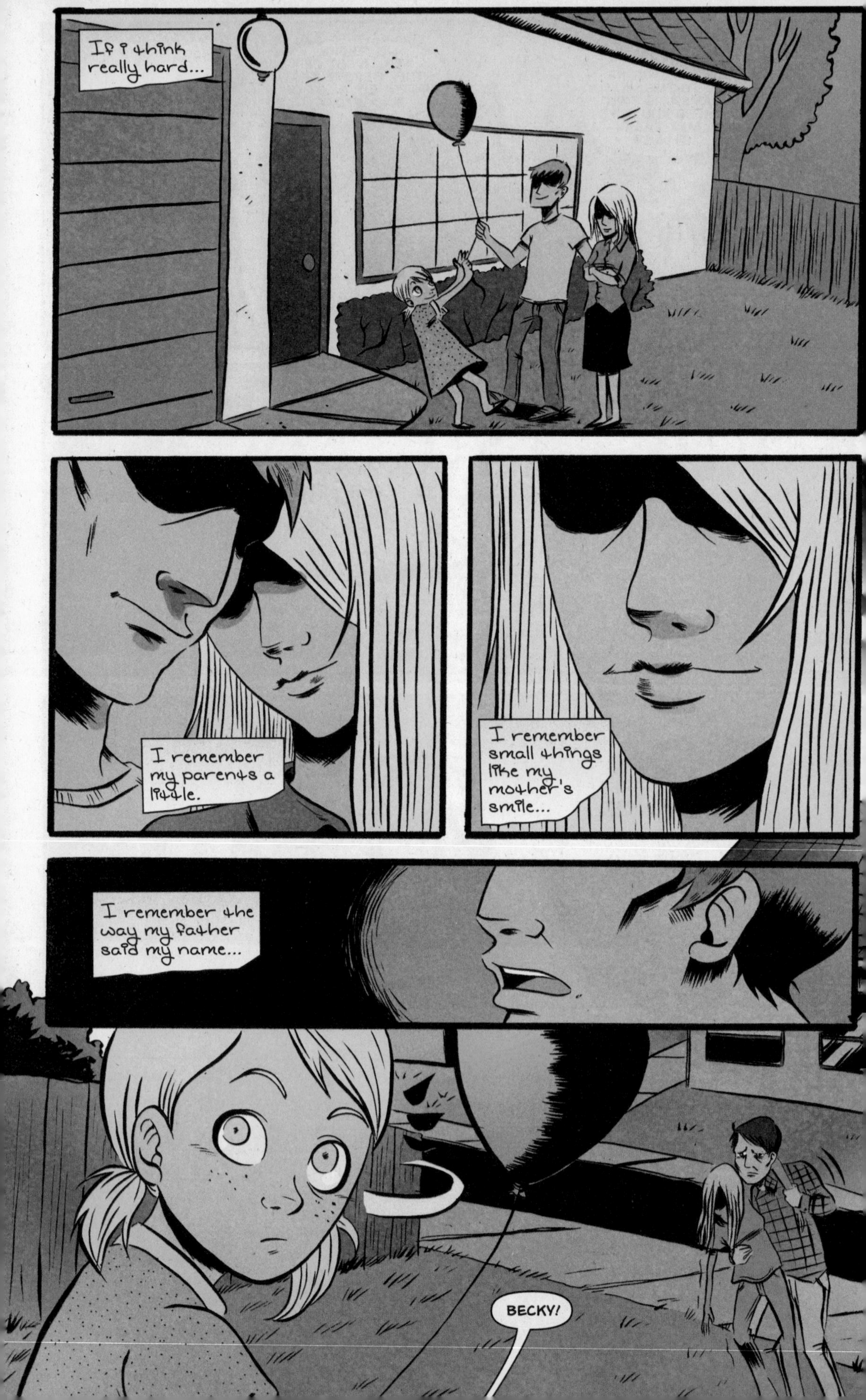
If I think really hard...
I remember my parents a little.
I remember small things like my mother's smile...
I remember the way my father said my name...
BECKY!

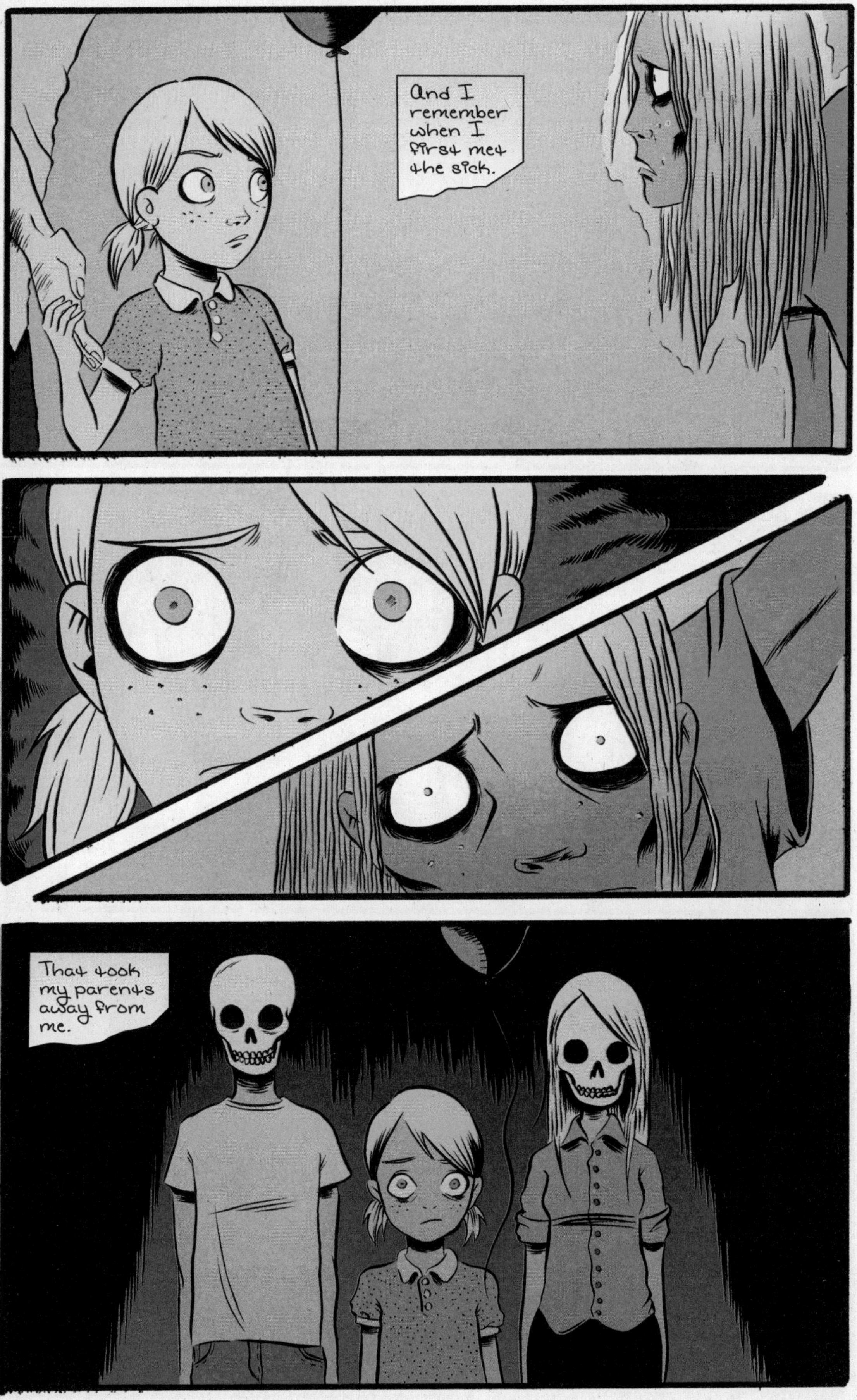
And I remember when I first met the sick.
That took my parents away from me.

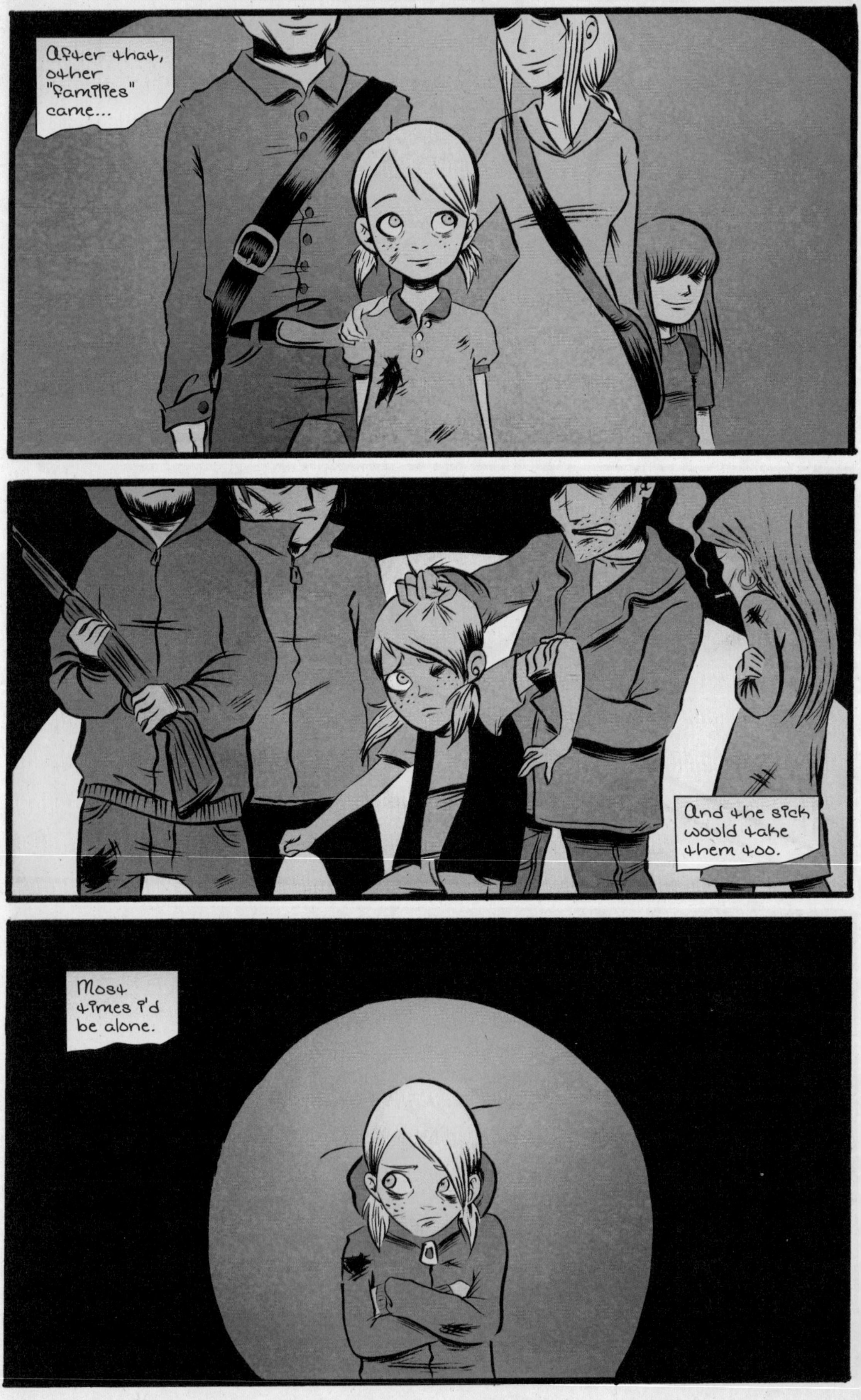
After that, other "families" came...
And the sick would take them too.
Most times I'd be alone.

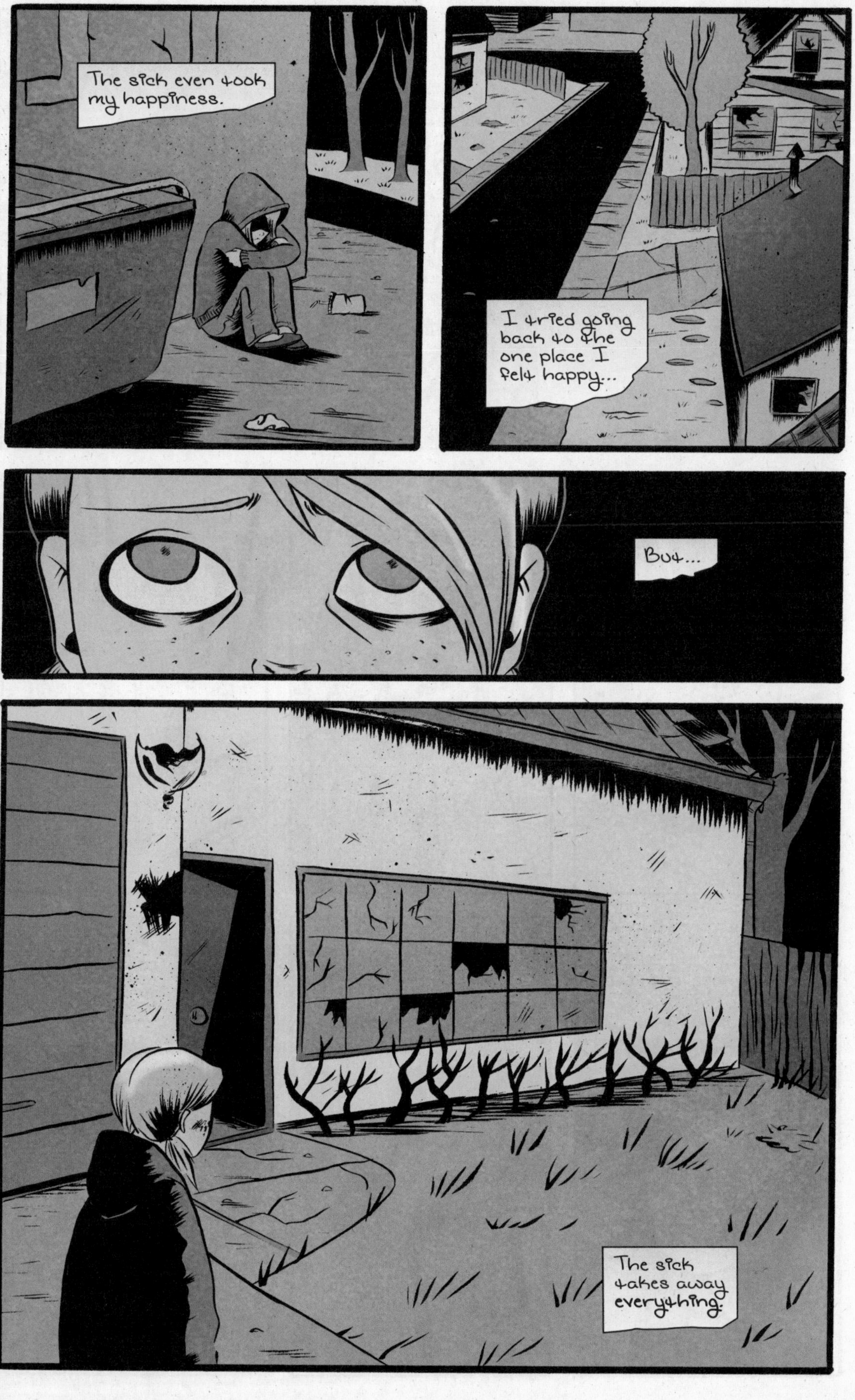
The sick even took my happiness.
I tried going back to the one place I felt happy...
But...
The sick takes away everything.

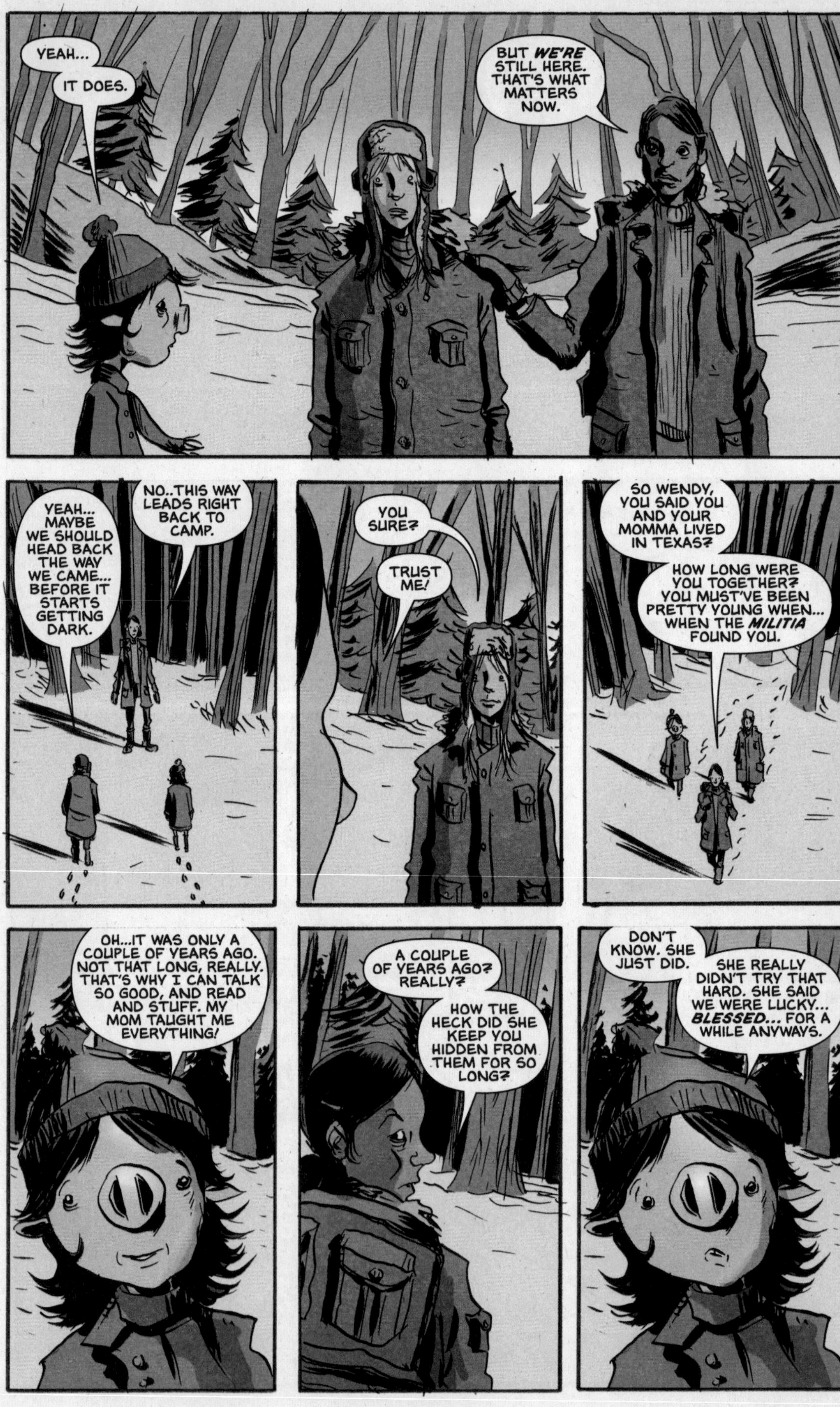
YEAH...
IT DOES.
BUT WE'RE STILL HERE. THAT'S WHAT MATTERS NOW.
YEAH... MAYBE WE SHOULD HEAD BACK THE WAY WE CAME... BEFORE IT STARTS GETTING DARK.
NO..THIS WAY LEADS RIGHT BACK TO CAMP.
YOU SURE?
TRUST ME!
SO WENDY, YOU SAID YOU AND YOUR MOMMA LIVED IN TEXAS?
HOW LONG WERE YOU TOGETHER? YOU MUST'VE BEEN PRETTY YOUNG WHEN... WHEN THE MILITIA FOUND YOU.
OH...IT WAS ONLY A COUPLE OF YEARS AGO. NOT THAT LONG, REALLY. THAT'S WHY I CAN TALK SO GOOD, AND READ AND STUFF. MY MOM TAUGHT ME EVERYTHING!
A COUPLE OF YEARS AGO? REALLY?
HOW THE HECK DID SHE KEEP YOU HIDDEN FROM THEM FOR SO LONG?
DON'T KNOW. SHE JUST DID.
SHE REALLY DIDN'T TRY THAT HARD. SHE SAID WE WERE LUCKY... BLESSED... FOR A WHILE ANYWAYS.

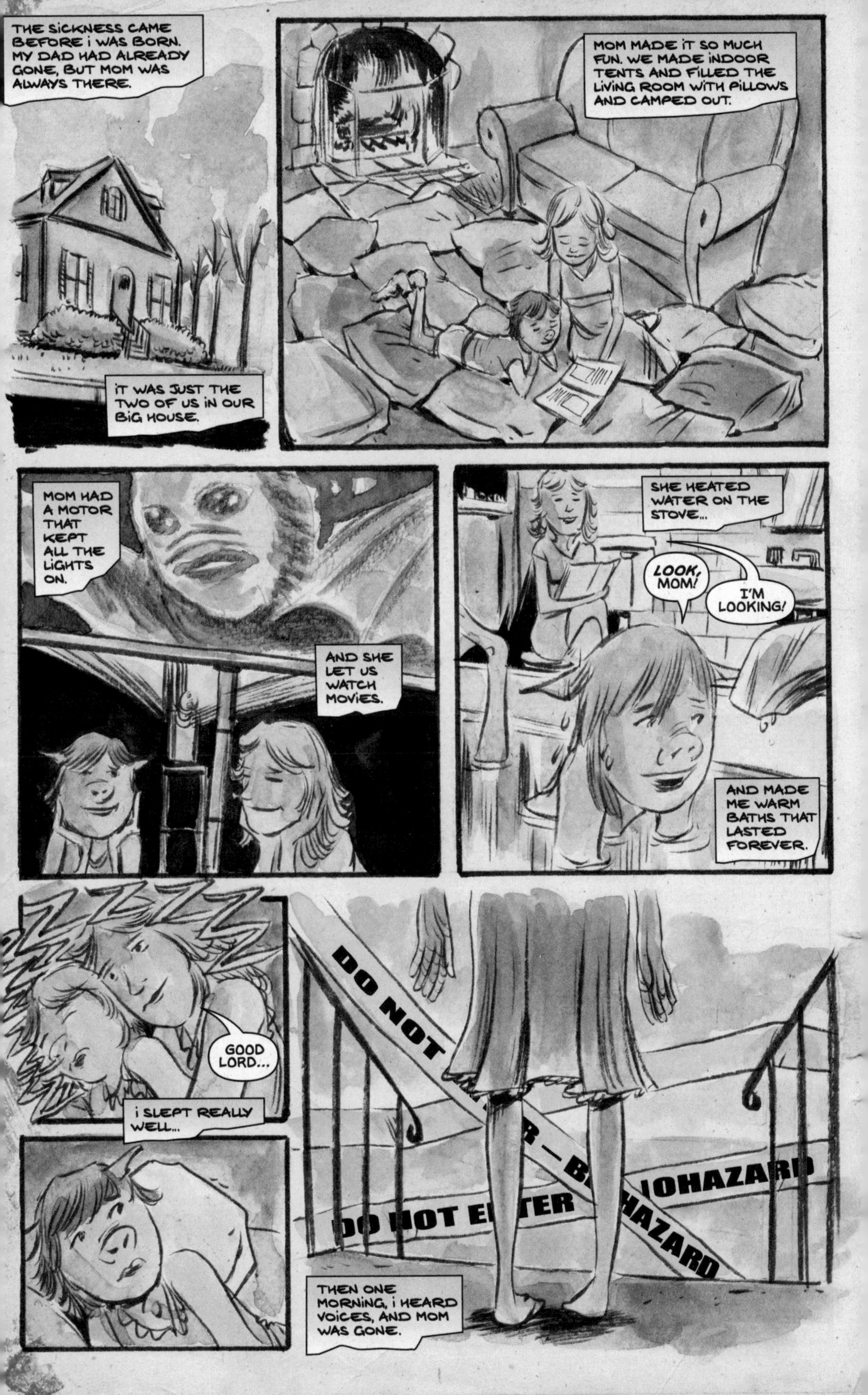
THE SICKNESS CAME BEFORE I WAS BORN. MY DAD HAD ALREADY GONE, BUT MOM WAS ALWAYS THERE.
IT WAS JUST THE TWO OF US IN OUR BIG HOUSE.
MOM MADE IT SO MUCH FUN. WE MADE INDOOR TENTS AND FILLED THE LIVING ROOM WITH PILLOWS AND CAMPED OUT.
MOM HAD A MOTOR THAT KEPT ALL THE LIGHTS ON.
AND SHE LET US WATCH MOVIES.
SHE HEATED WATER ON THE STOVE...
LOOK, MOM!
I'M LOOKING!
AND MADE ME WARM BATHS THAT LASTED FOREVER.
GOOD LORD...
I SLEPT REALLY WELL...
DO NOT
BIOHAZARD
DO NOT ENTER
HAZARD
THEN ONE MORNING, I HEARD VOICES, AND MOM WAS GONE.

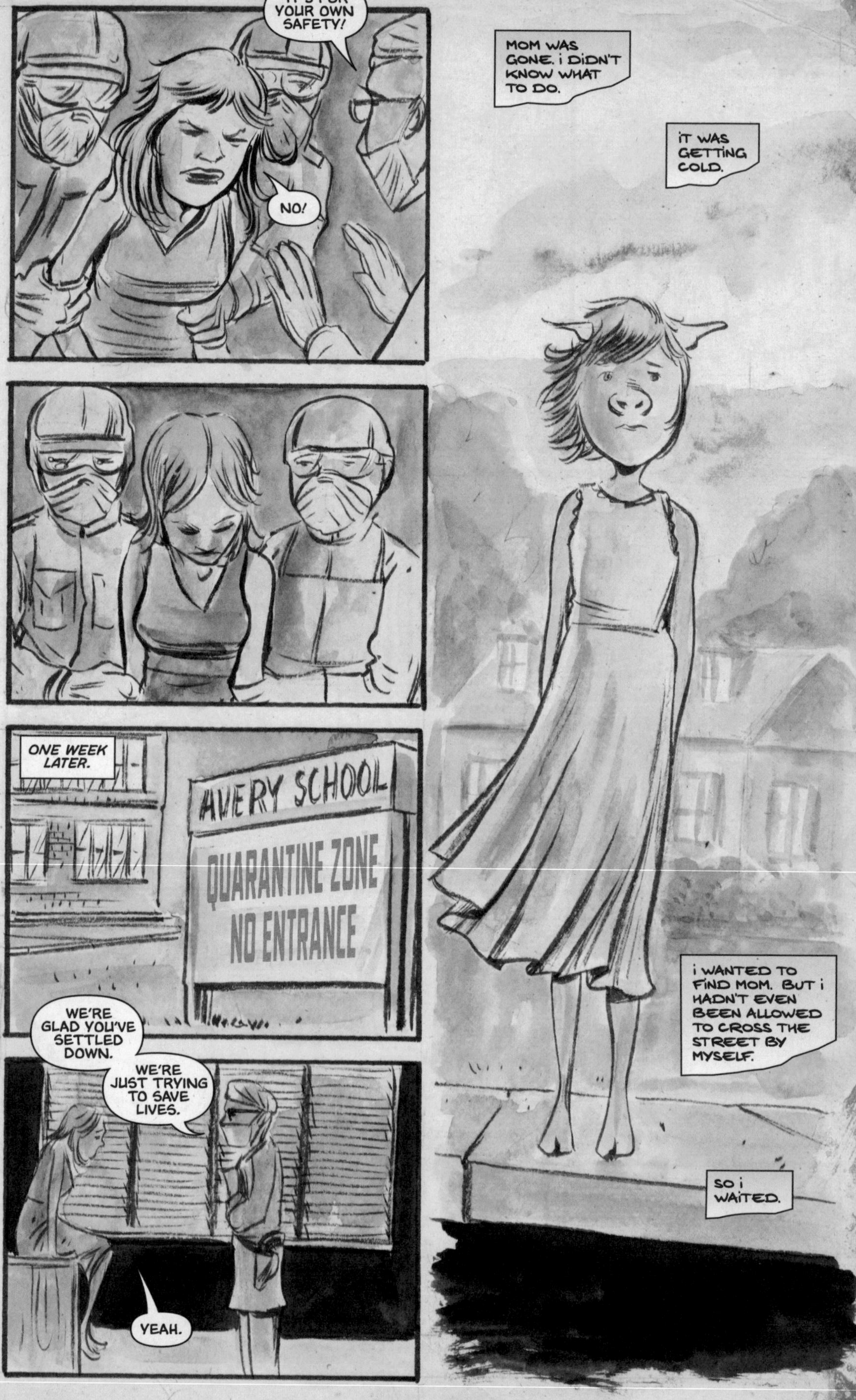

IT'S FOR YOUR OWN SAFETY!
NO!
ONE WEEK LATER.
AVERY SCHOOL
QUARANTINE ZONE NO ENTRANCE
WE'RE GLAD YOU'VE SETTLED DOWN.
WE'RE JUST TRYING TO SAVE LIVES.
YEAH.
MOM WAS GONE. I DIDN'T KNOW WHAT TO DO.
IT WAS GETTING COLD.
I WANTED TO FIND MOM. BUT I HADN'T EVEN BEEN ALLOWED TO CROSS THE STREET BY MYSELF.
SO I WAITED.

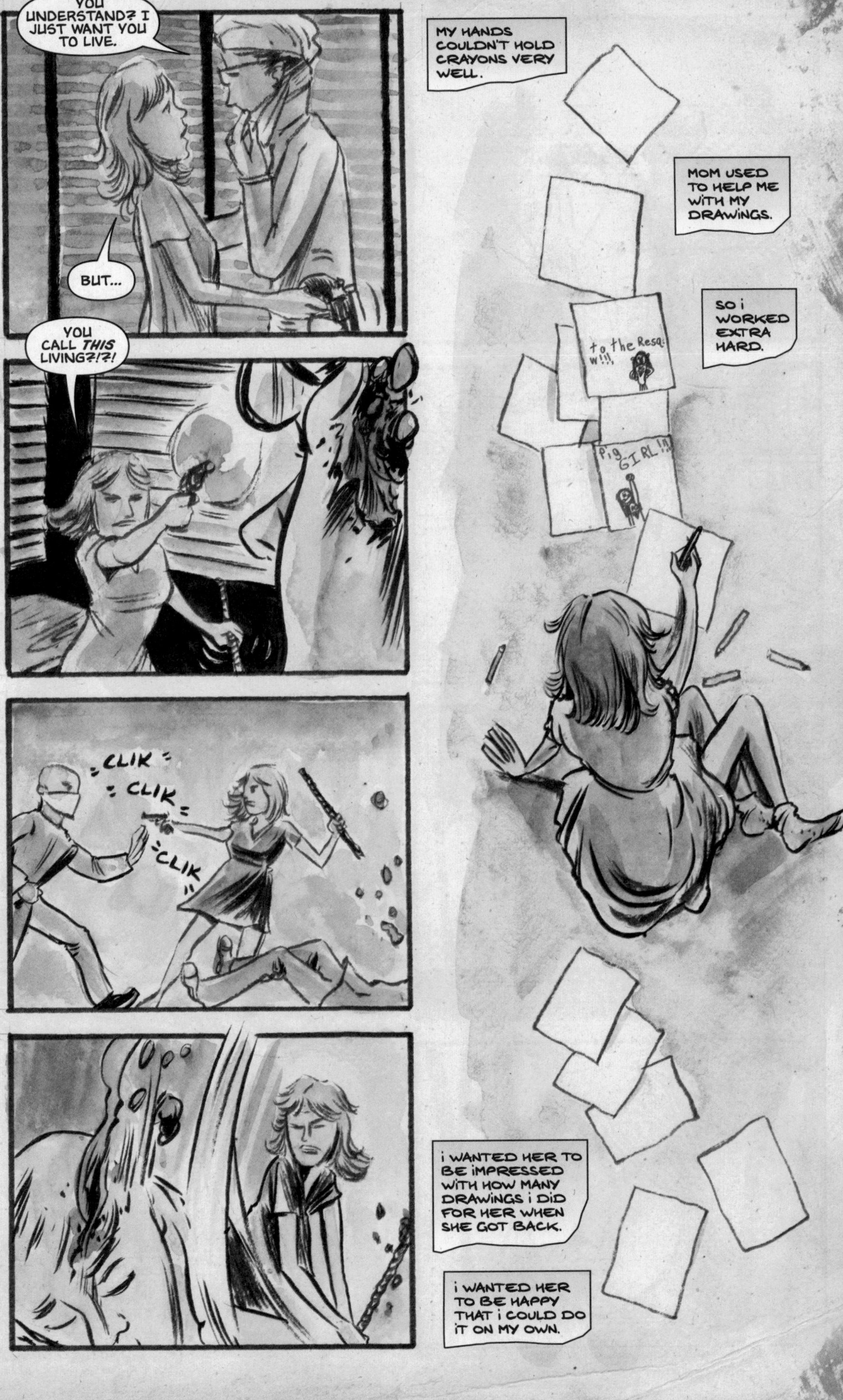
YOU UNDERSTAND? I JUST WANT YOU TO LIVE.
BUT...
YOU CALL THIS LIVING?!?!
CLIK
CLIK
CLIK
MY HANDS COULDN'T HOLD CRAYONS VERY WELL.
MOM USED TO HELP ME WITH MY DRAWINGS.
SO i WORKED EXTRA HARD.
to the Resq: w!!!
Pig GIRL!!!
i WANTED HER TO BE iMPRESSED WITH HOW MANY DRAWiNGS i DiD FOR HER WHEN SHE GOT BACK.
i WANTED HER TO BE HAPPY THAT i COULD DO iT ON MY OWN.

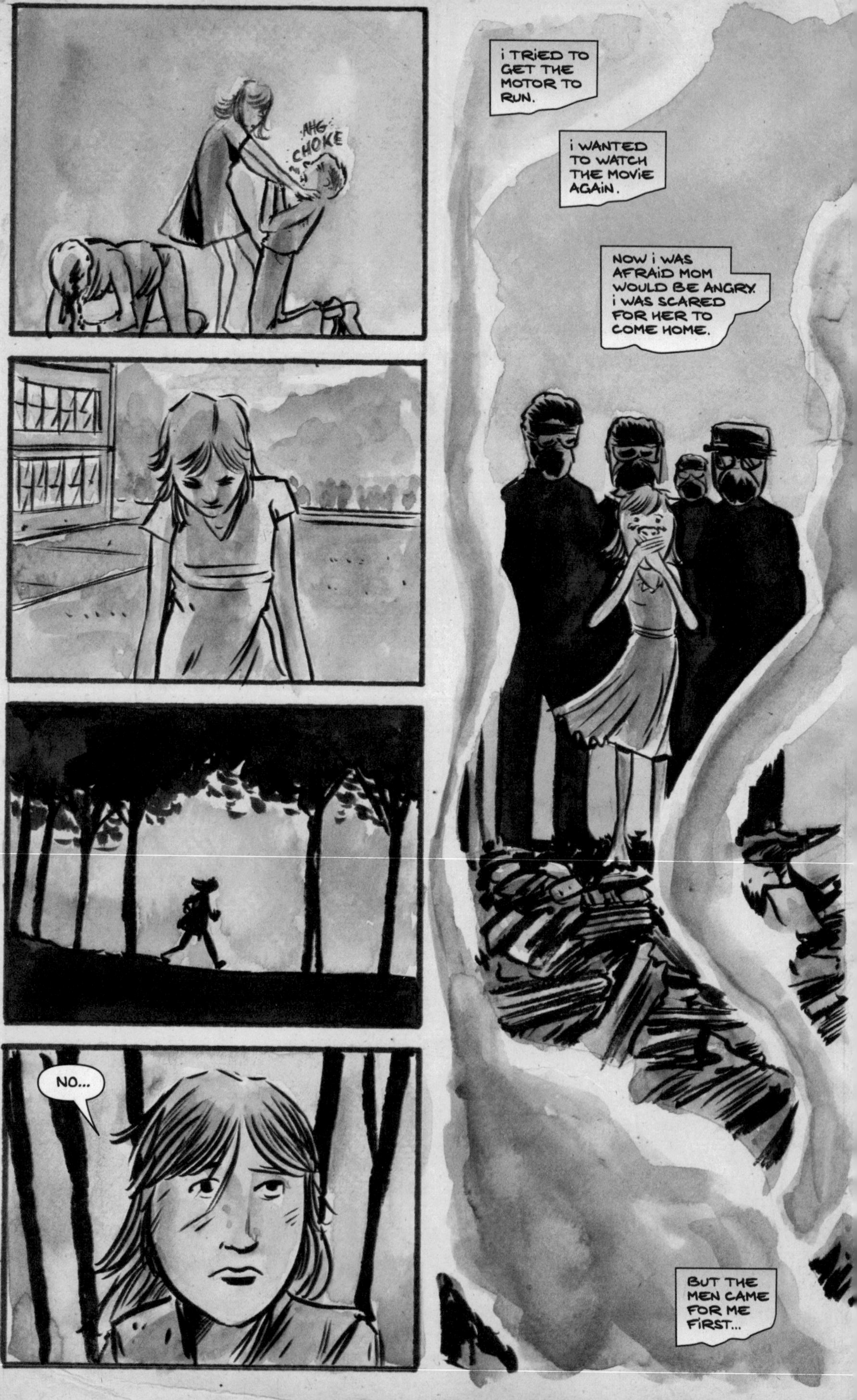
AHG
CHOKE
NO...
i TRiED TO GET THE MOTOR TO RUN.
i WANTED TO WATCH THE MOViE AGAiN.
NOW i WAS AFRAiD MOM WOULD BE ANGRY. i WAS SCARED FOR HER TO COME HOME.
BUT THE MEN CAME FOR ME FiRST...

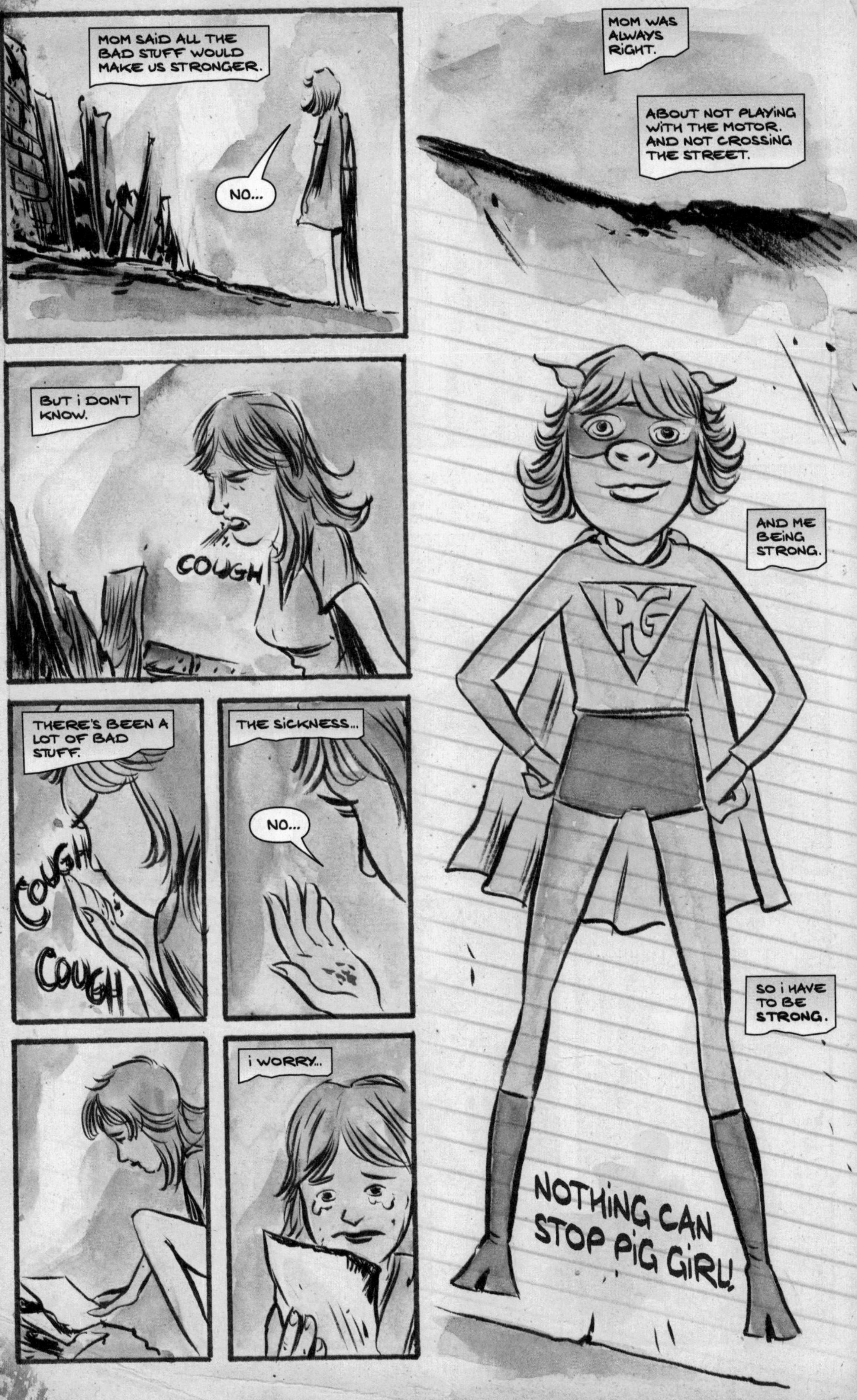
MOM SAID ALL THE BAD STUFF WOULD MAKE US STRONGER.
NO...
BUT I DON'T KNOW.
COUGH
THERE'S BEEN A LOT OF BAD STUFF.
COUGH
COUGH
THE SICKNESS...
NO...
I WORRY...
MOM WAS ALWAYS RIGHT.
ABOUT NOT PLAYING WITH THE MOTOR. AND NOT CROSSING THE STREET.
AND ME BEING STRONG.
PG
SO I HAVE TO BE STRONG.
NOTHING CAN STOP PIG GIRL!

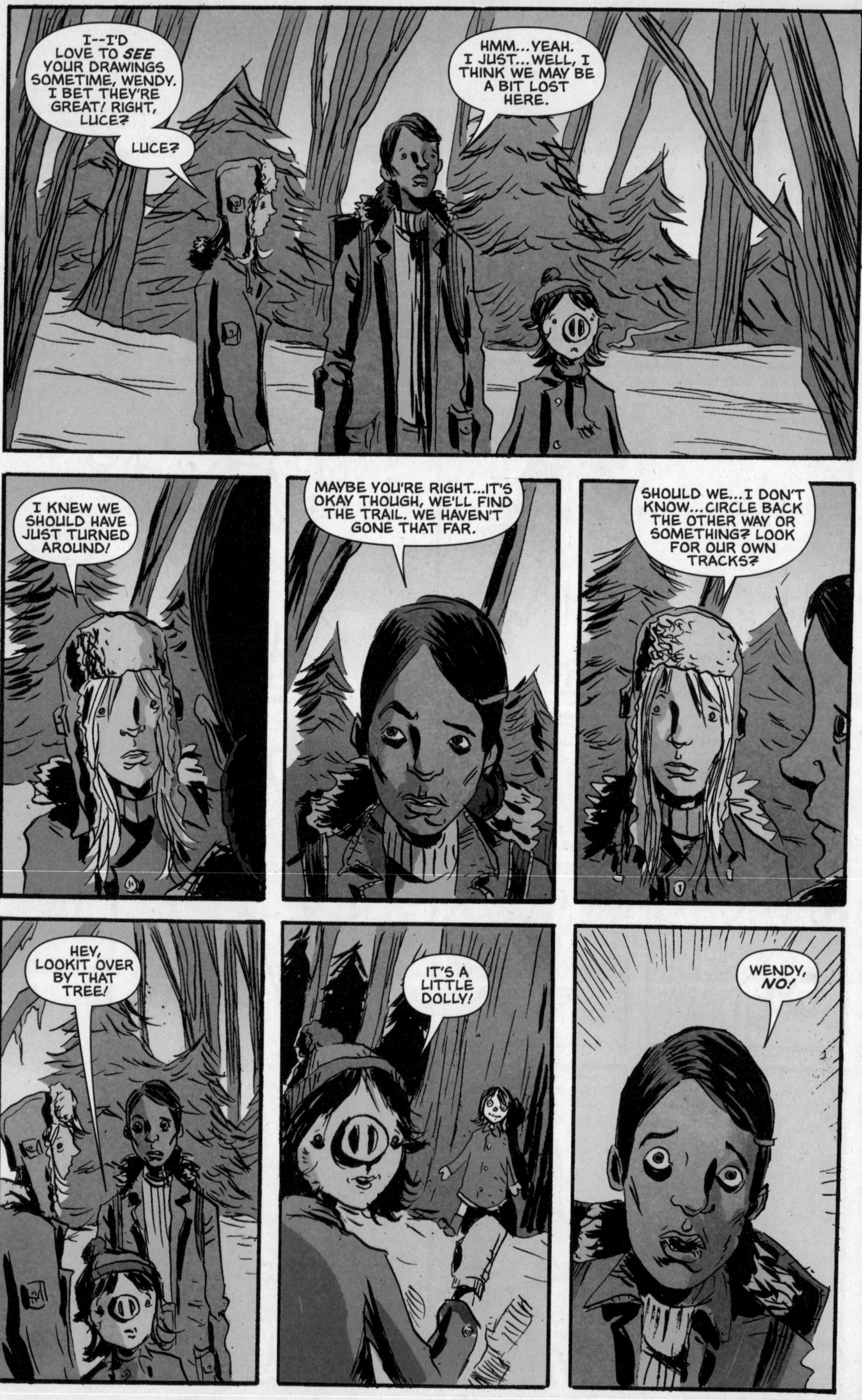
I--I'D LOVE TO SEE YOUR DRAWINGS SOMETIME, WENDY. I BET THEY'RE GREAT! RIGHT, LUCE?
LUCE?
HMM...YEAH. I JUST...WELL, I THINK WE MAY BE A BIT LOST HERE.
I KNEW WE SHOULD HAVE JUST TURNED AROUND!
MAYBE YOU'RE RIGHT...IT'S OKAY THOUGH, WE'LL FIND THE TRAIL. WE HAVEN'T GONE THAT FAR.
SHOULD WE...I DON'T KNOW...CIRCLE BACK THE OTHER WAY OR SOMETHING? LOOK FOR OUR OWN TRACKS?
HEY, LOOKIT OVER BY THAT TREE!
IT'S A LITTLE DOLLY!
WENDY, NO!

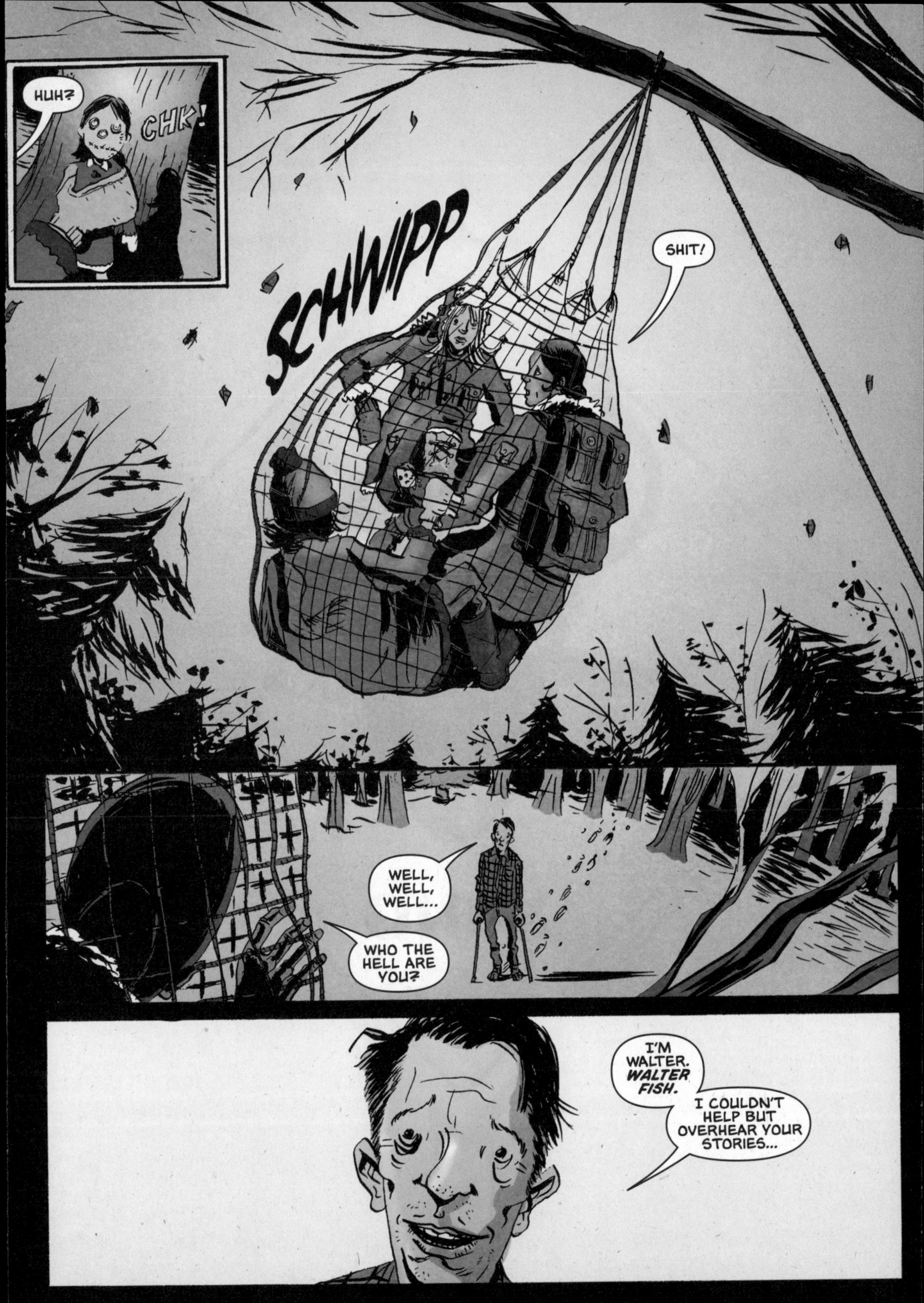
HUH?
CHK!
SCHWIPP
SHIT!
WELL, WELL, WELL...
WHO THE HELL ARE YOU?
I'M WALTER. *WALTER FISH.*
I COULDN'T HELP BUT OVERHEAR YOUR STORIES...

ENDANGERED SPECIES PRELUDE: LOST TRAILS

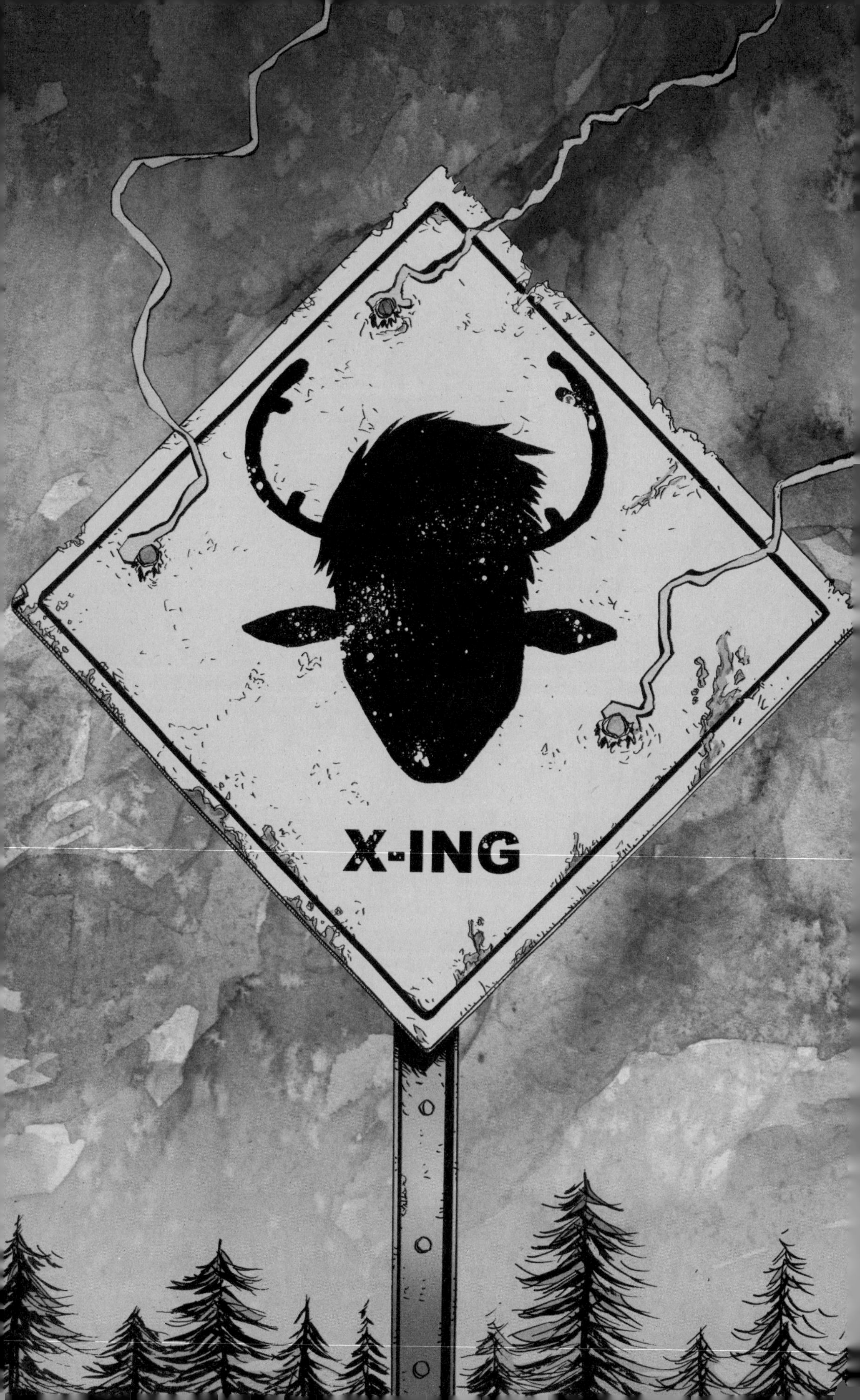
X-ING

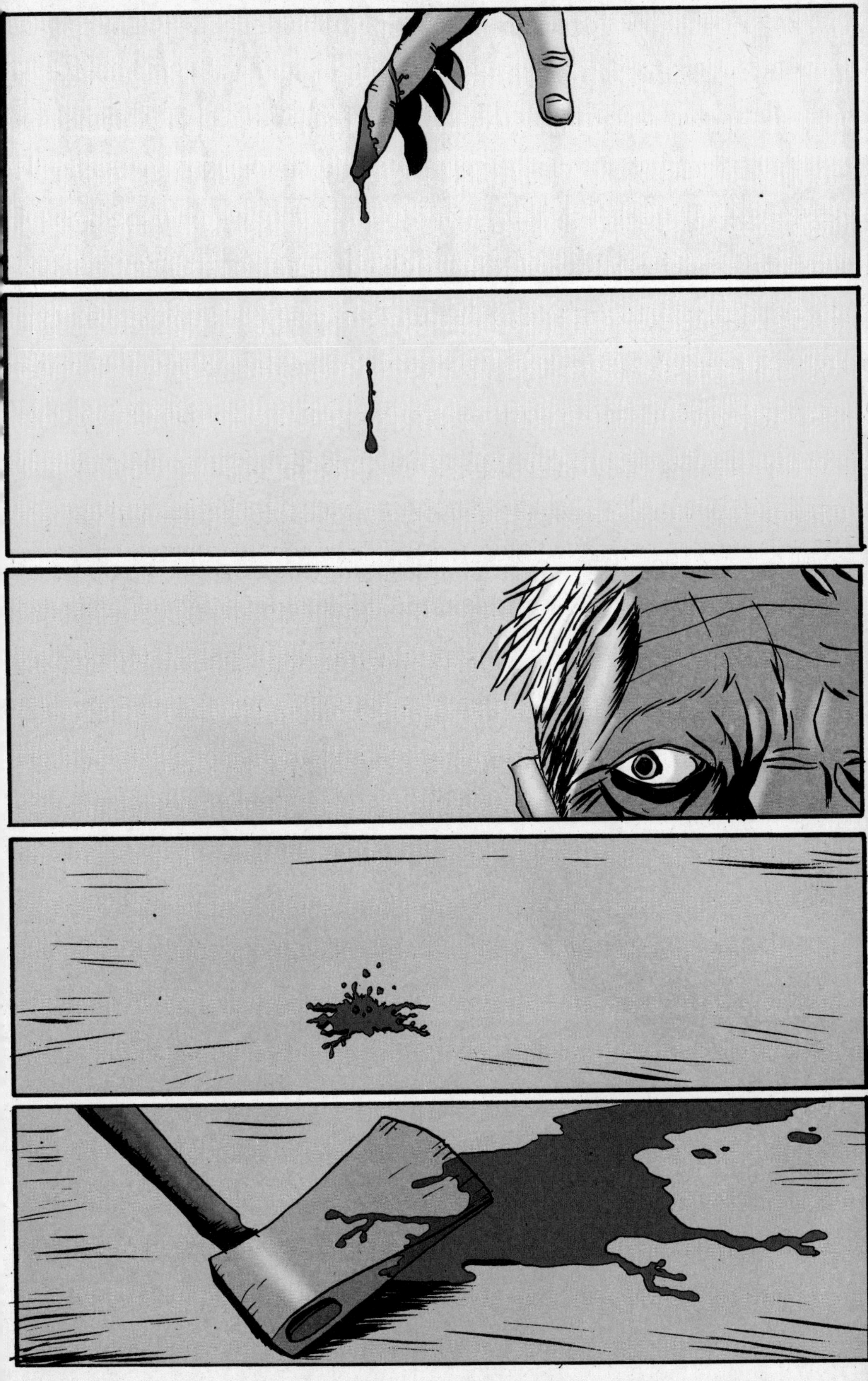

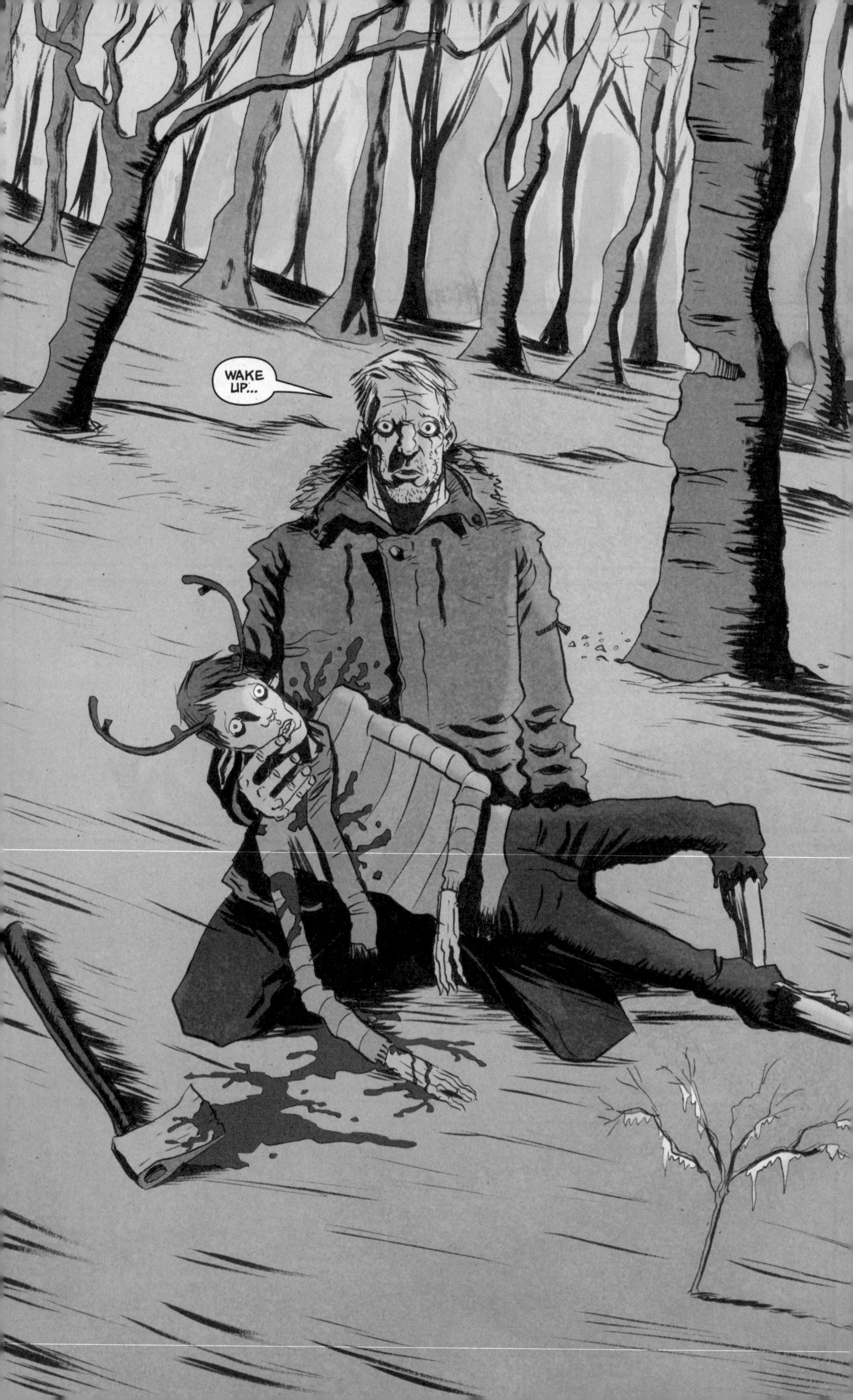
WAKE UP...

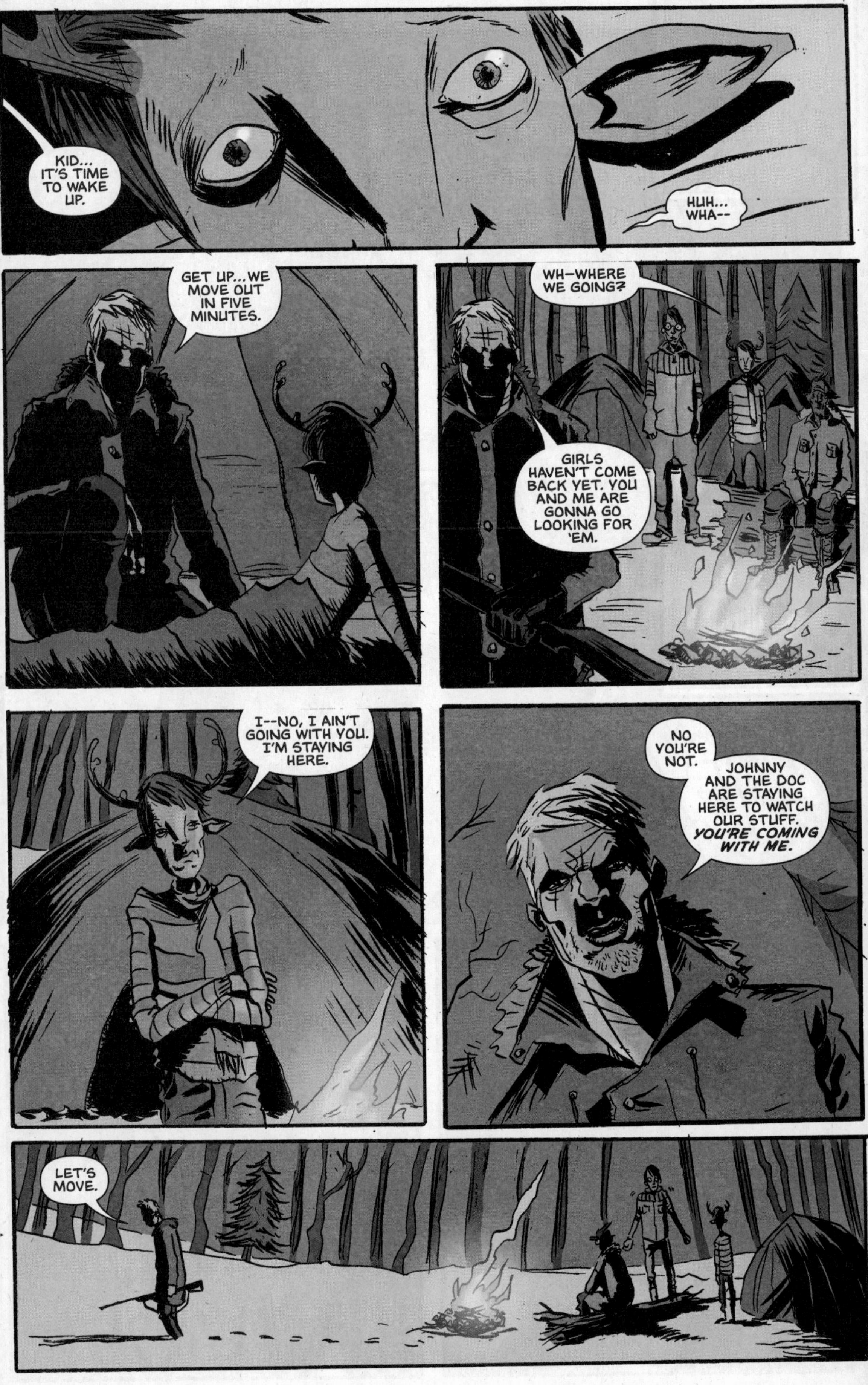
KID... IT'S TIME TO WAKE UP.
HUH... WHA--
GET UP... WE MOVE OUT IN FIVE MINUTES.
WH-WHERE WE GOING?
GIRLS HAVEN'T COME BACK YET. YOU AND ME ARE GONNA GO LOOKING FOR 'EM.
I--NO, I AIN'T GOING WITH YOU. I'M STAYING HERE.
NO YOU'RE NOT.
JOHNNY AND THE DOC ARE STAYING HERE TO WATCH OUR STUFF. *YOU'RE COMING WITH ME.*
LET'S MOVE.

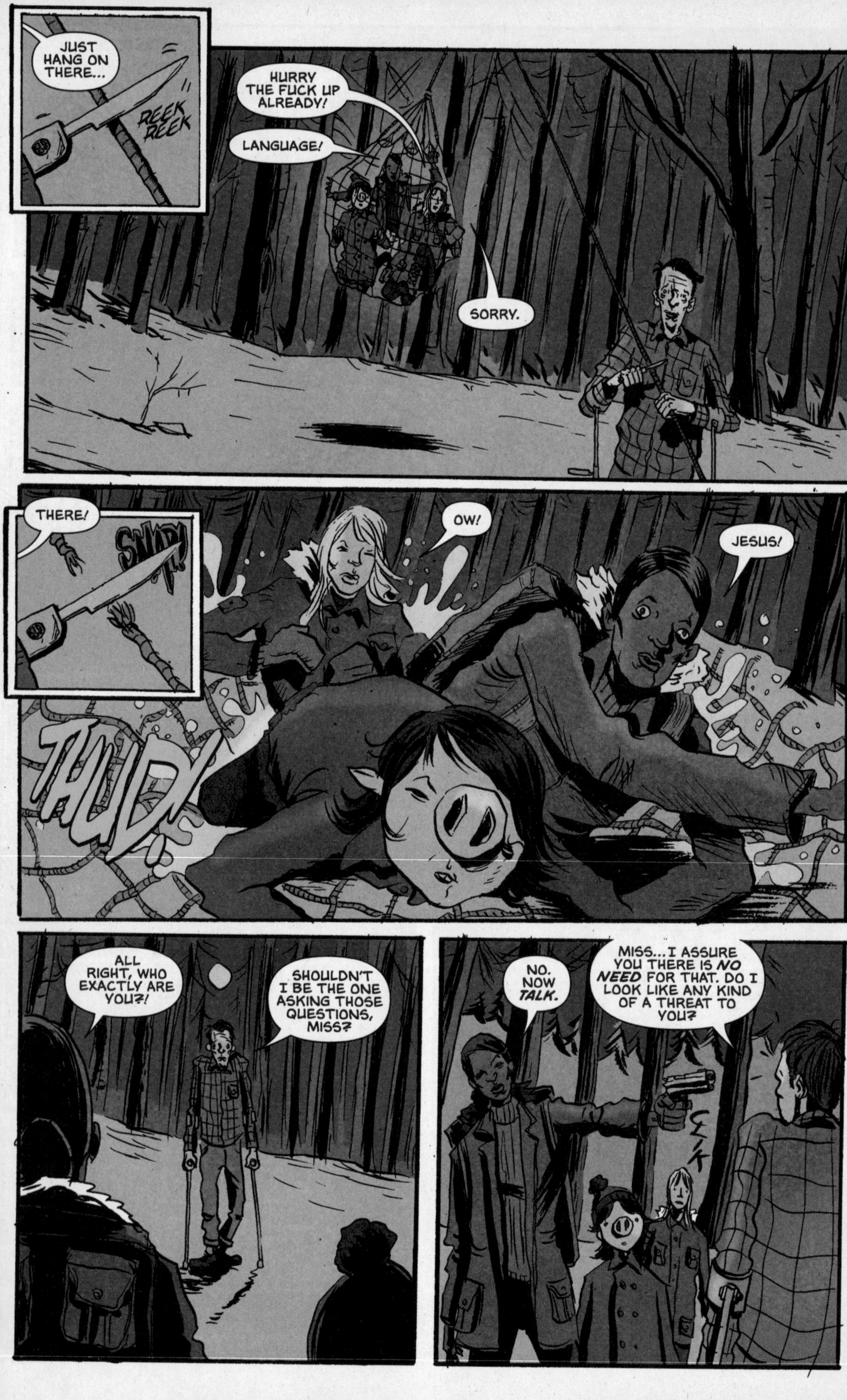
JUST HANG ON THERE...
REEK REEK
HURRY THE FUCK UP ALREADY!
LANGUAGE!
SORRY.
THERE!
SNAP!
OW!
JESUS!
THUD!
ALL RIGHT, WHO EXACTLY ARE YOU?!
SHOULDN'T I BE THE ONE ASKING THOSE QUESTIONS, MISS?
NO. NOW TALK.
MISS... I ASSURE YOU THERE IS NO NEED FOR THAT. DO I LOOK LIKE ANY KIND OF A THREAT TO YOU?
CLIK

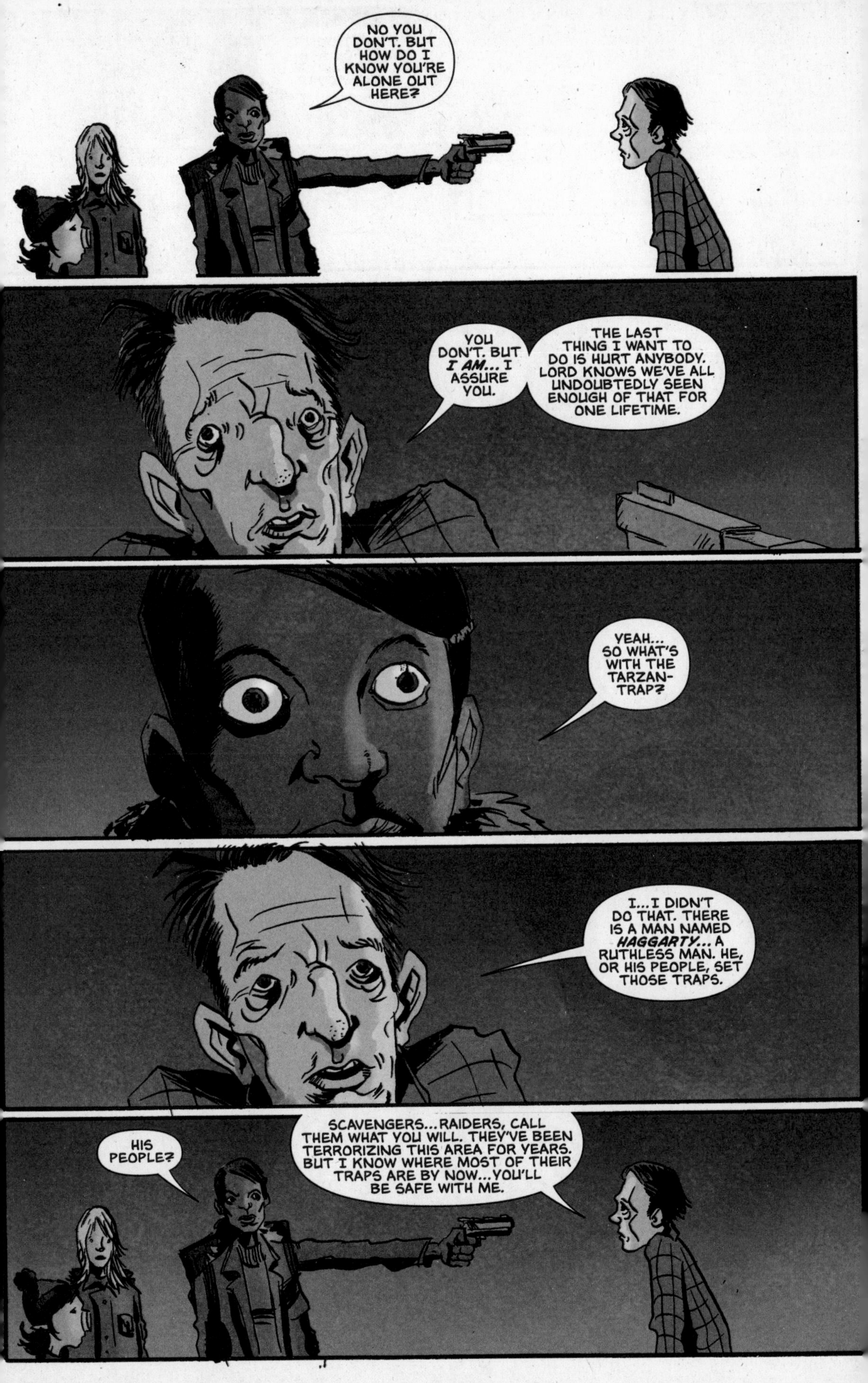
NO YOU DON'T. BUT HOW DO I KNOW YOU'RE ALONE OUT HERE?
YOU DON'T. BUT I AM... I ASSURE YOU.
THE LAST THING I WANT TO DO IS HURT ANYBODY. LORD KNOWS WE'VE ALL UNDOUBTEDLY SEEN ENOUGH OF THAT FOR ONE LIFETIME.
YEAH... SO WHAT'S WITH THE TARZAN-TRAP?
I...I DIDN'T DO THAT. THERE IS A MAN NAMED HAGGARTY... A RUTHLESS MAN. HE, OR HIS PEOPLE, SET THOSE TRAPS.
HIS PEOPLE?
SCAVENGERS...RAIDERS, CALL THEM WHAT YOU WILL. THEY'VE BEEN TERRORIZING THIS AREA FOR YEARS. BUT I KNOW WHERE MOST OF THEIR TRAPS ARE BY NOW...YOU'LL BE SAFE WITH ME.

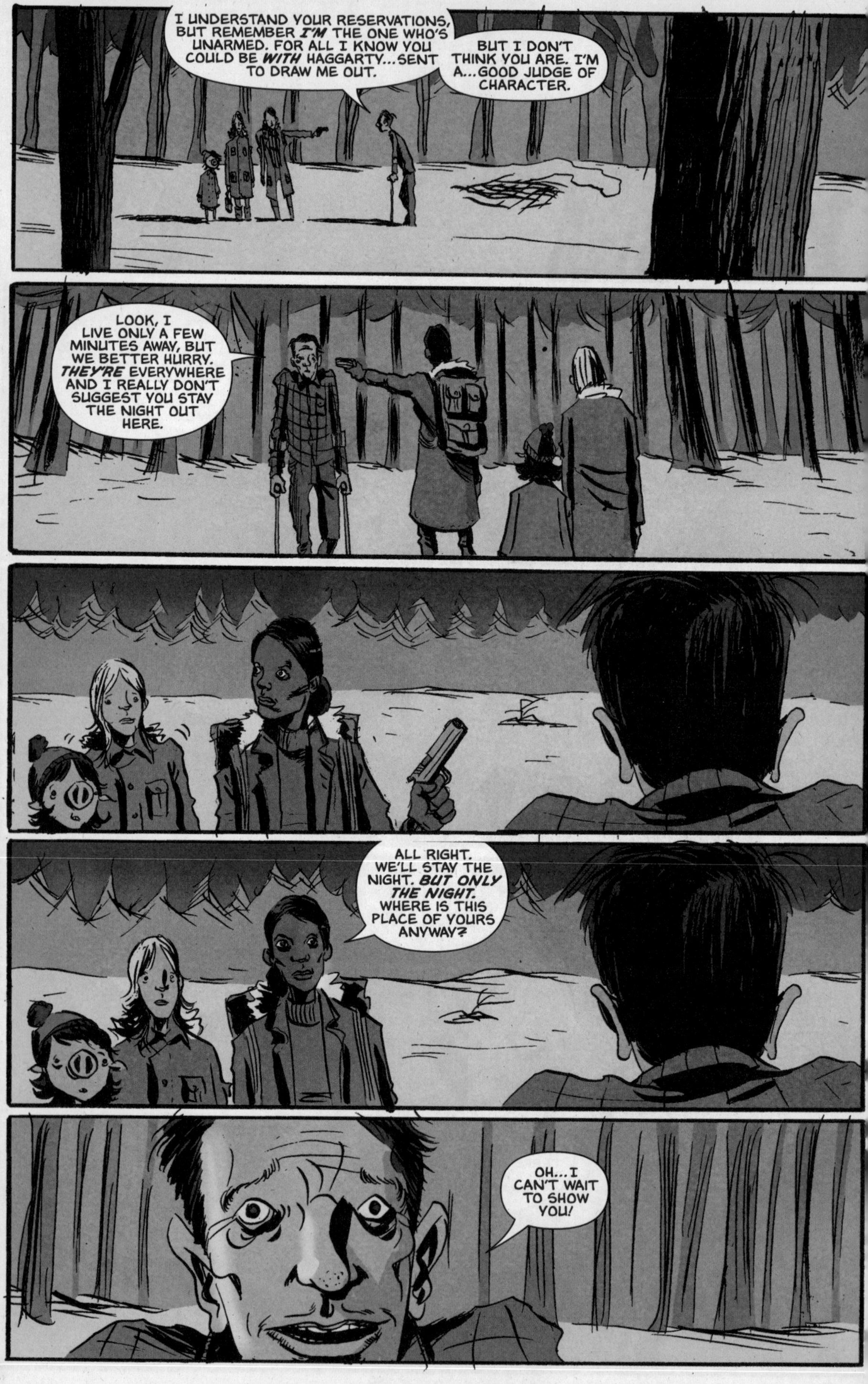
I UNDERSTAND YOUR RESERVATIONS, BUT REMEMBER I'M THE ONE WHO'S UNARMED. FOR ALL I KNOW YOU COULD BE WITH HAGGARTY...SENT TO DRAW ME OUT.
BUT I DON'T THINK YOU ARE. I'M A...GOOD JUDGE OF CHARACTER.
LOOK, I LIVE ONLY A FEW MINUTES AWAY, BUT WE BETTER HURRY. THEY'RE EVERYWHERE AND I REALLY DON'T SUGGEST YOU STAY THE NIGHT OUT HERE.
ALL RIGHT. WE'LL STAY THE NIGHT. BUT ONLY THE NIGHT. WHERE IS THIS PLACE OF YOURS ANYWAY?
OH...I CAN'T WAIT TO SHOW YOU!

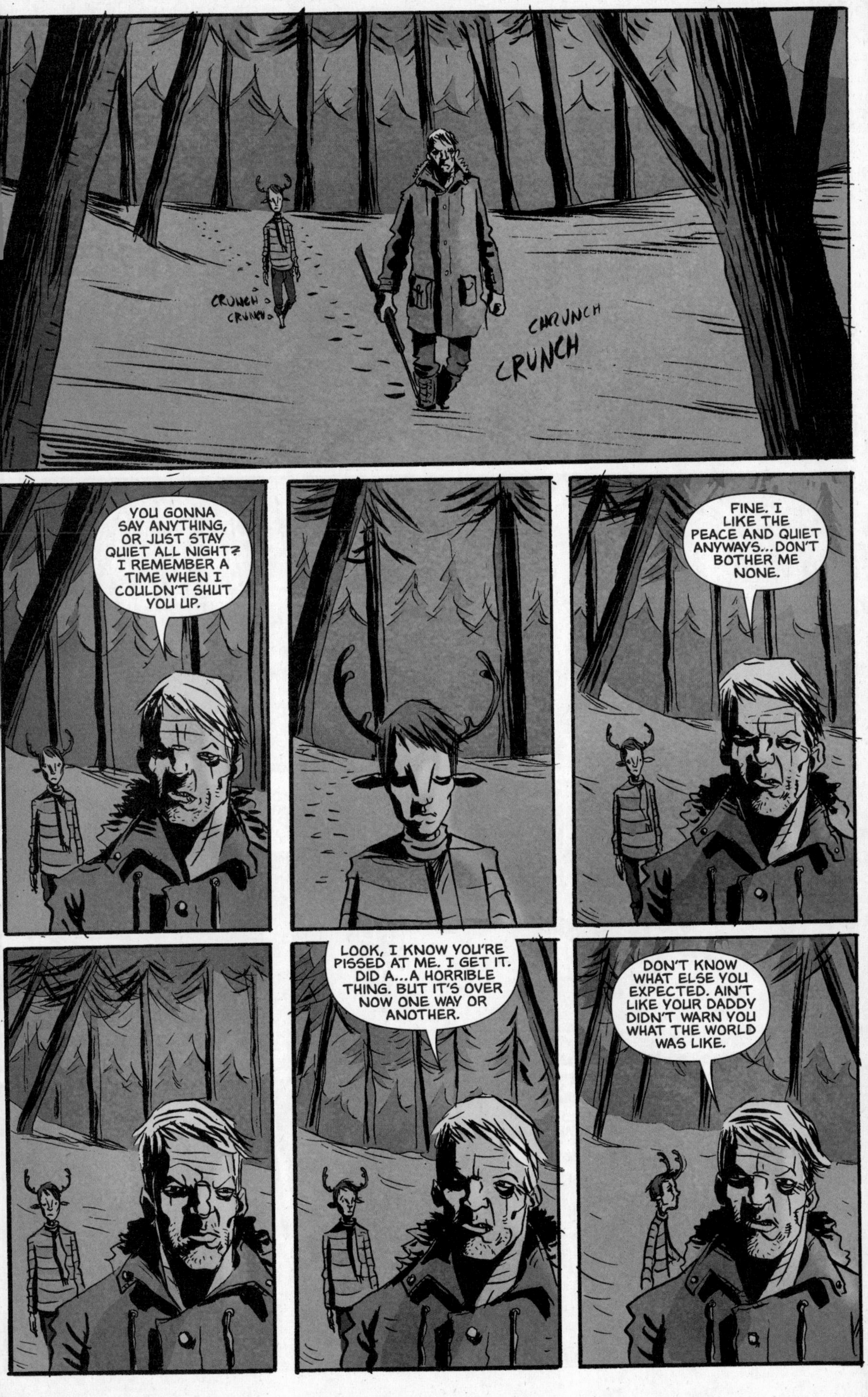
CRUNCH
CRUNCH
CRRUNCH
CRUNCH
YOU GONNA SAY ANYTHING, OR JUST STAY QUIET ALL NIGHT? I REMEMBER A TIME WHEN I COULDN'T SHUT YOU UP.
FINE. I LIKE THE PEACE AND QUIET ANYWAYS... DON'T BOTHER ME NONE.
LOOK, I KNOW YOU'RE PISSED AT ME. I GET IT. DID A... A HORRIBLE THING. BUT IT'S OVER NOW ONE WAY OR ANOTHER.
DON'T KNOW WHAT ELSE YOU EXPECTED. AIN'T LIKE YOUR DADDY DIDN'T WARN YOU WHAT THE WORLD WAS LIKE.

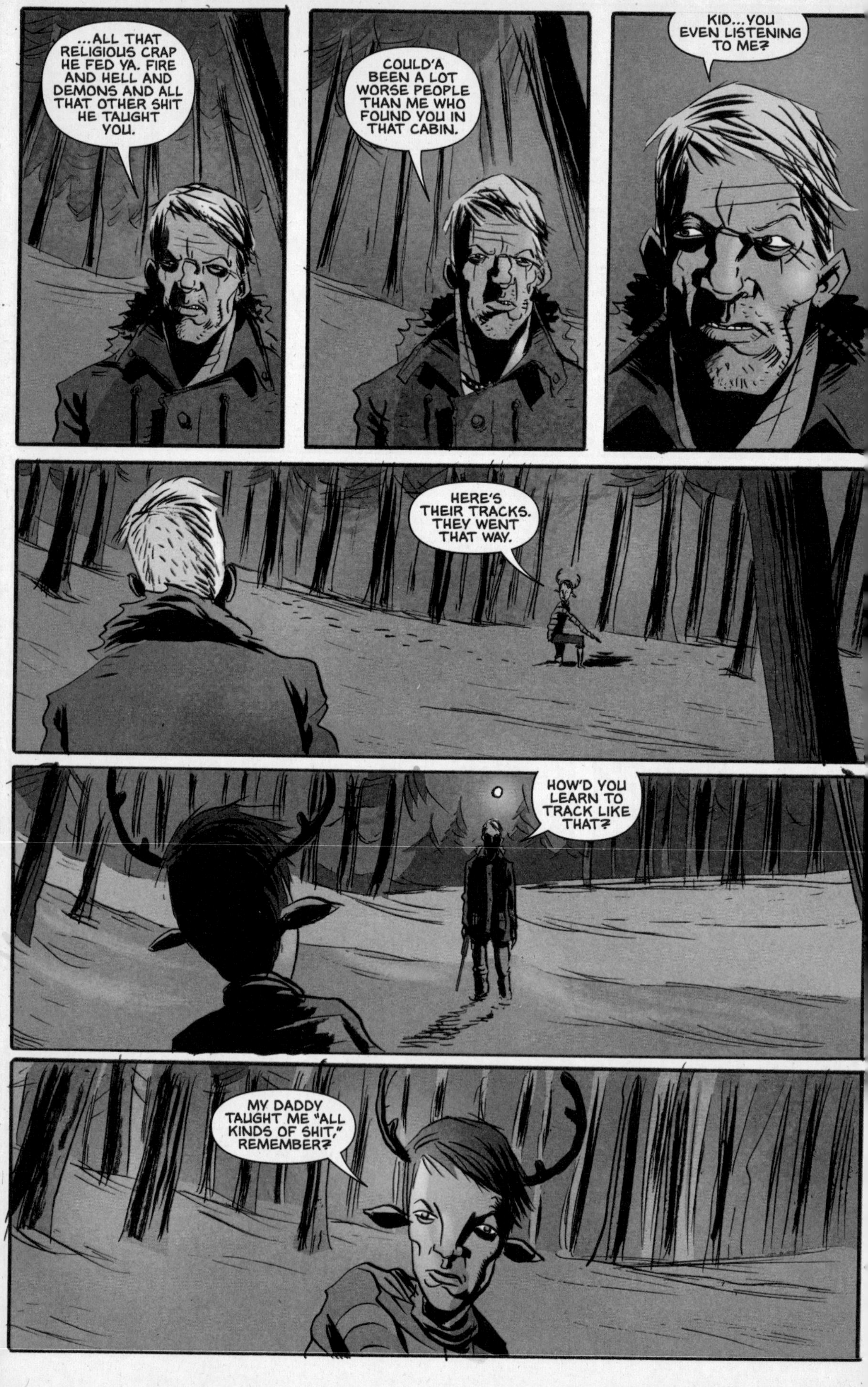
...ALL THAT RELIGIOUS CRAP HE FED YA. FIRE AND HELL AND DEMONS AND ALL THAT OTHER SHIT HE TAUGHT YOU.
COULD'A BEEN A LOT WORSE PEOPLE THAN ME WHO FOUND YOU IN THAT CABIN.
KID...YOU EVEN LISTENING TO ME?
HERE'S THEIR TRACKS. THEY WENT THAT WAY.
HOW'D YOU LEARN TO TRACK LIKE THAT?
MY DADDY TAUGHT ME "ALL KINDS OF SHIT," REMEMBER?

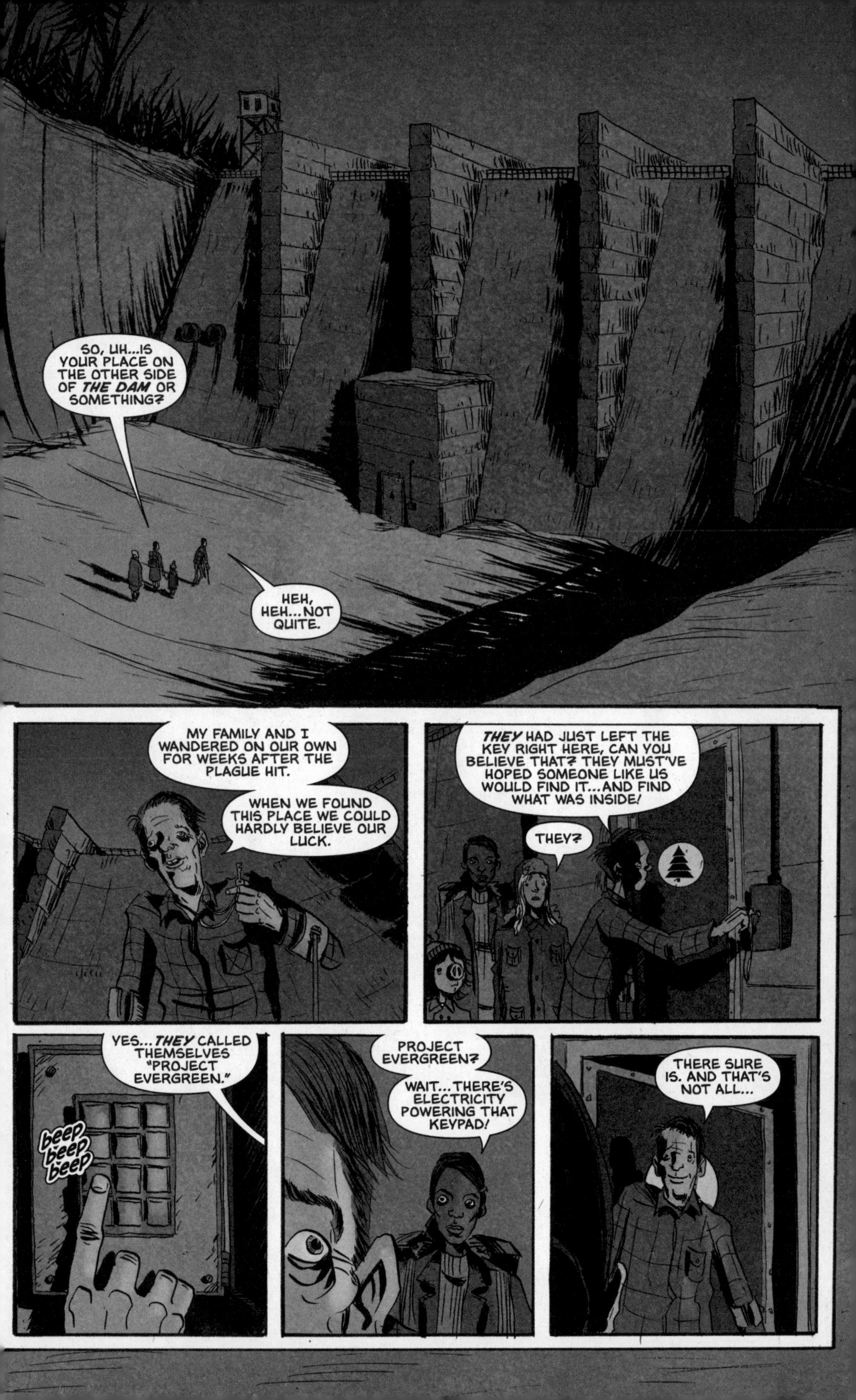

SO, UH...IS YOUR PLACE ON THE OTHER SIDE OF THE DAM OR SOMETHING?
HEH, HEH...NOT QUITE.
MY FAMILY AND I WANDERED ON OUR OWN FOR WEEKS AFTER THE PLAGUE HIT.
WHEN WE FOUND THIS PLACE WE COULD HARDLY BELIEVE OUR LUCK.
THEY HAD JUST LEFT THE KEY RIGHT HERE, CAN YOU BELIEVE THAT? THEY MUST'VE HOPED SOMEONE LIKE US WOULD FIND IT...AND FIND WHAT WAS INSIDE!
THEY?
YES...THEY CALLED THEMSELVES "PROJECT EVERGREEN."
beep beep beep
PROJECT EVERGREEN?
WAIT...THERE'S ELECTRICITY POWERING THAT KEYPAD!
THERE SURE IS. AND THAT'S NOT ALL...

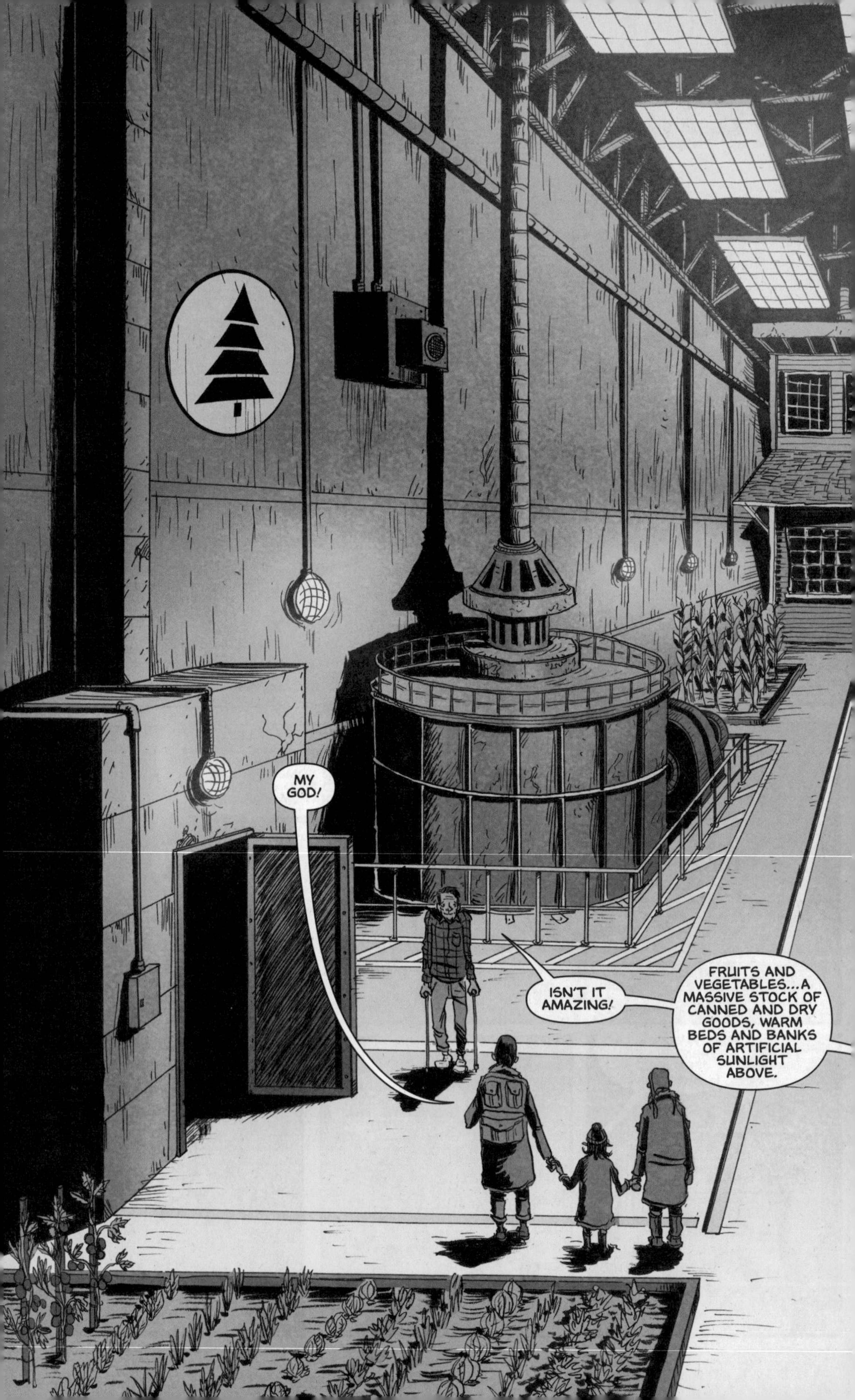
MY GOD!
ISN'T IT AMAZING!
FRUITS AND VEGETABLES...A MASSIVE STOCK OF CANNED AND DRY GOODS, WARM BEDS AND BANKS OF ARTIFICIAL SUNLIGHT ABOVE.

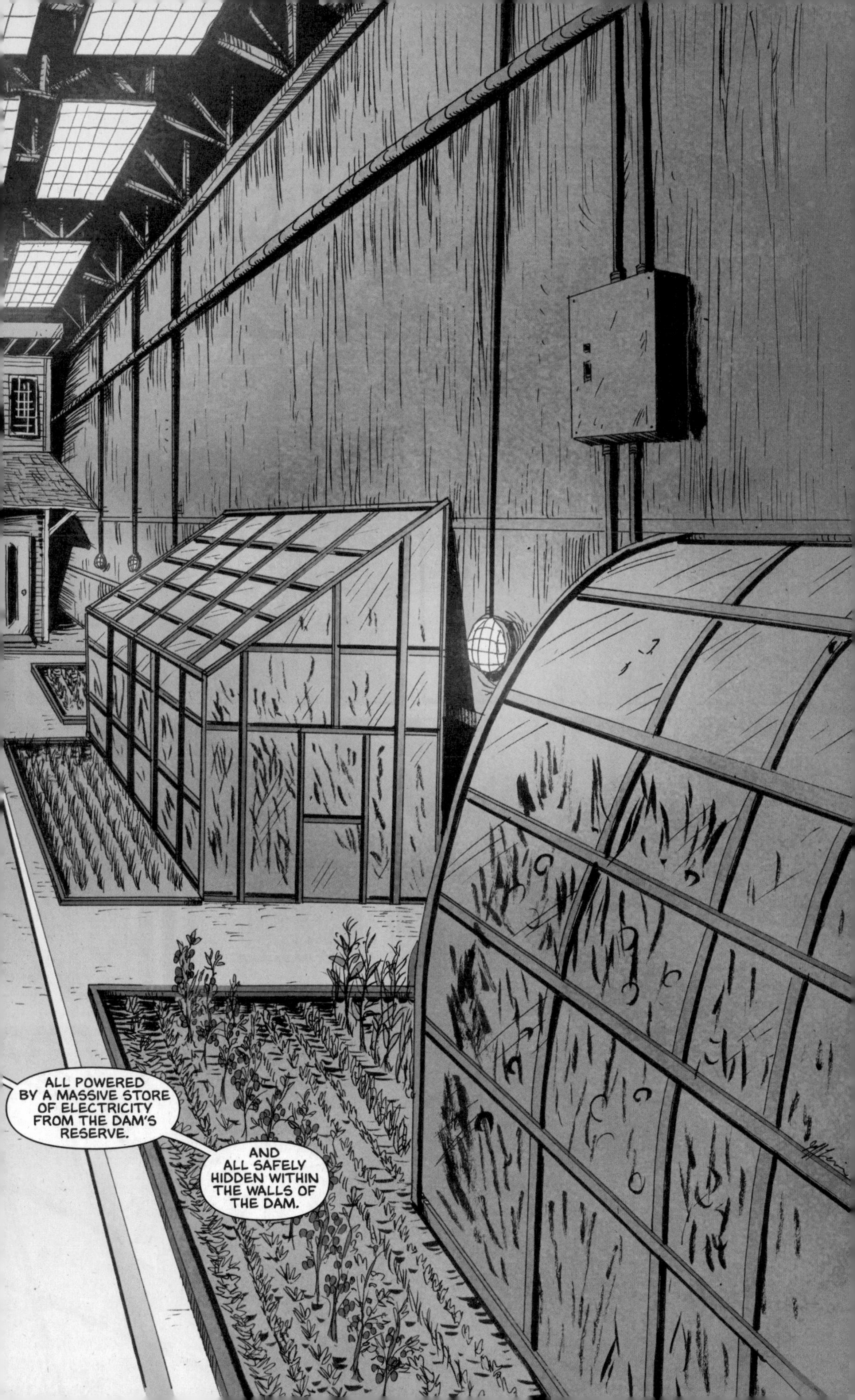
ALL POWERED BY A MASSIVE STORE OF ELECTRICITY FROM THE DAM'S RESERVE.
AND ALL SAFELY HIDDEN WITHIN THE WALLS OF THE DAM.

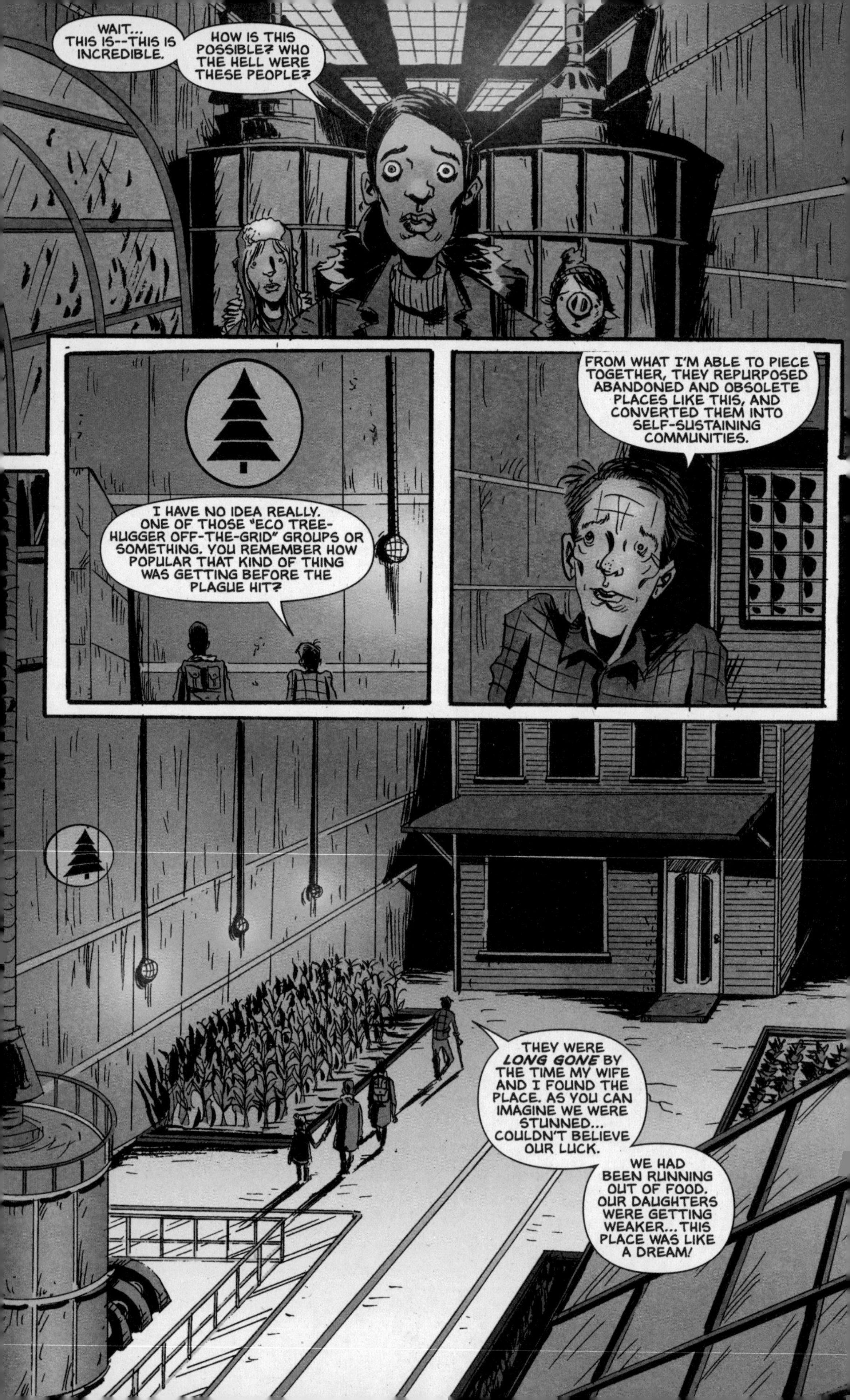
WAIT... THIS IS--THIS IS INCREDIBLE.
HOW IS THIS POSSIBLE? WHO THE HELL WERE THESE PEOPLE?
I HAVE NO IDEA REALLY. ONE OF THOSE "ECO TREE-HUGGER OFF-THE-GRID" GROUPS OR SOMETHING. YOU REMEMBER HOW POPULAR THAT KIND OF THING WAS GETTING BEFORE THE PLAGUE HIT?
FROM WHAT I'M ABLE TO PIECE TOGETHER, THEY REPURPOSED ABANDONED AND OBSOLETE PLACES LIKE THIS, AND CONVERTED THEM INTO SELF-SUSTAINING COMMUNITIES.
THEY WERE *LONG GONE* BY THE TIME MY WIFE AND I FOUND THE PLACE. AS YOU CAN IMAGINE WE WERE STUNNED... COULDN'T BELIEVE OUR LUCK.
WE HAD BEEN RUNNING OUT OF FOOD. OUR DAUGHTERS WERE GETTING WEAKER... THIS PLACE WAS LIKE A DREAM!

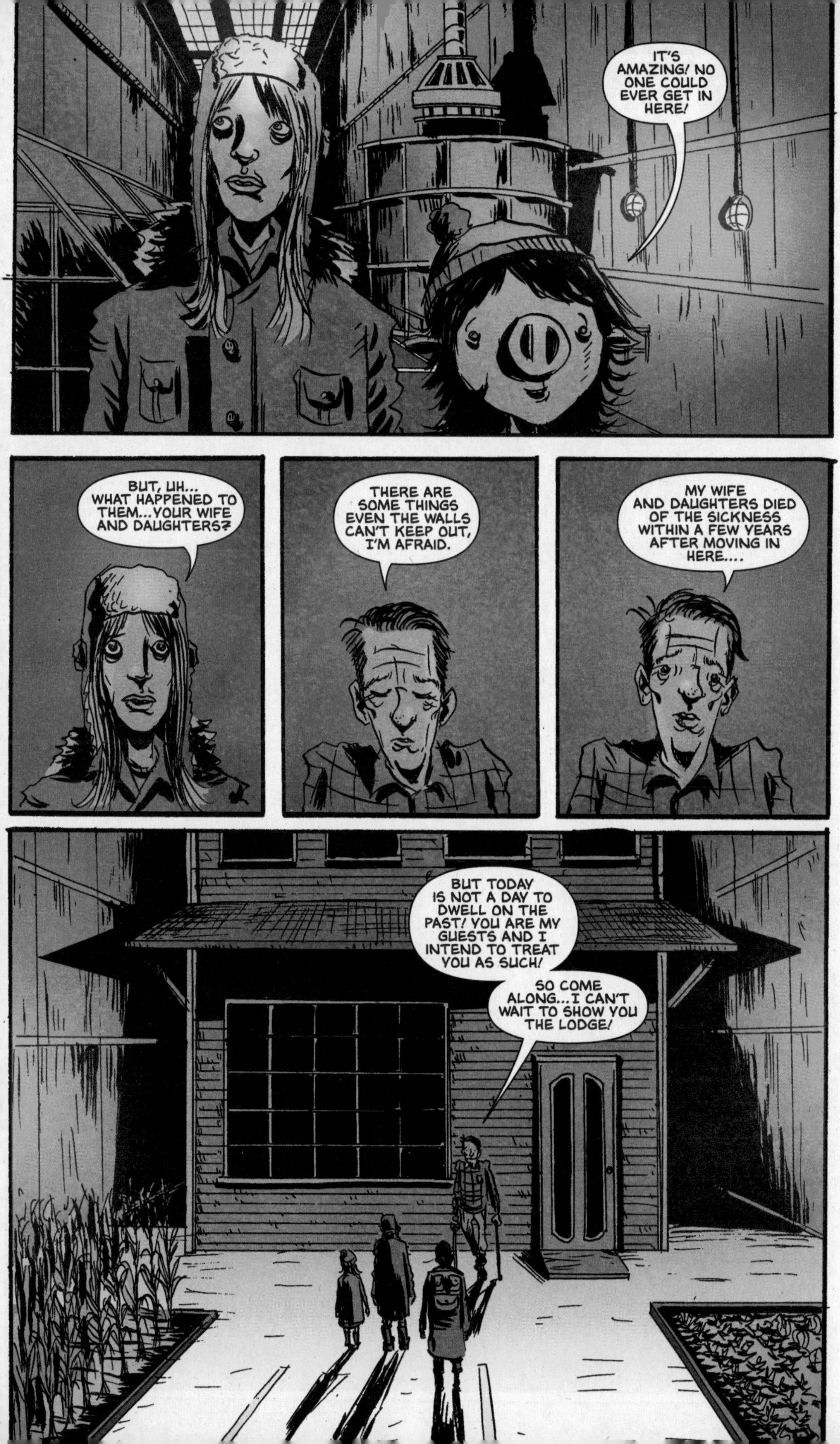
IT'S AMAZING! NO ONE COULD EVER GET IN HERE!
BUT, UH... WHAT HAPPENED TO THEM...YOUR WIFE AND DAUGHTERS?
THERE ARE SOME THINGS EVEN THE WALLS CAN'T KEEP OUT, I'M AFRAID.
MY WIFE AND DAUGHTERS DIED OF THE SICKNESS WITHIN A FEW YEARS AFTER MOVING IN HERE....
BUT TODAY IS NOT A DAY TO DWELL ON THE PAST! YOU ARE MY GUESTS AND I INTEND TO TREAT YOU AS SUCH!
SO COME ALONG...I CAN'T WAIT TO SHOW YOU THE LODGE!

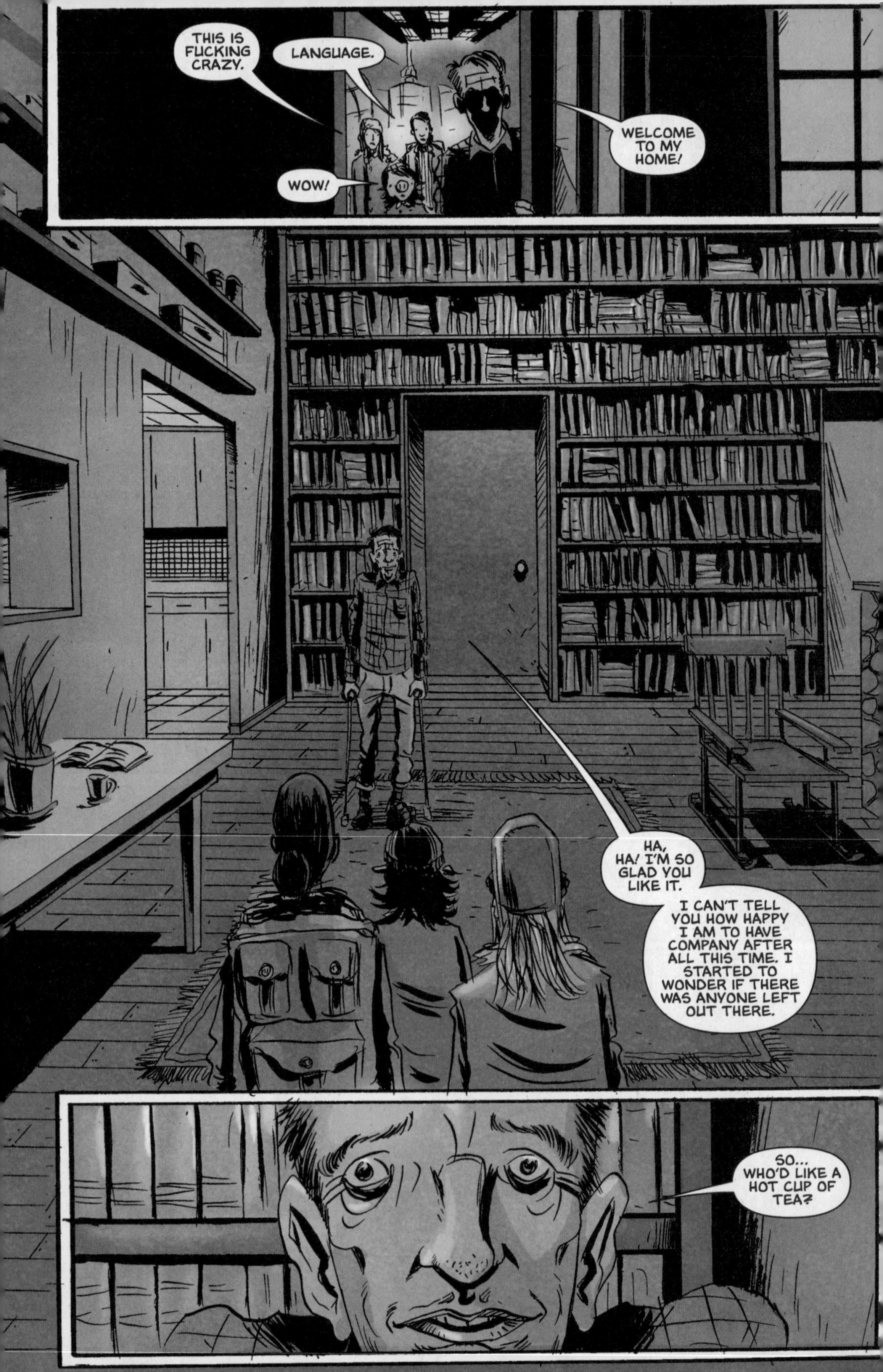
THIS IS FUCKING CRAZY.
LANGUAGE.
WELCOME TO MY HOME!
WOW!
HA, HA! I'M SO GLAD YOU LIKE IT.
I CAN'T TELL YOU HOW HAPPY I AM TO HAVE COMPANY AFTER ALL THIS TIME. I STARTED TO WONDER IF THERE WAS ANYONE LEFT OUT THERE.
SO... WHO'D LIKE A HOT CUP OF TEA?

HEY, DOC, YOU SEEN THE FURBALL ANYWHERE?

IF YOU'RE REFERRING TO BOBBY, THEN YES I HAVE. HE'S ACTUALLY *BENEATH* US SLEEPING.

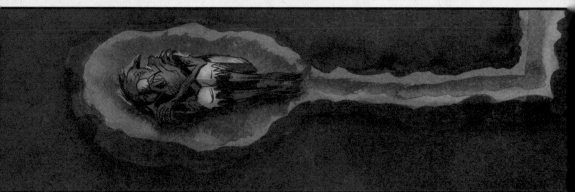

HUH? COME AGAIN?

THERE...HE'S *BURROWED* DOWN UNDER US. IT'S WHAT GROUNDHOGS DO.

NO SHIT! REALLY?

THAT'S CRAZY, MAN... I ALWAYS THOUGHT HE WAS A BEAVER OR SOME SHIT LIKE THAT.

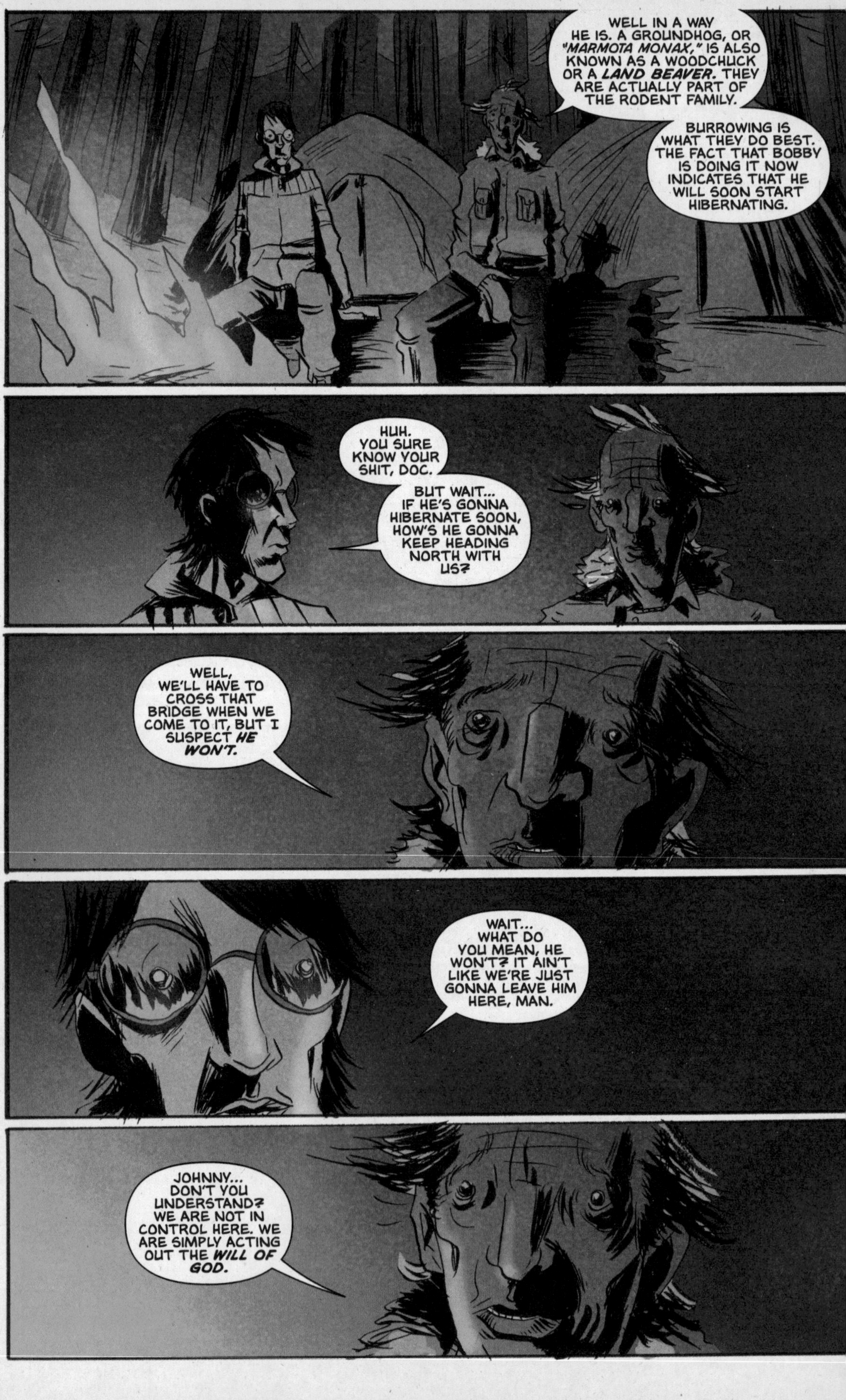
WELL IN A WAY HE IS. A GROUNDHOG, OR "MARMOTA MONAX," IS ALSO KNOWN AS A WOODCHUCK OR A LAND BEAVER. THEY ARE ACTUALLY PART OF THE RODENT FAMILY.
BURROWING IS WHAT THEY DO BEST. THE FACT THAT BOBBY IS DOING IT NOW INDICATES THAT HE WILL SOON START HIBERNATING.
HUH. YOU SURE KNOW YOUR SHIT, DOC.
BUT WAIT... IF HE'S GONNA HIBERNATE SOON, HOW'S HE GONNA KEEP HEADING NORTH WITH US?
WELL, WE'LL HAVE TO CROSS THAT BRIDGE WHEN WE COME TO IT, BUT I SUSPECT HE WON'T.
WAIT... WHAT DO YOU MEAN, HE WON'T? IT AIN'T LIKE WE'RE JUST GONNA LEAVE HIM HERE, MAN.
JOHNNY... DON'T YOU UNDERSTAND? WE ARE NOT IN CONTROL HERE. WE ARE SIMPLY ACTING OUT THE WILL OF GOD.

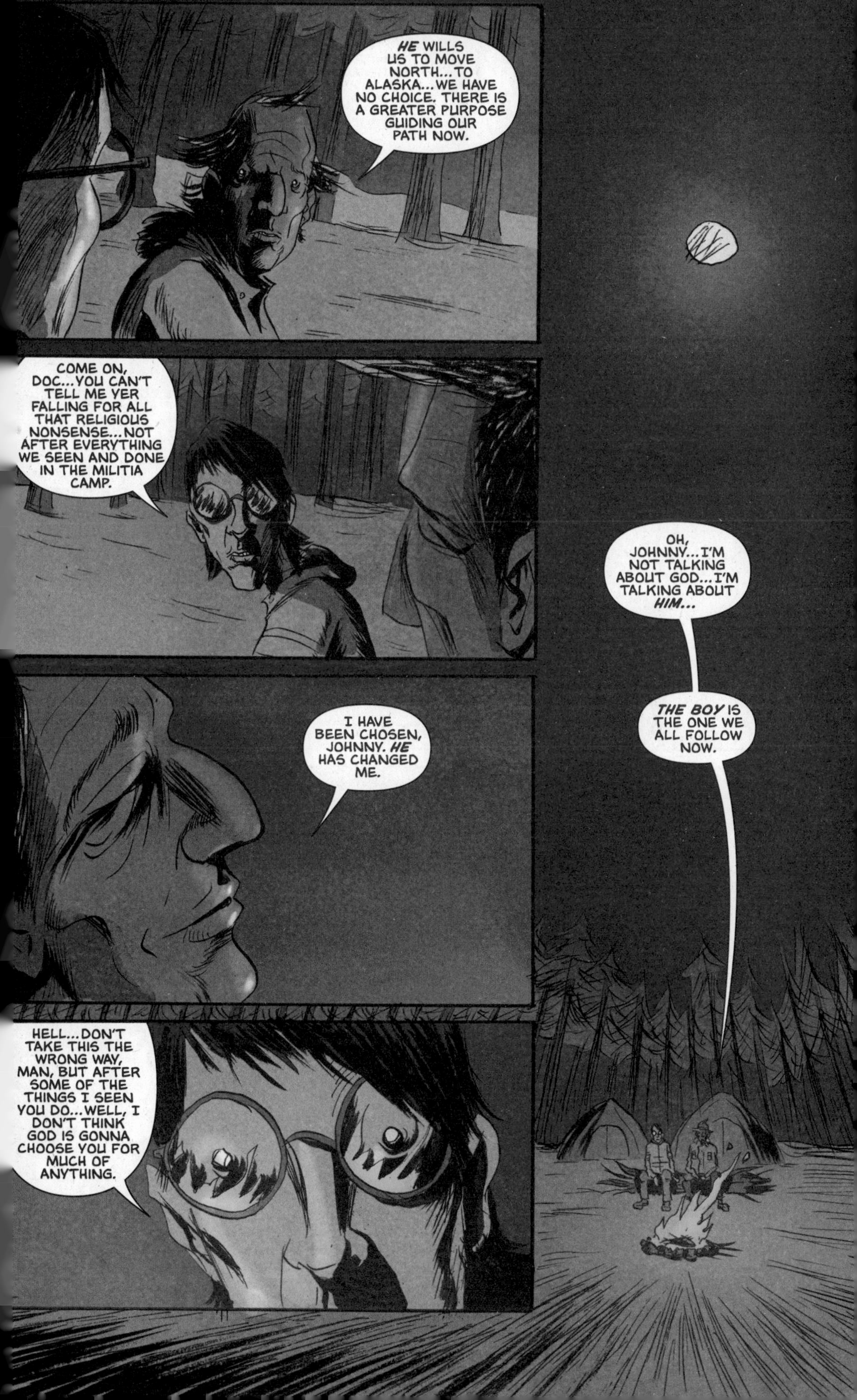
HE WILLS US TO MOVE NORTH...TO ALASKA...WE HAVE NO CHOICE. THERE IS A GREATER PURPOSE GUIDING OUR PATH NOW.
COME ON, DOC...YOU CAN'T TELL ME YER FALLING FOR ALL THAT RELIGIOUS NONSENSE...NOT AFTER EVERYTHING WE SEEN AND DONE IN THE MILITIA CAMP.
I HAVE BEEN CHOSEN, JOHNNY. HE HAS CHANGED ME.
HELL...DON'T TAKE THIS THE WRONG WAY, MAN, BUT AFTER SOME OF THE THINGS I SEEN YOU DO...WELL, I DON'T THINK GOD IS GONNA CHOOSE YOU FOR MUCH OF ANYTHING.
OH, JOHNNY...I'M NOT TALKING ABOUT GOD...I'M TALKING ABOUT HIM...
THE BOY IS THE ONE WE ALL FOLLOW NOW.

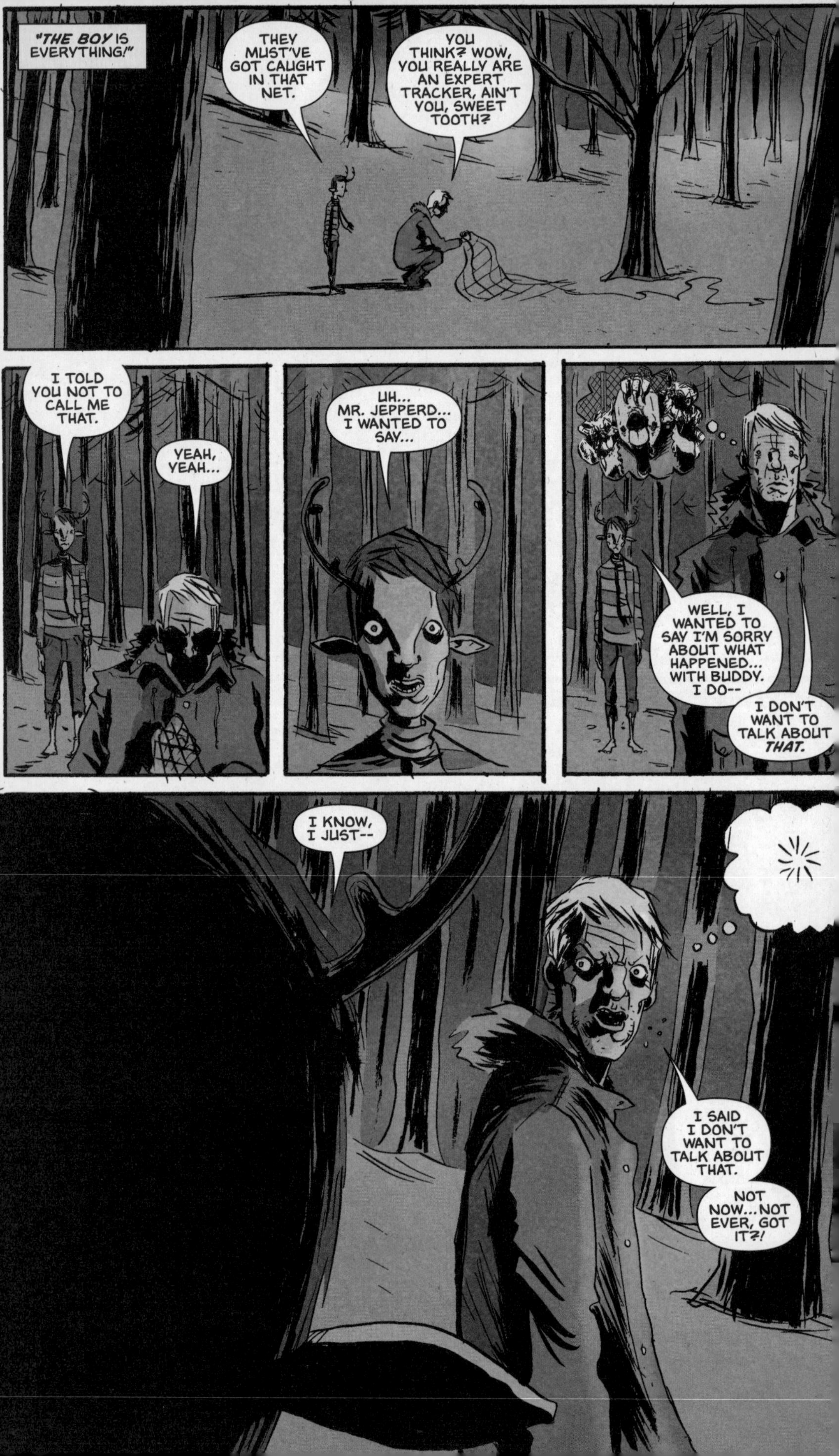
"THE BOY IS EVERYTHING!"
THEY MUST'VE GOT CAUGHT IN THAT NET.
YOU THINK? WOW, YOU REALLY ARE AN EXPERT TRACKER, AIN'T YOU, SWEET TOOTH?
I TOLD YOU NOT TO CALL ME THAT.
YEAH, YEAH...
UH... MR. JEPPERD... I WANTED TO SAY...
WELL, I WANTED TO SAY I'M SORRY ABOUT WHAT HAPPENED... WITH BUDDY. I DO--
I DON'T WANT TO TALK ABOUT *THAT.*
I KNOW, I JUST--
I SAID I DON'T WANT TO TALK ABOUT THAT.
NOT NOW... NOT EVER, GOT IT?!

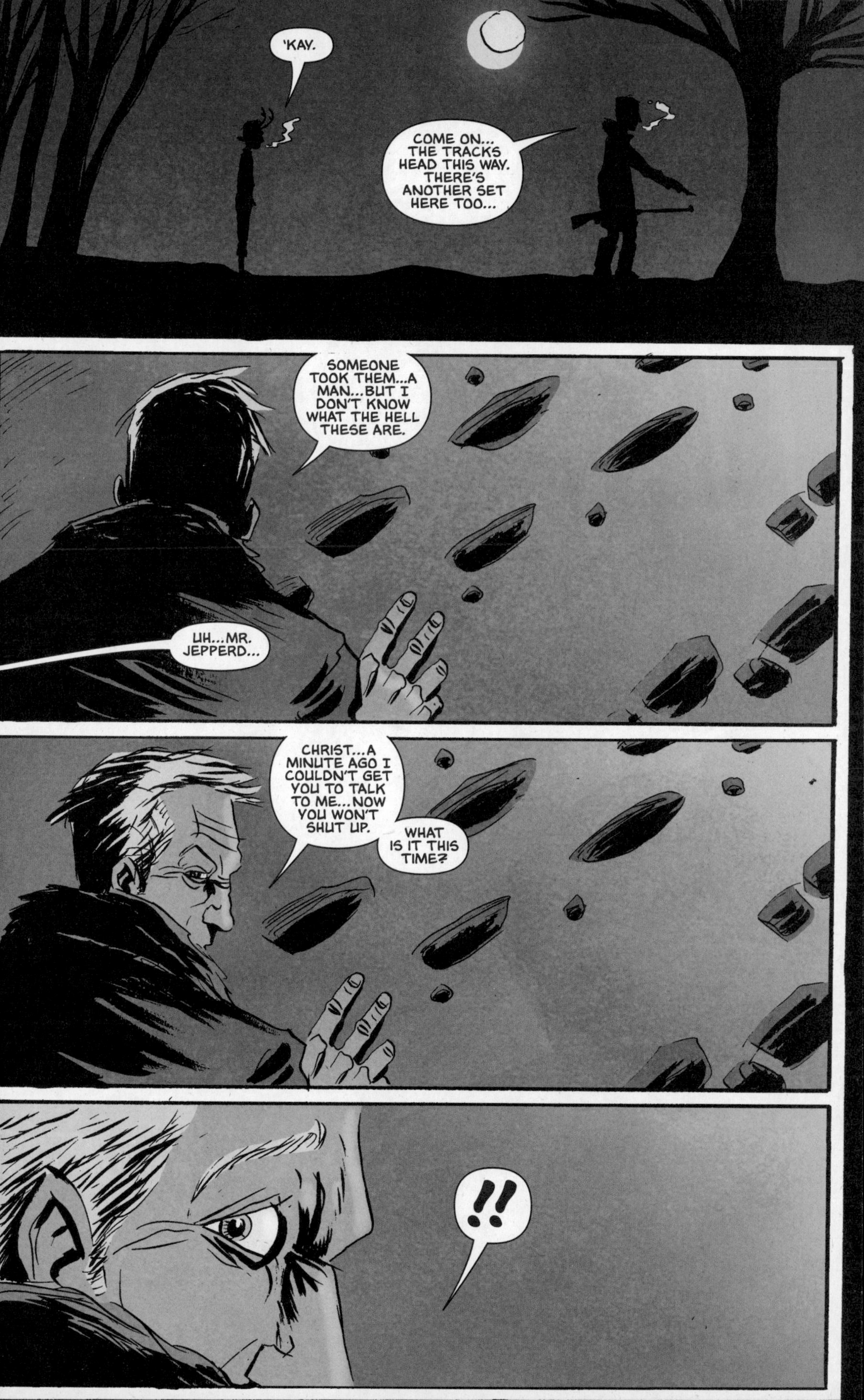
'KAY.
COME ON... THE TRACKS HEAD THIS WAY. THERE'S ANOTHER SET HERE TOO...
SOMEONE TOOK THEM...A MAN...BUT I DON'T KNOW WHAT THE HELL THESE ARE.
UH...MR. JEPPERD...
CHRIST...A MINUTE AGO I COULDN'T GET YOU TO TALK TO ME...NOW YOU WON'T SHUT UP.
WHAT IS IT THIS TIME?
!!

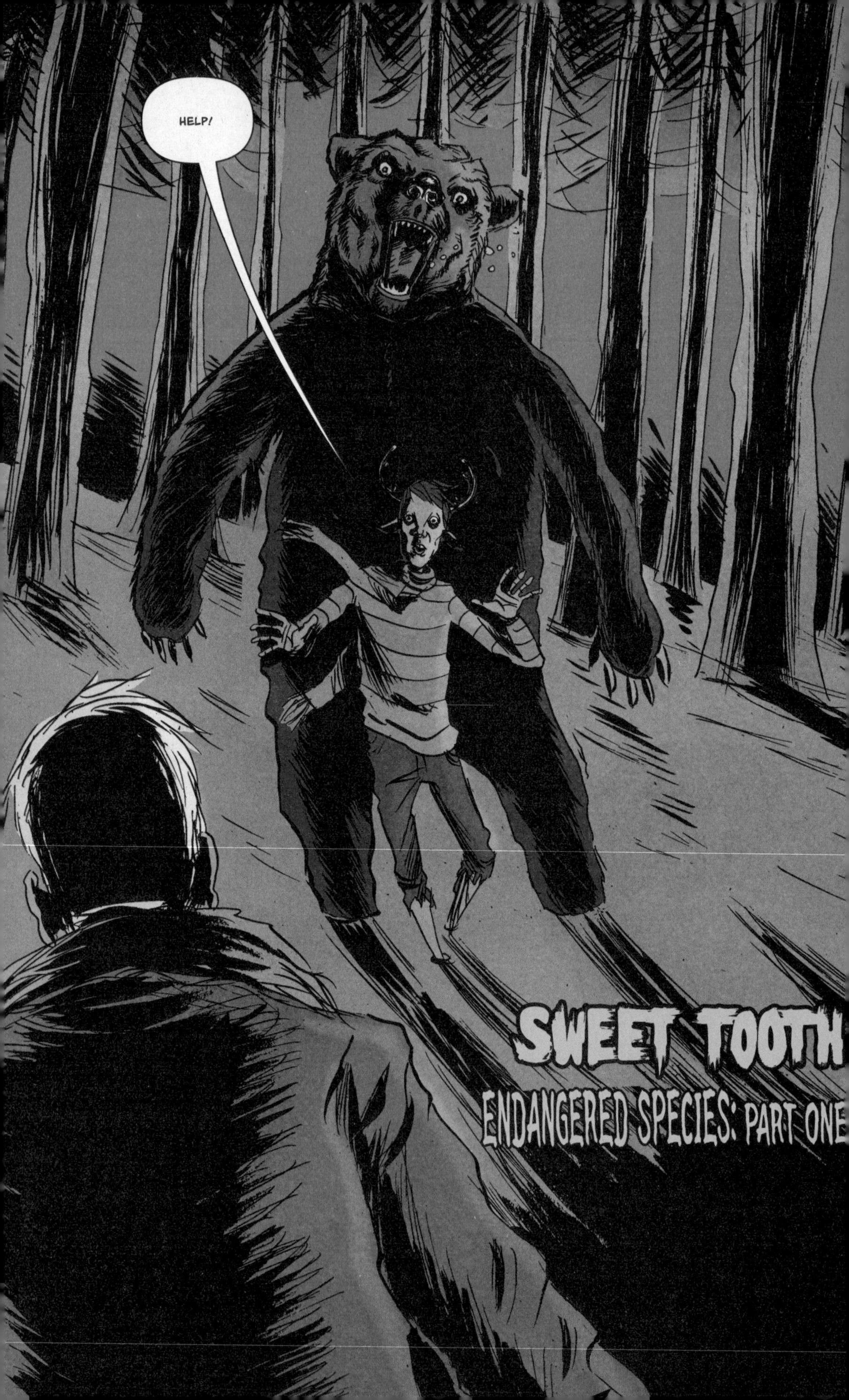
HELP!
SWEET TOOTH
ENDANGERED SPECIES: PART ONE

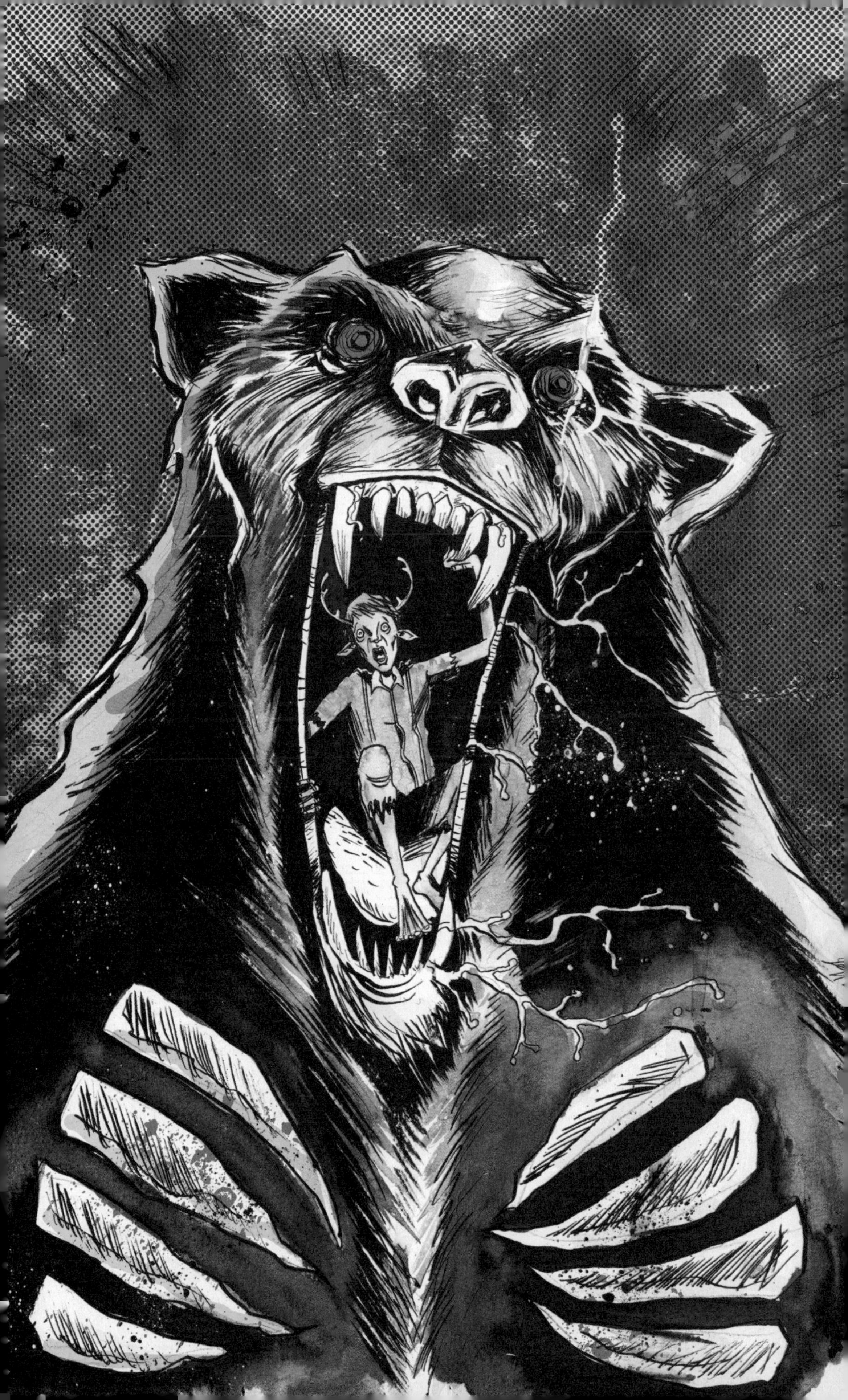

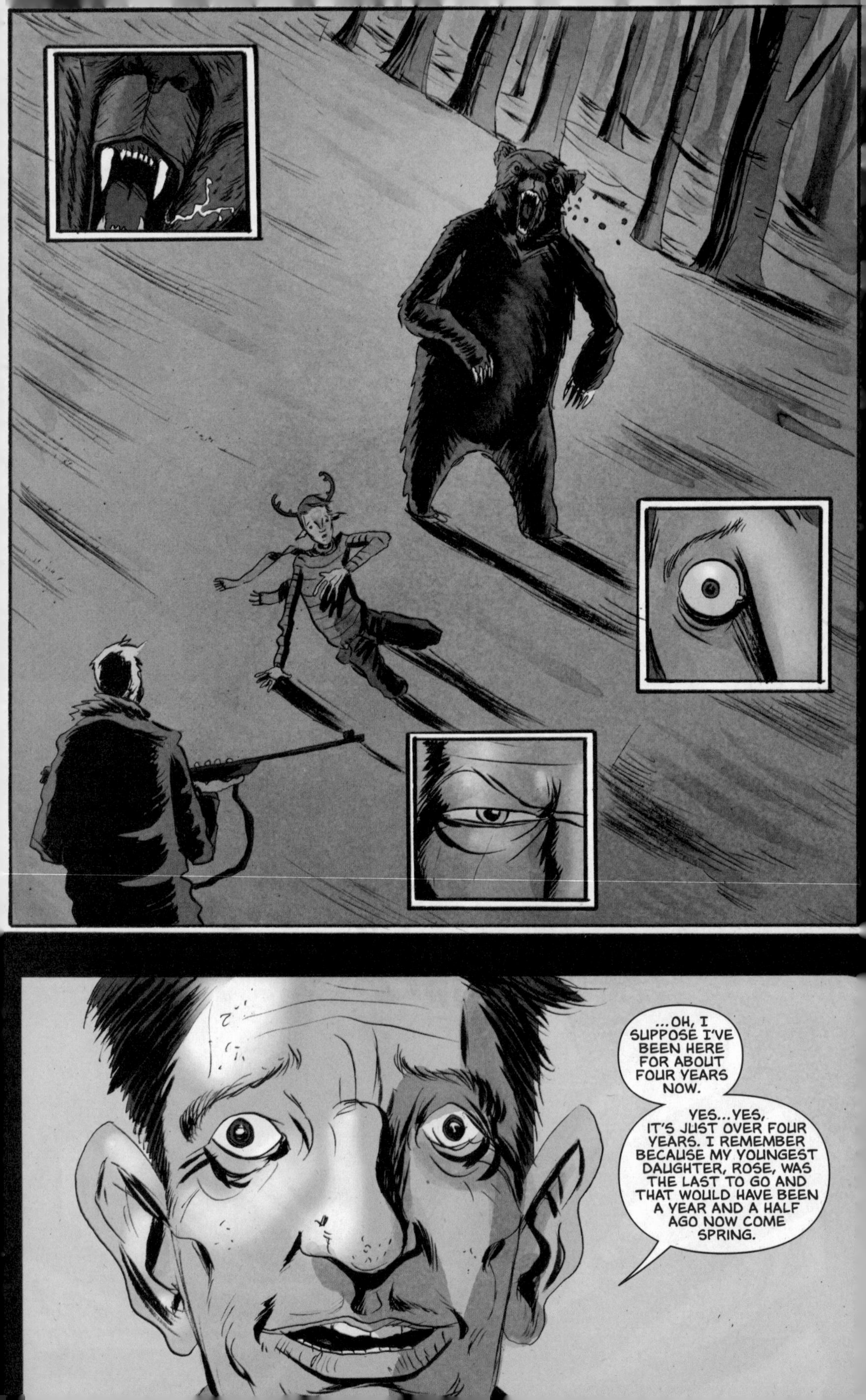
...OH, I SUPPOSE I'VE BEEN HERE FOR ABOUT FOUR YEARS NOW.
YES...YES, IT'S JUST OVER FOUR YEARS. I REMEMBER BECAUSE MY YOUNGEST DAUGHTER, ROSE, WAS THE LAST TO GO AND THAT WOULD HAVE BEEN A YEAR AND A HALF AGO NOW COME SPRING.

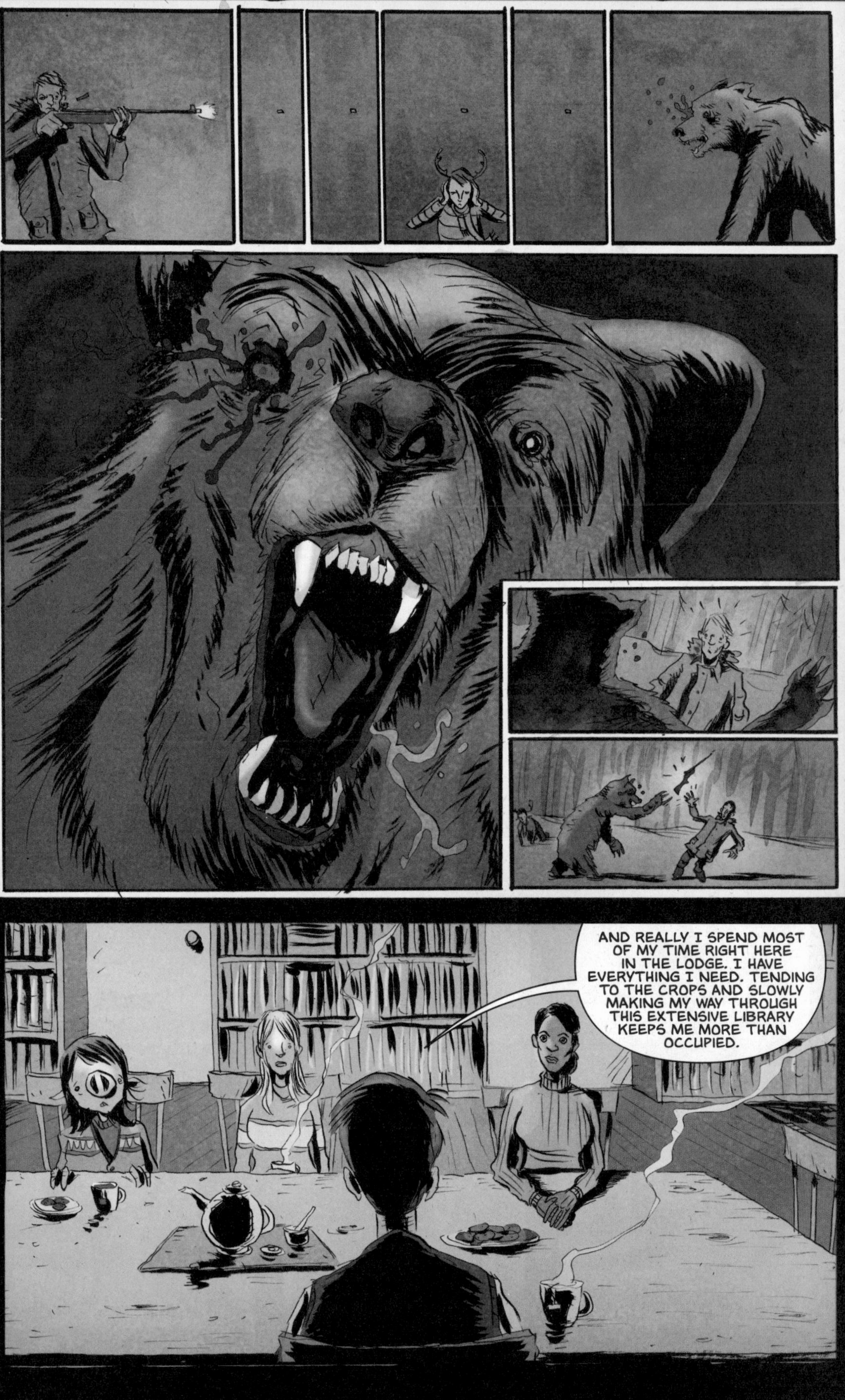
AND REALLY I SPEND MOST OF MY TIME RIGHT HERE IN THE LODGE. I HAVE EVERYTHING I NEED. TENDING TO THE CROPS AND SLOWLY MAKING MY WAY THROUGH THIS EXTENSIVE LIBRARY KEEPS ME MORE THAN OCCUPIED.

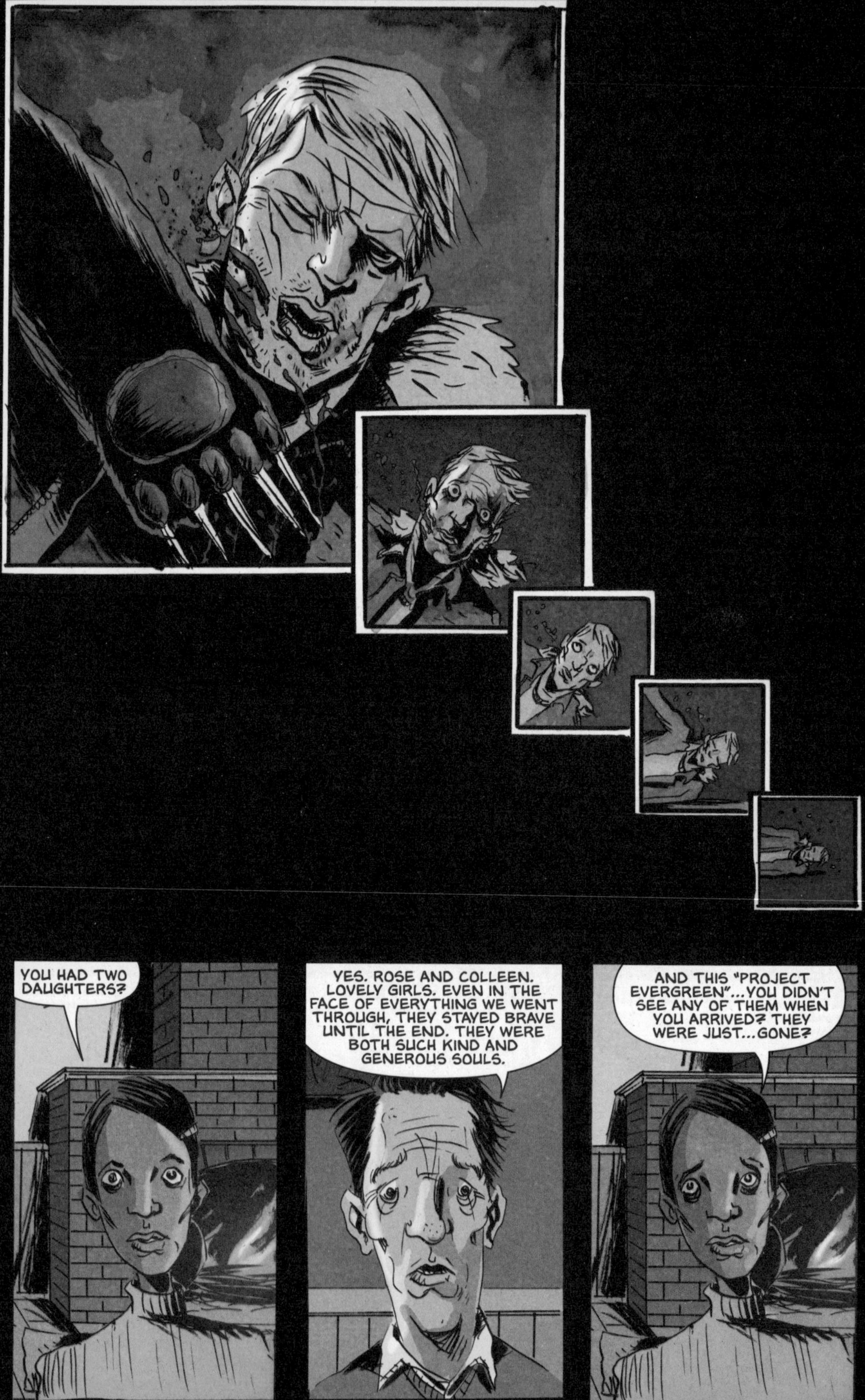
YOU HAD TWO DAUGHTERS?
YES. ROSE AND COLLEEN. LOVELY GIRLS. EVEN IN THE FACE OF EVERYTHING WE WENT THROUGH, THEY STAYED BRAVE UNTIL THE END. THEY WERE BOTH SUCH KIND AND GENEROUS SOULS.
AND THIS "PROJECT EVERGREEN"...YOU DIDN'T SEE ANY OF THEM WHEN YOU ARRIVED? THEY WERE JUST...GONE?

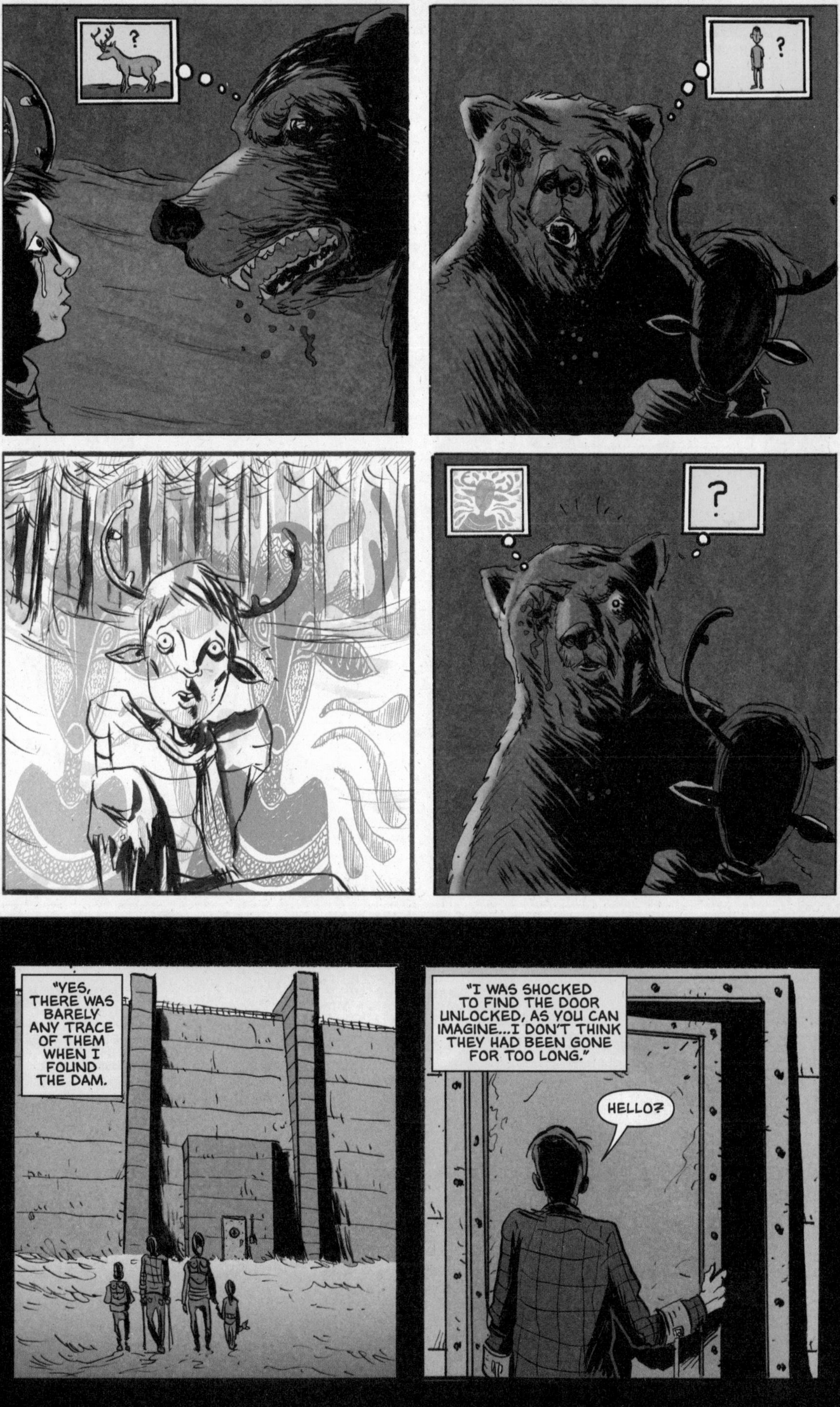
?
?
?
"YES, THERE WAS BARELY ANY TRACE OF THEM WHEN I FOUND THE DAM.
"I WAS SHOCKED TO FIND THE DOOR UNLOCKED, AS YOU CAN IMAGINE...I DON'T THINK THEY HAD BEEN GONE FOR TOO LONG."
HELLO?

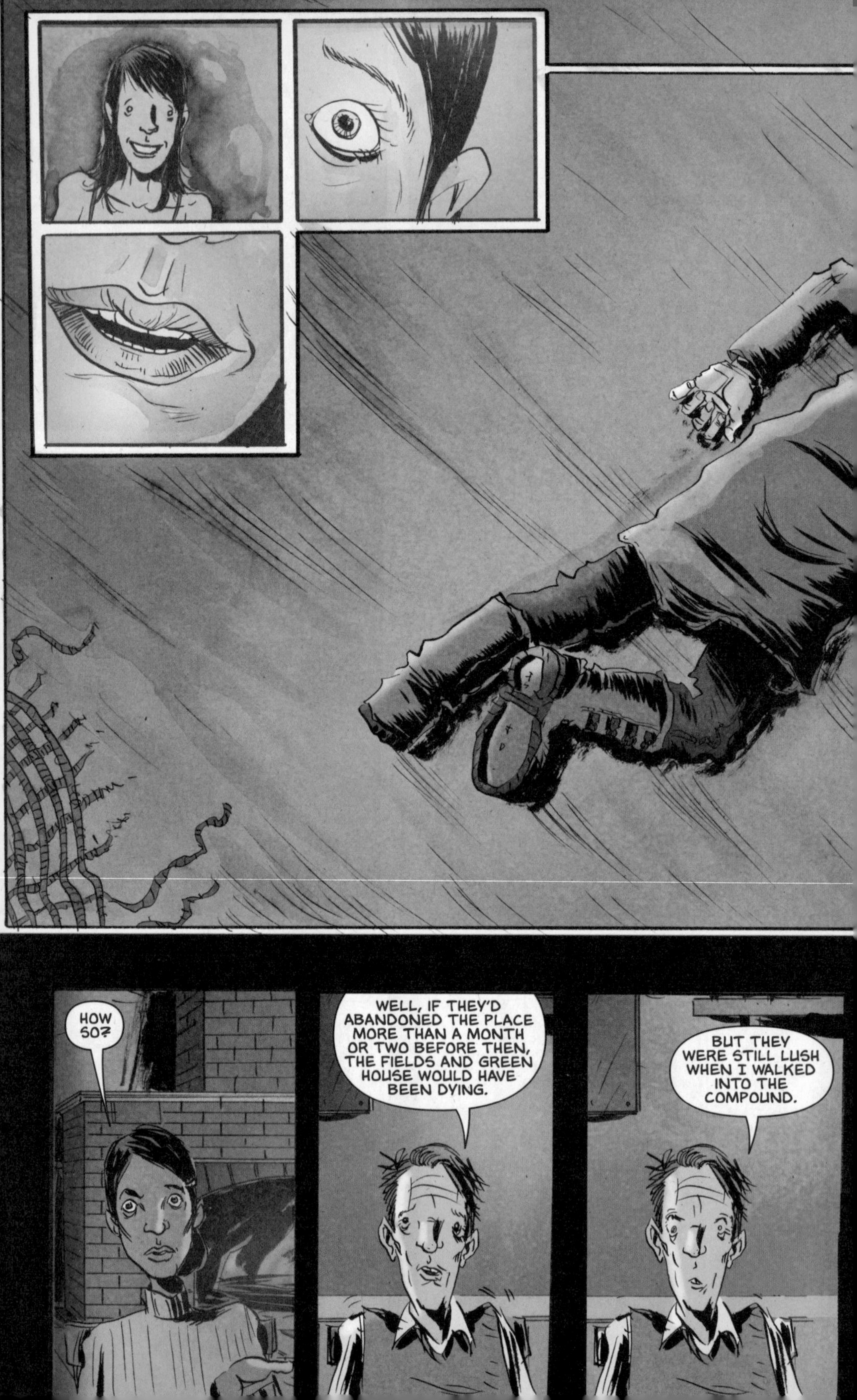
HOW SO?
WELL, IF THEY'D ABANDONED THE PLACE MORE THAN A MONTH OR TWO BEFORE THEN, THE FIELDS AND GREEN HOUSE WOULD HAVE BEEN DYING.
BUT THEY WERE STILL LUSH WHEN I WALKED INTO THE COMPOUND.

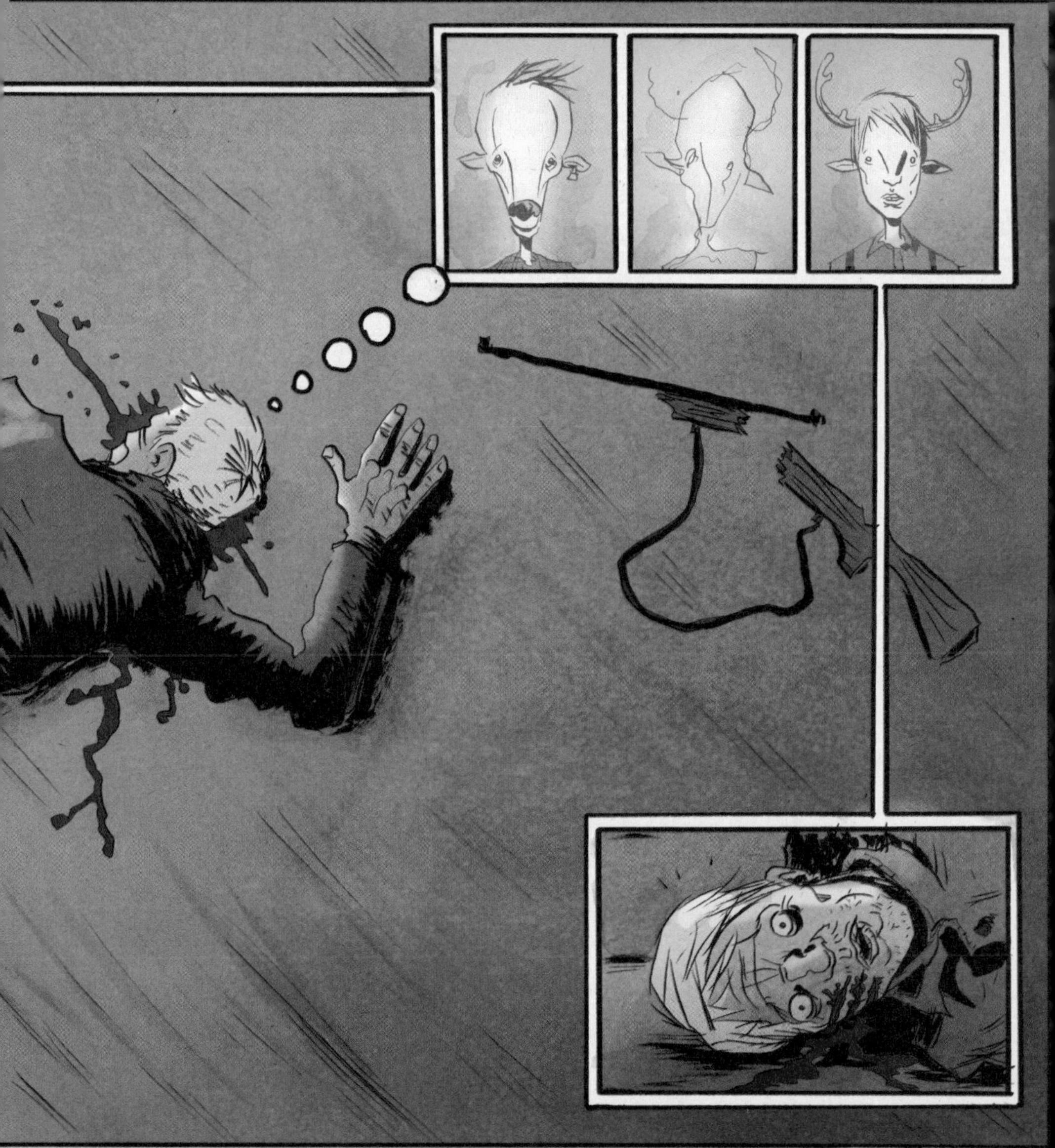

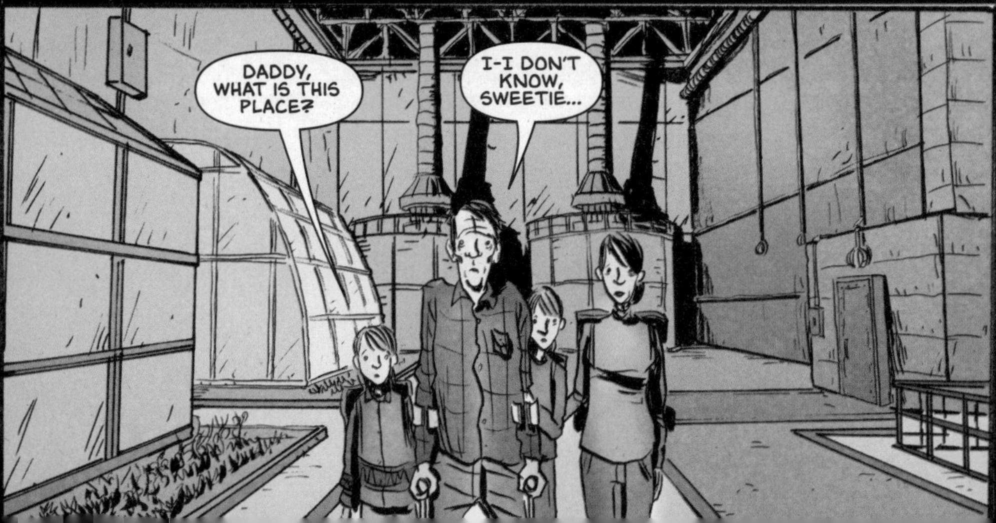
DADDY, WHAT IS THIS PLACE?
I-I DON'T KNOW, SWEETIE...

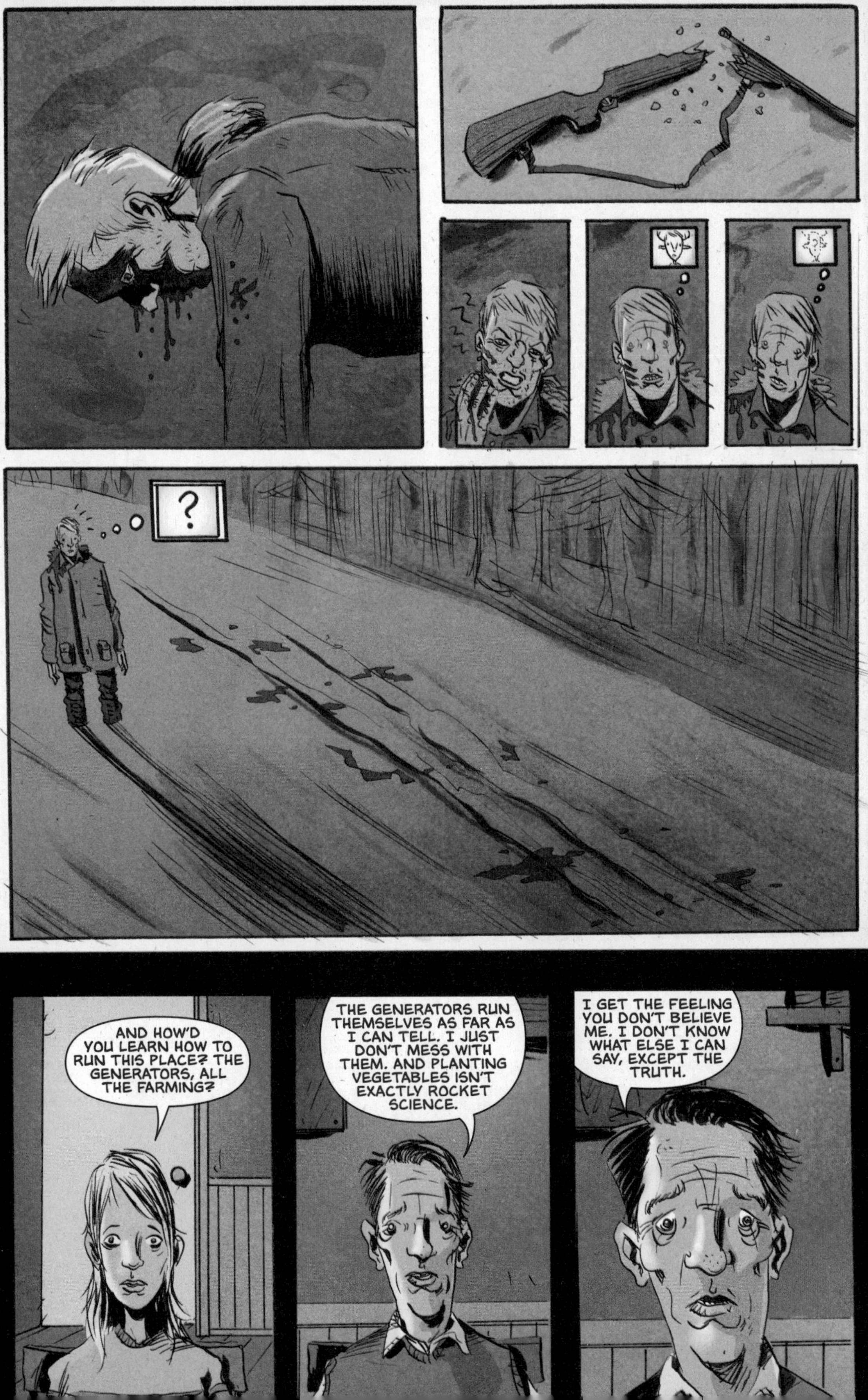
?
AND HOW'D YOU LEARN HOW TO RUN THIS PLACE? THE GENERATORS, ALL THE FARMING?
THE GENERATORS RUN THEMSELVES AS FAR AS I CAN TELL. I JUST DON'T MESS WITH THEM. AND PLANTING VEGETABLES ISN'T EXACTLY ROCKET SCIENCE.
I GET THE FEELING YOU DON'T BELIEVE ME. I DON'T KNOW WHAT ELSE I CAN SAY, EXCEPT THE TRUTH.

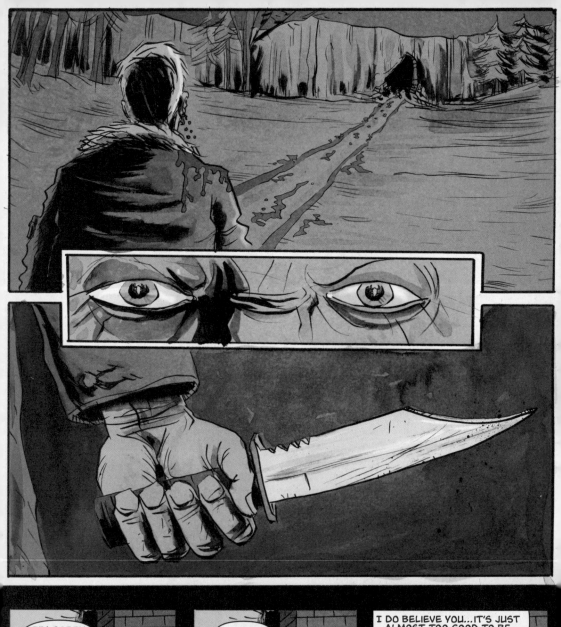

I'M SORRY, WALTER...I DO BELIEVE YOU--≶COUGH!≶

≶COUGH≶ ≶COUGH!≶ EXCUSE ME...

I DO BELIEVE YOU...IT'S JUST ALMOST TOO GOOD TO BE TRUE, YOU KNOW? I MEAN WHY WOULD THE PROJECT EVERGREEN PEOPLE EVER LEAVE THIS PLACE?

THEY HAD EVERYTHING THEY COULD POSSIBLY NEED RIGHT HERE!

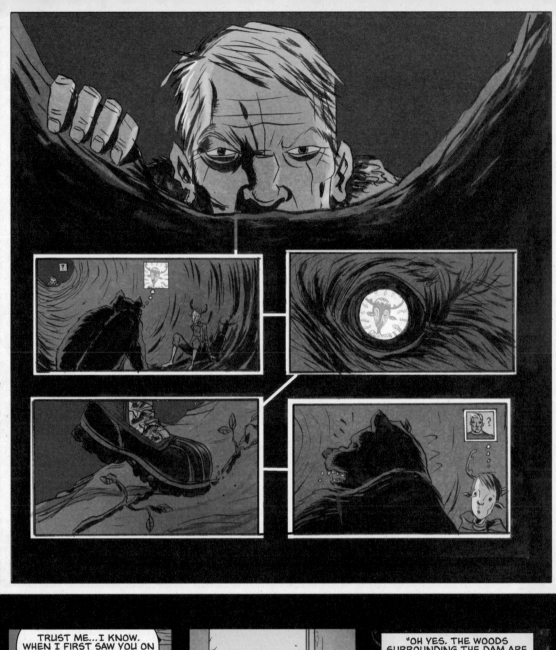

TRUST ME... I KNOW. WHEN I FIRST SAW YOU ON THE MONITORS I THOUGHT YOU MIGHT BE SOME OF THEM COMING BACK.

MONITORS?

"OH YES. THE WOODS SURROUNDING THE DAM ARE LITTERED WITH CAMERAS. AT FIRST I JUST THOUGHT THAT THE EVERGREENS WERE BEING PARANOID."

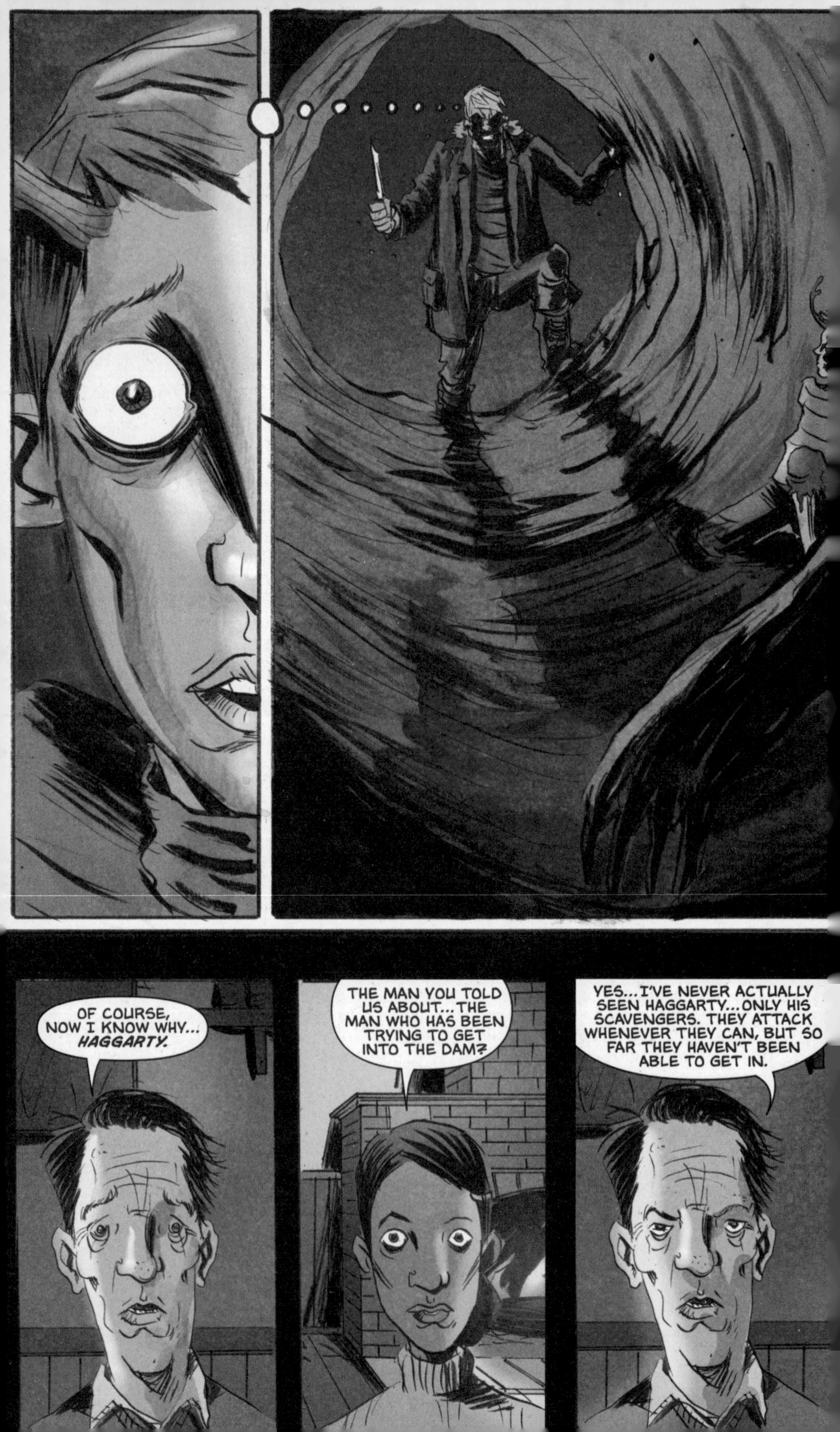
OF COURSE, NOW I KNOW WHY... *HAGGARTY.*
THE MAN YOU TOLD US ABOUT... THE MAN WHO HAS BEEN TRYING TO GET INTO THE DAM?
YES... I'VE NEVER ACTUALLY SEEN HAGGARTY... ONLY HIS SCAVENGERS. THEY ATTACK WHENEVER THEY CAN, BUT SO FAR THEY HAVEN'T BEEN ABLE TO GET IN.

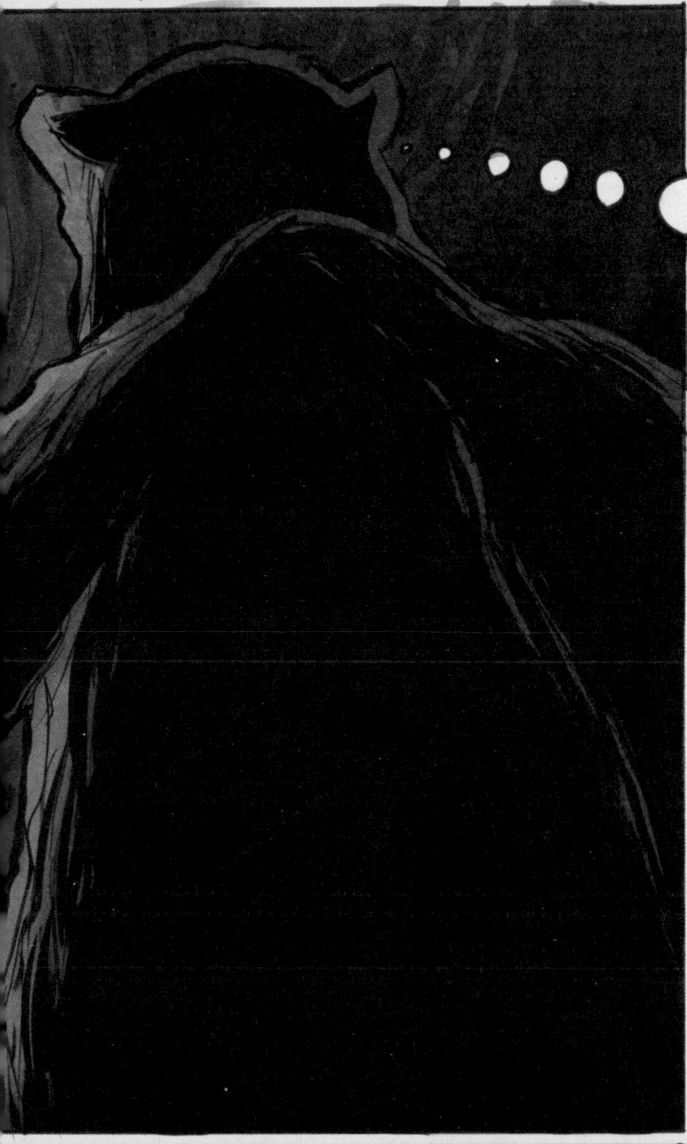

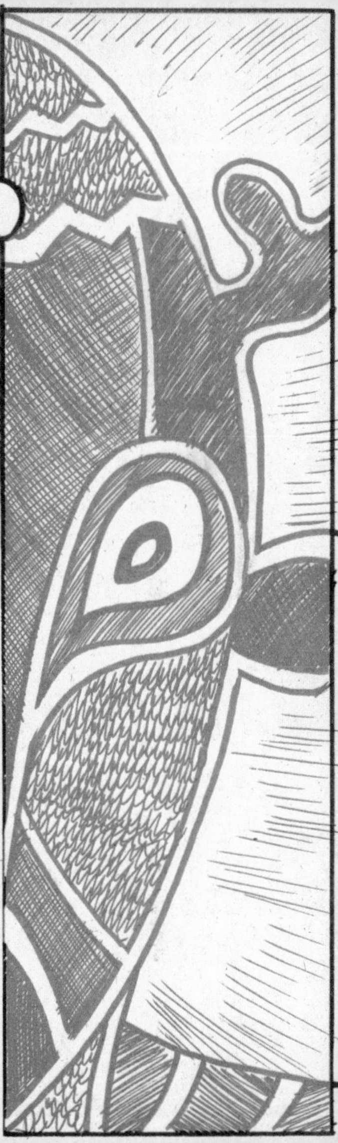

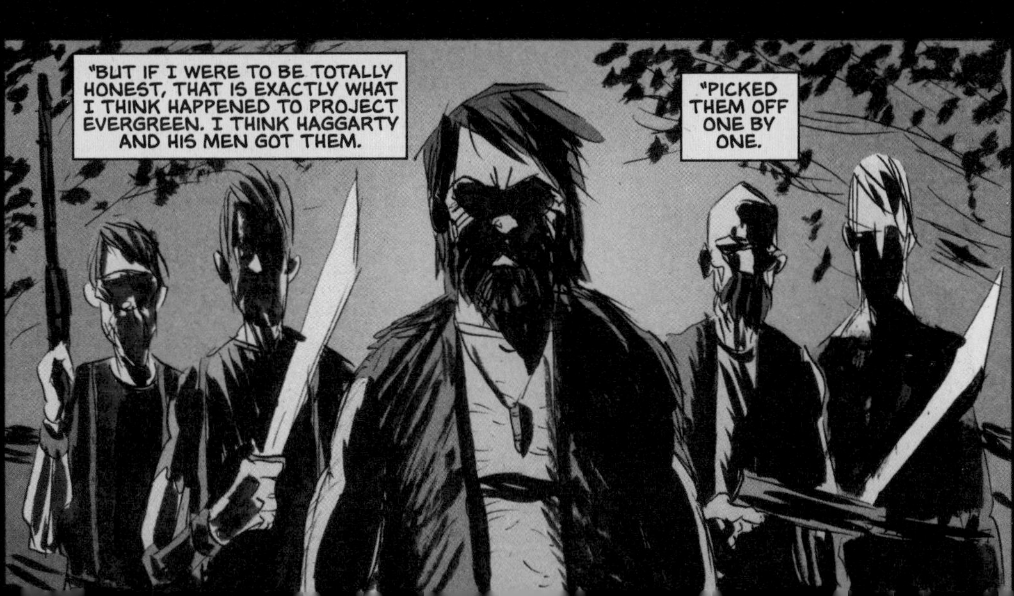
"BUT IF I WERE TO BE TOTALLY HONEST, THAT IS EXACTLY WHAT I THINK HAPPENED TO PROJECT EVERGREEN. I THINK HAGGARTY AND HIS MEN GOT THEM.
"PICKED THEM OFF ONE BY ONE.

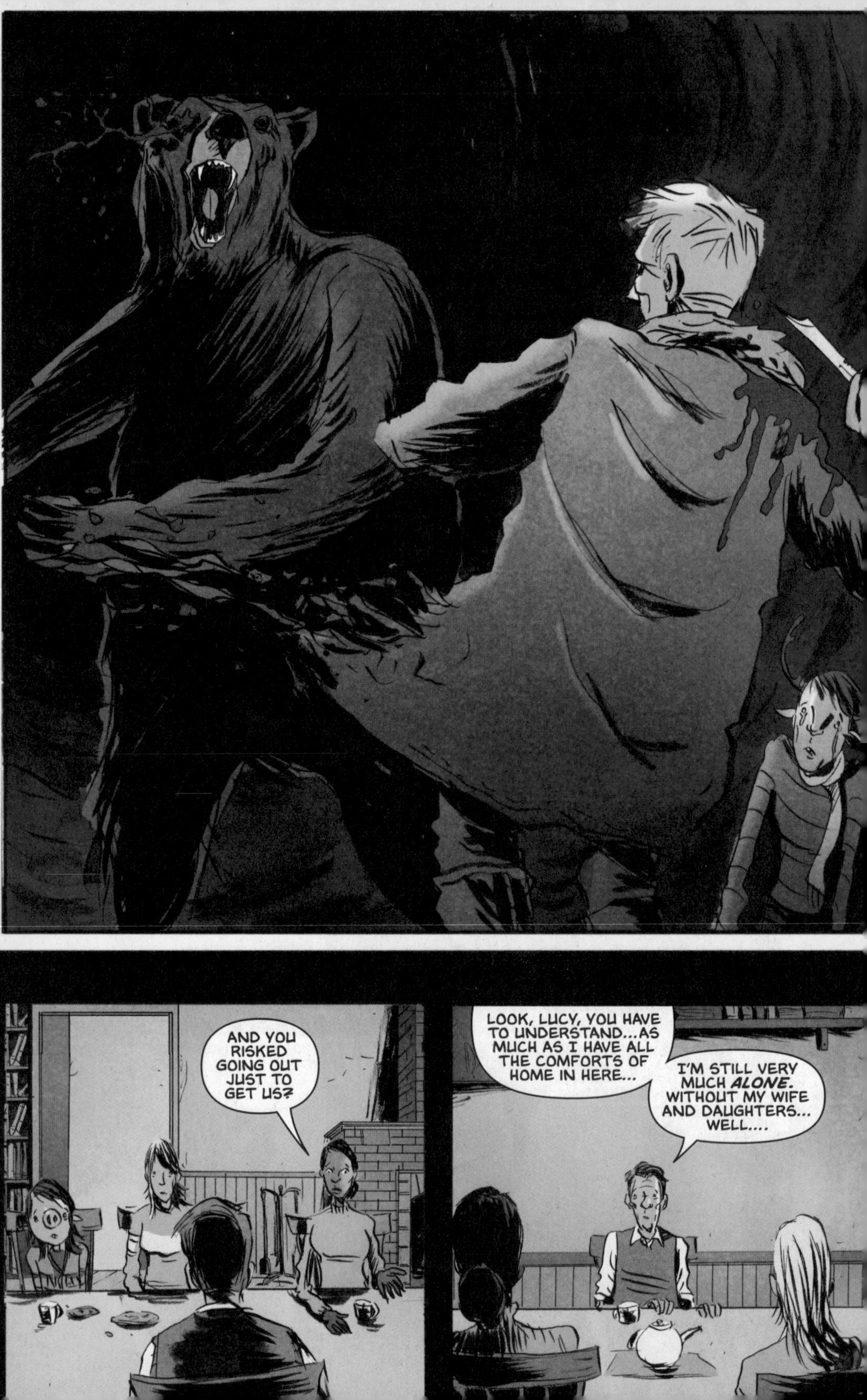
AND YOU RISKED GOING OUT JUST TO GET US?
LOOK, LUCY, YOU HAVE TO UNDERSTAND...AS MUCH AS I HAVE ALL THE COMFORTS OF HOME IN HERE...
I'M STILL VERY MUCH *ALONE.* WITHOUT MY WIFE AND DAUGHTERS... WELL....

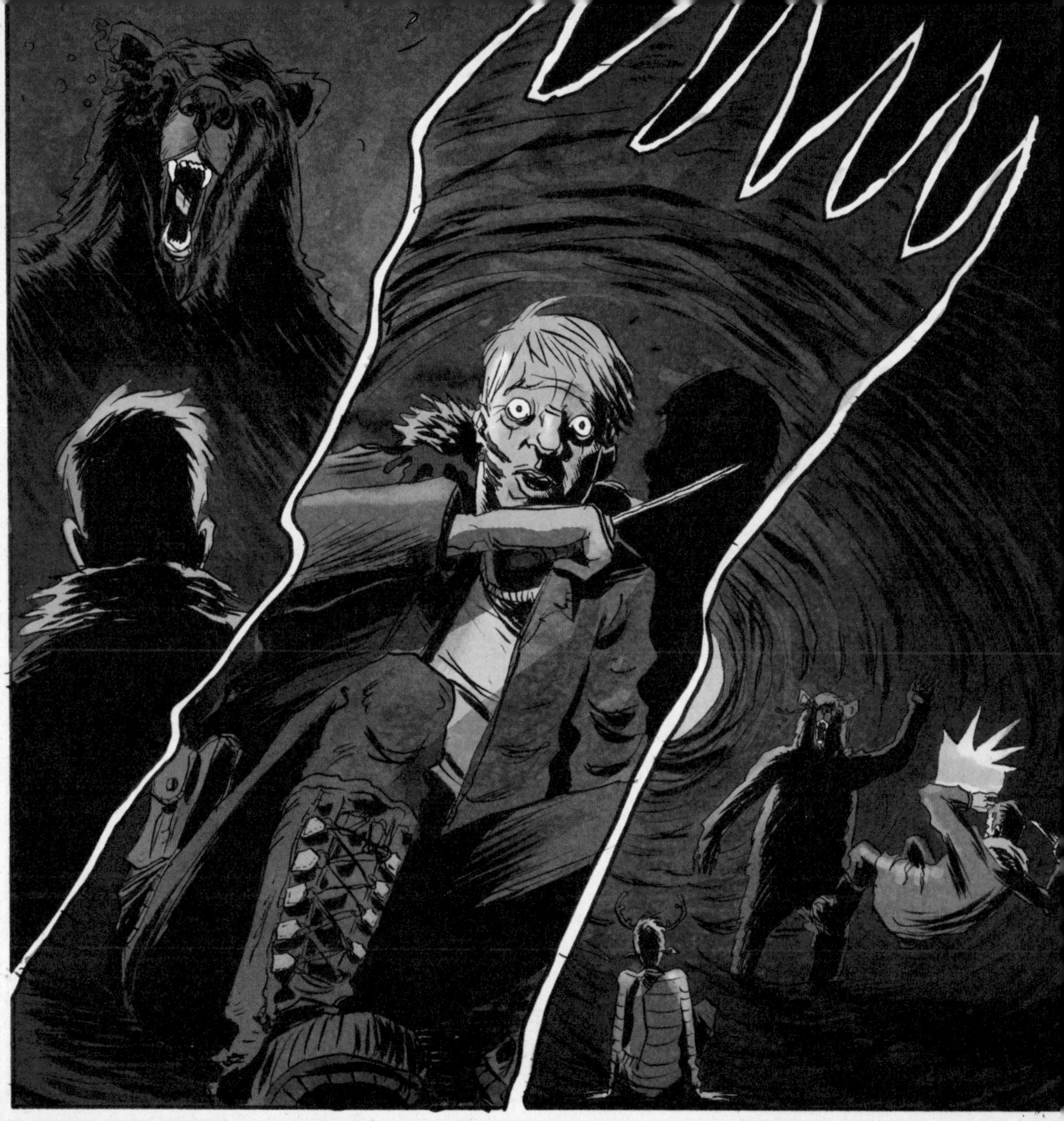

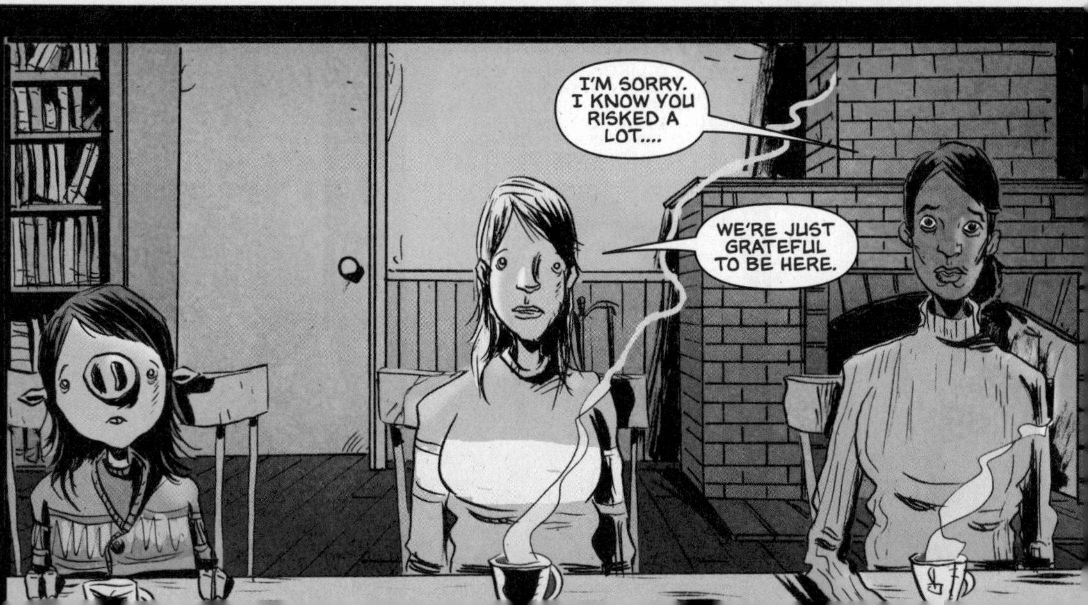
I'M SORRY. I KNOW YOU RISKED A LOT....
WE'RE JUST GRATEFUL TO BE HERE.

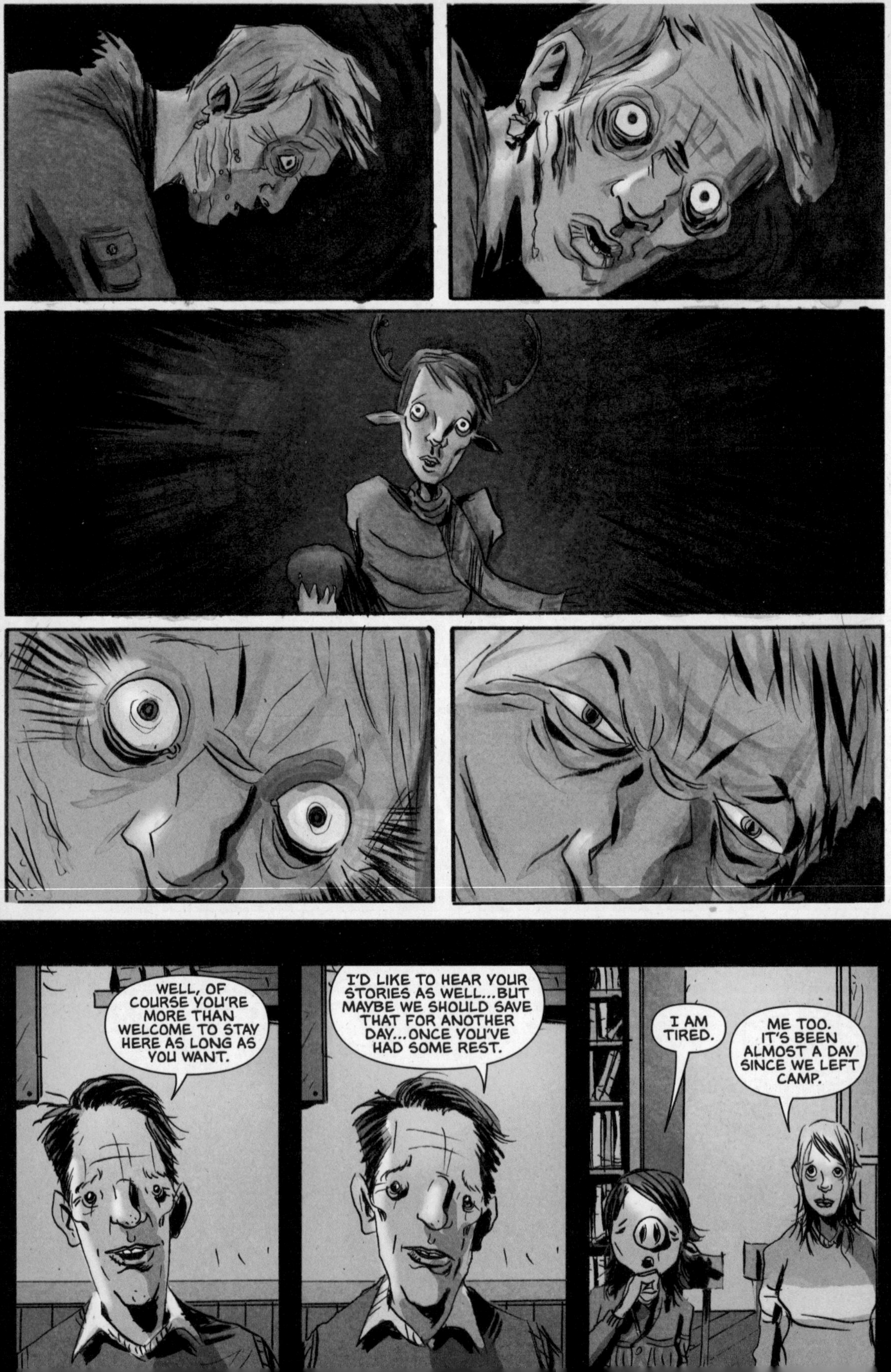

WELL, OF COURSE YOU'RE MORE THAN WELCOME TO STAY HERE AS LONG AS YOU WANT.
I'D LIKE TO HEAR YOUR STORIES AS WELL...BUT MAYBE WE SHOULD SAVE THAT FOR ANOTHER DAY...ONCE YOU'VE HAD SOME REST.
I AM TIRED.
ME TOO. IT'S BEEN ALMOST A DAY SINCE WE LEFT CAMP.

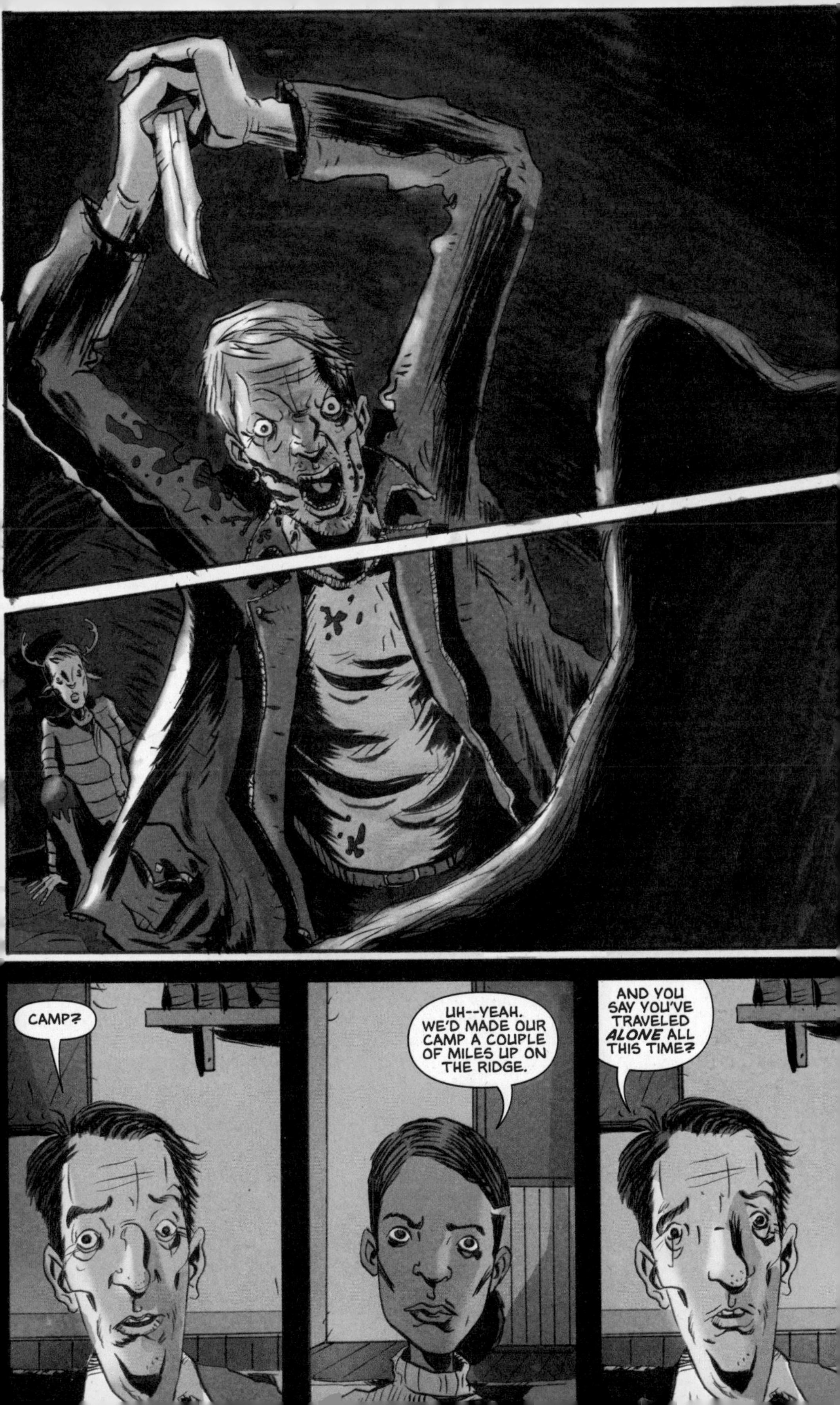
CAMP?
UH--YEAH. WE'D MADE OUR CAMP A COUPLE OF MILES UP ON THE RIDGE.
AND YOU SAY YOU'VE TRAVELED ALONE ALL THIS TIME?

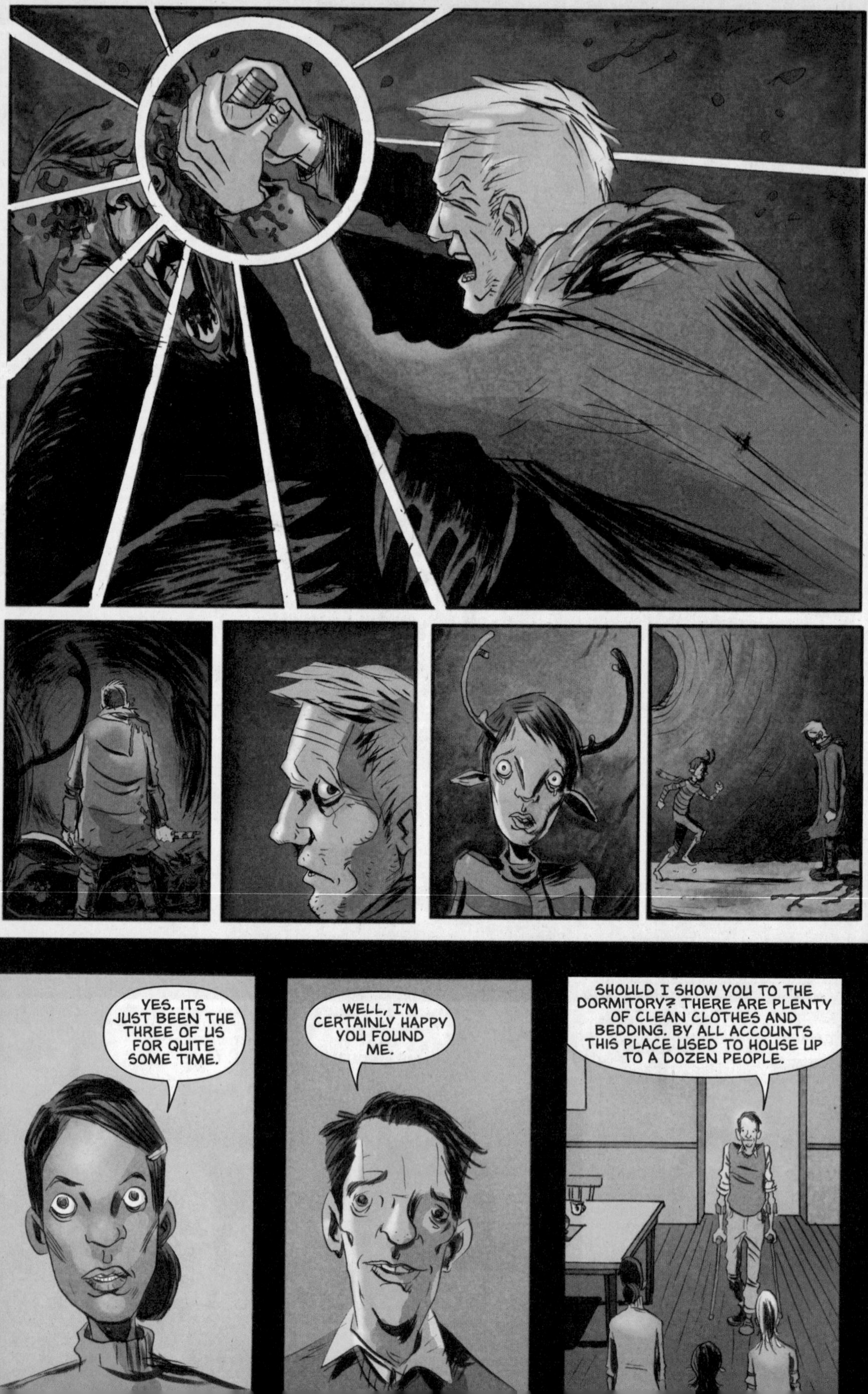
YES. ITS JUST BEEN THE THREE OF US FOR QUITE SOME TIME.
WELL, I'M CERTAINLY HAPPY YOU FOUND ME.
SHOULD I SHOW YOU TO THE DORMITORY? THERE ARE PLENTY OF CLEAN CLOTHES AND BEDDING. BY ALL ACCOUNTS THIS PLACE USED TO HOUSE UP TO A DOZEN PEOPLE.

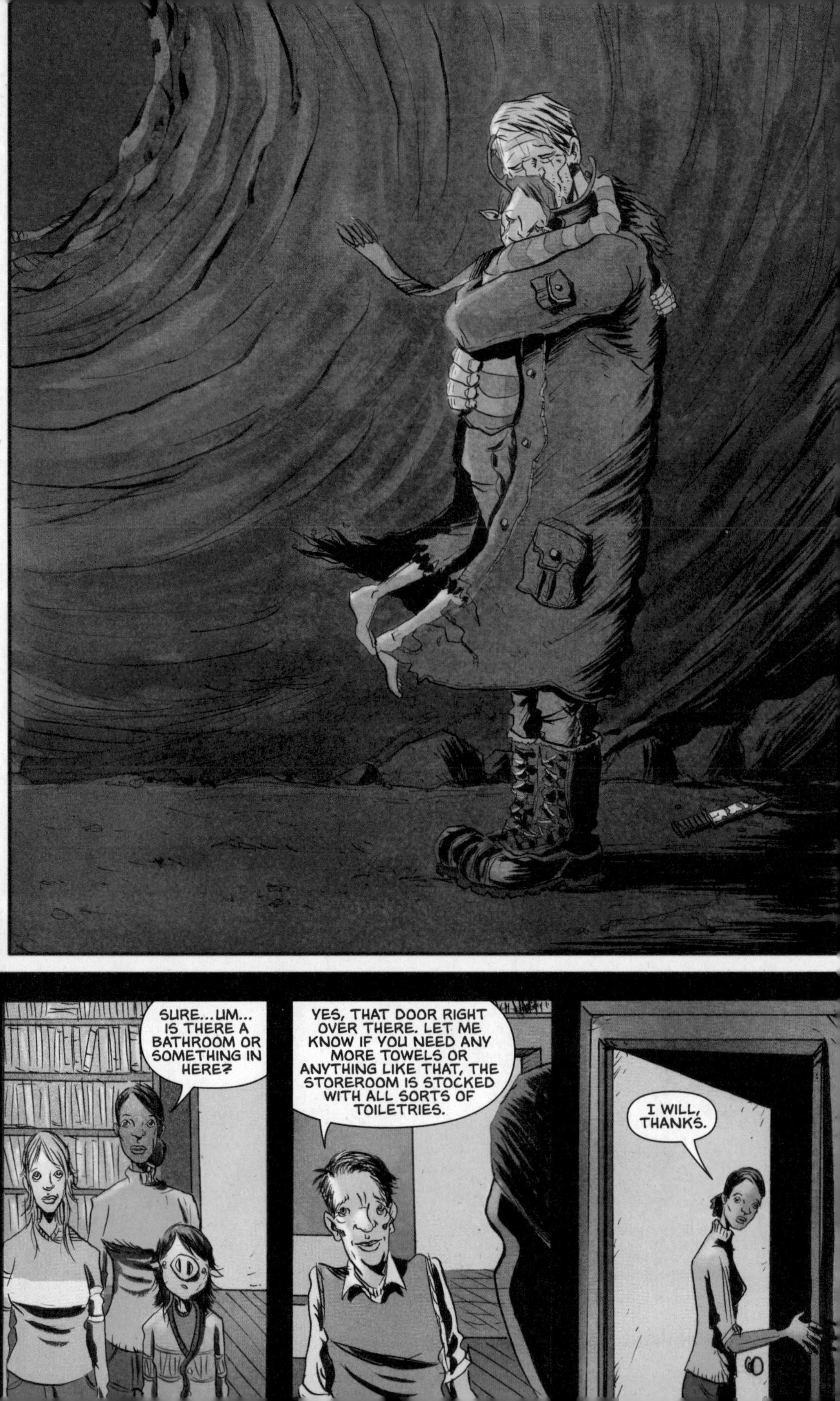
SURE...UM... IS THERE A BATHROOM OR SOMETHING IN HERE?
YES, THAT DOOR RIGHT OVER THERE. LET ME KNOW IF YOU NEED ANY MORE TOWELS OR ANYTHING LIKE THAT, THE STOREROOM IS STOCKED WITH ALL SORTS OF TOILETRIES.
I WILL, THANKS.

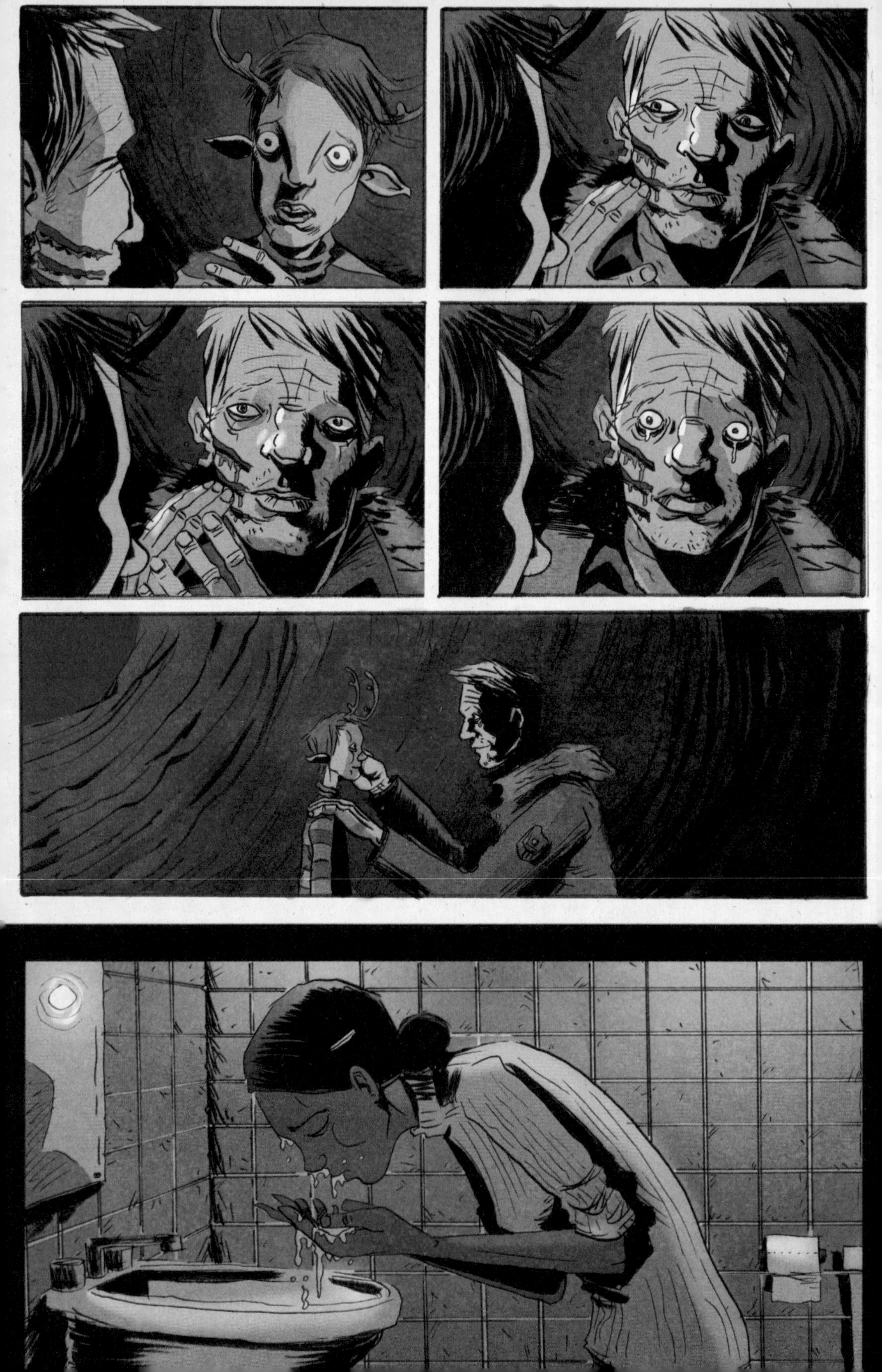

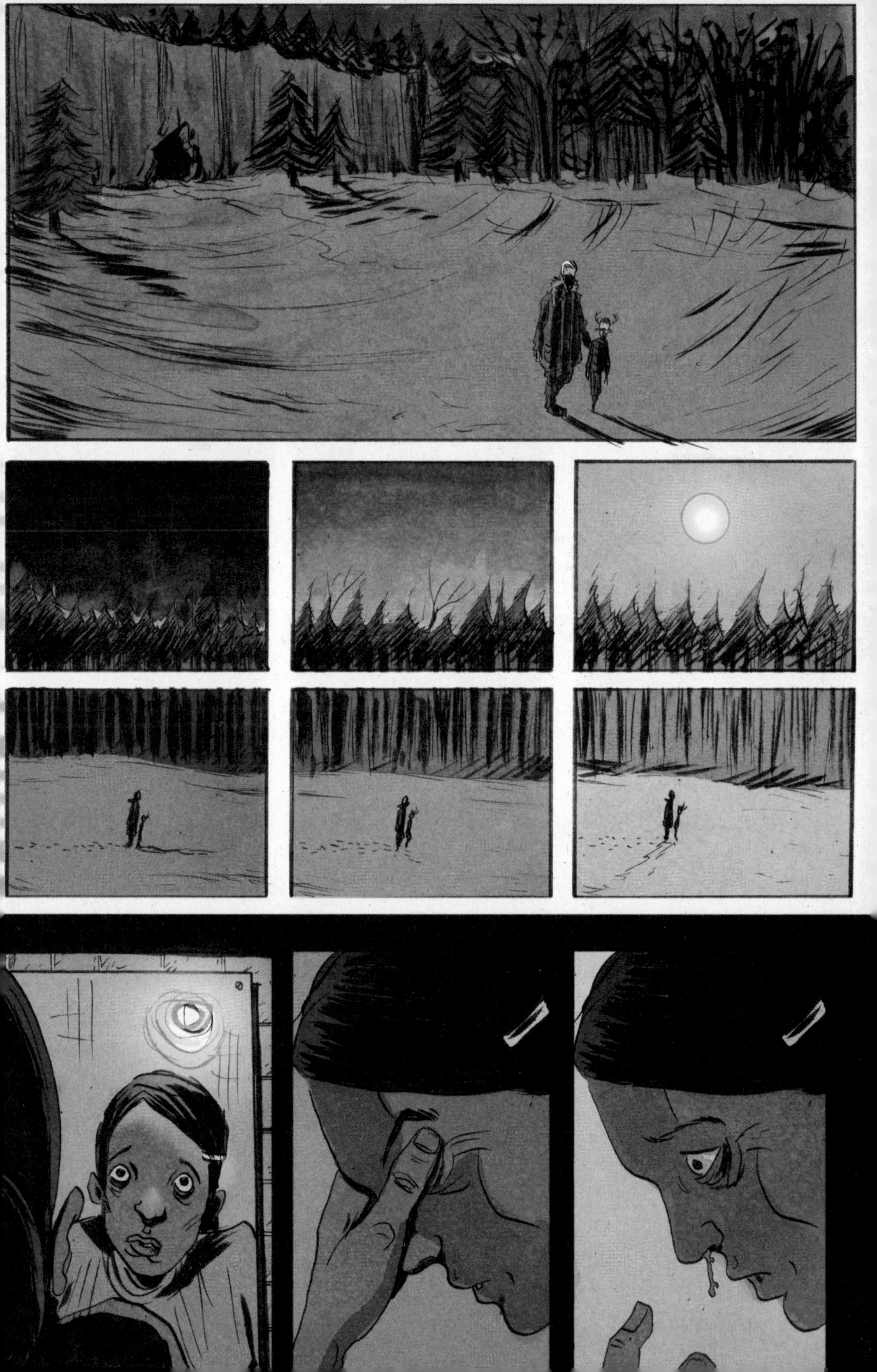

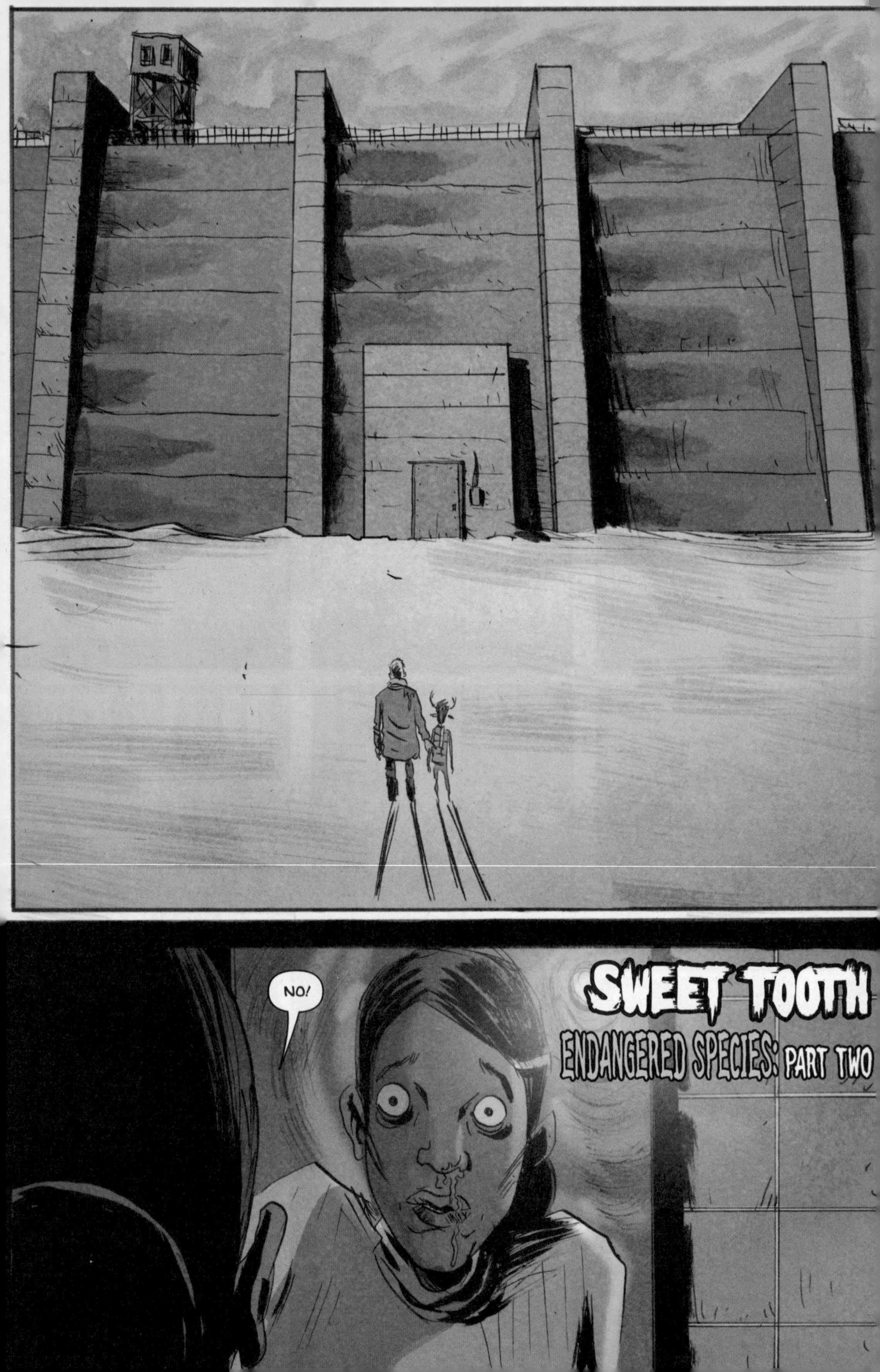
NO!
SWEET TOOTH
ENDANGERED SPECIES: PART TWO

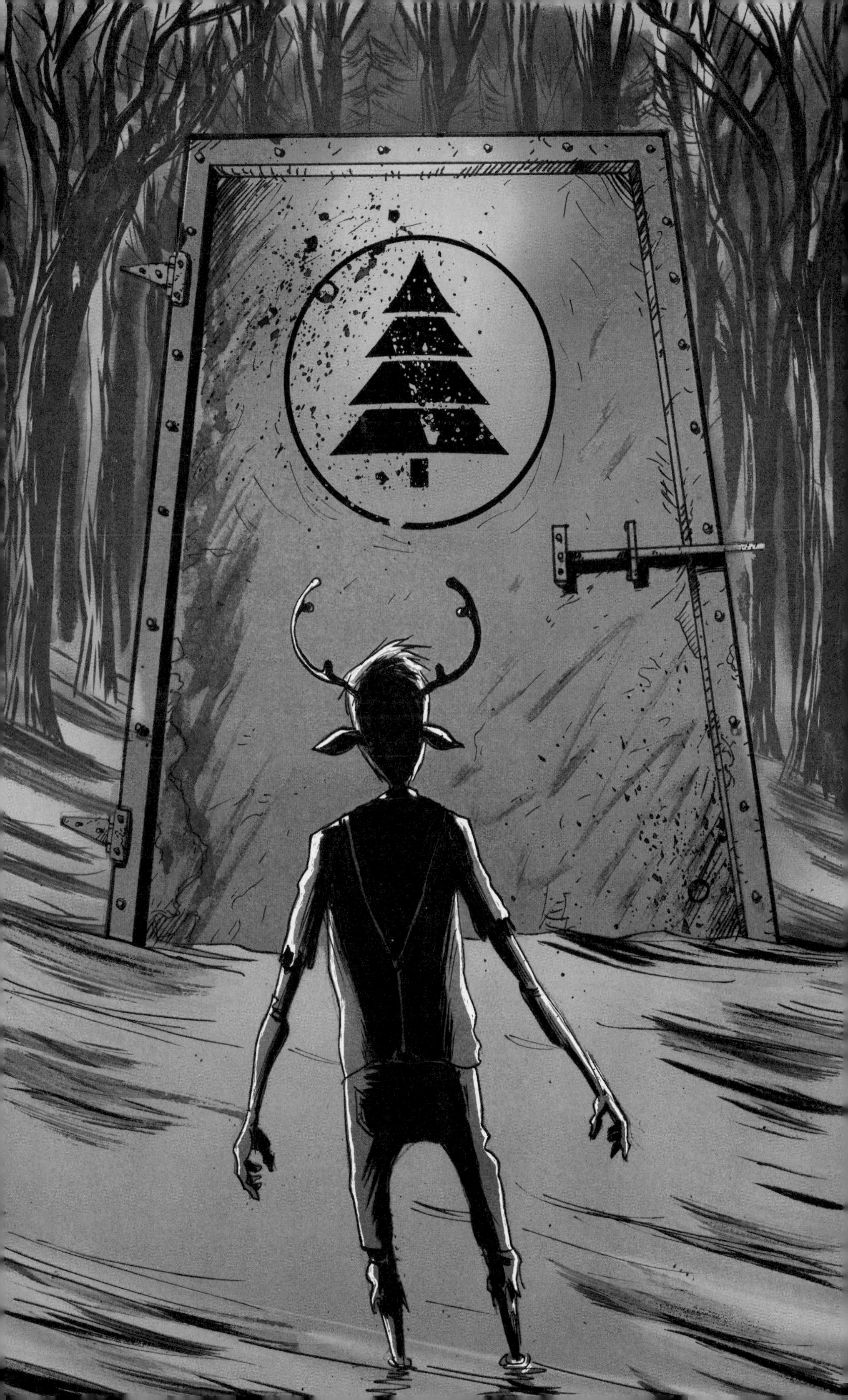

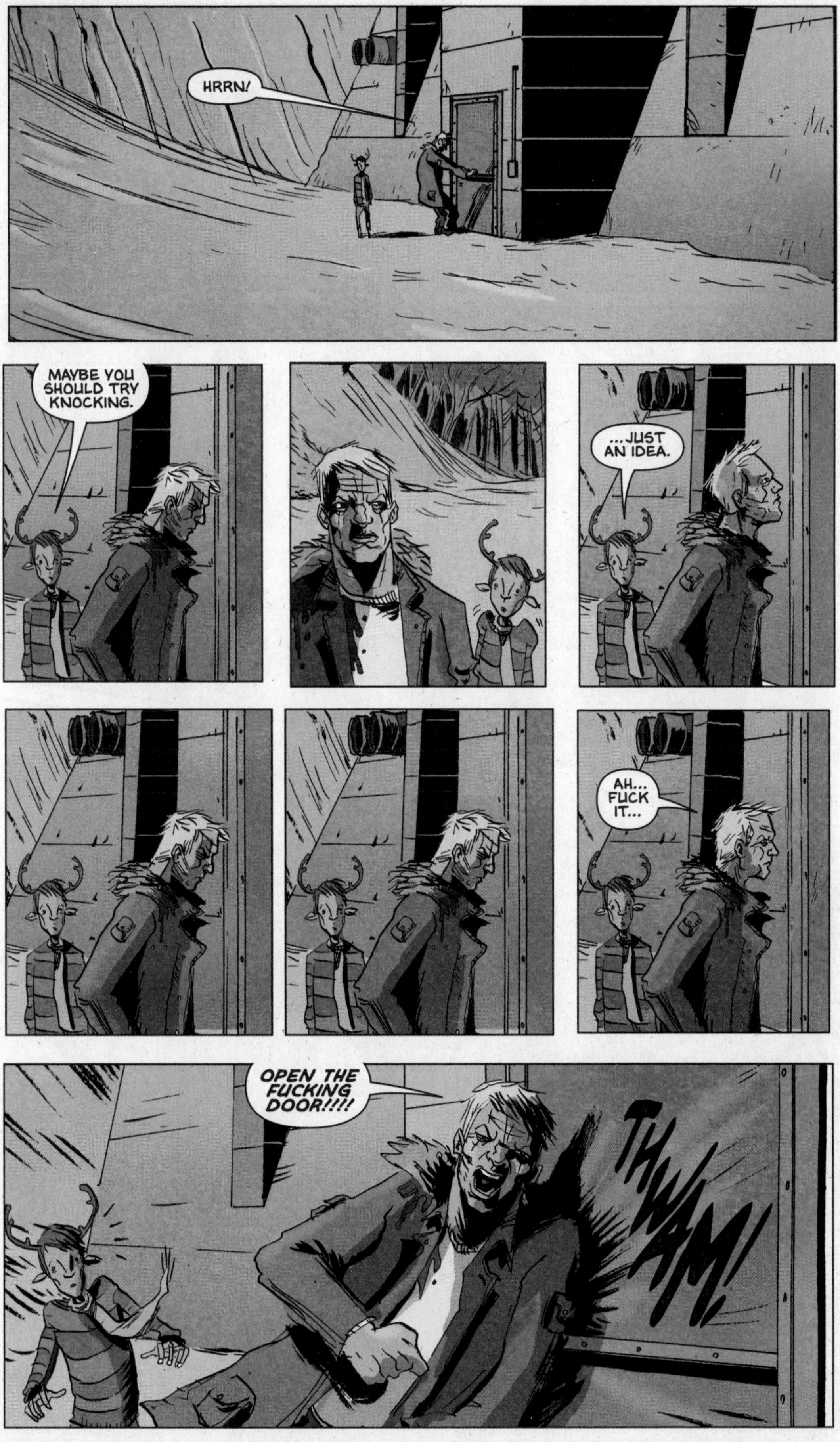
HRRN!
MAYBE YOU SHOULD TRY KNOCKING.
...JUST AN IDEA.
AH... FUCK IT...
OPEN THE FUCKING DOOR!!!!
THWAM!

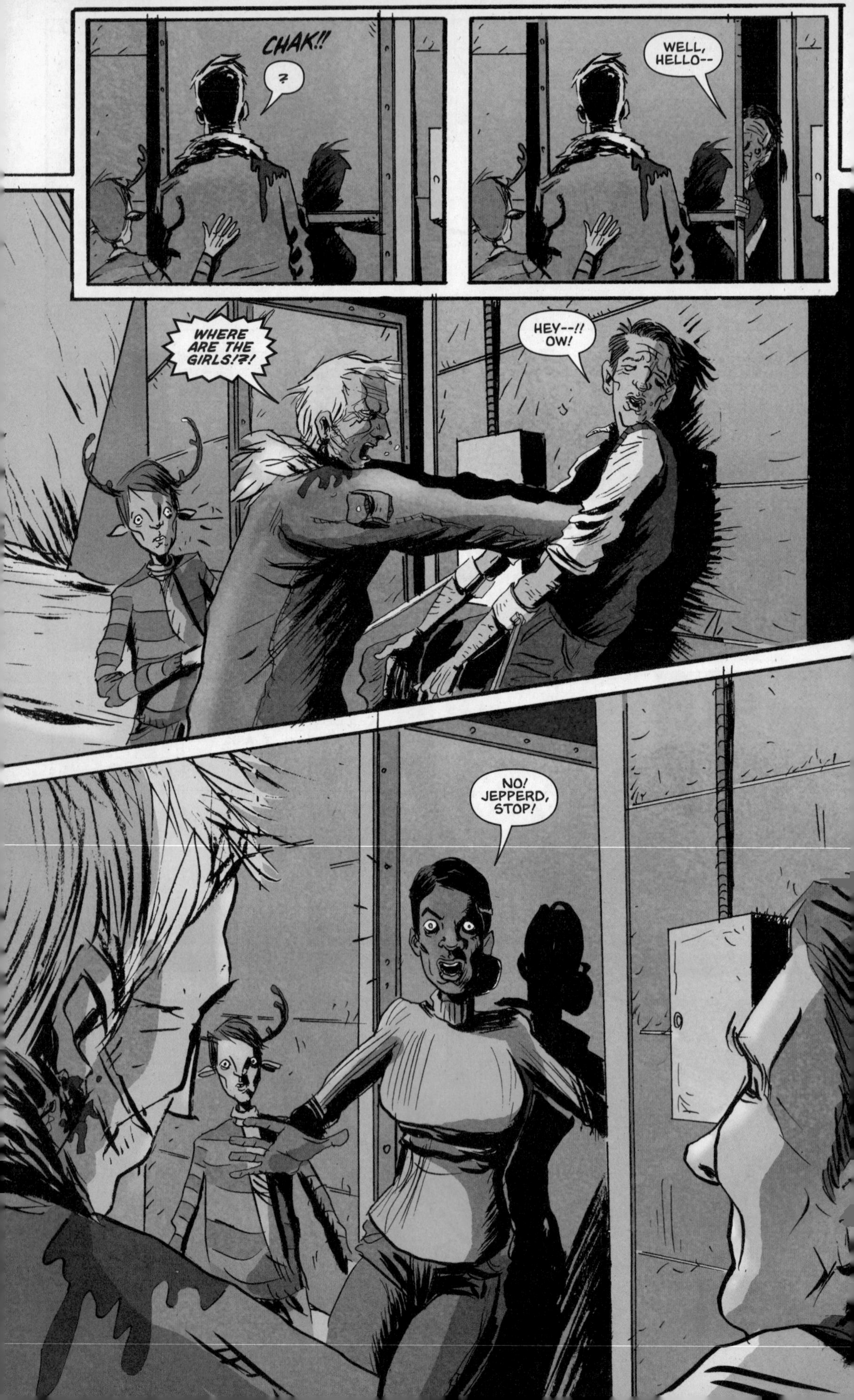
CHAK!!
?
WELL, HELLO--
WHERE ARE THE GIRLS!?!
HEY--!! OW!
NO! JEPPERD, STOP!

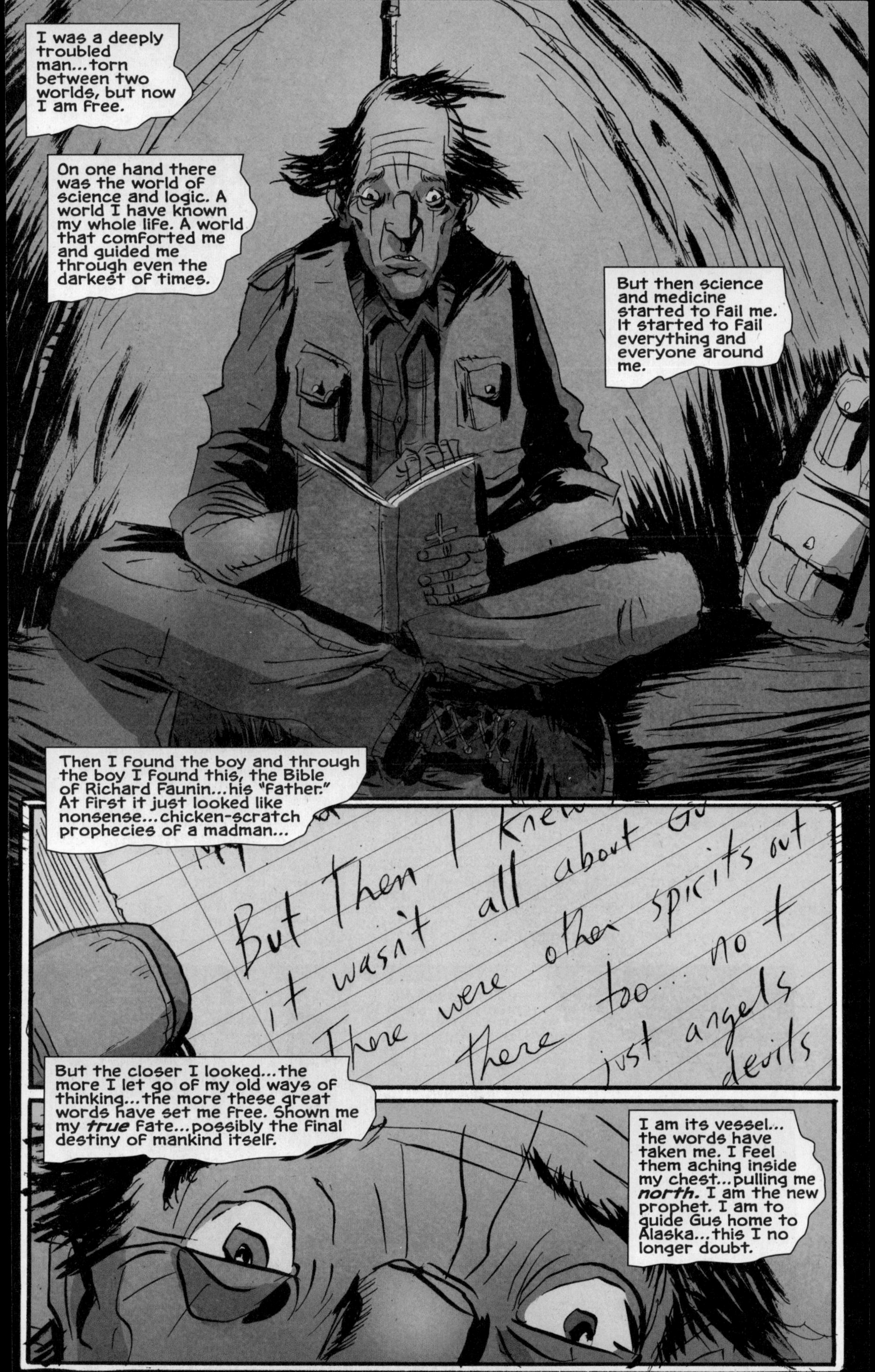
I was a deeply troubled man...torn between two worlds, but now I am free.
On one hand there was the world of science and logic. A world I have known my whole life. A world that comforted me and guided me through even the darkest of times.
But then science and medicine started to fail me. It started to fail everything and everyone around me.
Then I found the boy and through the boy I found this, the Bible of Richard Faunin...his "Father." At first it just looked like nonsense...chicken-scratch prophecies of a madman...
But then I knew it wasn't all about
There were other spirits out there too... not just angels devils
But the closer I looked...the more I let go of my old ways of thinking...the more these great words have set me free. Shown me my *true* fate...possibly the final destiny of mankind itself.
I am its vessel... the words have taken me. I feel them aching inside my chest...pulling me ***north.*** I am the new prophet. I am to guide Gus home to Alaska...this I no longer doubt.

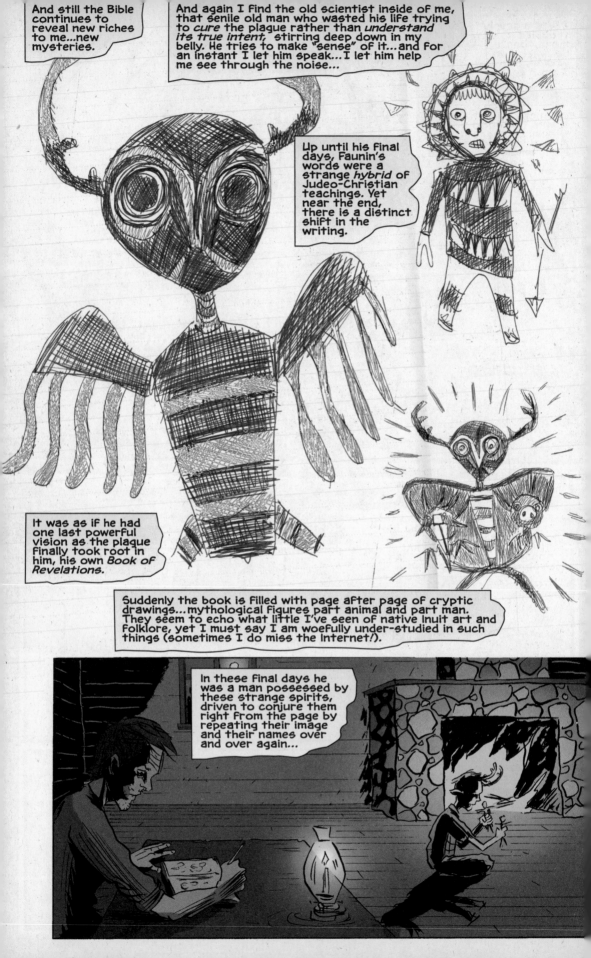

And still the Bible continues to reveal new riches to me...new mysteries.

And again I find the old scientist inside of me, that senile old man who wasted his life trying to *cure* the plague rather than *understand its true intent*, stirring deep down in my belly. He tries to make "sense" of it...and for an instant I let him speak...I let him help me see through the noise...

Up until his final days, Faunin's words were a strange *hybrid* of Judeo-Christian teachings. Yet near the end, there is a distinct shift in the writing.

It was as if he had one last powerful vision as the plague finally took root in him, his own *Book of Revelations.*

Suddenly the book is filled with page after page of cryptic drawings...mythological figures part animal and part man. They seem to echo what little I've seen of native Inuit art and folklore, yet I must say I am woefully under-studied in such things (sometimes I do miss the internet!).

In these final days he was a man possessed by these strange spirits, driven to conjure them right from the page by repeating their image and their names over and over again...

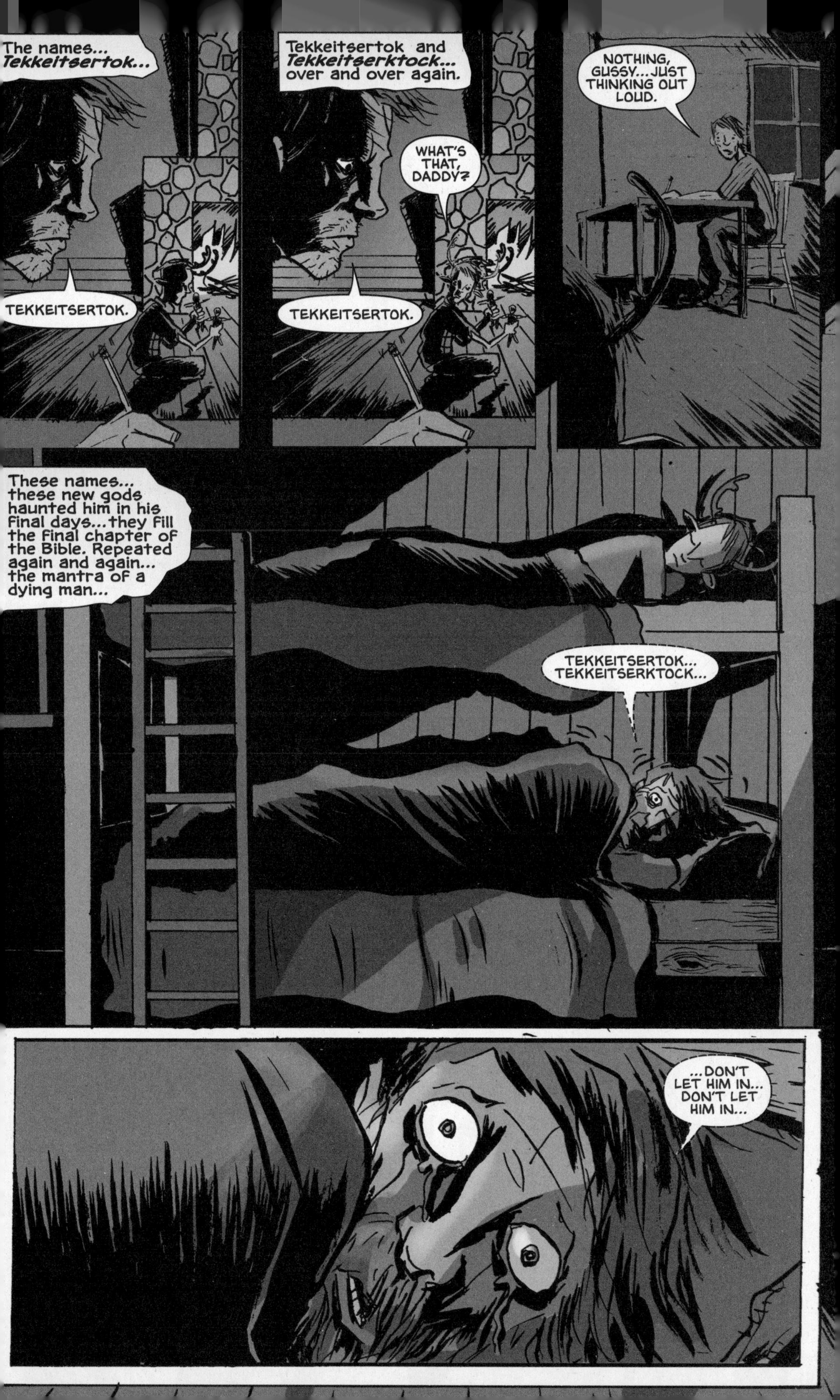

The names... *Tekkeitsertok...*
TEKKEITSERTOK.
Tekkeitsertok and *Tekkeitserktock...* over and over again.
WHAT'S THAT, DADDY?
TEKKEITSERTOK.
NOTHING, GUSSY... JUST THINKING OUT LOUD.
These names... these new gods haunted him in his final days... they fill the final chapter of the Bible. Repeated again and again... the mantra of a dying man...
TEKKEITSERTOK... TEKKEITSERKTOCK...
...DON'T LET HIM IN... DON'T LET HIM IN...

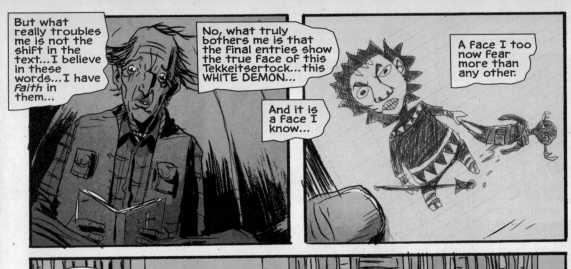

But what really troubles me is not the shift in the text...I believe in these words...I have *faith* in them...

No, what truly bothers me is that the final entries show the true face of this Tekkeitsertock...this WHITE DEMON...

And it is a face I know...

A face I too now fear more than any other.

THOSE STITCHES SHOULD DO...TRY TO KEEP THEM CLEAN.

SORRY I COULDN'T SAVE THE EARLOBE.

...

DON'T NEED IT.

HOW ARE YOU FEELING, WALTER?

A BIT STIFF, BUT I'LL LIVE.

I'M MORE CONCERNED WITH THE FACT THAT *YOU LIED TO ME,* LUCY.

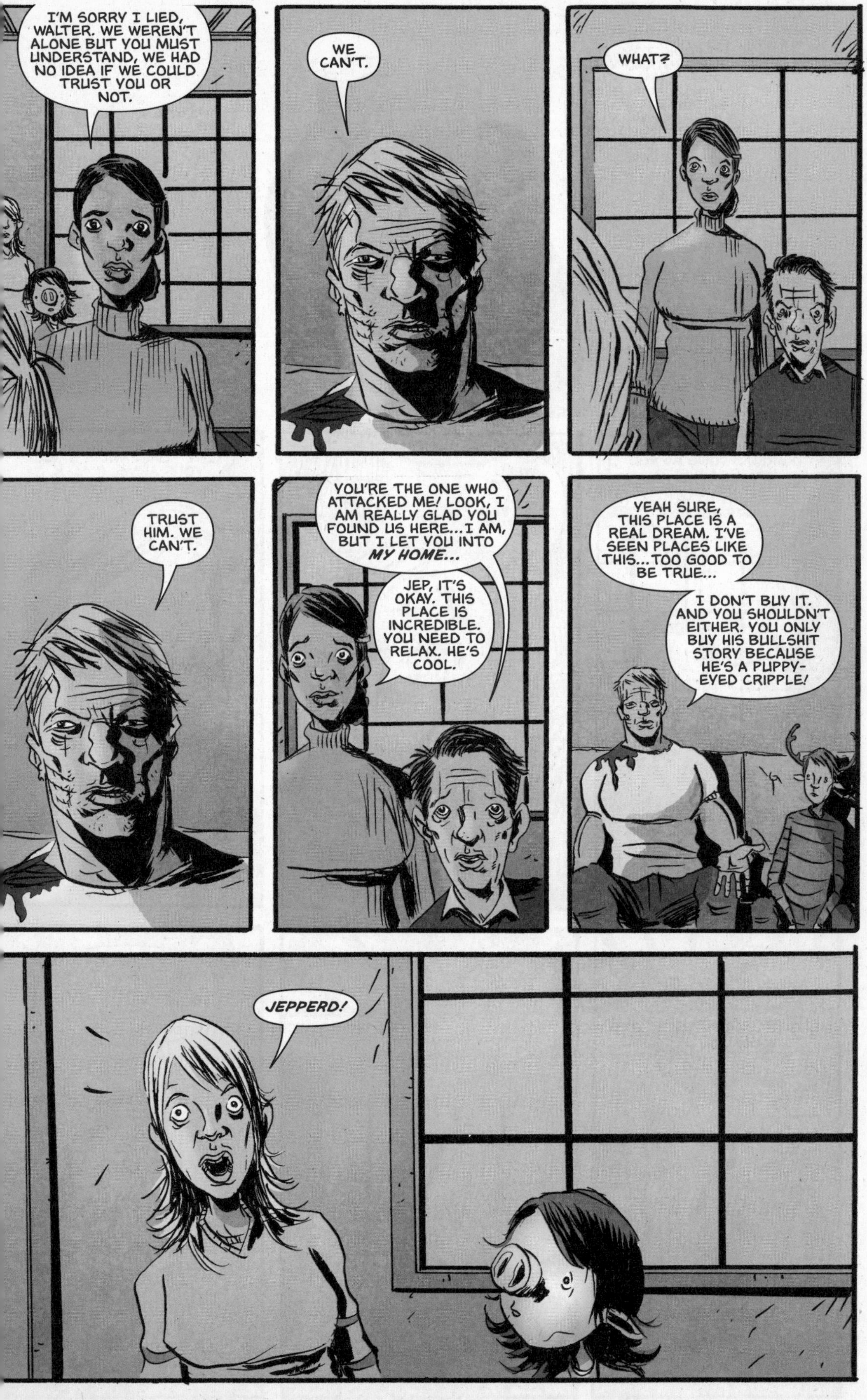
I'M SORRY I LIED, WALTER. WE WEREN'T ALONE BUT YOU MUST UNDERSTAND, WE HAD NO IDEA IF WE COULD TRUST YOU OR NOT.
WE CAN'T.
WHAT?
TRUST HIM. WE CAN'T.
YOU'RE THE ONE WHO ATTACKED ME! LOOK, I AM REALLY GLAD YOU FOUND US HERE...I AM, BUT I LET YOU INTO *MY HOME...*
JEP, IT'S OKAY. THIS PLACE IS INCREDIBLE. YOU NEED TO RELAX. HE'S COOL.
YEAH SURE, THIS PLACE IS A REAL DREAM. I'VE SEEN PLACES LIKE THIS...TOO GOOD TO BE TRUE...
I DON'T BUY IT. AND YOU SHOULDN'T EITHER. YOU ONLY BUY HIS BULLSHIT STORY BECAUSE HE'S A PUPPY-EYED CRIPPLE!
JEPPERD!

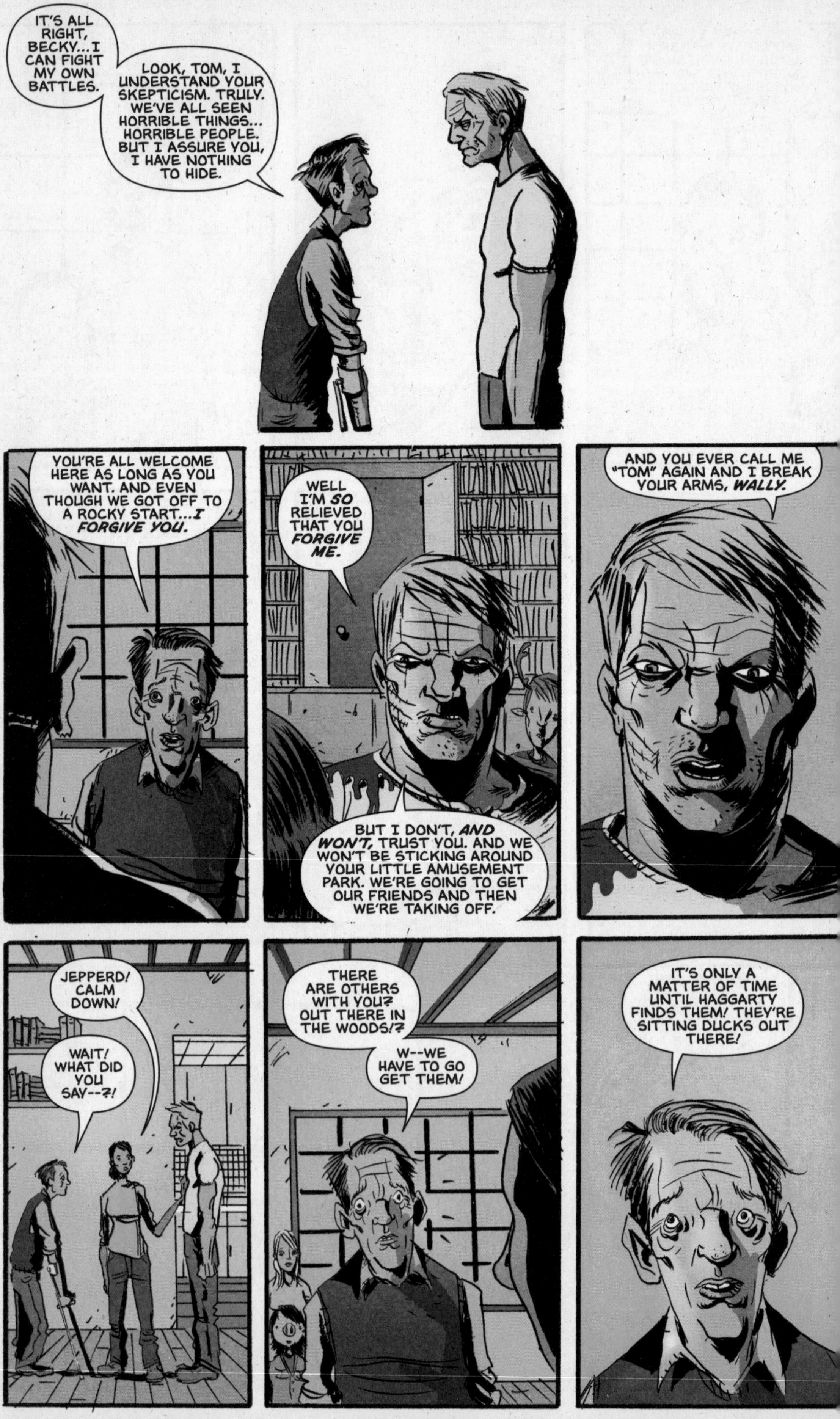
IT'S ALL RIGHT, BECKY...I CAN FIGHT MY OWN BATTLES.
LOOK, TOM, I UNDERSTAND YOUR SKEPTICISM. TRULY. WE'VE ALL SEEN HORRIBLE THINGS... HORRIBLE PEOPLE. BUT I ASSURE YOU, I HAVE NOTHING TO HIDE.
YOU'RE ALL WELCOME HERE AS LONG AS YOU WANT. AND EVEN THOUGH WE GOT OFF TO A ROCKY START...I FORGIVE YOU.
WELL I'M SO RELIEVED THAT YOU FORGIVE ME.
BUT I DON'T, AND WON'T, TRUST YOU. AND WE WON'T BE STICKING AROUND YOUR LITTLE AMUSEMENT PARK. WE'RE GOING TO GET OUR FRIENDS AND THEN WE'RE TAKING OFF.
AND YOU EVER CALL ME "TOM" AGAIN AND I BREAK YOUR ARMS, WALLY.
JEPPERD! CALM DOWN!
WAIT! WHAT DID YOU SAY--?!
THERE ARE OTHERS WITH YOU? OUT THERE IN THE WOODS!?
W--WE HAVE TO GO GET THEM!
IT'S ONLY A MATTER OF TIME UNTIL HAGGARTY FINDS THEM! THEY'RE SITTING DUCKS OUT THERE!

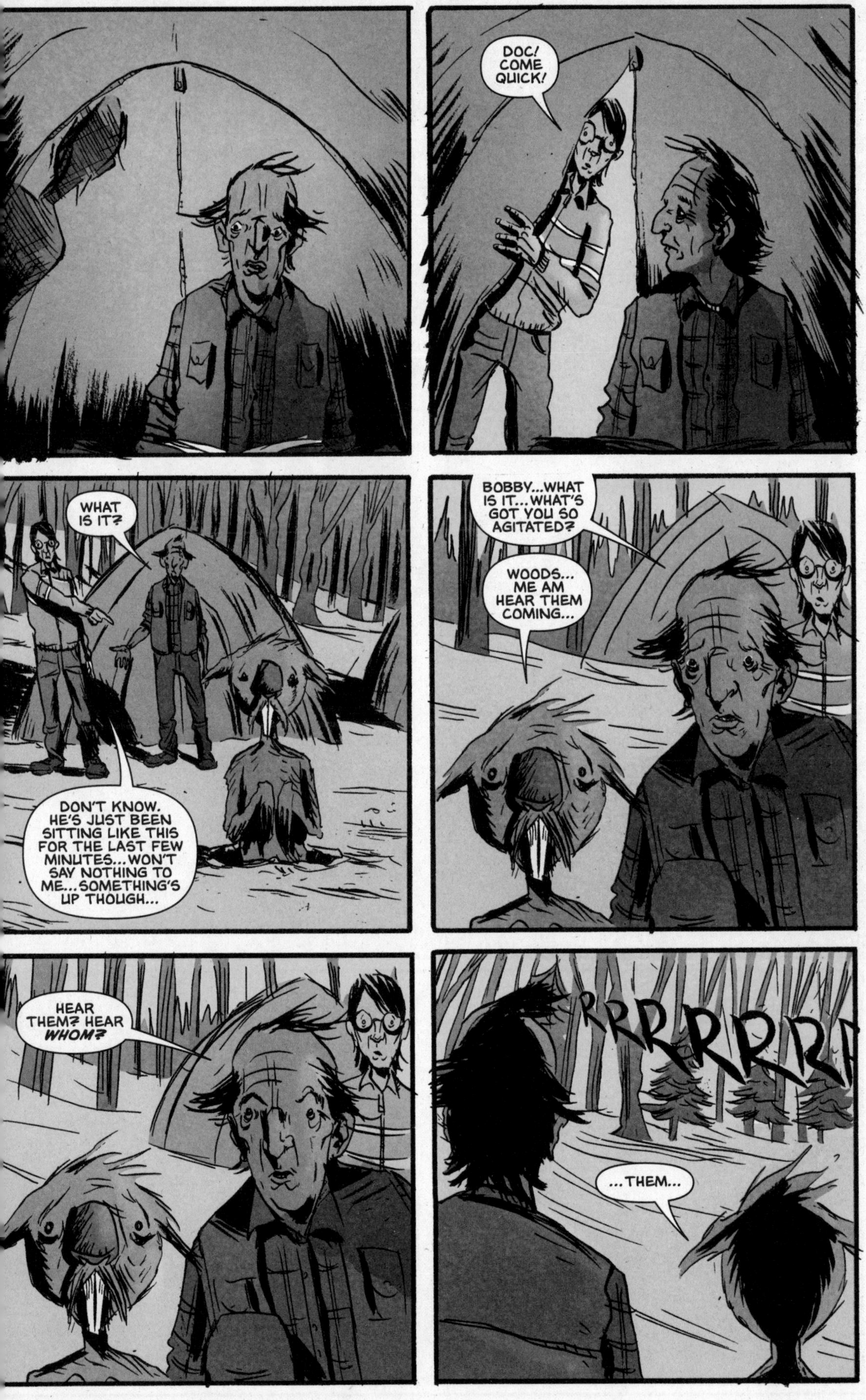
DOC! COME QUICK!
WHAT IS IT?
DON'T KNOW. HE'S JUST BEEN SITTING LIKE THIS FOR THE LAST FEW MINUTES...WON'T SAY NOTHING TO ME...SOMETHING'S UP THOUGH...
BOBBY...WHAT IS IT...WHAT'S GOT YOU SO AGITATED?
WOODS... ME AM HEAR THEM COMING...
HEAR THEM? HEAR *WHOM?*
RRRRRRRR
...THEM...

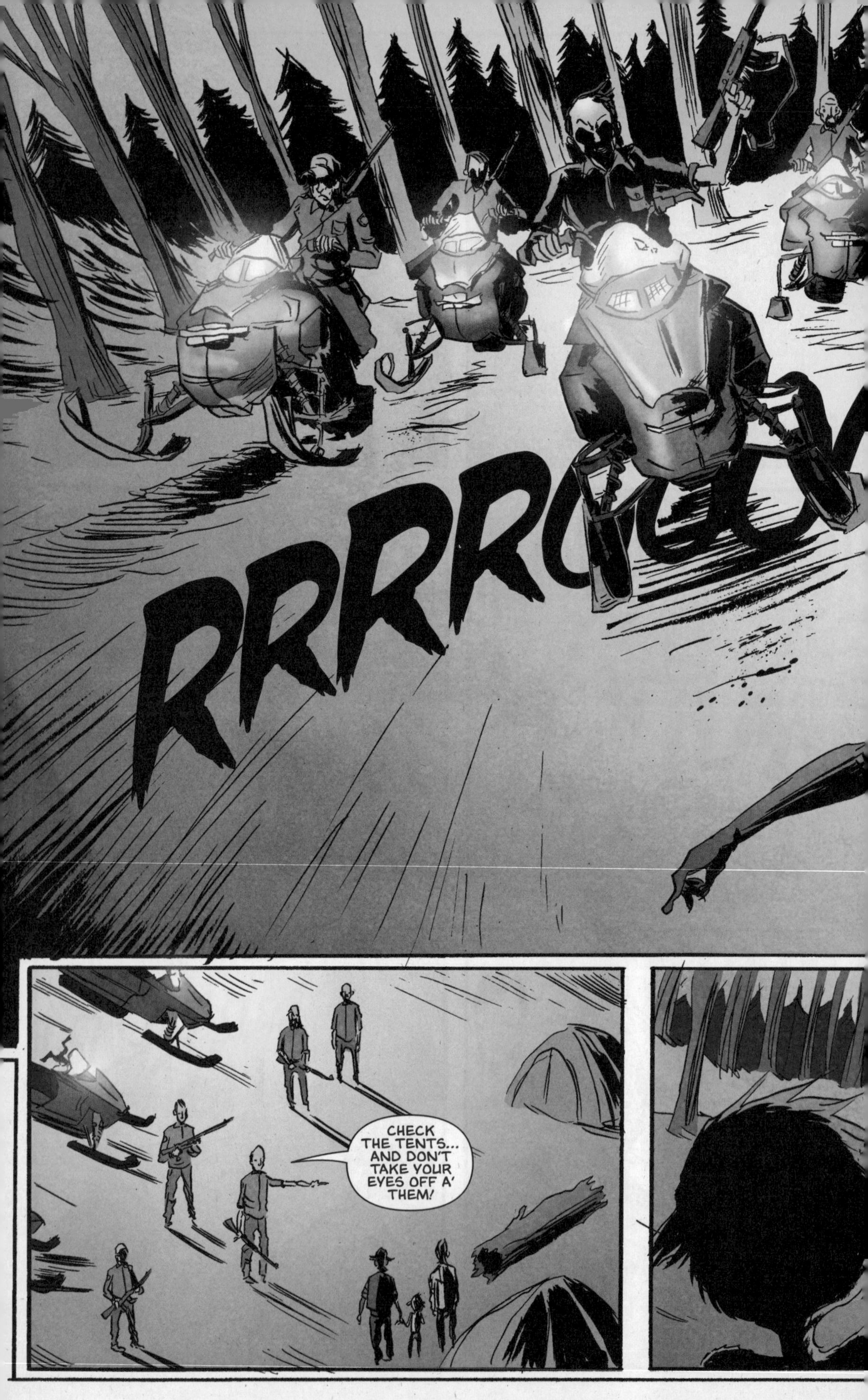
CHECK THE TENTS... AND DON'T TAKE YOUR EYES OFF A' THEM!

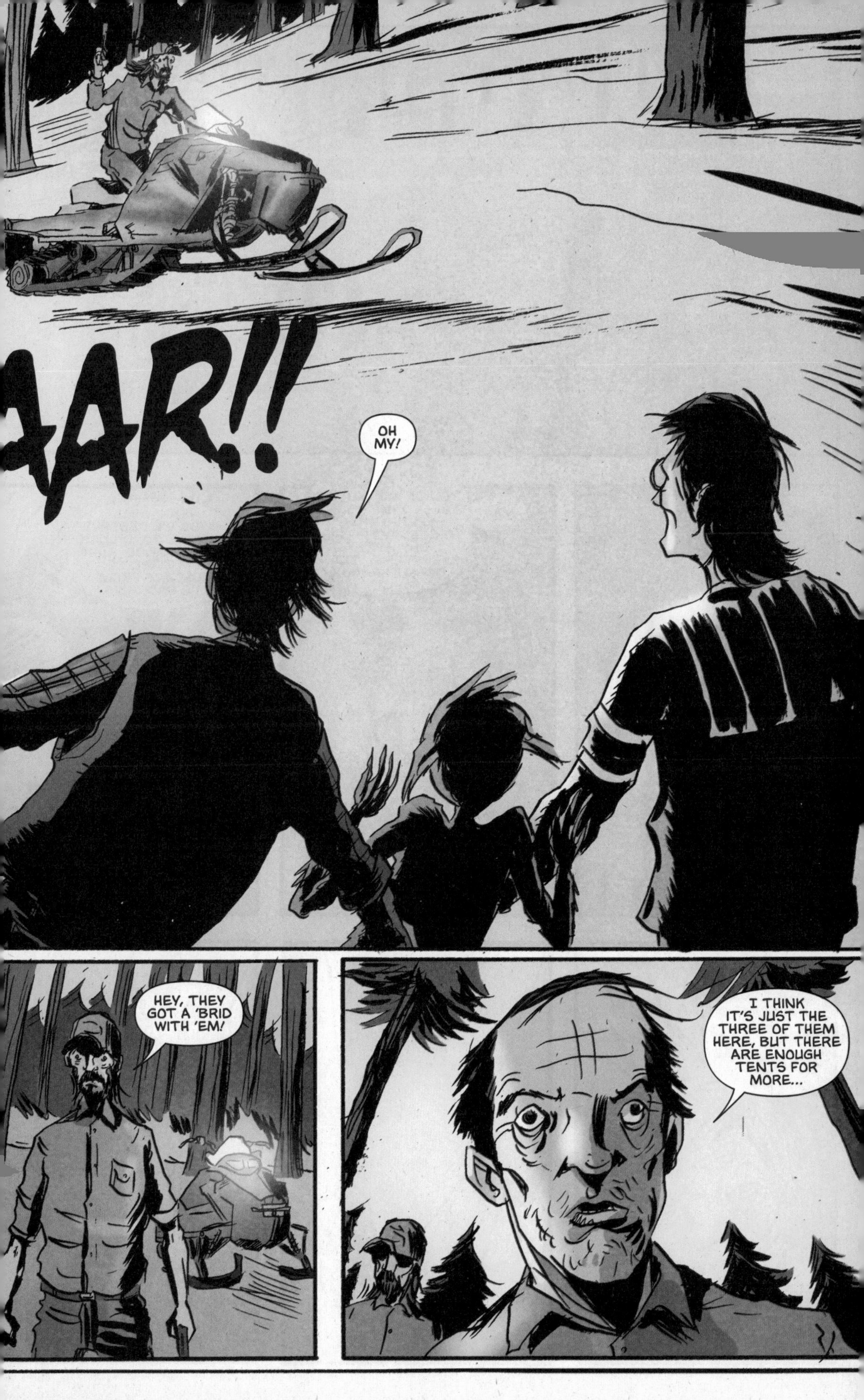
AAR!!
OH MY!
HEY, THEY GOT A 'BRID WITH 'EM!
I THINK IT'S JUST THE THREE OF THEM HERE, BUT THERE ARE ENOUGH TENTS FOR MORE...

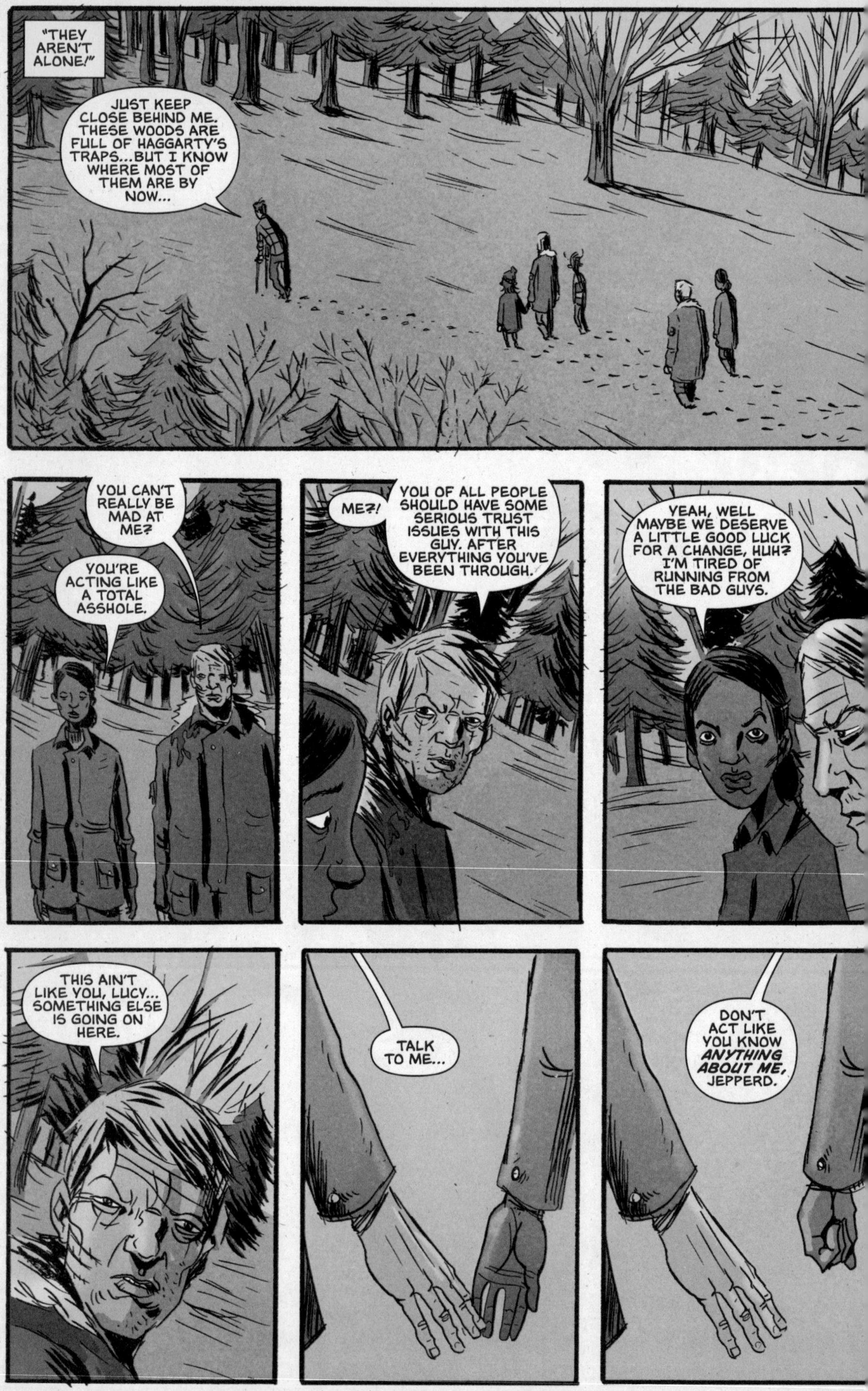
"THEY AREN'T ALONE!"
JUST KEEP CLOSE BEHIND ME. THESE WOODS ARE FULL OF HAGGARTY'S TRAPS...BUT I KNOW WHERE MOST OF THEM ARE BY NOW...
YOU CAN'T REALLY BE MAD AT ME?
YOU'RE ACTING LIKE A TOTAL ASSHOLE.
ME?!
YOU OF ALL PEOPLE SHOULD HAVE SOME SERIOUS TRUST ISSUES WITH THIS GUY. AFTER EVERYTHING YOU'VE BEEN THROUGH.
YEAH, WELL MAYBE WE DESERVE A LITTLE GOOD LUCK FOR A CHANGE, HUH? I'M TIRED OF RUNNING FROM THE BAD GUYS.
THIS AIN'T LIKE YOU, LUCY... SOMETHING ELSE IS GOING ON HERE.
TALK TO ME...
DON'T ACT LIKE YOU KNOW *ANYTHING ABOUT ME,* JEPPERD.

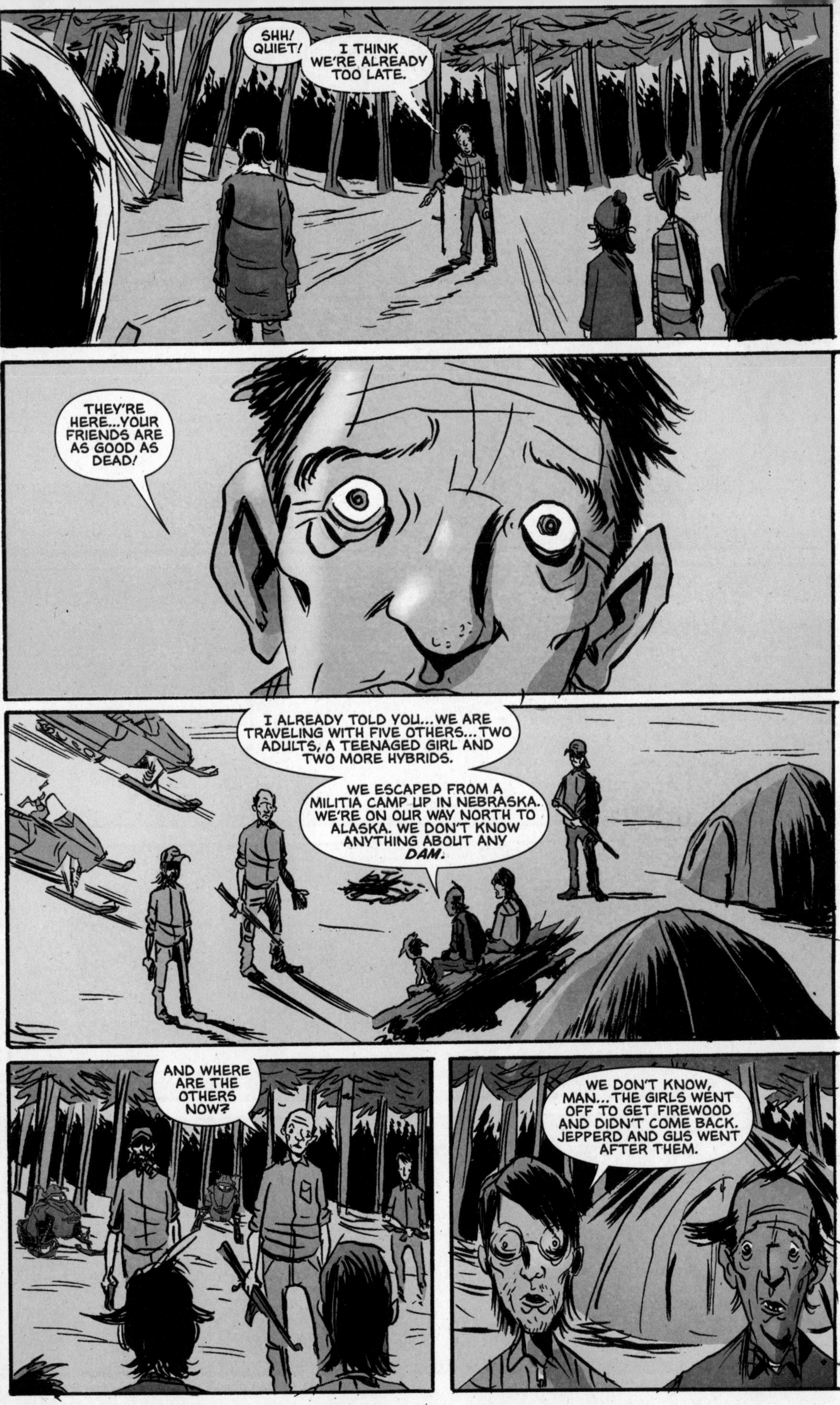
SHH! QUIET!
I THINK WE'RE ALREADY TOO LATE.
THEY'RE HERE...YOUR FRIENDS ARE AS GOOD AS DEAD!
I ALREADY TOLD YOU...WE ARE TRAVELING WITH FIVE OTHERS...TWO ADULTS, A TEENAGED GIRL AND TWO MORE HYBRIDS.
WE ESCAPED FROM A MILITIA CAMP UP IN NEBRASKA. WE'RE ON OUR WAY NORTH TO ALASKA. WE DON'T KNOW ANYTHING ABOUT ANY *DAM*.
AND WHERE ARE THE OTHERS NOW?
WE DON'T KNOW, MAN...THE GIRLS WENT OFF TO GET FIREWOOD AND DIDN'T COME BACK. JEPPERD AND GUS WENT AFTER THEM.

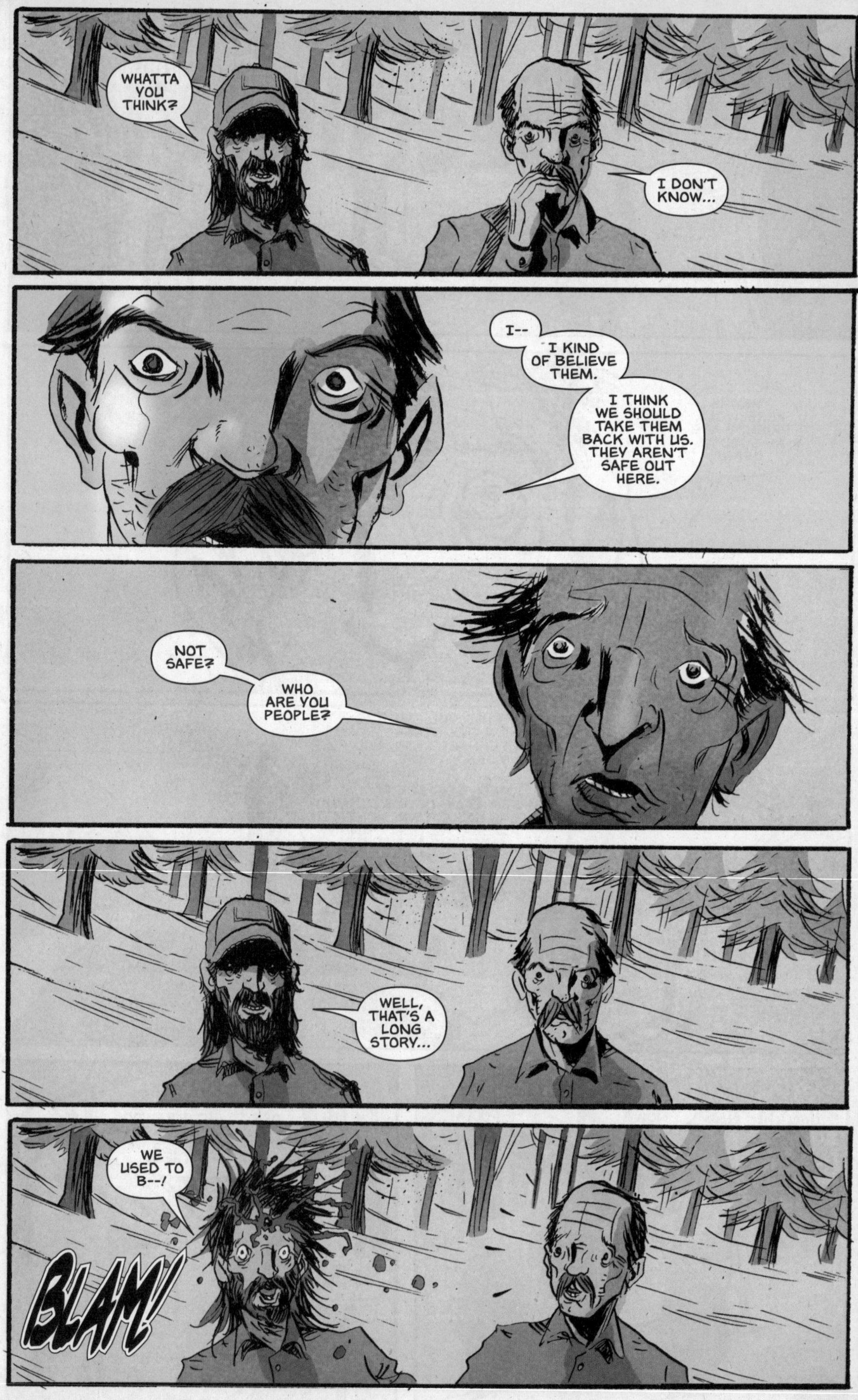

WHATTA YOU THINK?
I DON'T KNOW...
I--
I KIND OF BELIEVE THEM.
I THINK WE SHOULD TAKE THEM BACK WITH US. THEY AREN'T SAFE OUT HERE.
NOT SAFE?
WHO ARE YOU PEOPLE?
WELL, THAT'S A LONG STORY...
WE USED TO B--!
BLAM!

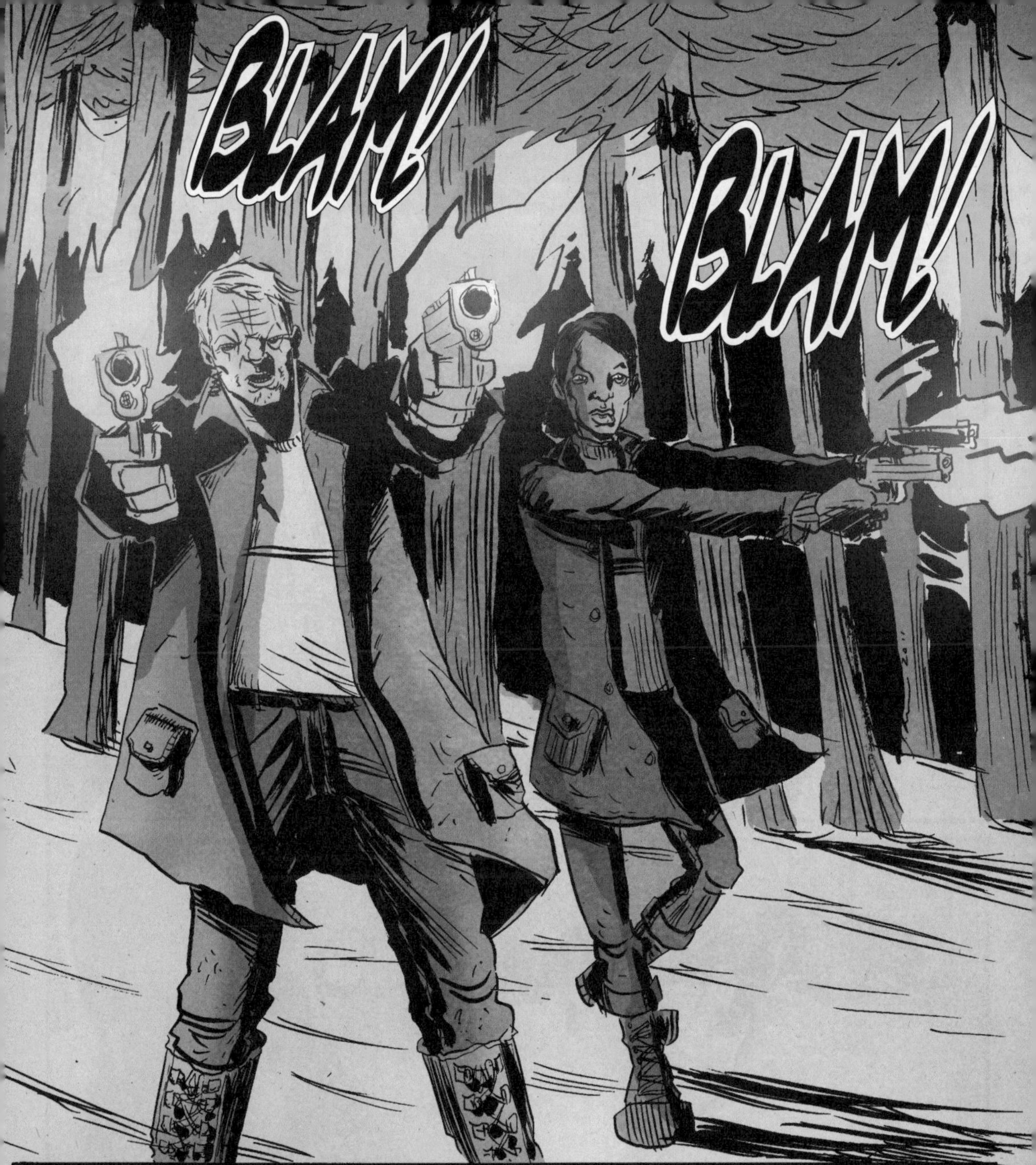
BLAM!
BLAM!

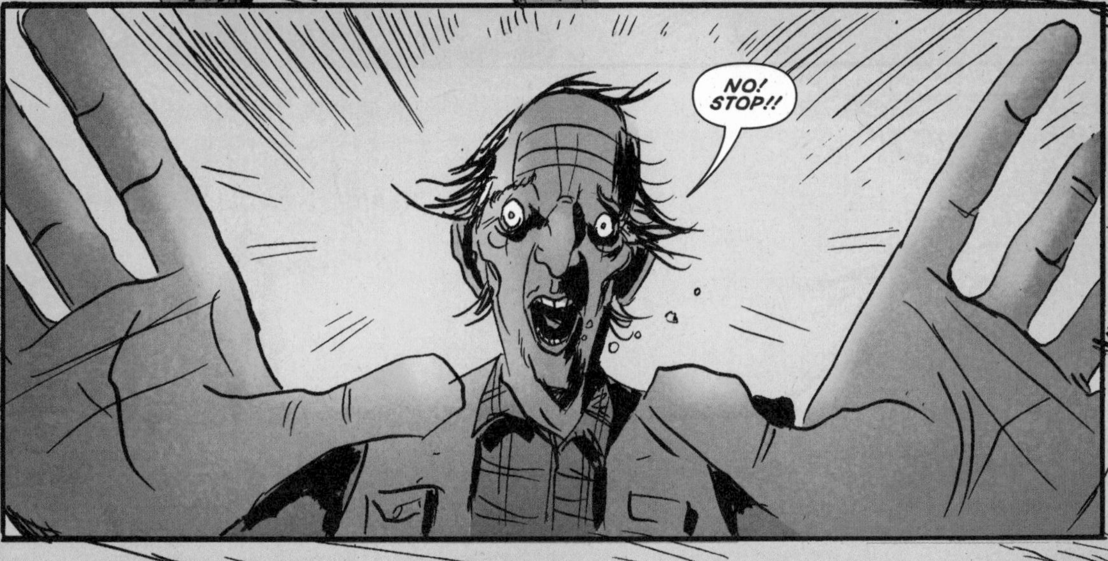
NO! STOP!!

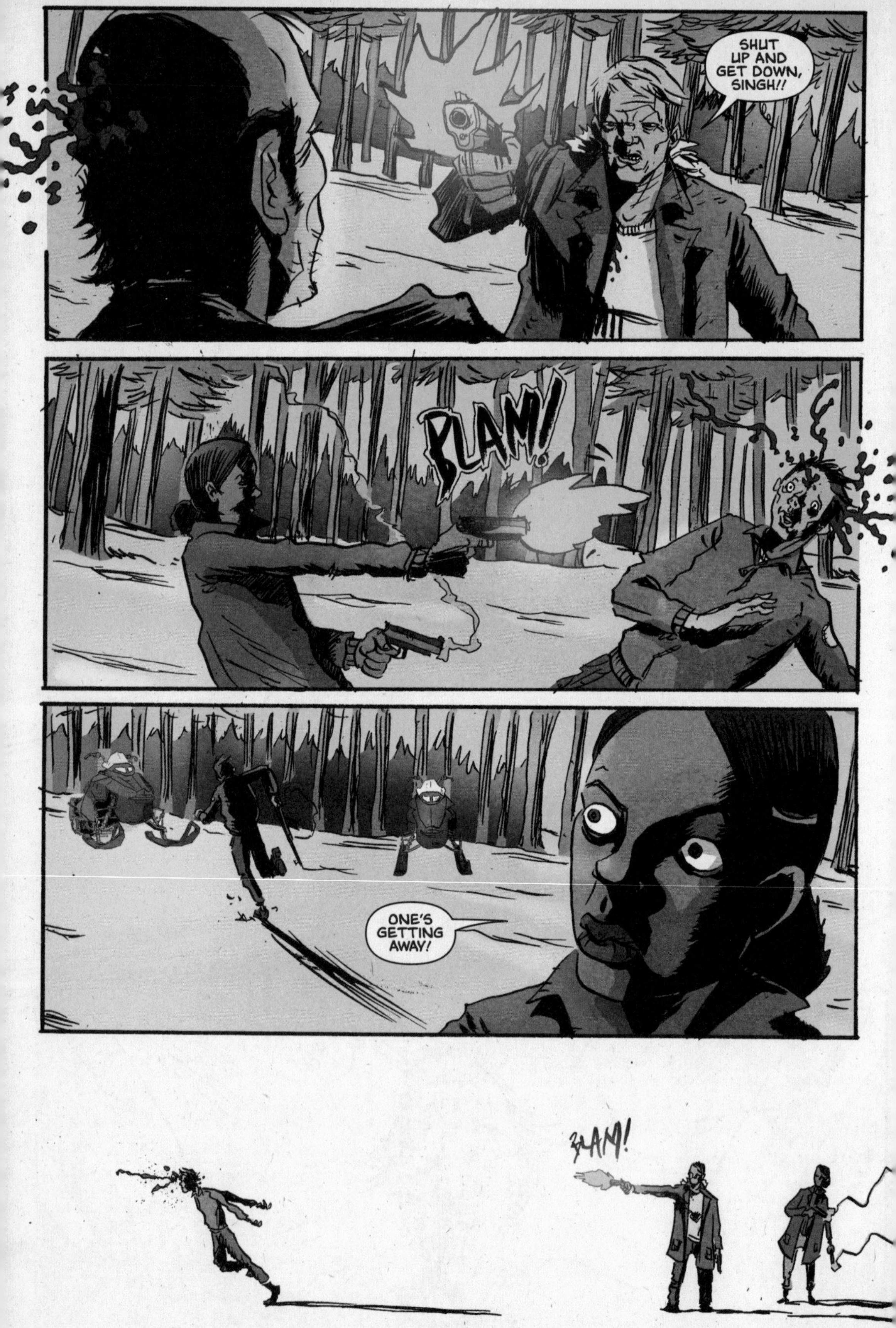
SHUT UP AND GET DOWN, SINGH!!
BLAM!
ONE'S GETTING AWAY!
BLAM!

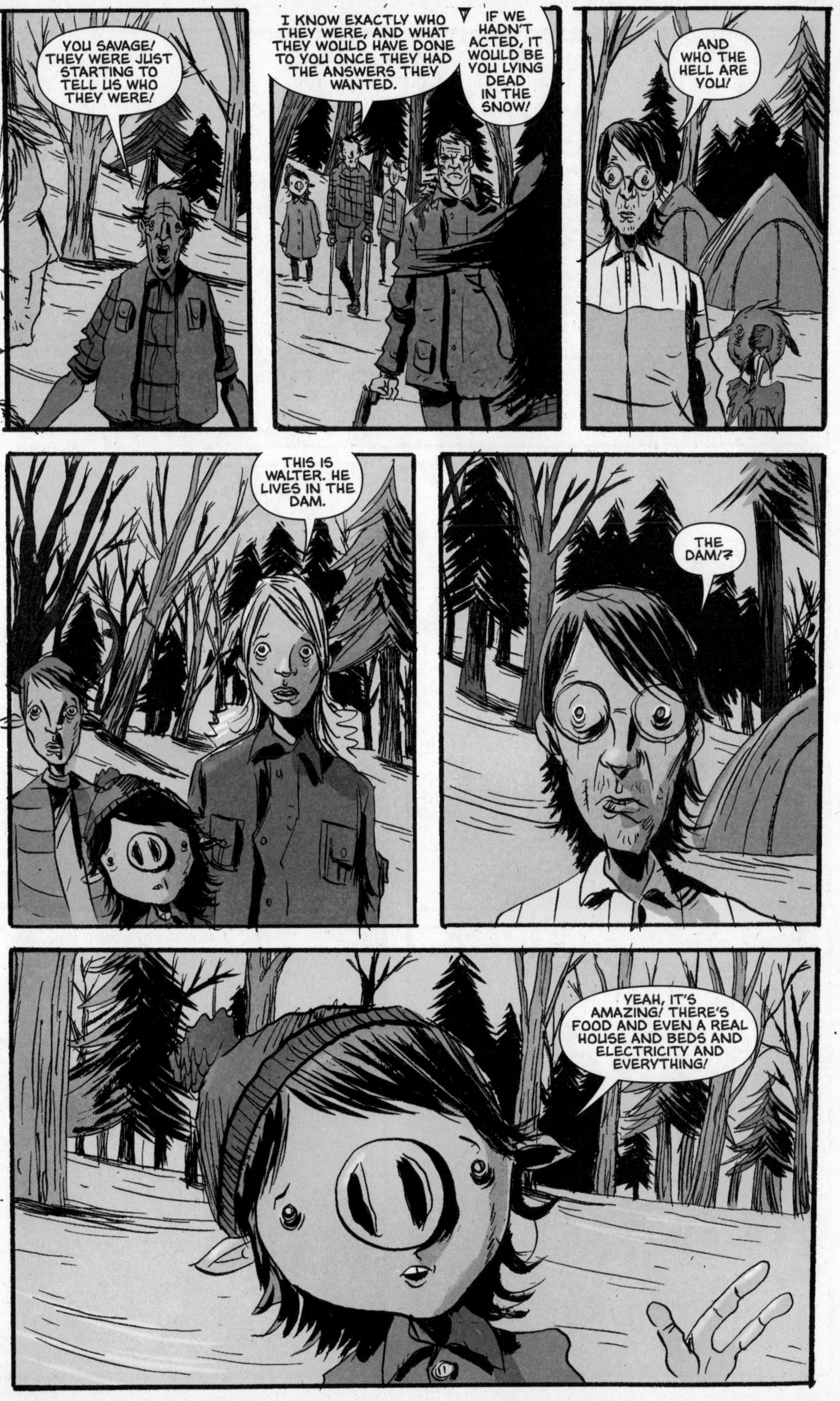
YOU SAVAGE! THEY WERE JUST STARTING TO TELL US WHO THEY WERE!
I KNOW EXACTLY WHO THEY WERE, AND WHAT THEY WOULD HAVE DONE TO YOU ONCE THEY HAD THE ANSWERS THEY WANTED.
IF WE HADN'T ACTED, IT WOULD BE YOU LYING DEAD IN THE SNOW!
AND WHO THE HELL ARE YOU!
THIS IS WALTER. HE LIVES IN THE DAM.
THE DAM!?
YEAH, IT'S AMAZING! THERE'S FOOD AND EVEN A REAL HOUSE AND BEDS AND ELECTRICITY AND EVERYTHING!

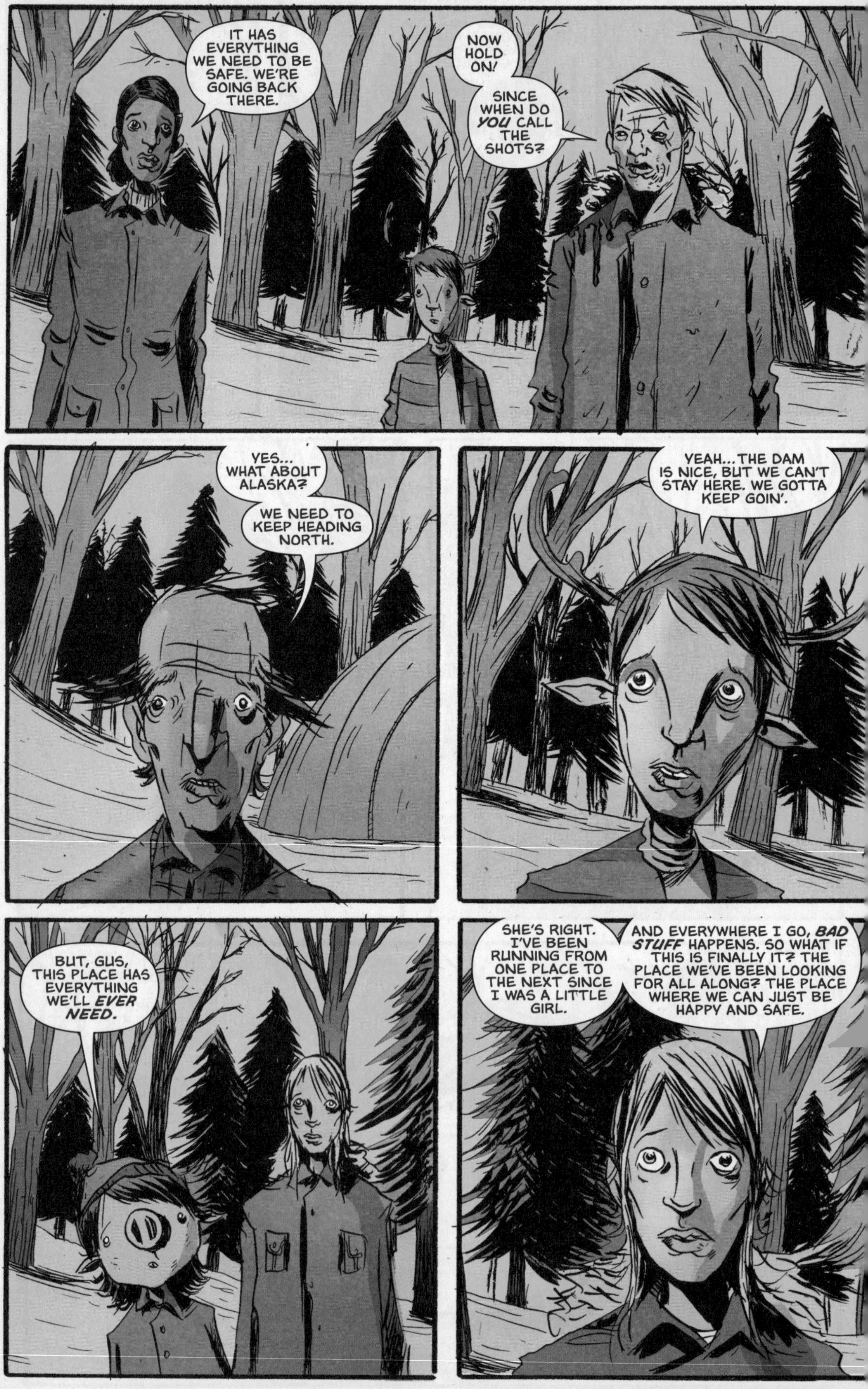
IT HAS EVERYTHING WE NEED TO BE SAFE. WE'RE GOING BACK THERE.
NOW HOLD ON!
SINCE WHEN DO *YOU* CALL THE SHOTS?
YES... WHAT ABOUT ALASKA?
WE NEED TO KEEP HEADING NORTH.
YEAH... THE DAM IS NICE, BUT WE CAN'T STAY HERE. WE GOTTA KEEP GOIN'.
BUT, GUS, THIS PLACE HAS EVERYTHING WE'LL *EVER NEED.*
SHE'S RIGHT. I'VE BEEN RUNNING FROM ONE PLACE TO THE NEXT SINCE I WAS A LITTLE GIRL.
AND EVERYWHERE I GO, *BAD STUFF* HAPPENS. SO WHAT IF THIS IS FINALLY IT? THE PLACE WE'VE BEEN LOOKING FOR ALL ALONG? THE PLACE WHERE WE CAN JUST BE HAPPY AND SAFE.

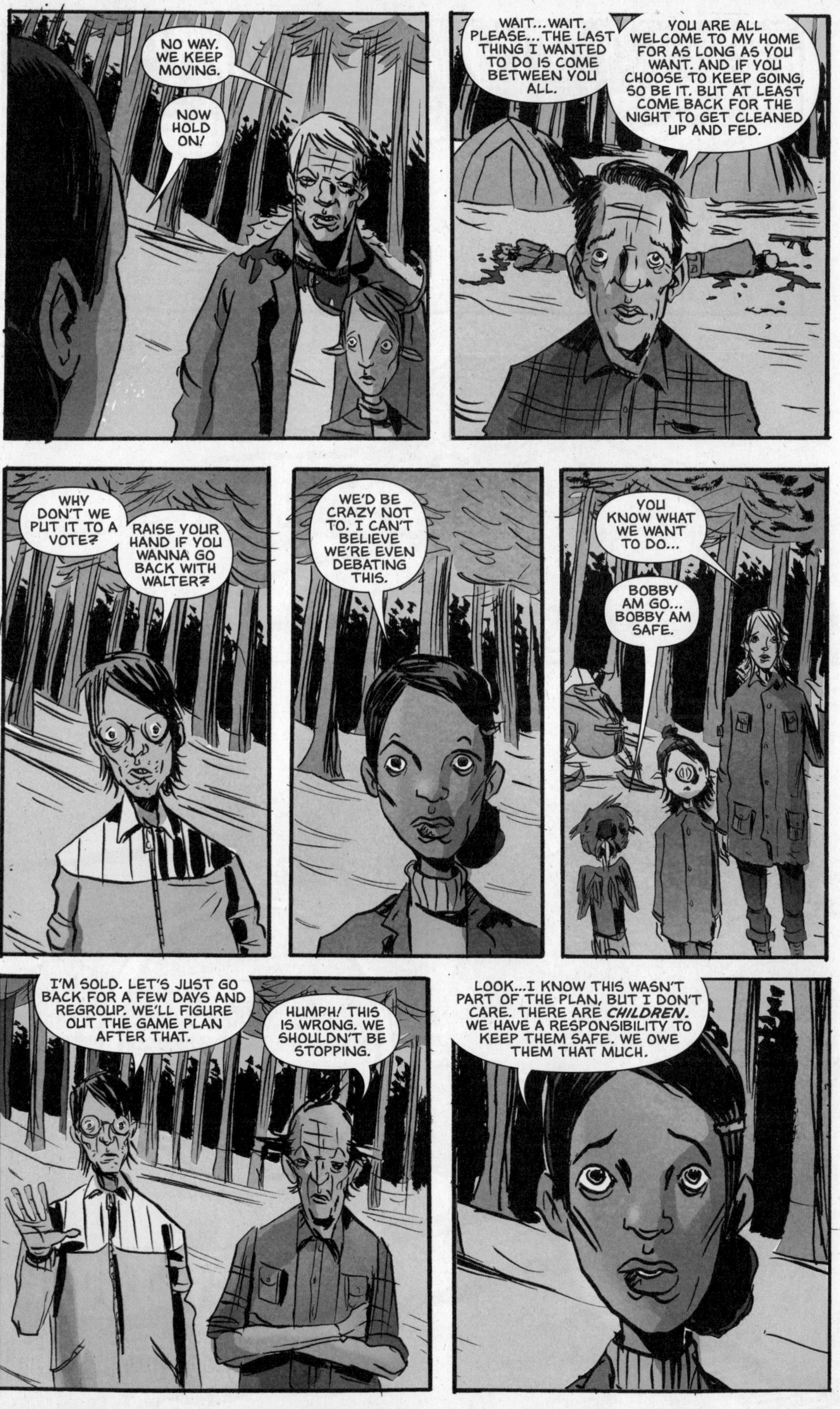
NO WAY. WE KEEP MOVING.
NOW HOLD ON!
WAIT...WAIT. PLEASE...THE LAST THING I WANTED TO DO IS COME BETWEEN YOU ALL.
YOU ARE ALL WELCOME TO MY HOME FOR AS LONG AS YOU WANT. AND IF YOU CHOOSE TO KEEP GOING, SO BE IT. BUT AT LEAST COME BACK FOR THE NIGHT TO GET CLEANED UP AND FED.
WHY DON'T WE PUT IT TO A VOTE?
RAISE YOUR HAND IF YOU WANNA GO BACK WITH WALTER?
WE'D BE CRAZY NOT TO. I CAN'T BELIEVE WE'RE EVEN DEBATING THIS.
YOU KNOW WHAT WE WANT TO DO...
BOBBY AM GO... BOBBY AM SAFE.
I'M SOLD. LET'S JUST GO BACK FOR A FEW DAYS AND REGROUP. WE'LL FIGURE OUT THE GAME PLAN AFTER THAT.
HUMPH! THIS IS WRONG. WE SHOULDN'T BE STOPPING.
LOOK...I KNOW THIS WASN'T PART OF THE PLAN, BUT I DON'T CARE. THERE ARE *CHILDREN*. WE HAVE A RESPONSIBILITY TO KEEP THEM SAFE. WE OWE THEM THAT MUCH.

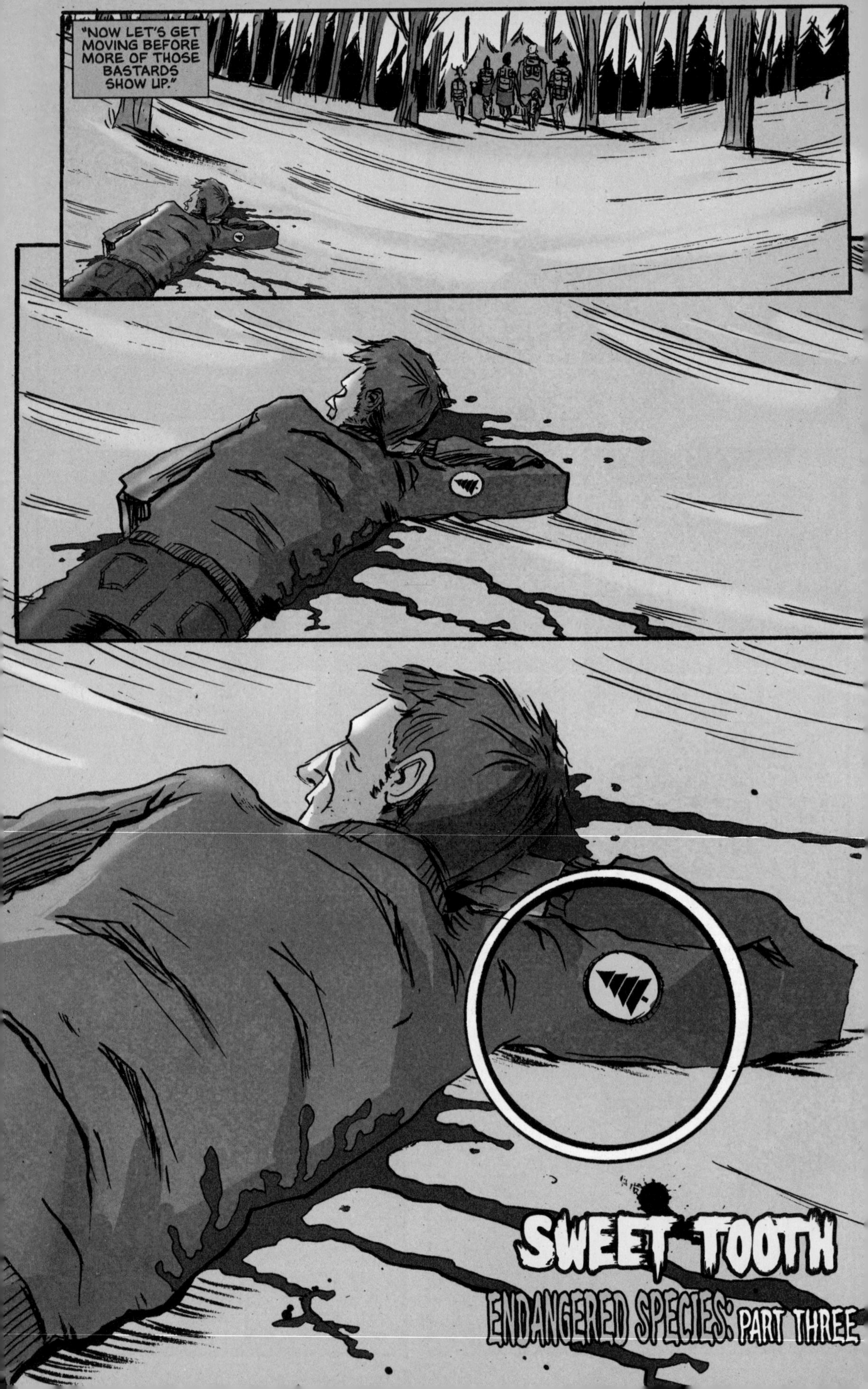
"NOW LET'S GET MOVING BEFORE MORE OF THOSE BASTARDS SHOW UP."
SWEET TOOTH
ENDANGERED SPECIES: PART THREE

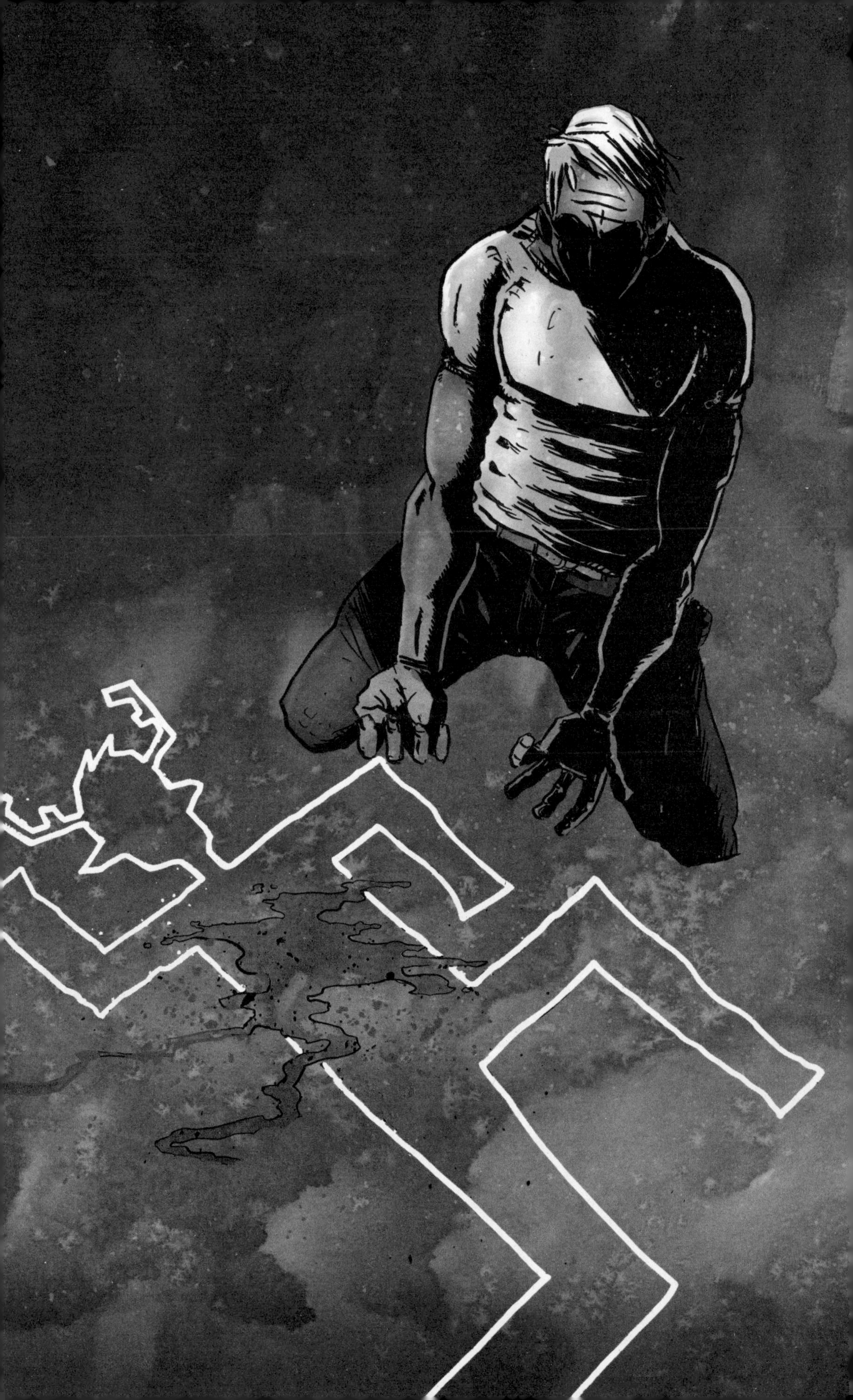

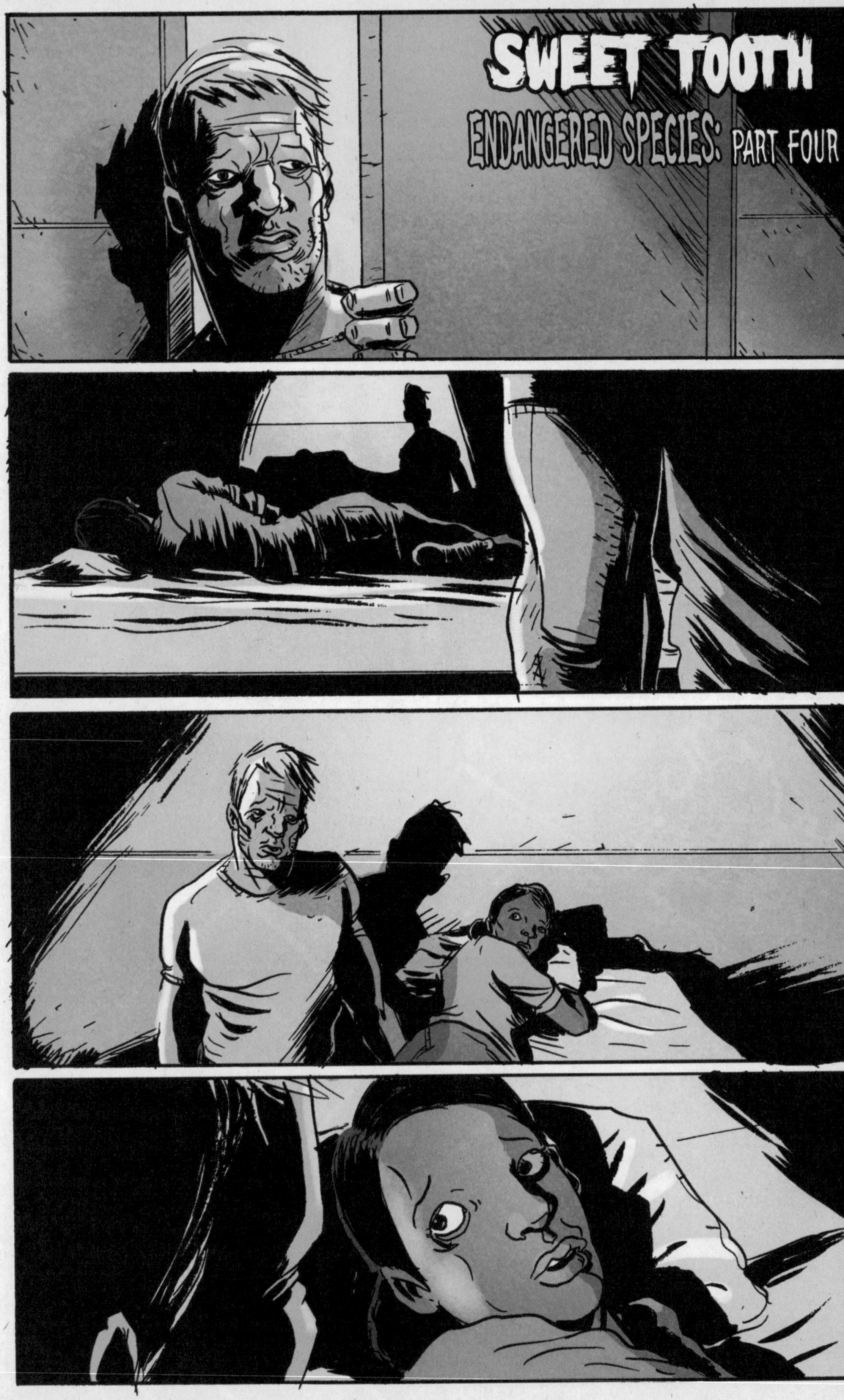
SWEET TOOTH
ENDANGERED SPECIES: PART FOUR

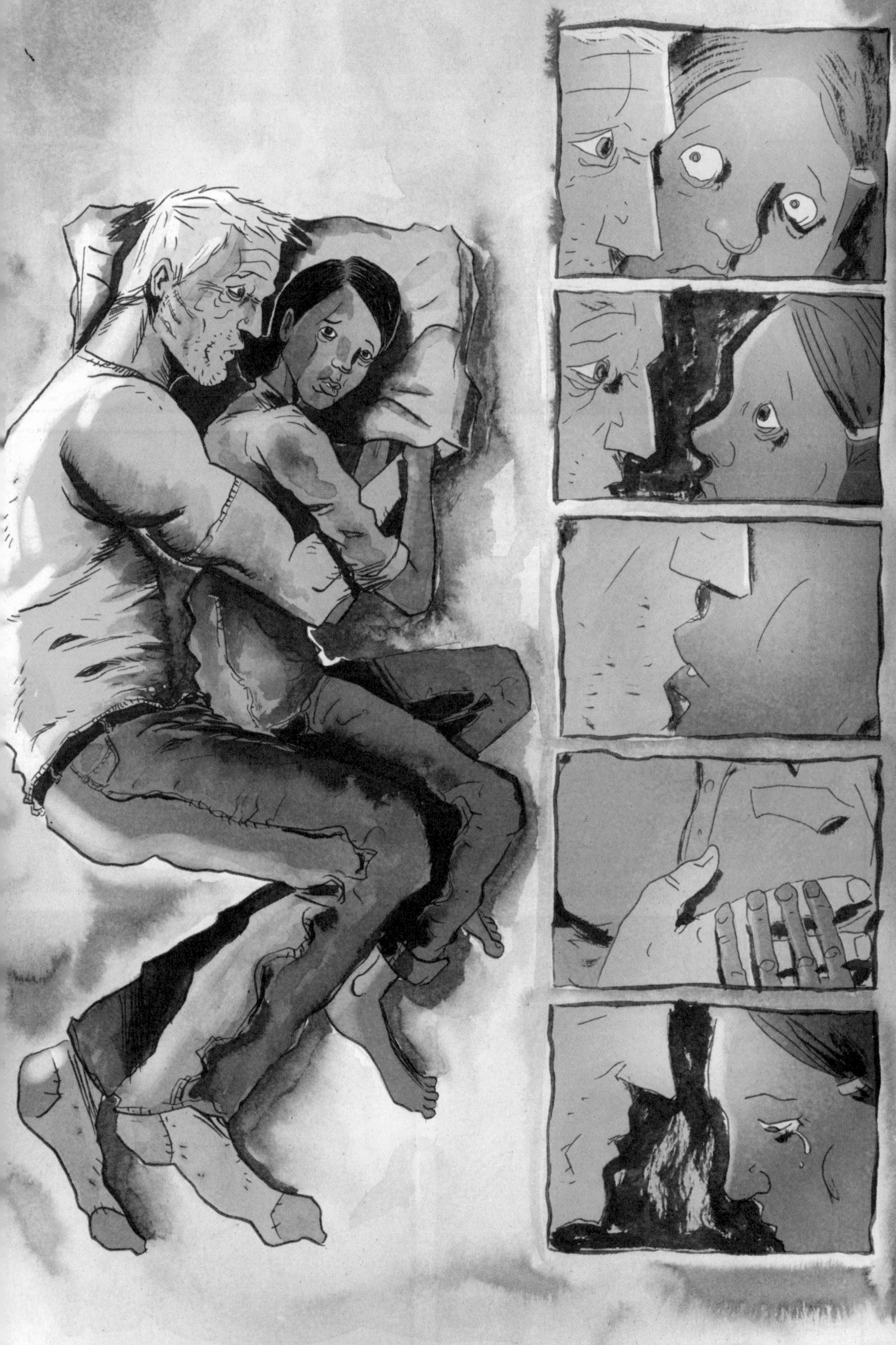

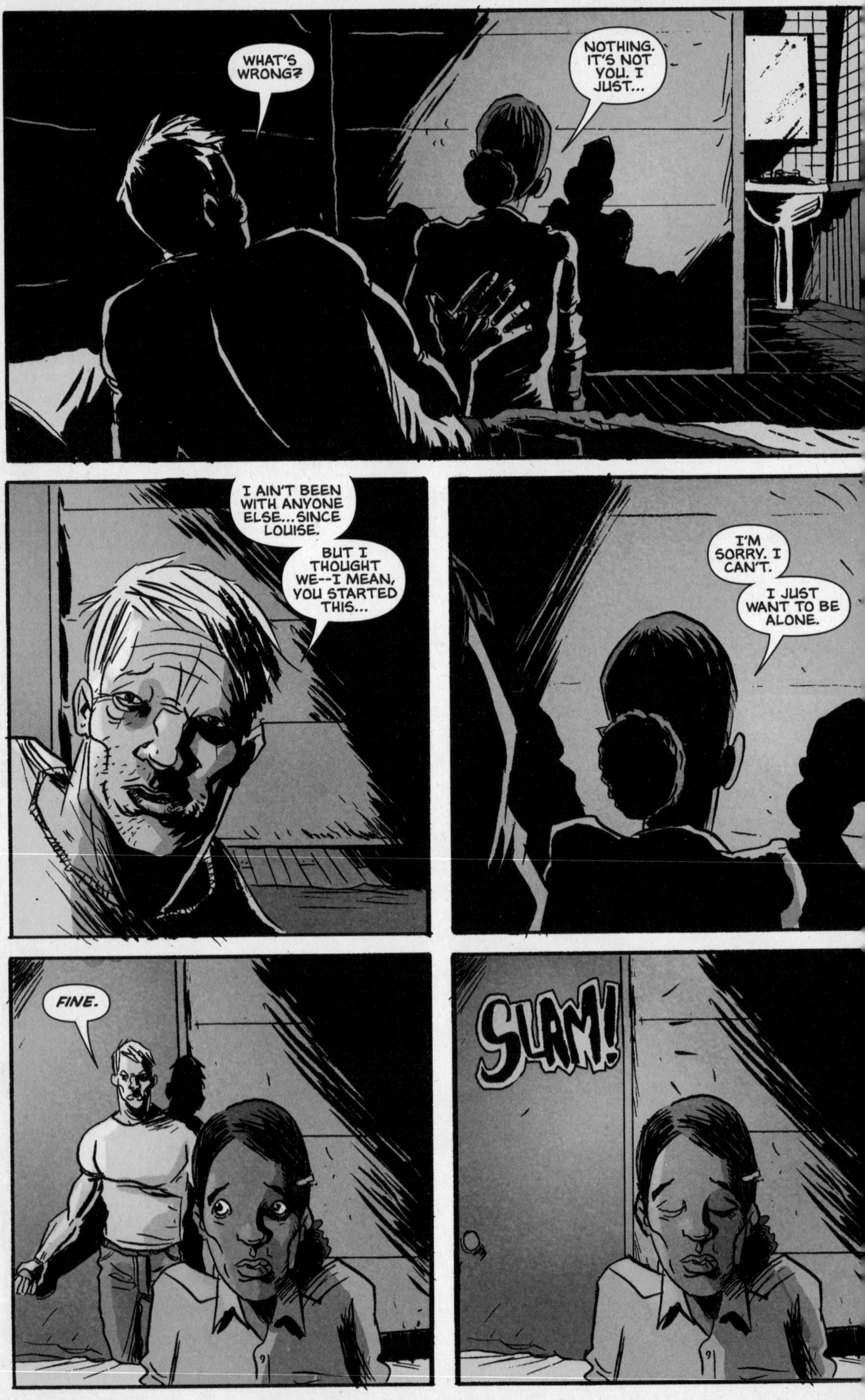
WHAT'S WRONG?
NOTHING. IT'S NOT YOU. I JUST...
I AIN'T BEEN WITH ANYONE ELSE...SINCE LOUISE.
BUT I THOUGHT WE--I MEAN, YOU STARTED THIS...
I'M SORRY. I CAN'T.
I JUST WANT TO BE ALONE.
FINE.
SLAM!

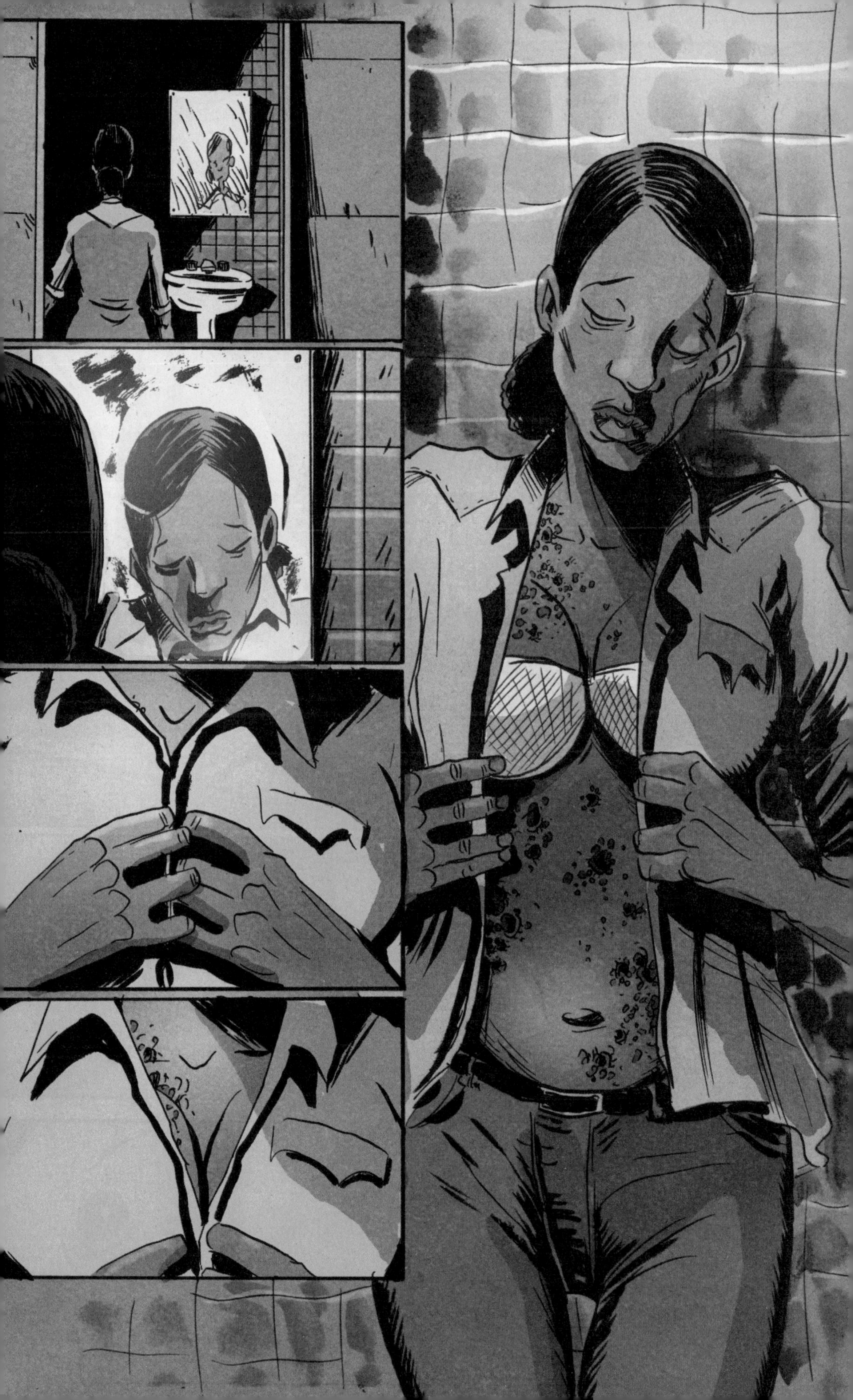

SKRITCH...
SKRITCH...

SKRITCH
SKRITCH

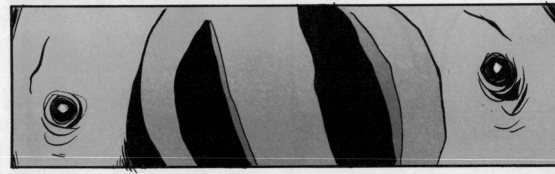

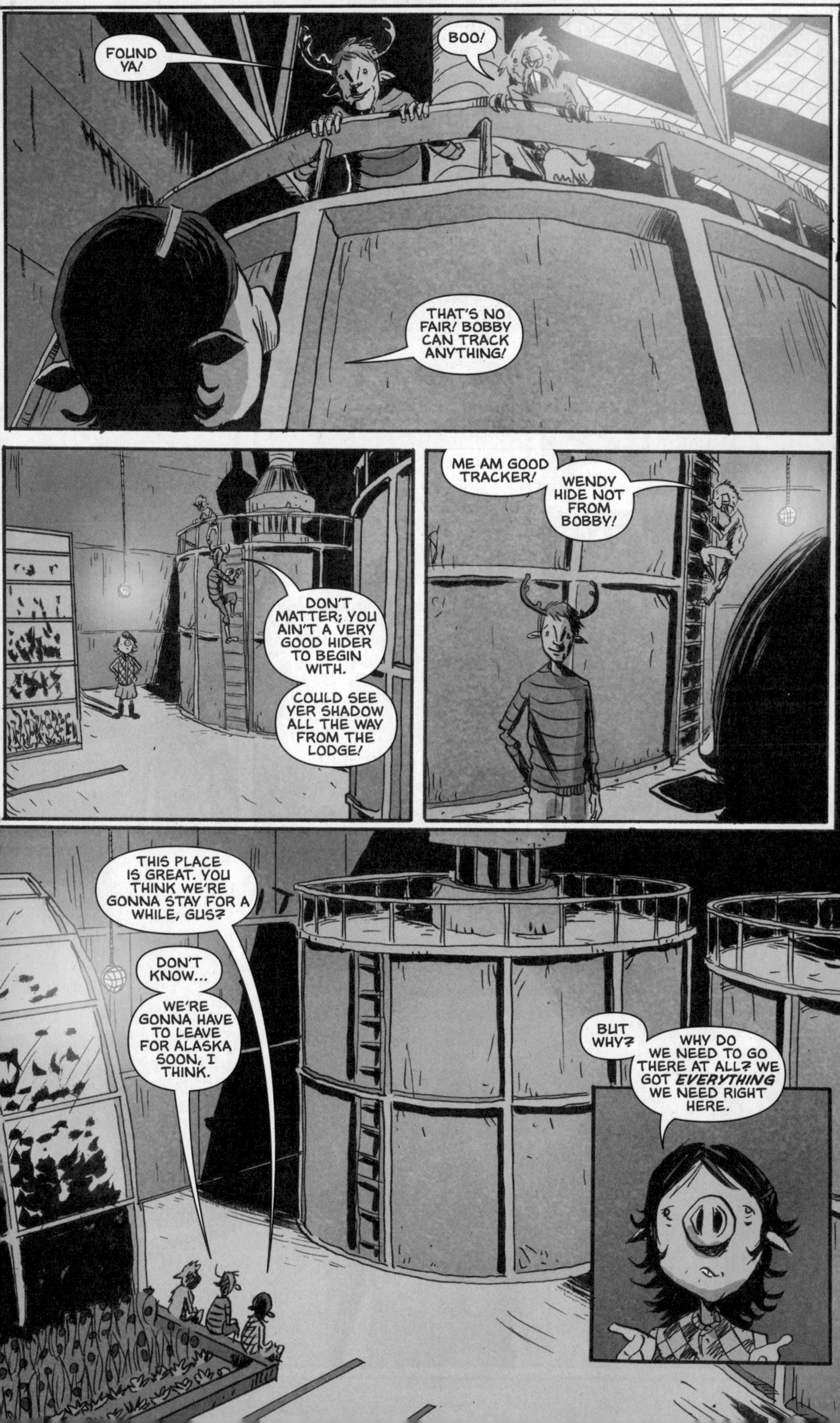
FOUND YA!
BOO!
THAT'S NO FAIR! BOBBY CAN TRACK ANYTHING!
DON'T MATTER; YOU AIN'T A VERY GOOD HIDER TO BEGIN WITH.
COULD SEE YER SHADOW ALL THE WAY FROM THE LODGE!
ME AM GOOD TRACKER!
WENDY HIDE NOT FROM BOBBY!
THIS PLACE IS GREAT. YOU THINK WE'RE GONNA STAY FOR A WHILE, GUS?
DON'T KNOW...
WE'RE GONNA HAVE TO LEAVE FOR ALASKA SOON, I THINK.
BUT WHY?
WHY DO WE NEED TO GO THERE AT ALL? WE GOT *EVERYTHING* WE NEED RIGHT HERE.

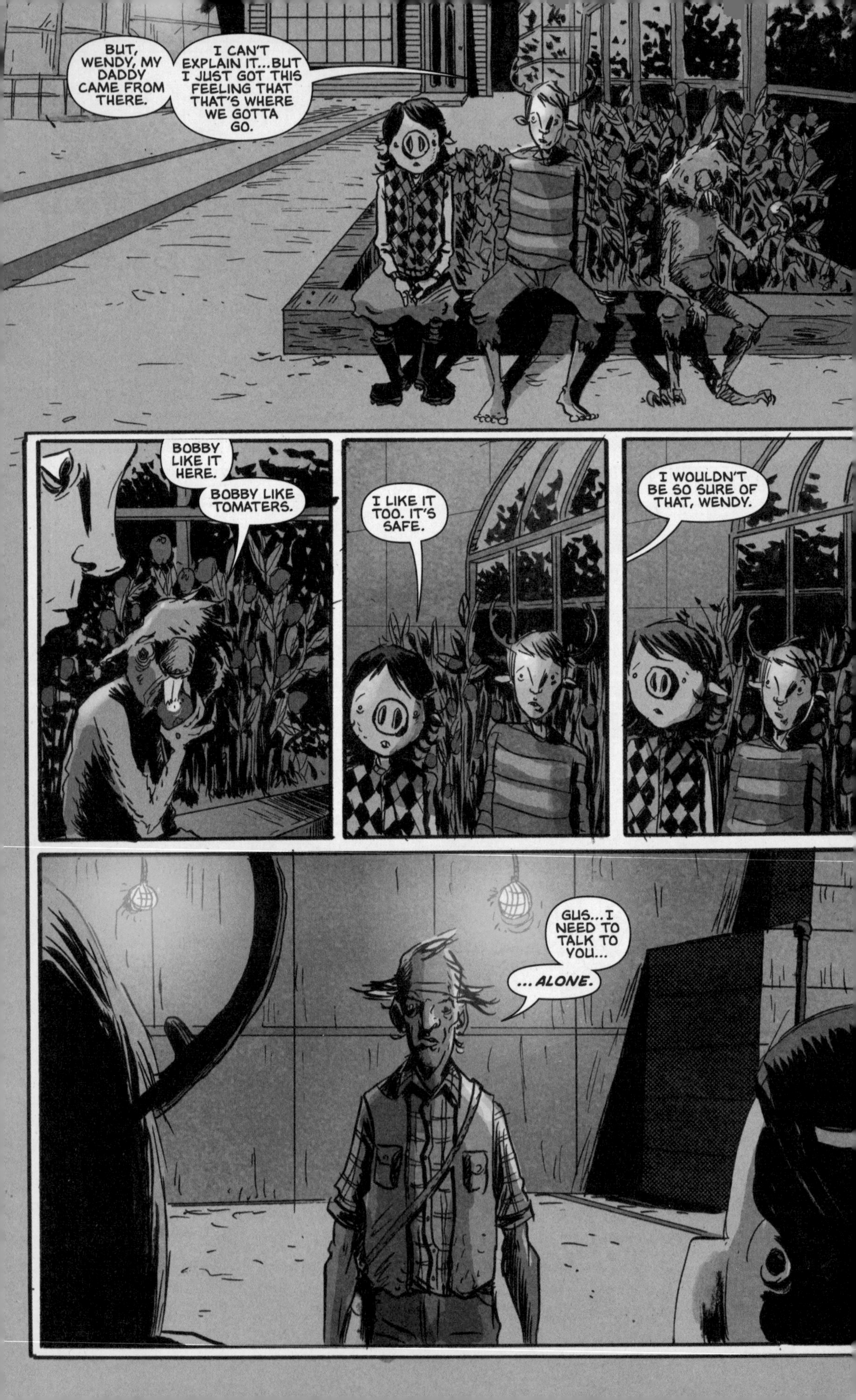
BUT, WENDY, MY DADDY CAME FROM THERE.
I CAN'T EXPLAIN IT...BUT I JUST GOT THIS FEELING THAT THAT'S WHERE WE GOTTA GO.
BOBBY LIKE IT HERE.
BOBBY LIKE TOMATERS.
I LIKE IT TOO. IT'S SAFE.
I WOULDN'T BE SO SURE OF THAT, WENDY.
GUS...I NEED TO TALK TO YOU...
...ALONE.

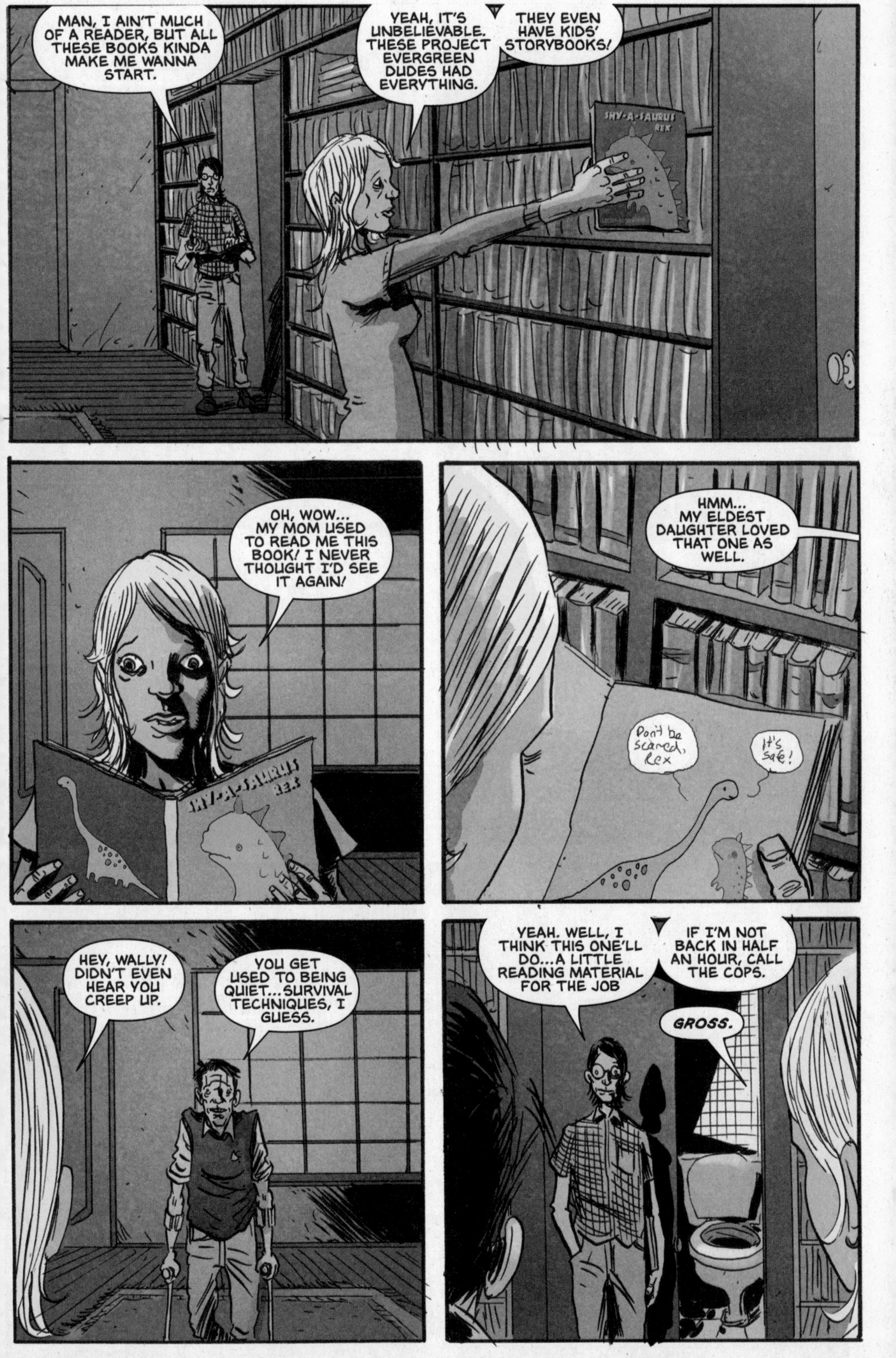
MAN, I AIN'T MUCH OF A READER, BUT ALL THESE BOOKS KINDA MAKE ME WANNA START.
YEAH, IT'S UNBELIEVABLE. THESE PROJECT EVERGREEN DUDES HAD EVERYTHING.
THEY EVEN HAVE KIDS' STORYBOOKS!
SHY-A-SAURUS REX
OH, WOW... MY MOM USED TO READ ME THIS BOOK! I NEVER THOUGHT I'D SEE IT AGAIN!
SHY-A-SAURUS REX
HMM... MY ELDEST DAUGHTER LOVED THAT ONE AS WELL.
Don't be scared, Rex
It's safe!
HEY, WALLY! DIDN'T EVEN HEAR YOU CREEP UP.
YOU GET USED TO BEING QUIET...SURVIVAL TECHNIQUES, I GUESS.
YEAH. WELL, I THINK THIS ONE'LL DO...A LITTLE READING MATERIAL FOR THE JOB
IF I'M NOT BACK IN HALF AN HOUR, CALL THE COPS.
GROSS.

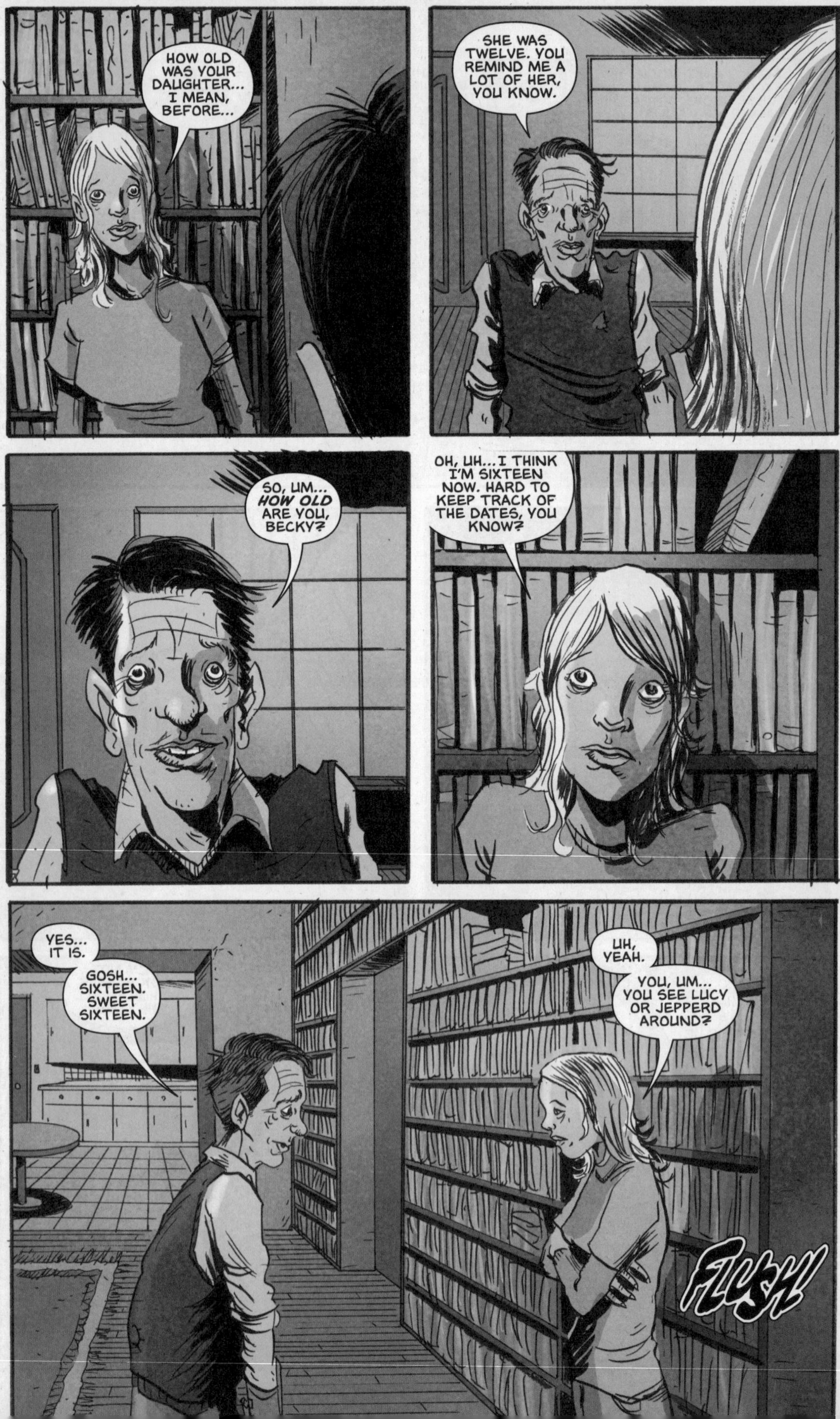
HOW OLD WAS YOUR DAUGHTER... I MEAN, BEFORE...
SHE WAS TWELVE. YOU REMIND ME A LOT OF HER, YOU KNOW.
SO, UM... *HOW OLD* ARE YOU, BECKY?
OH, UH... I THINK I'M SIXTEEN NOW. HARD TO KEEP TRACK OF THE DATES, YOU KNOW?
YES... IT IS.
GOSH... SIXTEEN. SWEET SIXTEEN.
UH, YEAH.
YOU, UM... YOU SEE LUCY OR JEPPERD AROUND?
FLUSH!

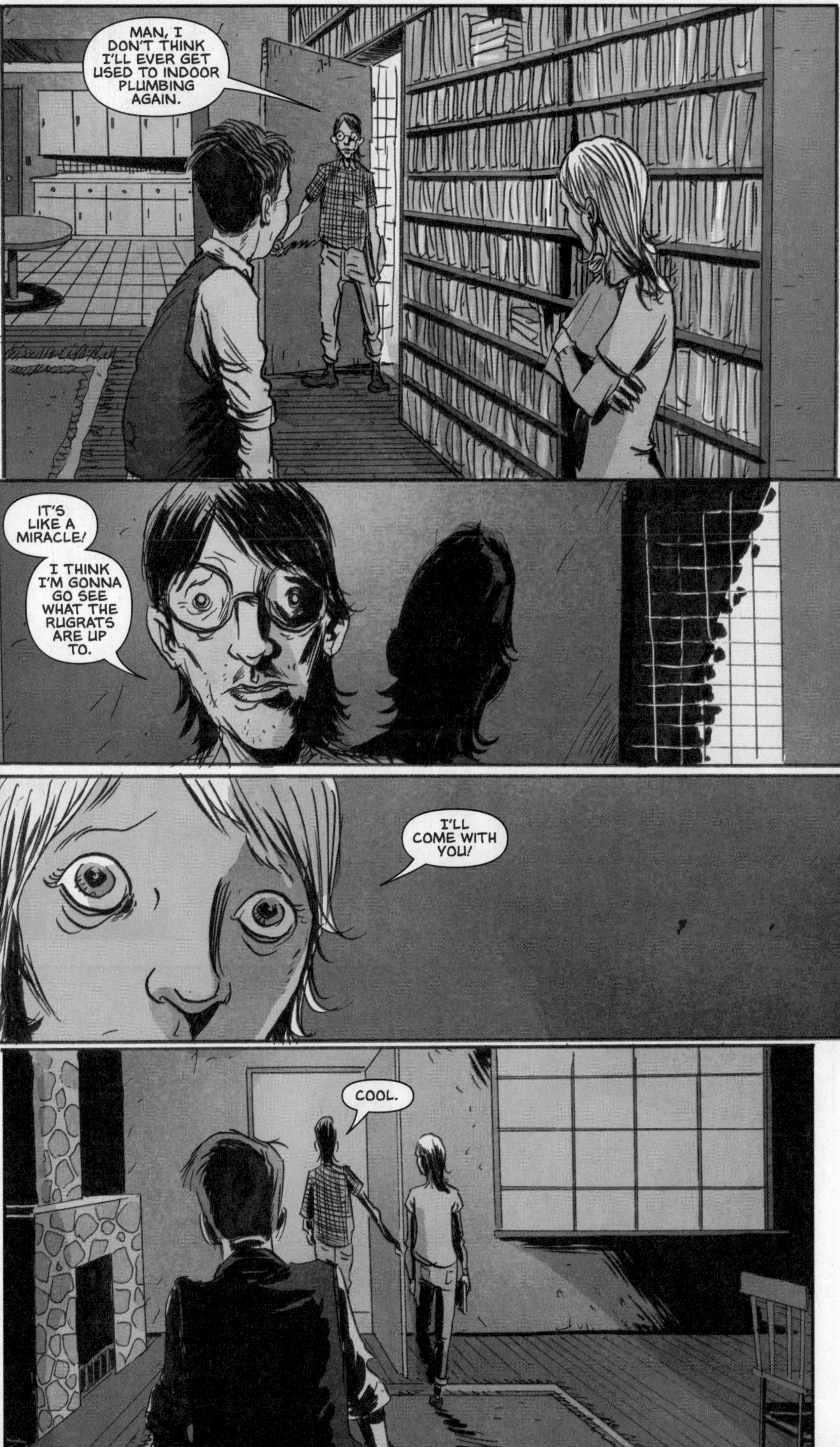
MAN, I DON'T THINK I'LL EVER GET USED TO INDOOR PLUMBING AGAIN.
IT'S LIKE A MIRACLE!
I THINK I'M GONNA GO SEE WHAT THE RUGRATS ARE UP TO.
I'LL COME WITH YOU!
COOL.

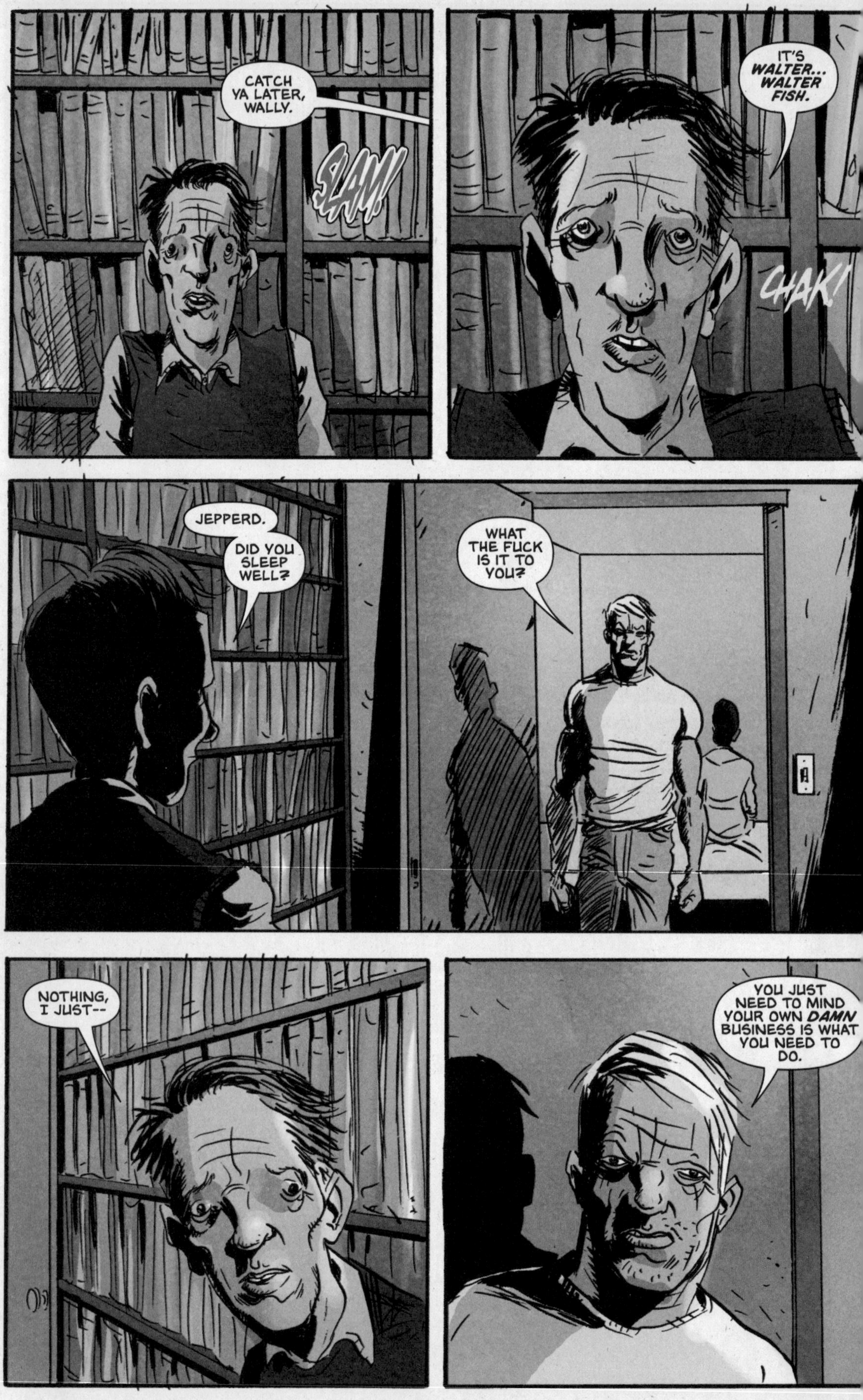
CATCH YA LATER, WALLY.
SLAM!
IT'S WALTER... WALTER FISH.
CHAK!
JEPPERD.
DID YOU SLEEP WELL?
WHAT THE FUCK IS IT TO YOU?
NOTHING, I JUST--
YOU JUST NEED TO MIND YOUR OWN DAMN BUSINESS IS WHAT YOU NEED TO DO.

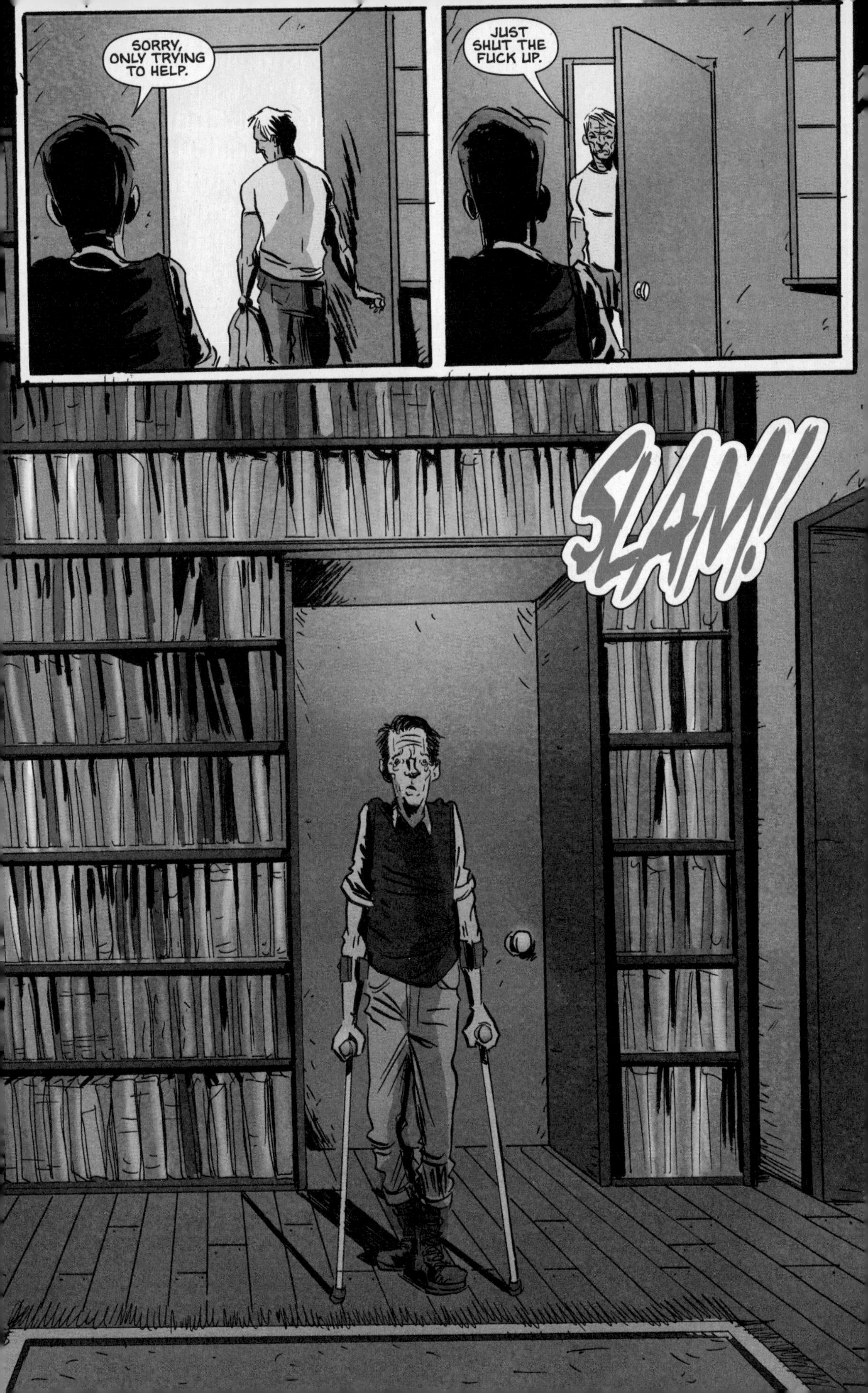
SORRY, ONLY TRYING TO HELP.
JUST SHUT THE FUCK UP.
SLAM!

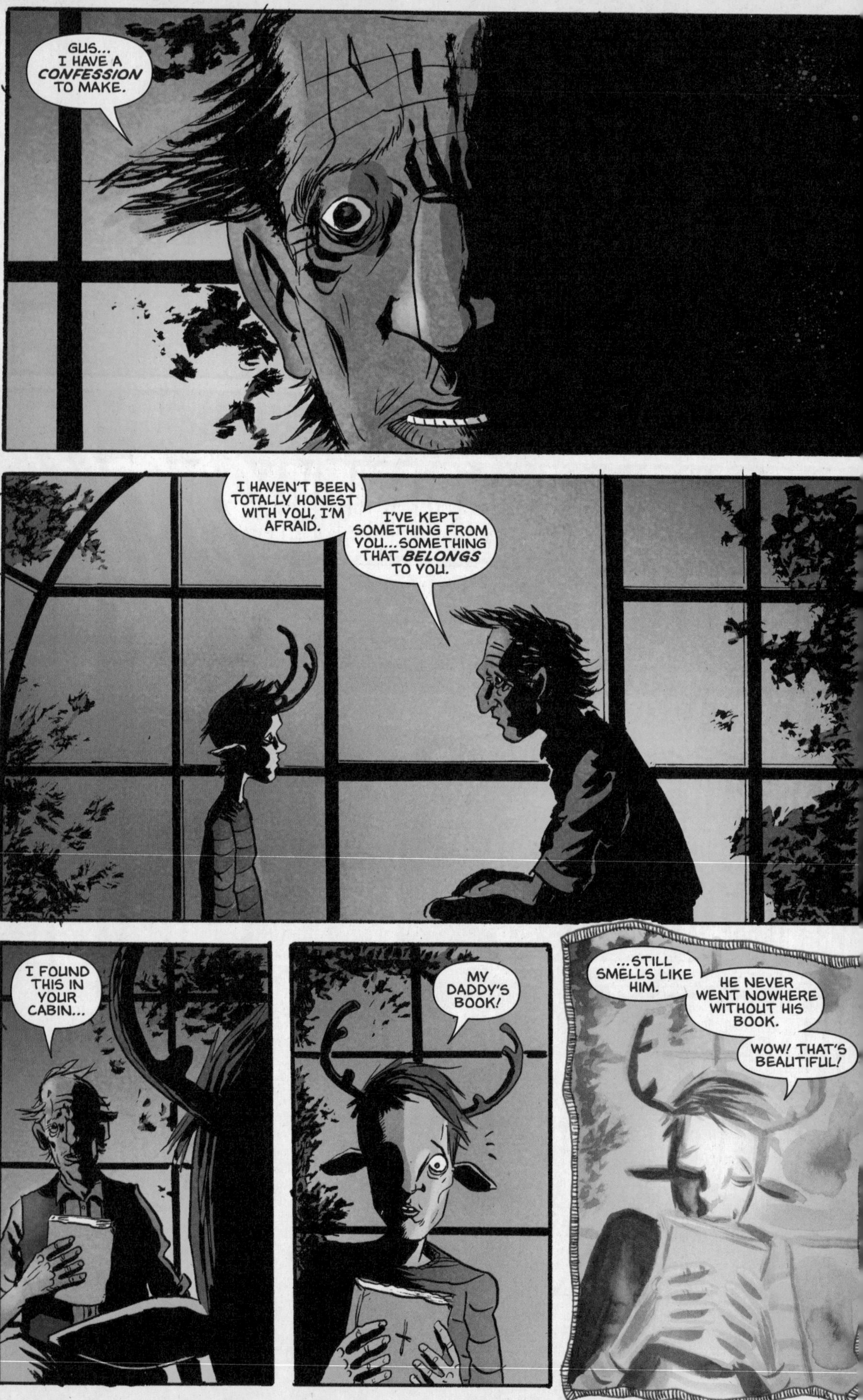
GUS...
I HAVE A *CONFESSION* TO MAKE.
I HAVEN'T BEEN TOTALLY HONEST WITH YOU, I'M AFRAID.
I'VE KEPT SOMETHING FROM YOU...SOMETHING THAT *BELONGS* TO YOU.
I FOUND THIS IN YOUR CABIN...
MY DADDY'S BOOK!
...STILL SMELLS LIKE HIM.
HE NEVER WENT NOWHERE WITHOUT HIS BOOK.
WOW! THAT'S BEAUTIFUL!

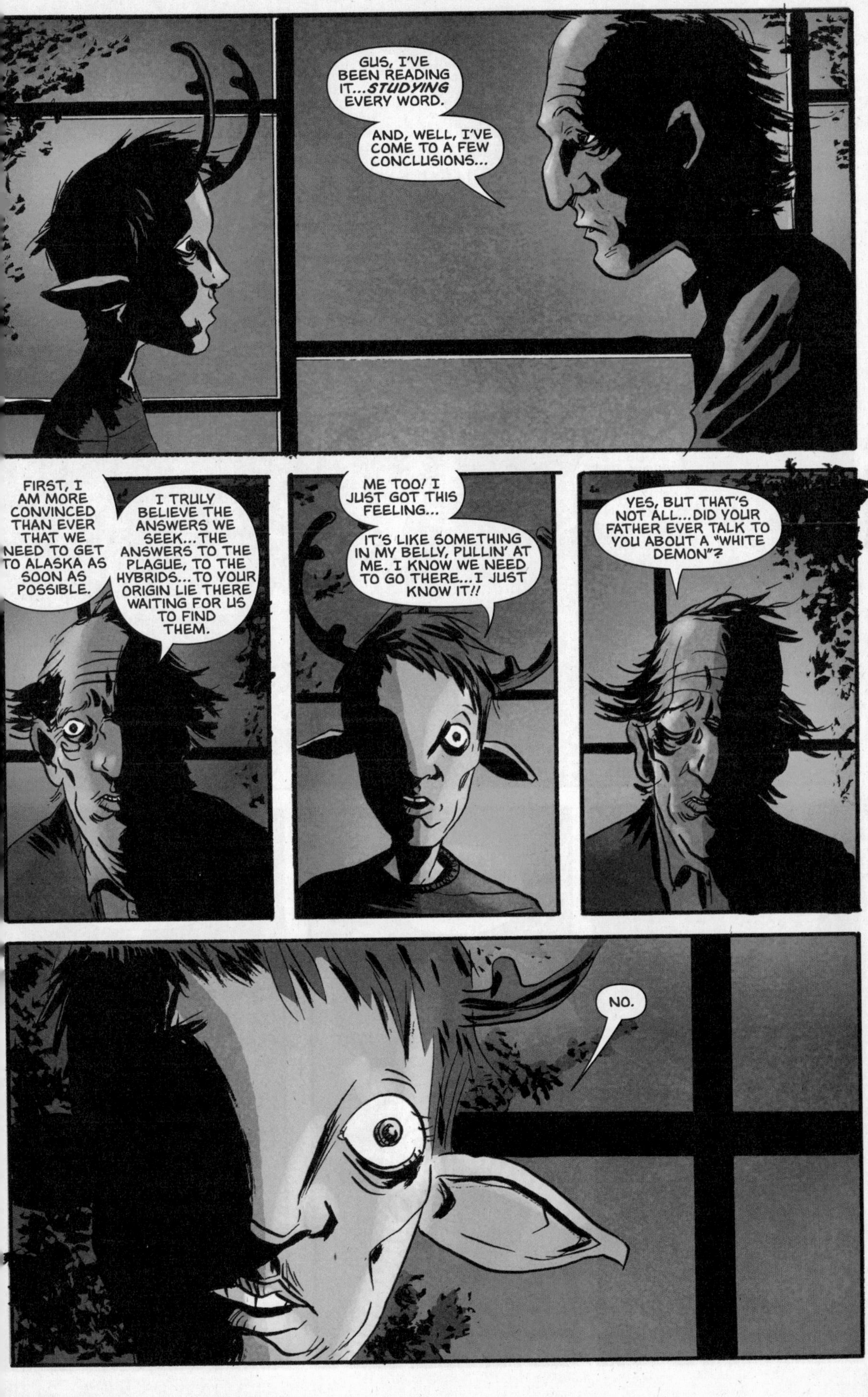
GUS, I'VE BEEN READING IT...STUDYING EVERY WORD.
AND, WELL, I'VE COME TO A FEW CONCLUSIONS...
FIRST, I AM MORE CONVINCED THAN EVER THAT WE NEED TO GET TO ALASKA AS SOON AS POSSIBLE.
I TRULY BELIEVE THE ANSWERS WE SEEK...THE ANSWERS TO THE PLAGUE, TO THE HYBRIDS...TO YOUR ORIGIN LIE THERE WAITING FOR US TO FIND THEM.
ME TOO! I JUST GOT THIS FEELING...
IT'S LIKE SOMETHING IN MY BELLY, PULLIN' AT ME. I KNOW WE NEED TO GO THERE...I JUST KNOW IT!!
YES, BUT THAT'S NOT ALL...DID YOUR FATHER EVER TALK TO YOU ABOUT A "WHITE DEMON"?
NO.

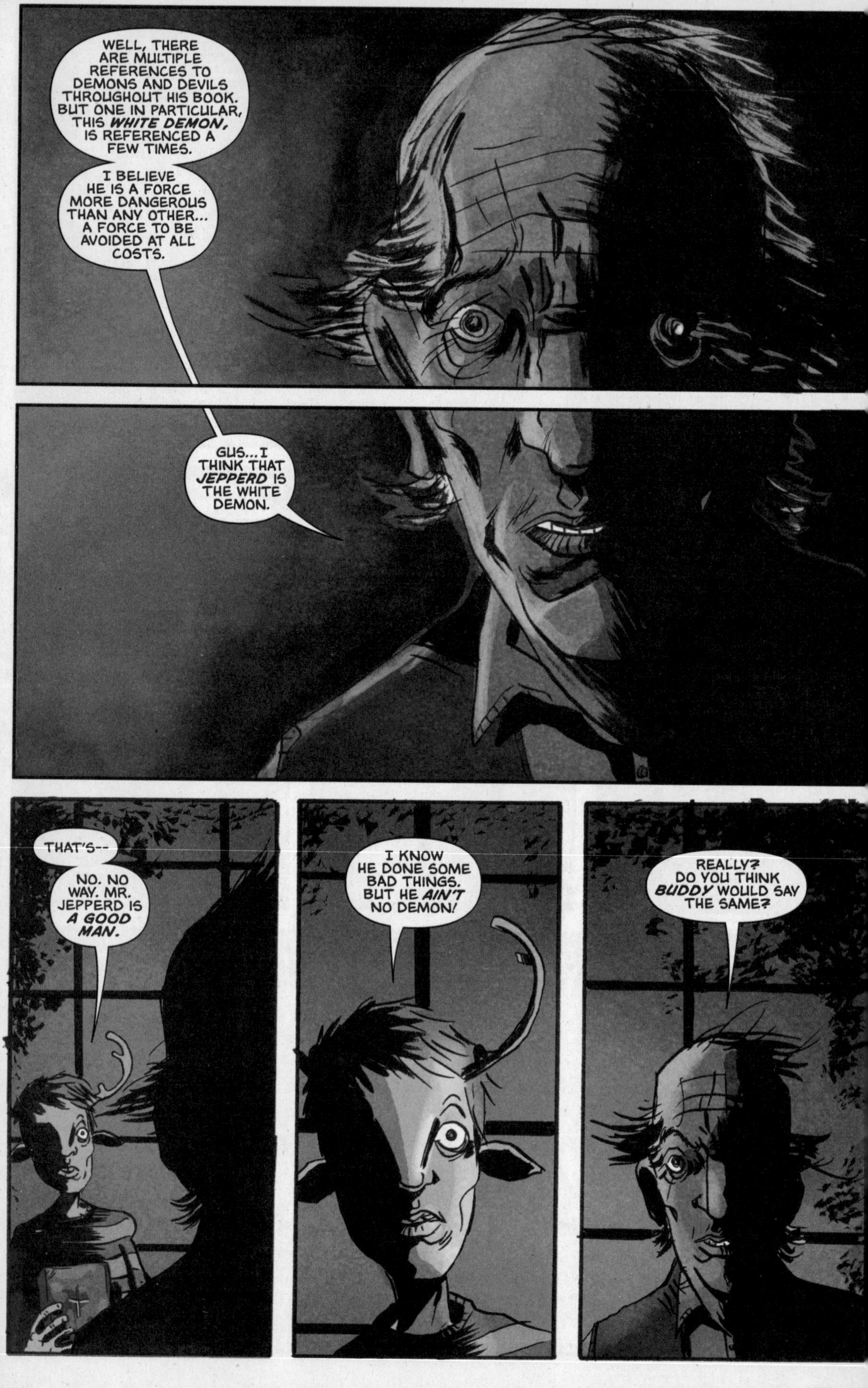

WELL, THERE ARE MULTIPLE REFERENCES TO DEMONS AND DEVILS THROUGHOUT HIS BOOK. BUT ONE IN PARTICULAR, THIS *WHITE DEMON,* IS REFERENCED A FEW TIMES.
I BELIEVE HE IS A FORCE MORE DANGEROUS THAN ANY OTHER... A FORCE TO BE AVOIDED AT ALL COSTS.
GUS...I THINK THAT *JEPPERD* IS THE WHITE DEMON.
THAT'S--
NO. NO WAY. MR. JEPPERD IS *A GOOD MAN.*
I KNOW HE DONE SOME BAD THINGS. BUT HE *AIN'T* NO DEMON!
REALLY? DO YOU THINK *BUDDY* WOULD SAY THE SAME?

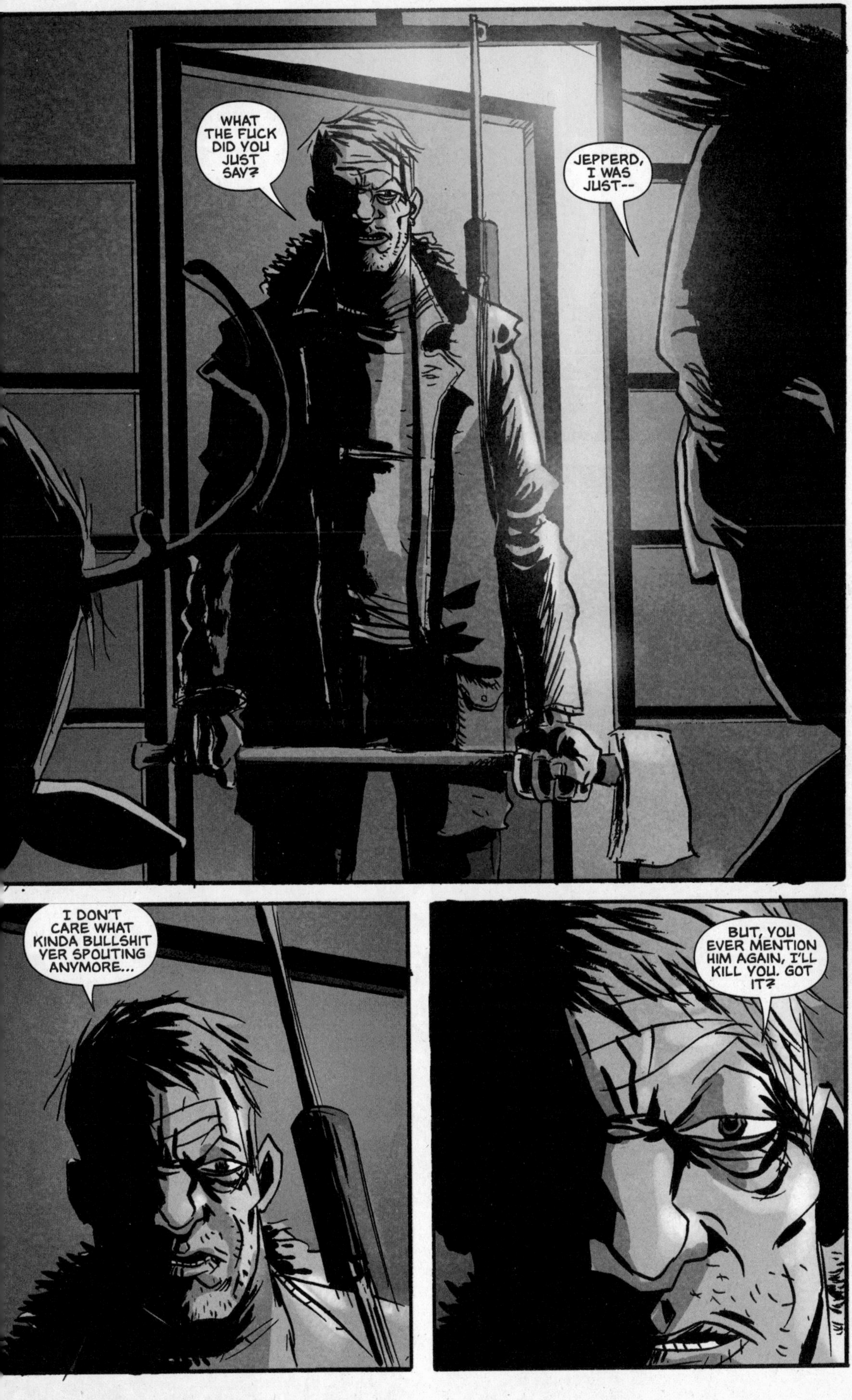
WHAT THE FUCK DID YOU JUST SAY?
JEPPERD, I WAS JUST--
I DON'T CARE WHAT KINDA BULLSHIT YER SPOUTING ANYMORE...
BUT, YOU EVER MENTION HIM AGAIN, I'LL KILL YOU. GOT IT?

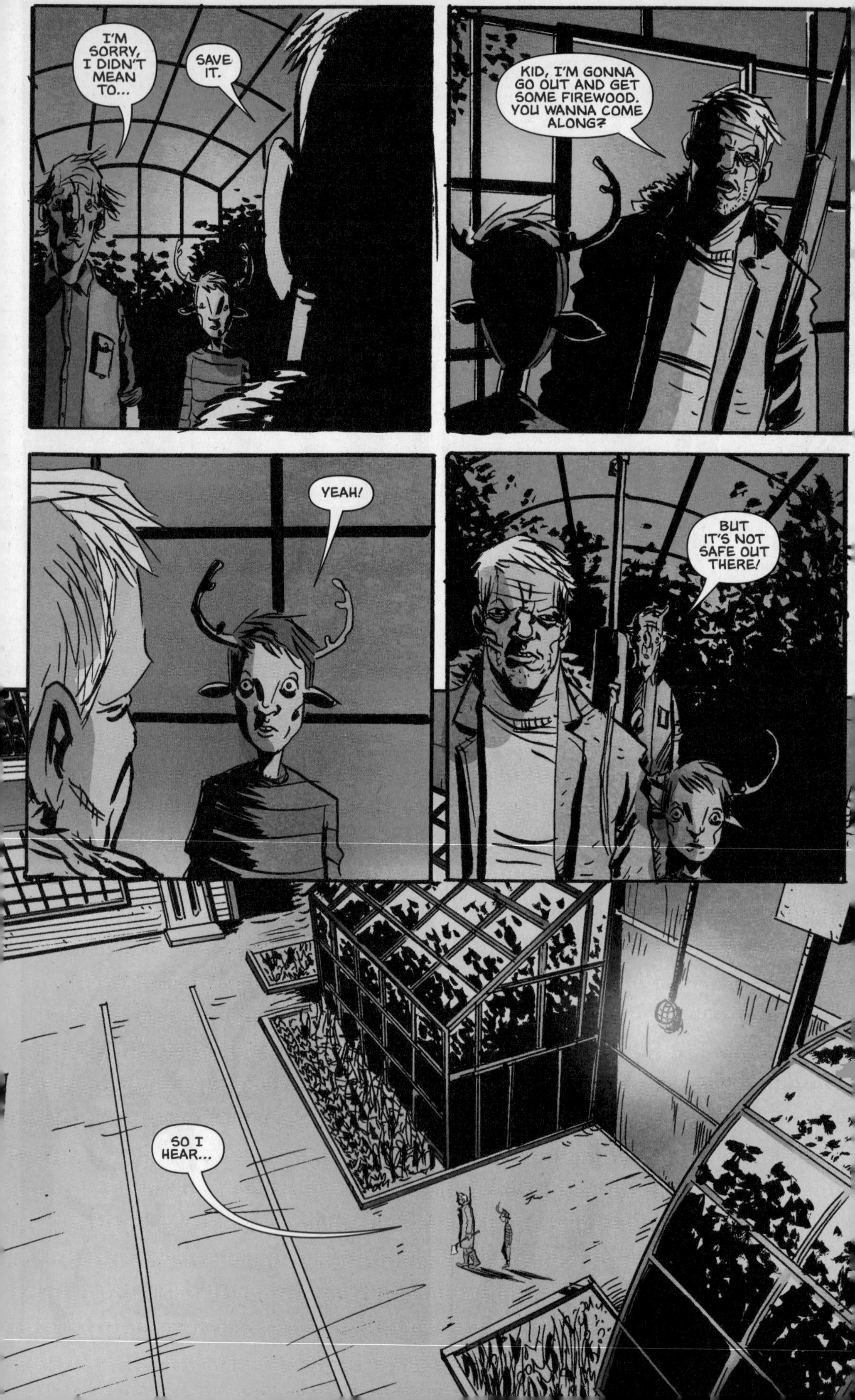
I'M SORRY, I DIDN'T MEAN TO...
SAVE IT.
KID, I'M GONNA GO OUT AND GET SOME FIREWOOD. YOU WANNA COME ALONG?
YEAH!
BUT IT'S NOT SAFE OUT THERE!
SO I HEAR...

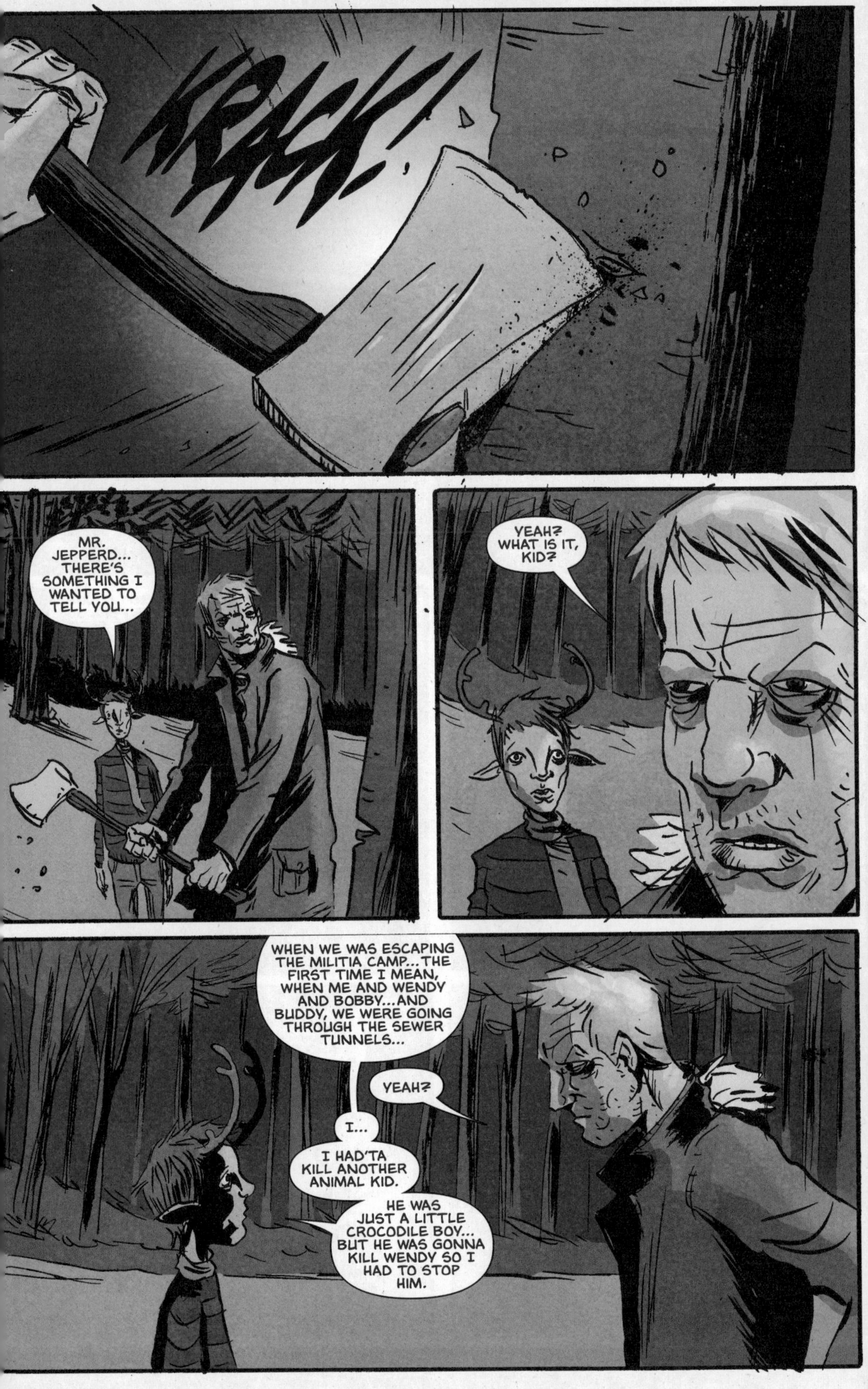
KRACK!
MR. JEPPERD... THERE'S SOMETHING I WANTED TO TELL YOU...
YEAH? WHAT IS IT, KID?
WHEN WE WAS ESCAPING THE MILITIA CAMP... THE FIRST TIME I MEAN, WHEN ME AND WENDY AND BOBBY...AND BUDDY, WE WERE GOING THROUGH THE SEWER TUNNELS...
YEAH?
I...
I HAD'TA KILL ANOTHER ANIMAL KID.
HE WAS JUST A LITTLE CROCODILE BOY... BUT HE WAS GONNA KILL WENDY SO I HAD TO STOP HIM.

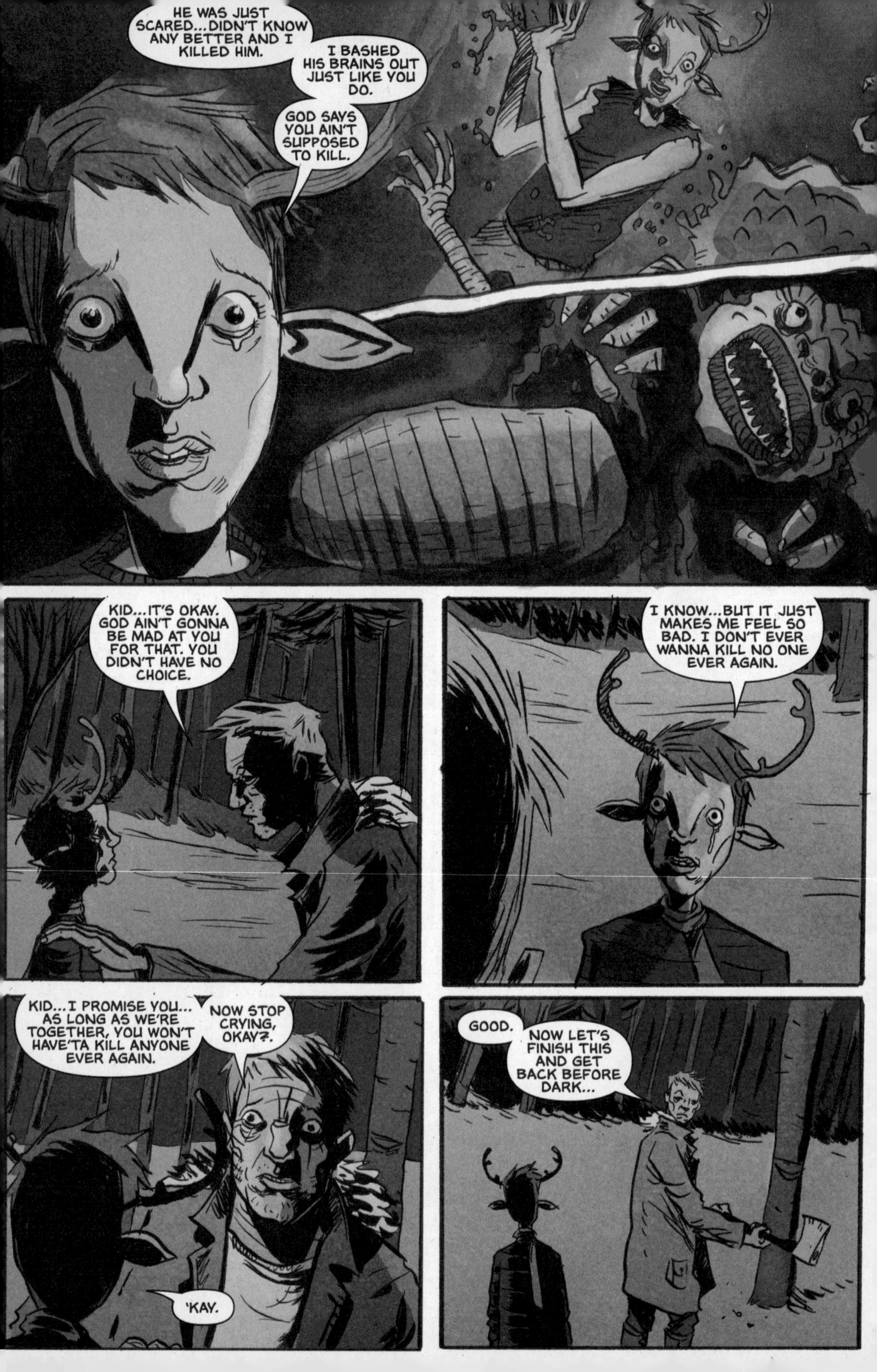
HE WAS JUST SCARED...DIDN'T KNOW ANY BETTER AND I KILLED HIM.
I BASHED HIS BRAINS OUT JUST LIKE YOU DO.
GOD SAYS YOU AIN'T SUPPOSED TO KILL.
KID...IT'S OKAY. GOD AIN'T GONNA BE MAD AT YOU FOR THAT. YOU DIDN'T HAVE NO CHOICE.
I KNOW...BUT IT JUST MAKES ME FEEL SO BAD. I DON'T EVER WANNA KILL NO ONE EVER AGAIN.
KID...I PROMISE YOU... AS LONG AS WE'RE TOGETHER, YOU WON'T HAVE'TA KILL ANYONE EVER AGAIN.
NOW STOP CRYING, OKAY?.
'KAY.
GOOD.
NOW LET'S FINISH THIS AND GET BACK BEFORE DARK...

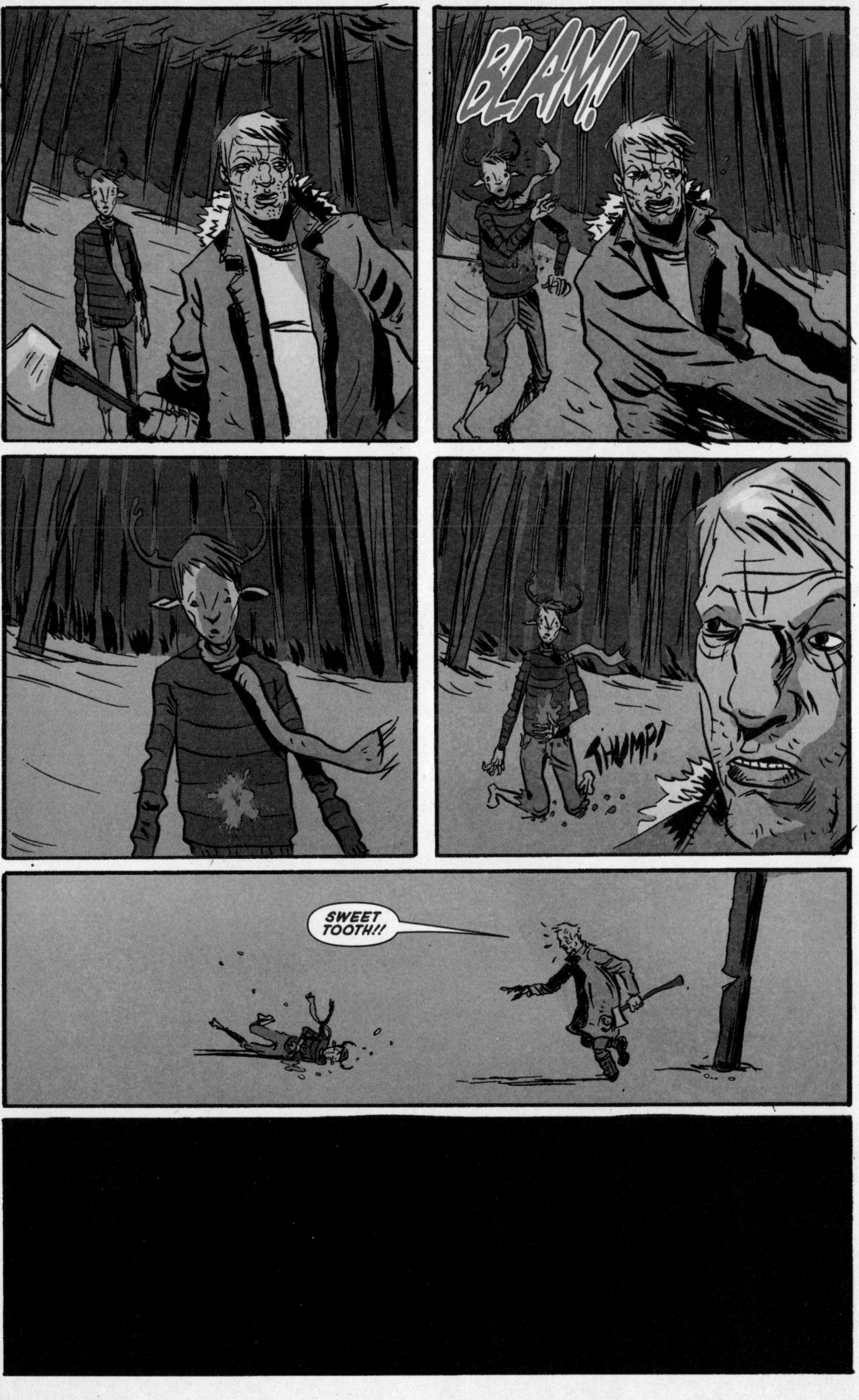
BLAM!
THUMP!
SWEET TOOTH!!

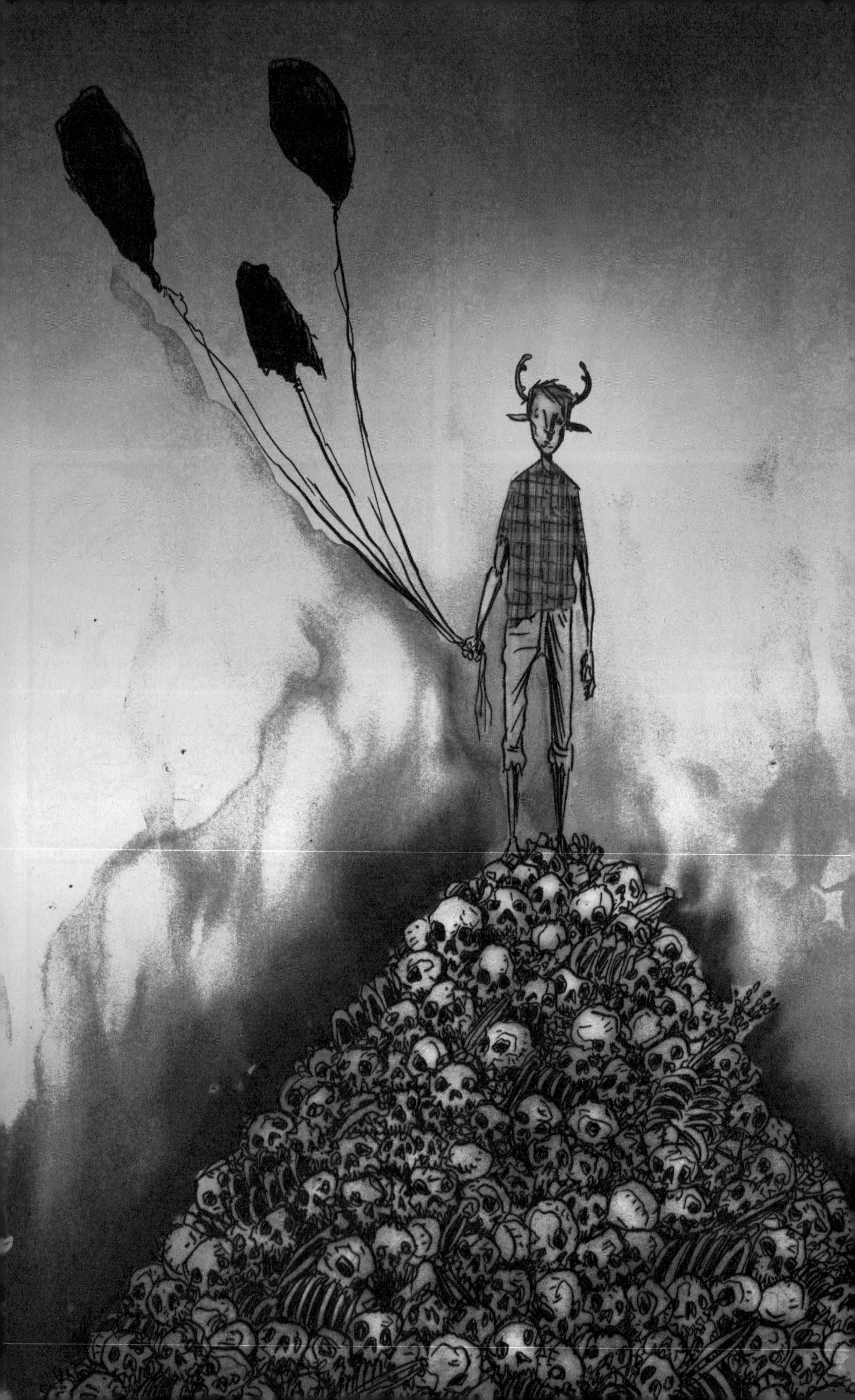

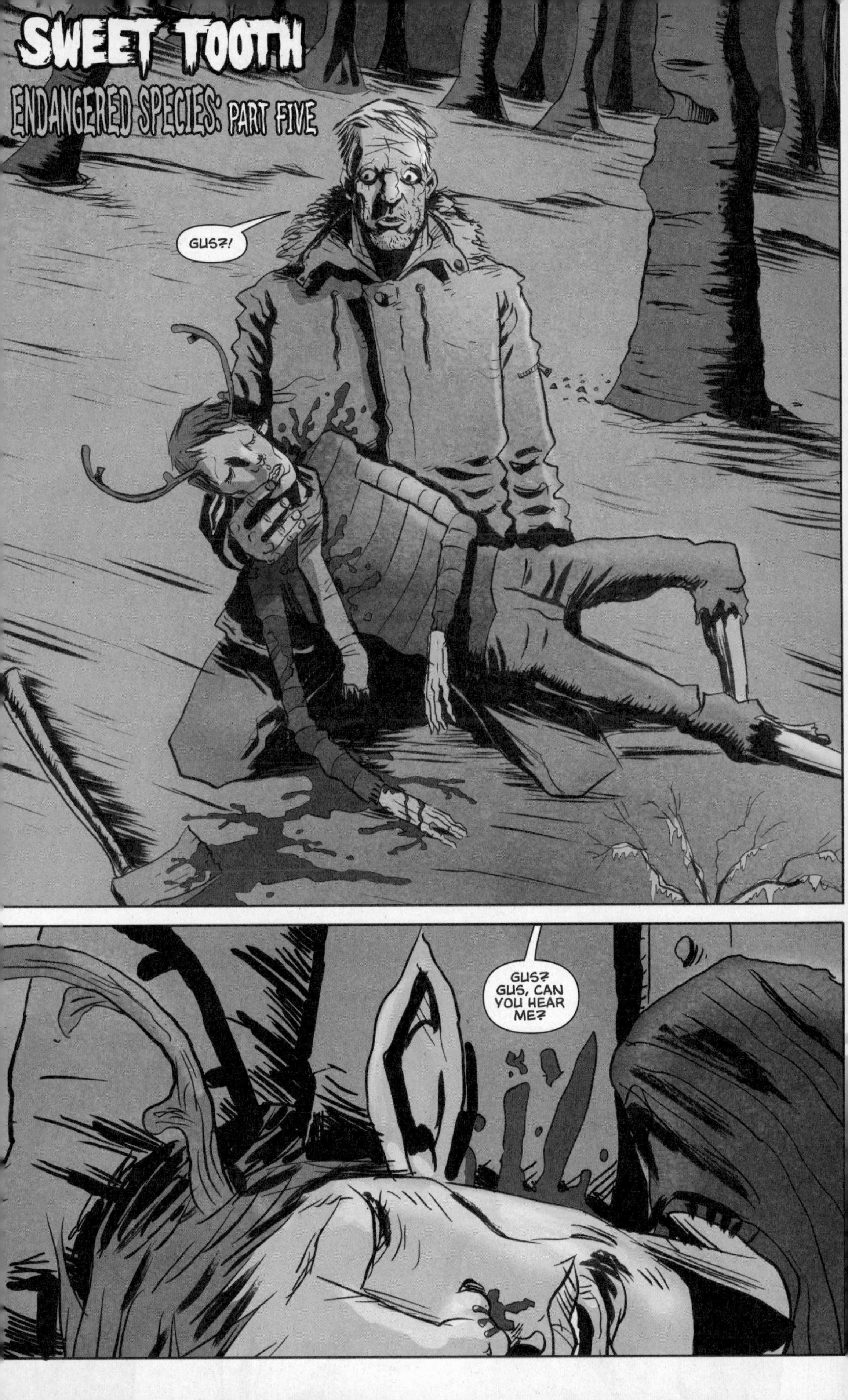
SWEET TOOTH
ENDANGERED SPECIES: PART FIVE
GUS?!
GUS? GUS, CAN YOU HEAR ME?

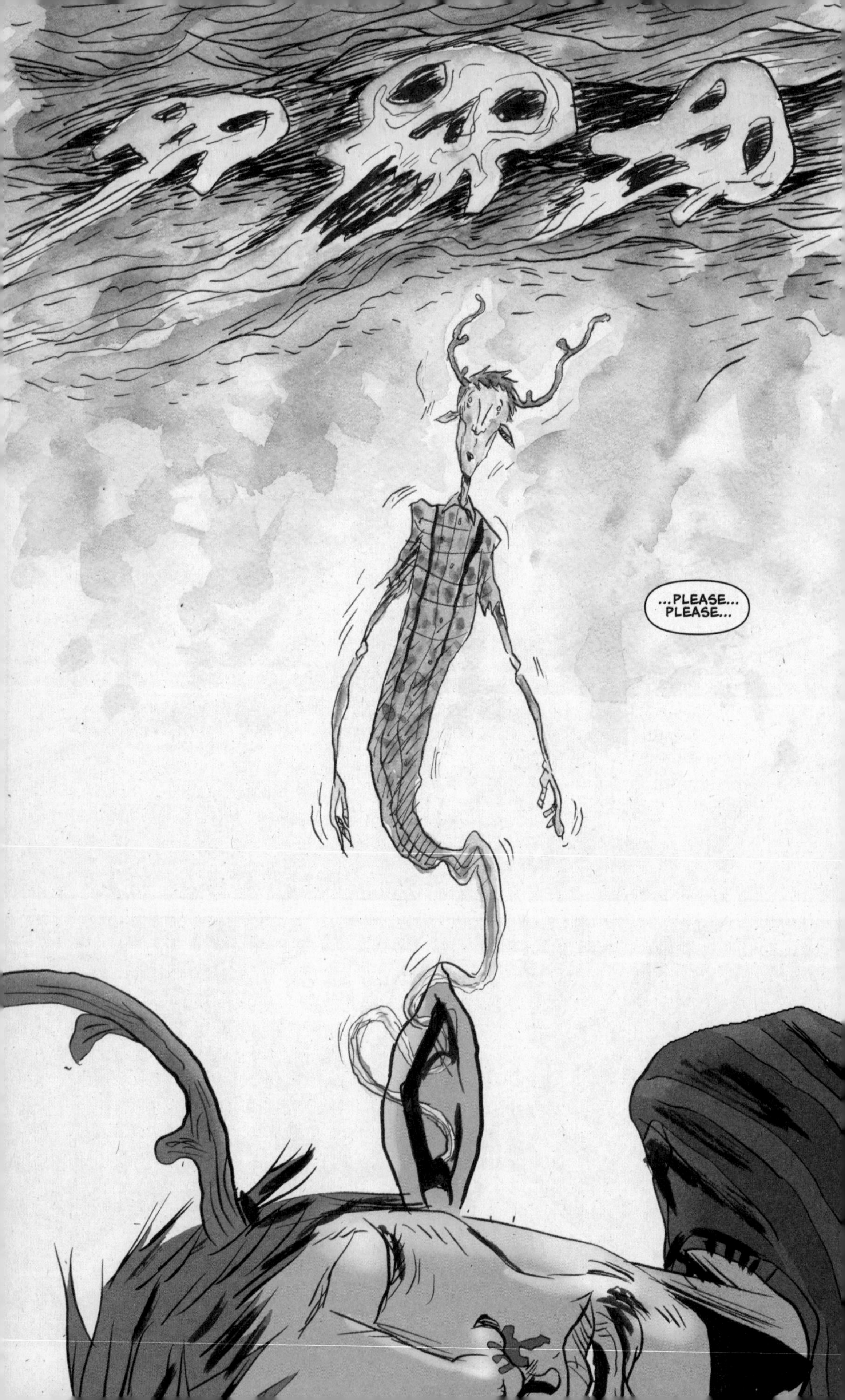
...PLEASE... PLEASE...

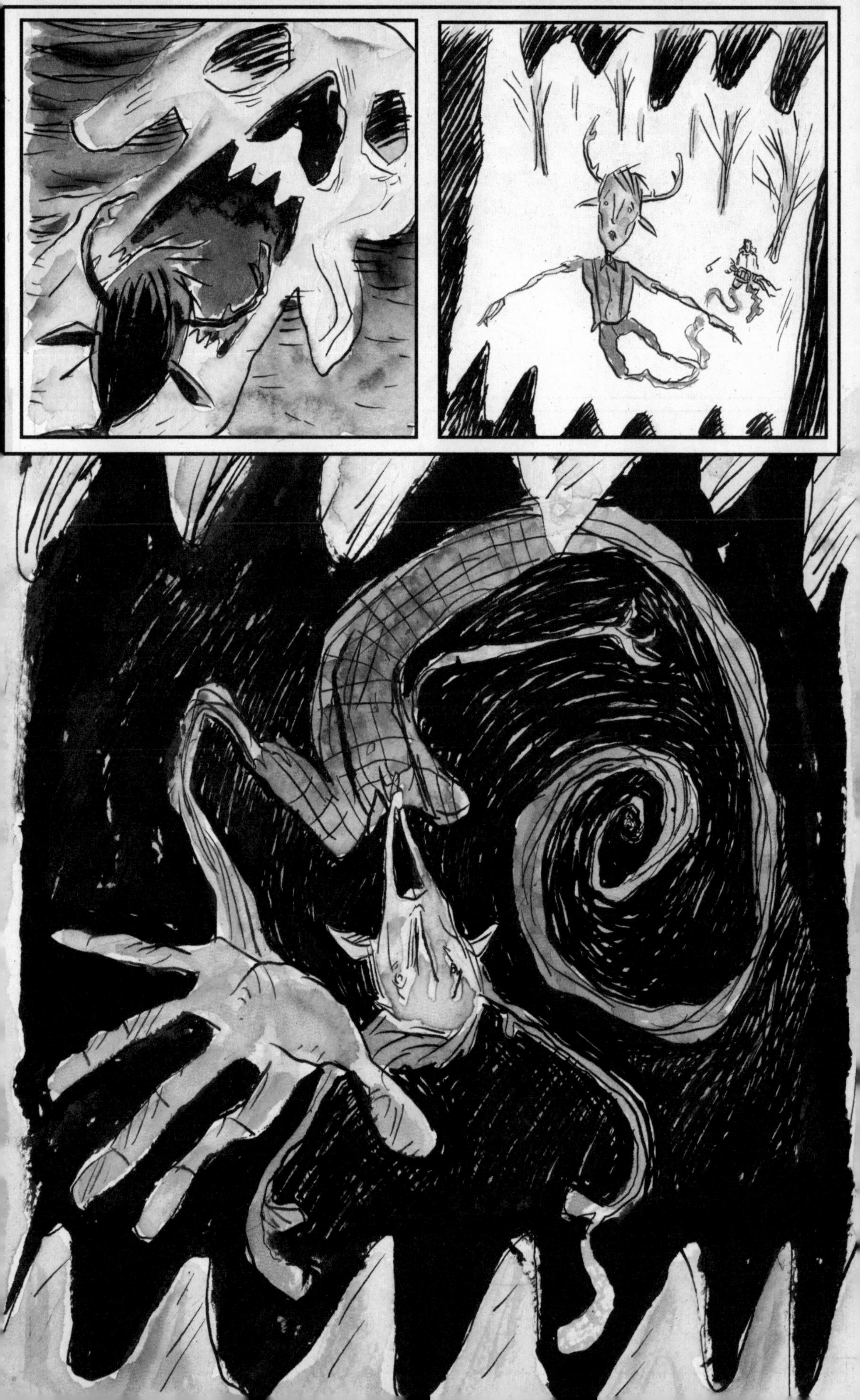

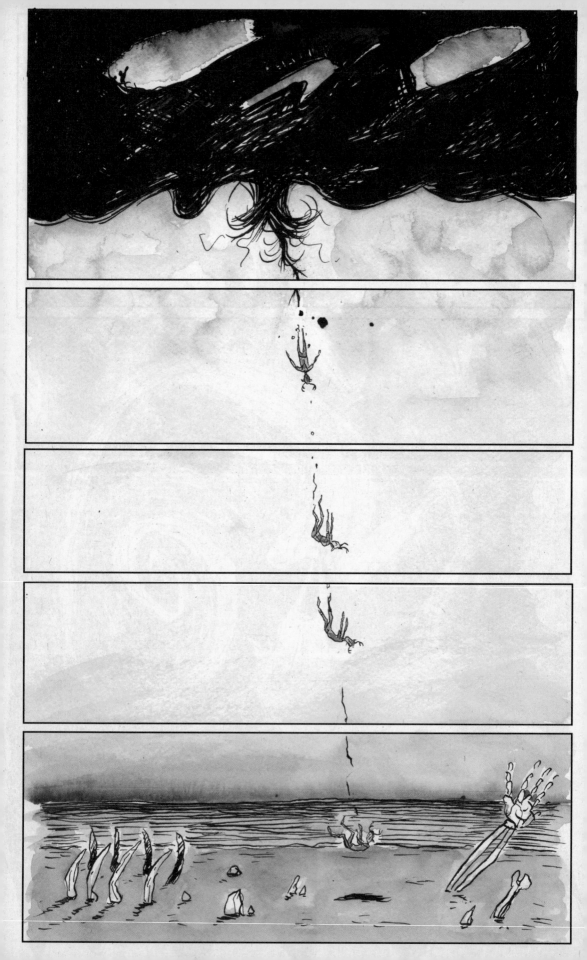

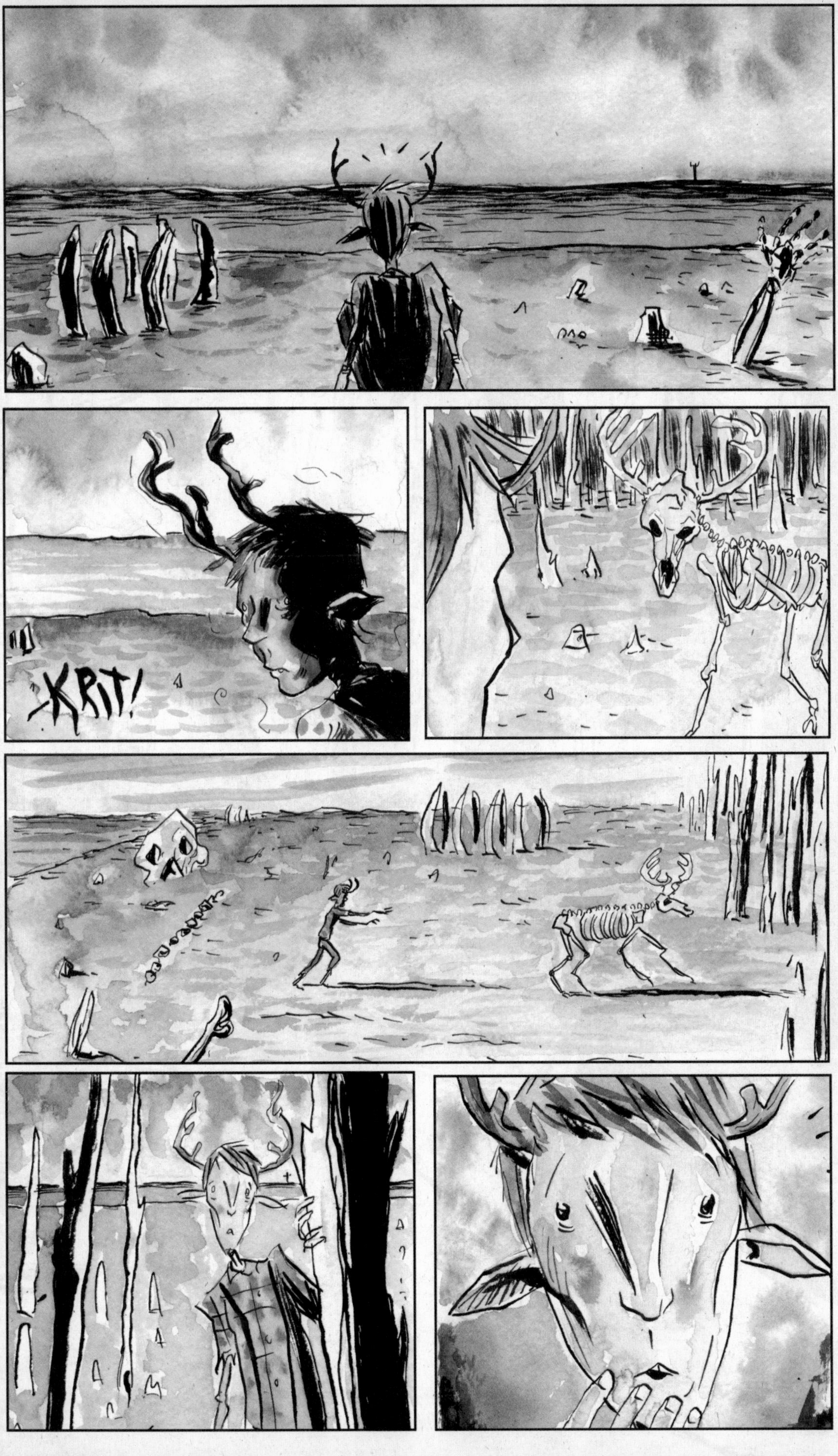
KRIT!

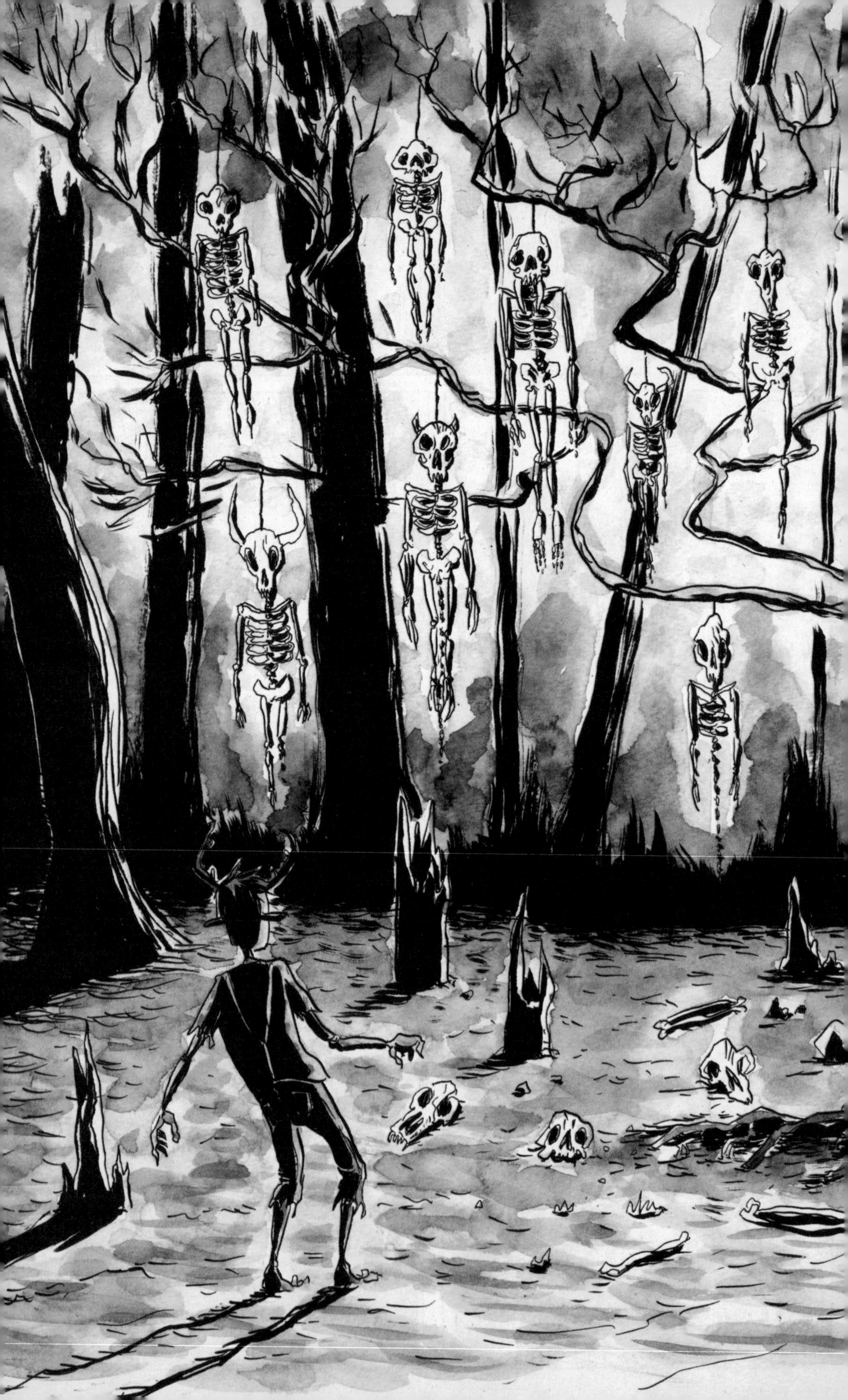

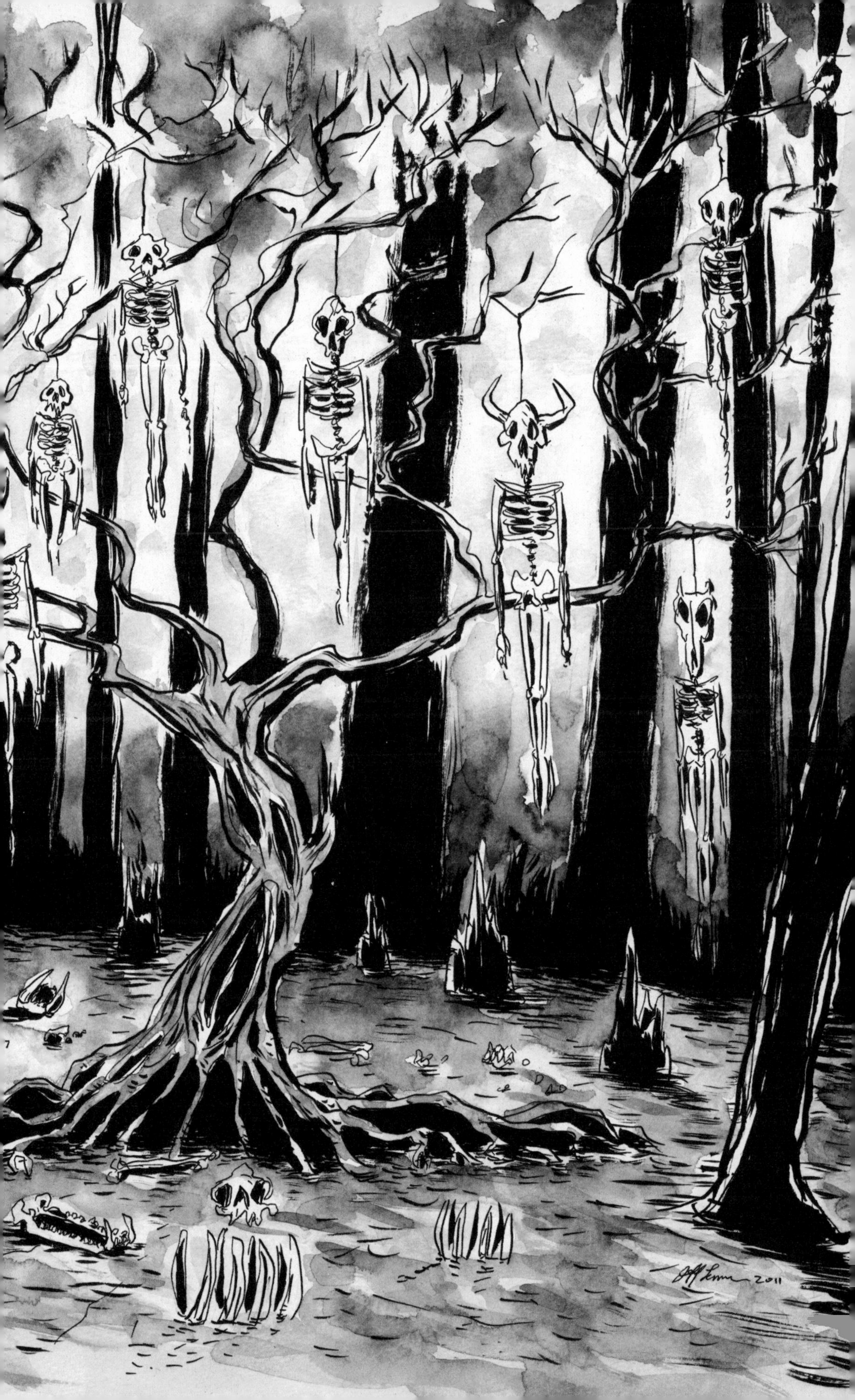

GUS...
WAKE UP!

BLAM!

CRACK!

SHIT!

ZING!

ZING!

HUFF HUFF HUFF HUFF

HANG
ON, KID, WE'RE
ALMOST...

HUFF HUFF HUFF

...THERE...

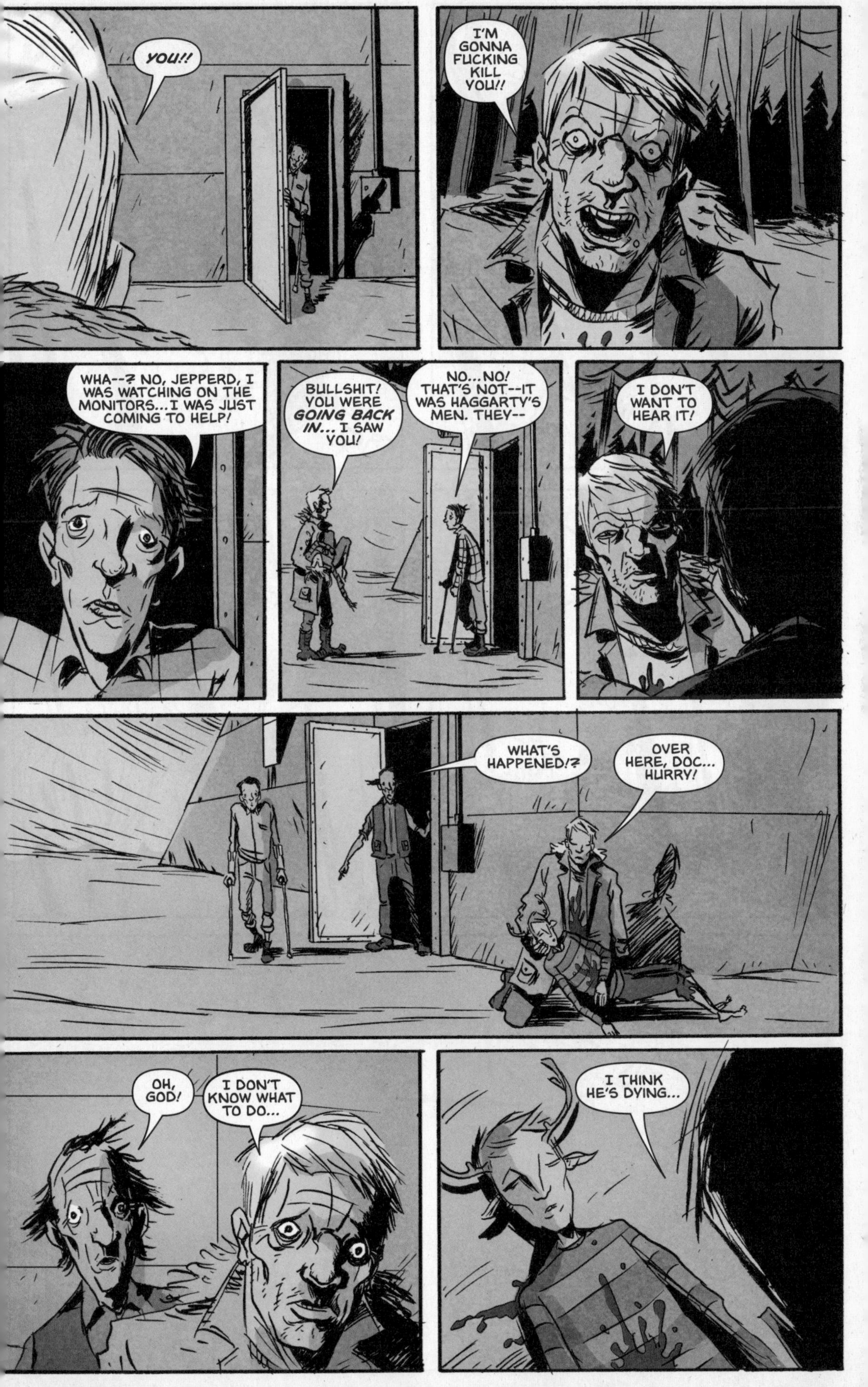
YOU!!
I'M GONNA FUCKING KILL YOU!!
WHA--? NO, JEPPERD, I WAS WATCHING ON THE MONITORS...I WAS JUST COMING TO HELP!
BULLSHIT! YOU WERE GOING BACK IN... I SAW YOU!
NO...NO! THAT'S NOT--IT WAS HAGGARTY'S MEN. THEY--
I DON'T WANT TO HEAR IT!
WHAT'S HAPPENED!?
OVER HERE, DOC... HURRY!
OH, GOD!
I DON'T KNOW WHAT TO DO...
I THINK HE'S DYING...

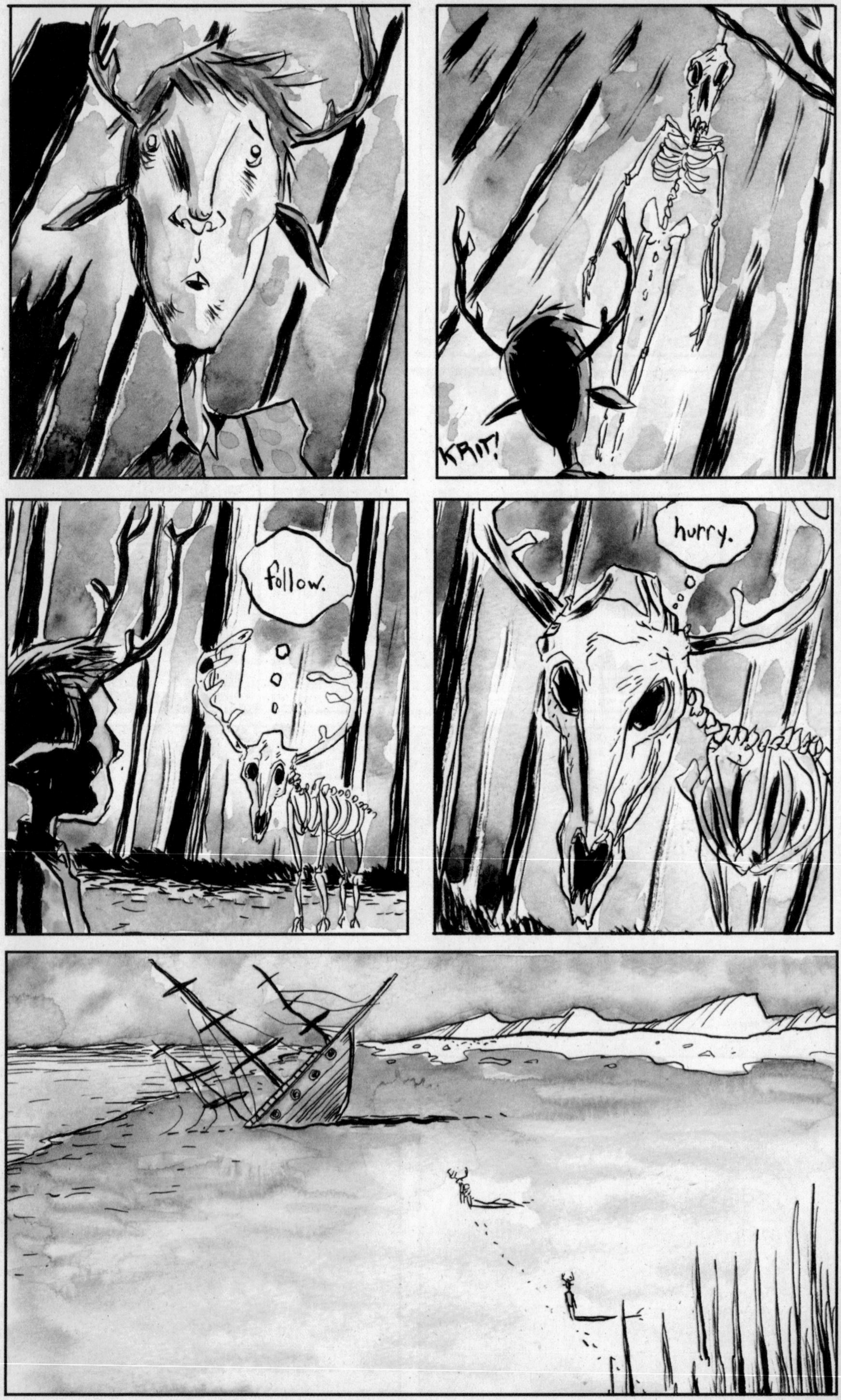
KRIT!
follow.
hurry.

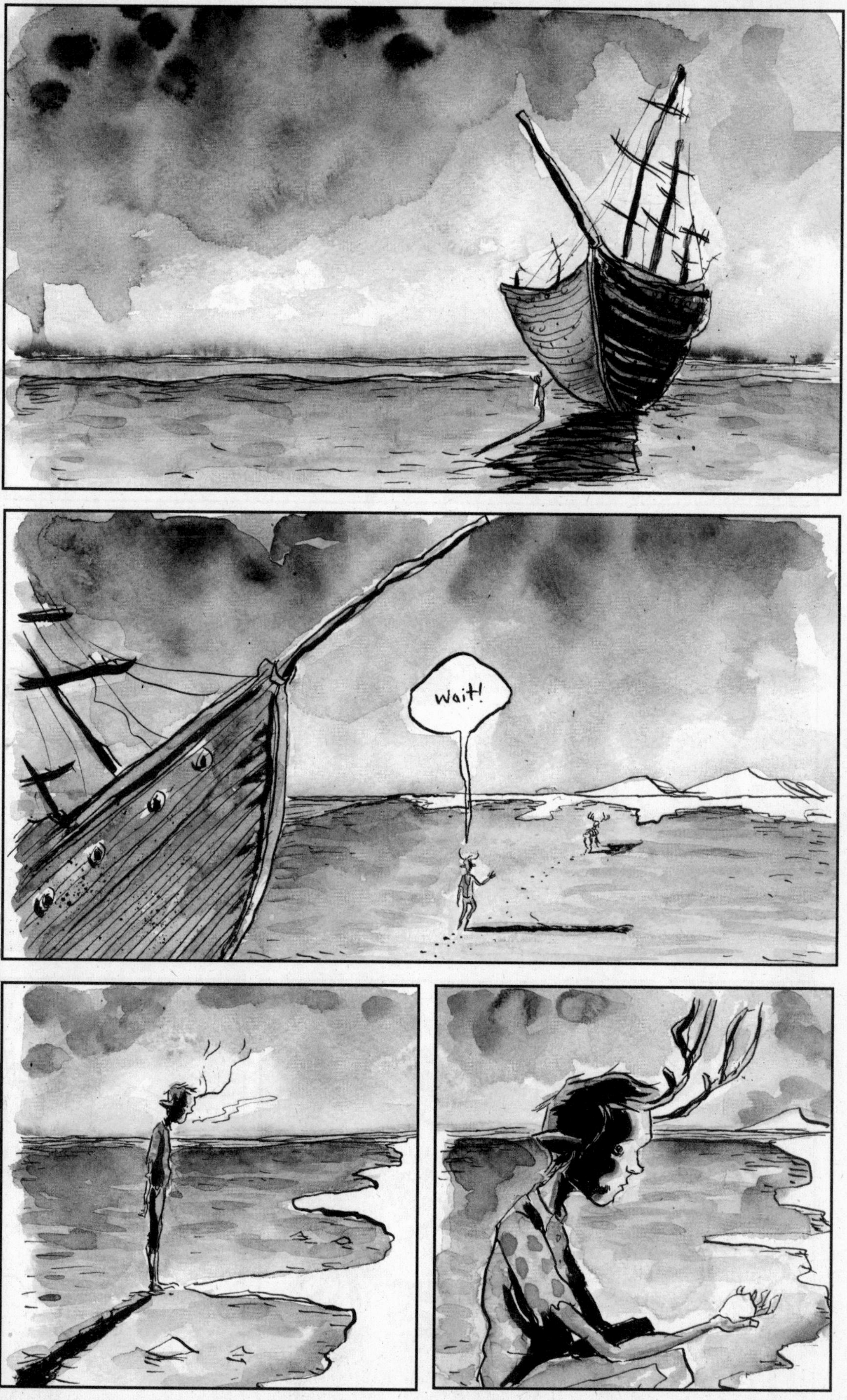
Wait!

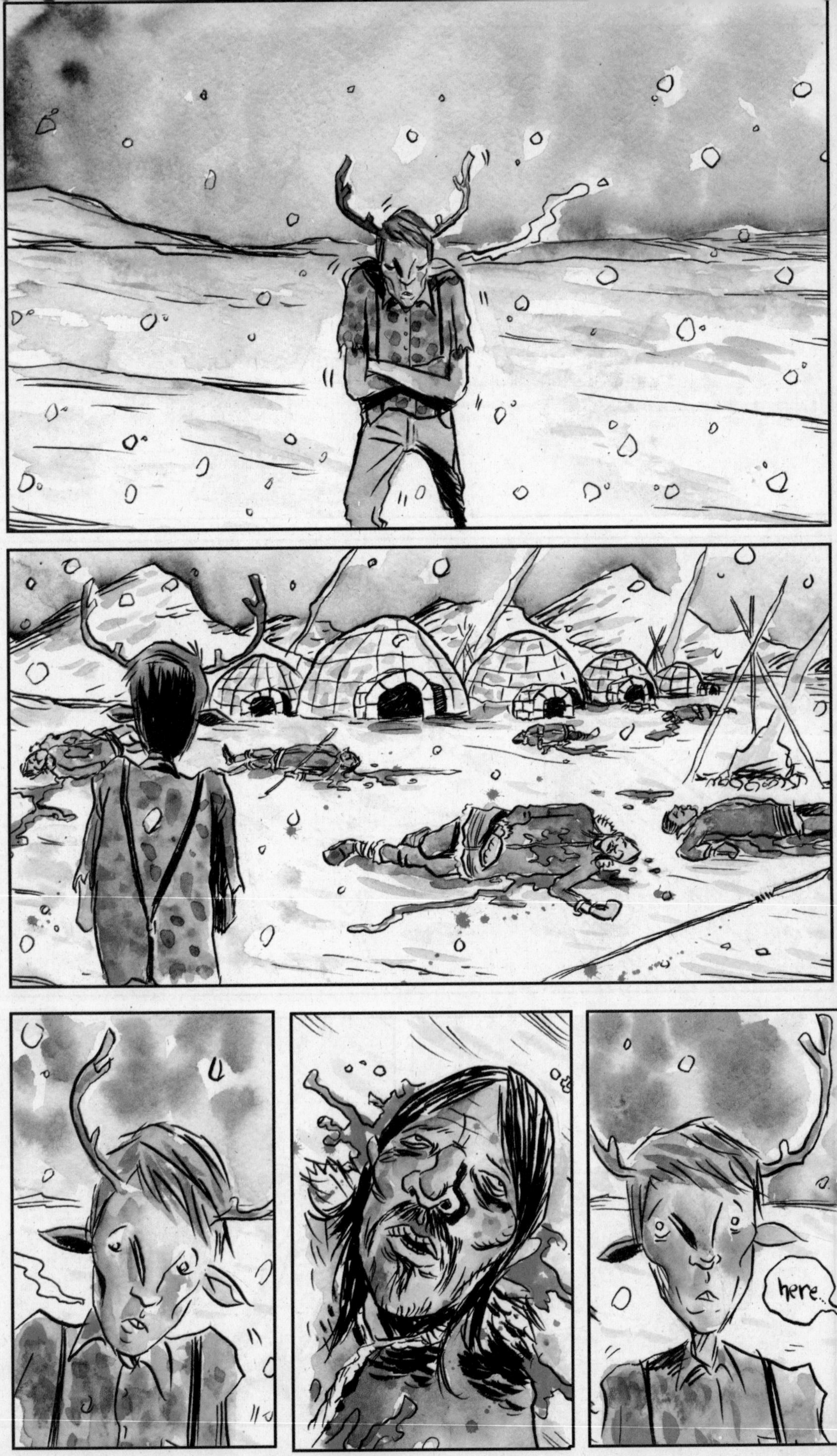
here...

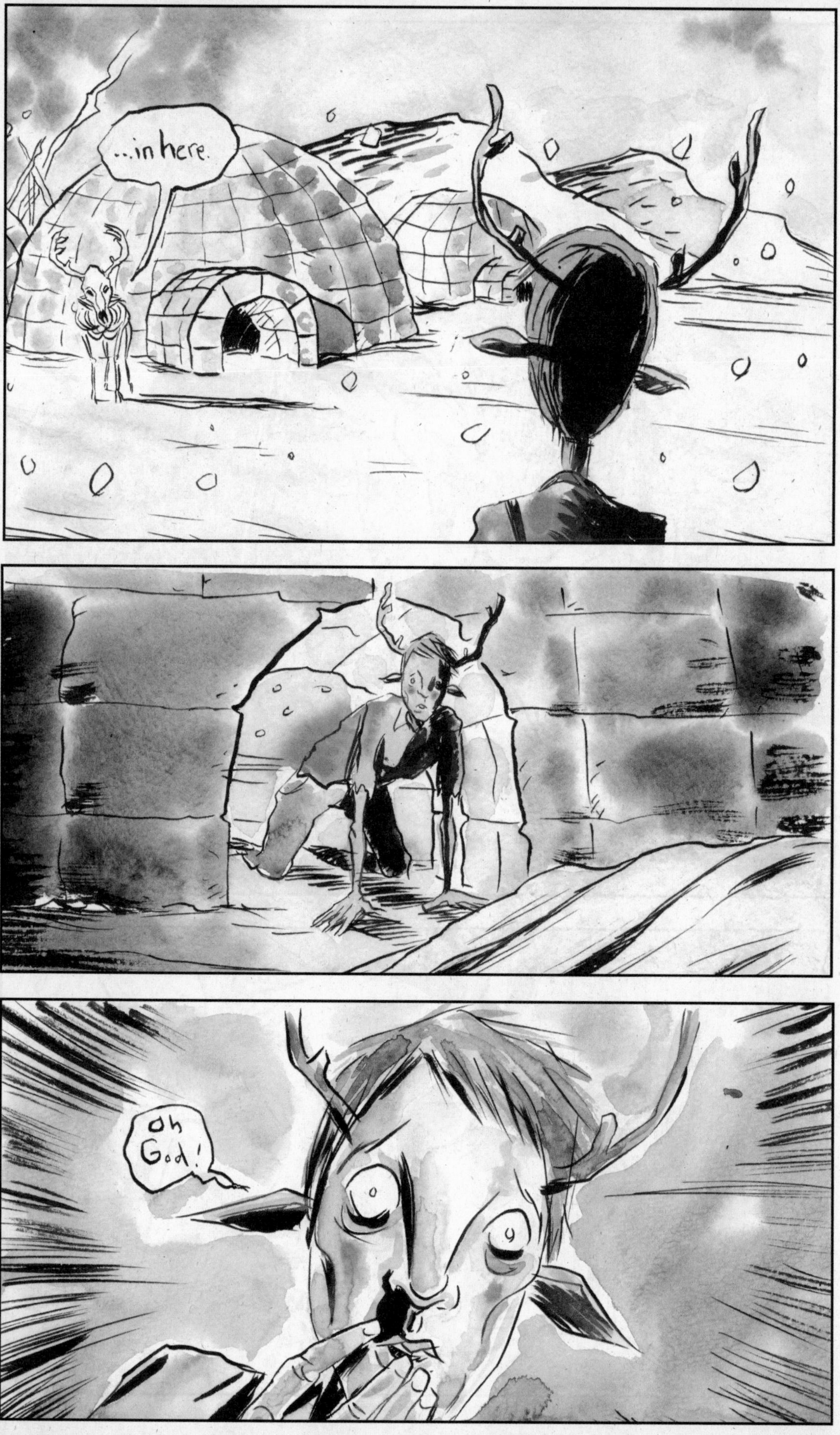
...in here.
Oh God!

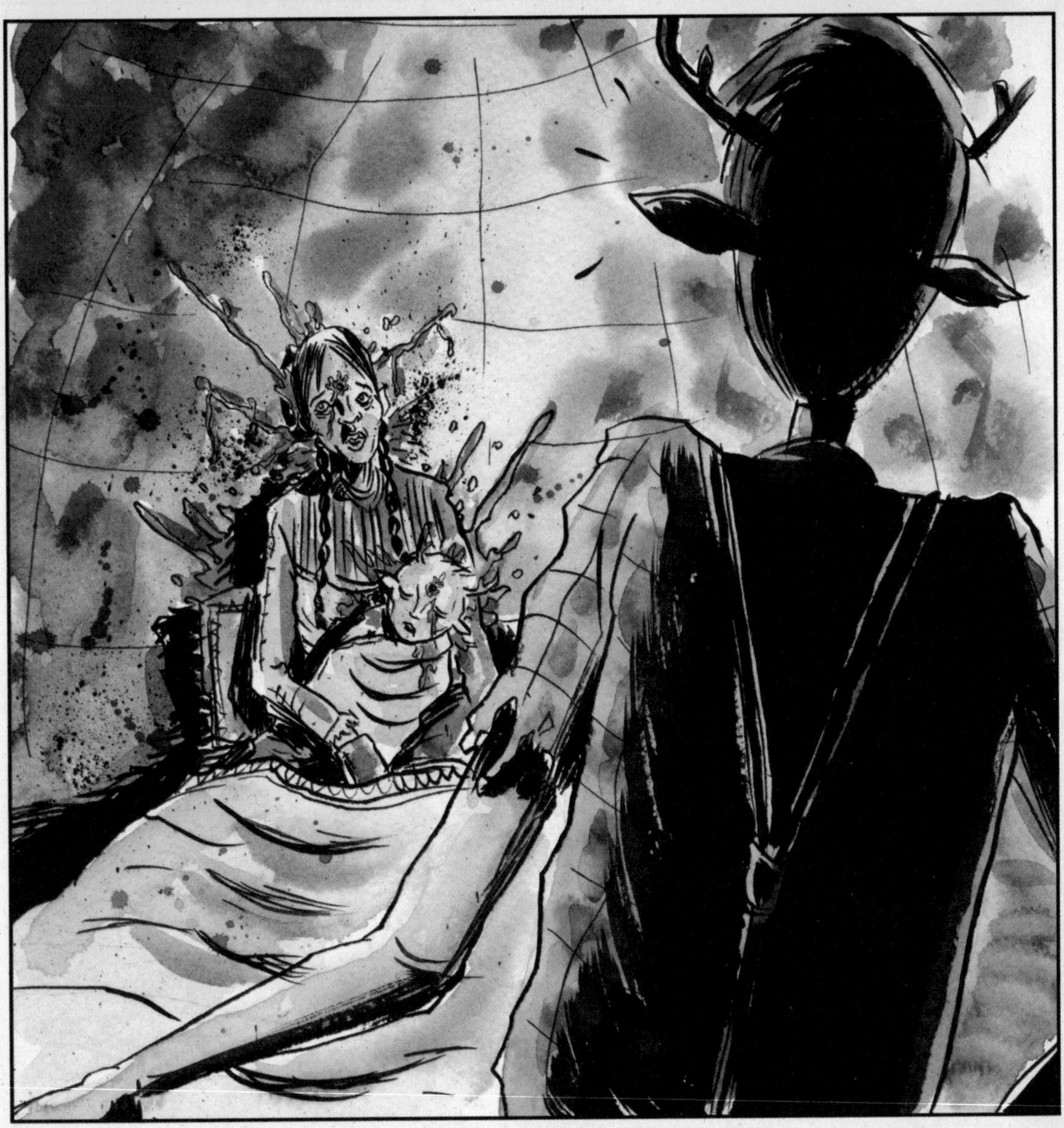

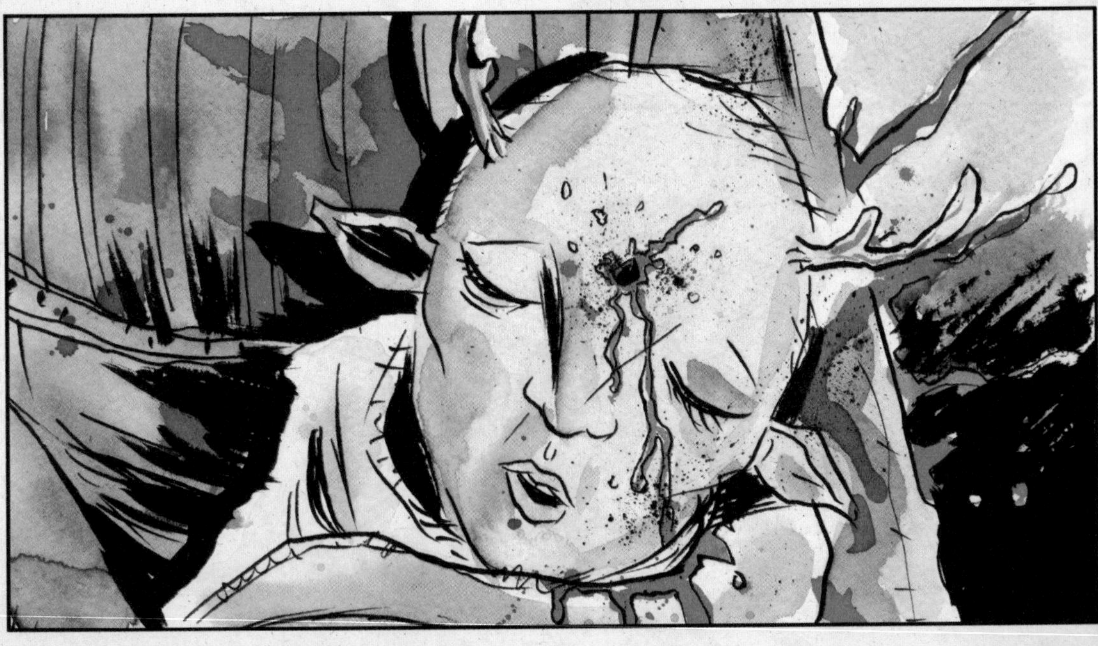

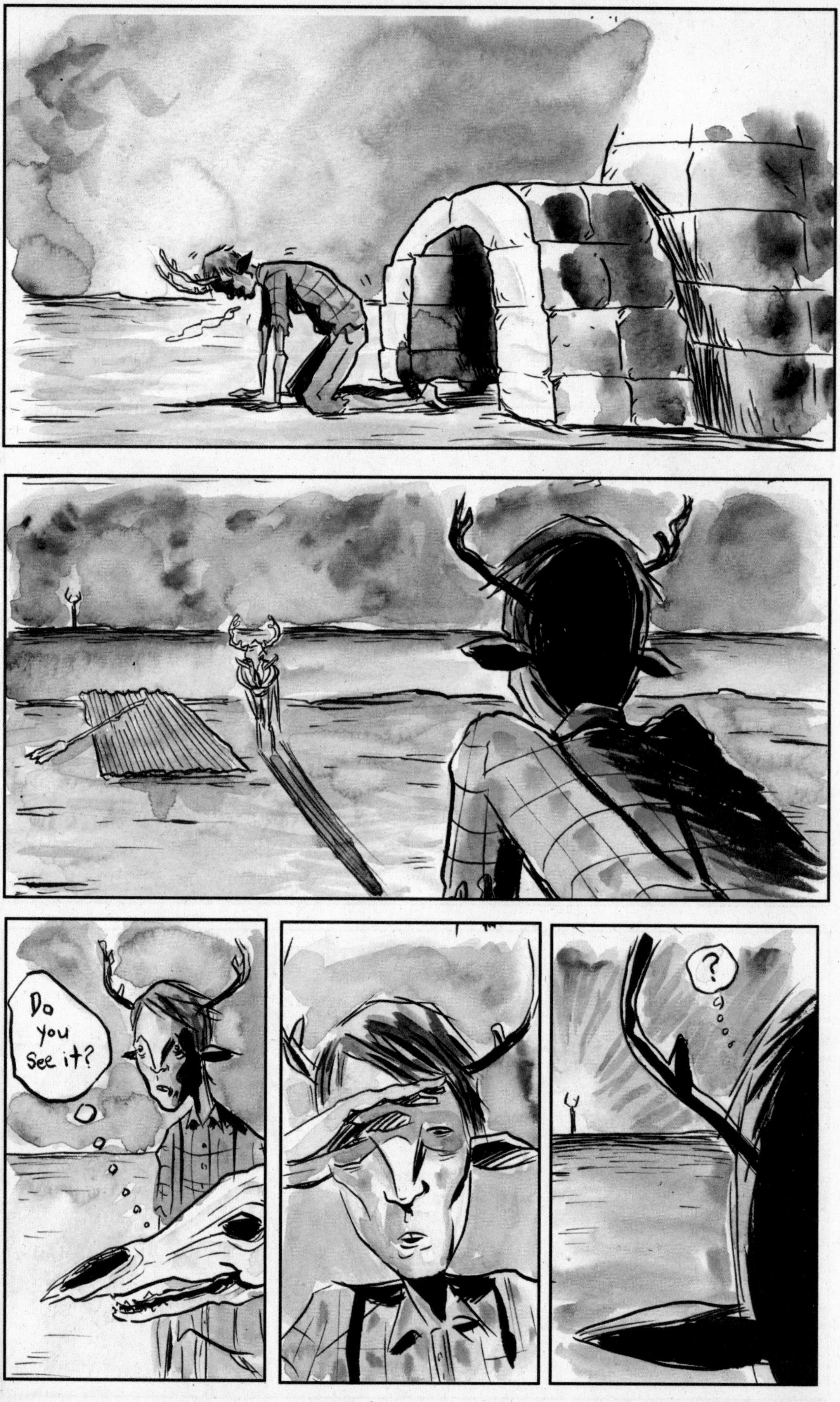
Do you see it?
?

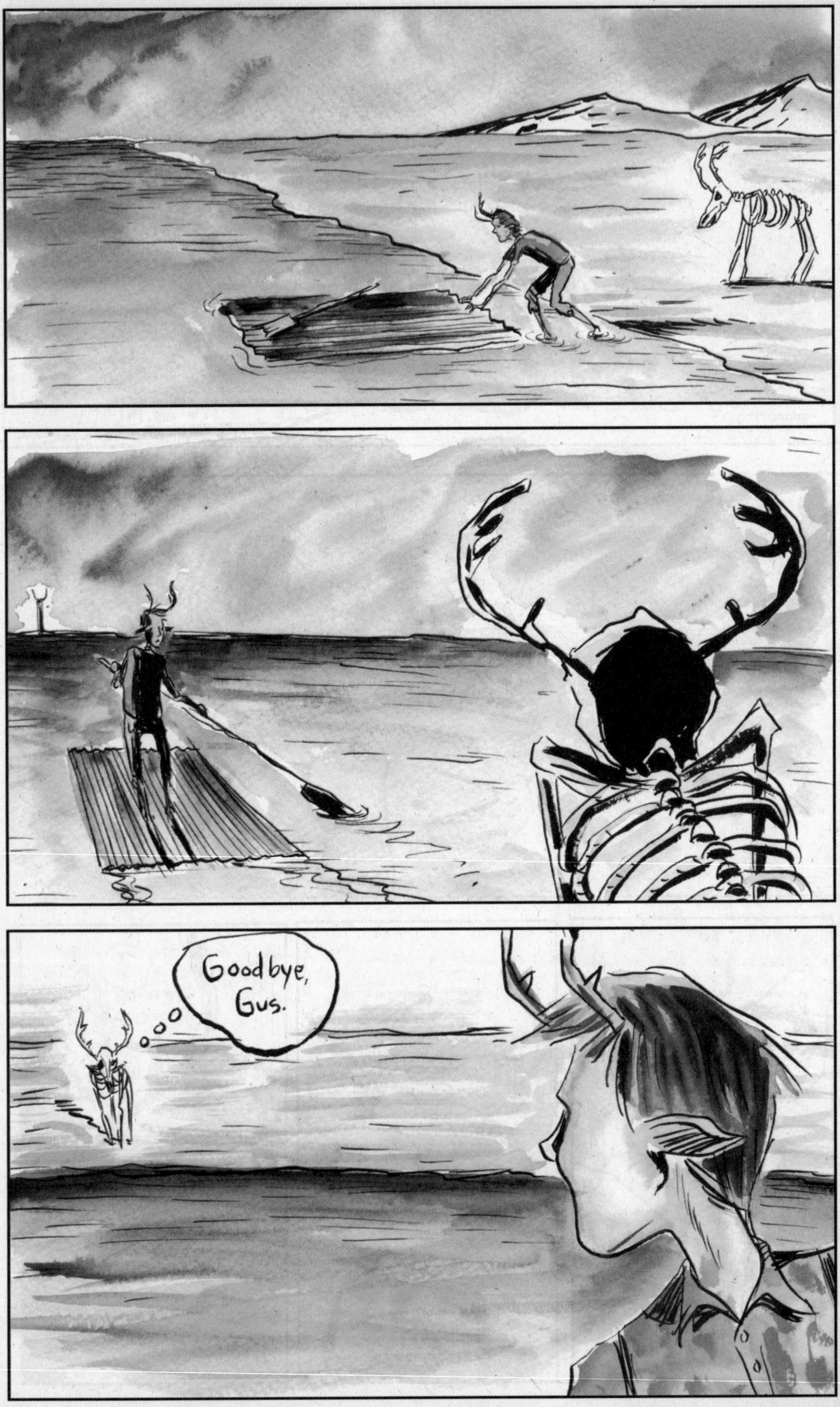
Goodbye, Gus.

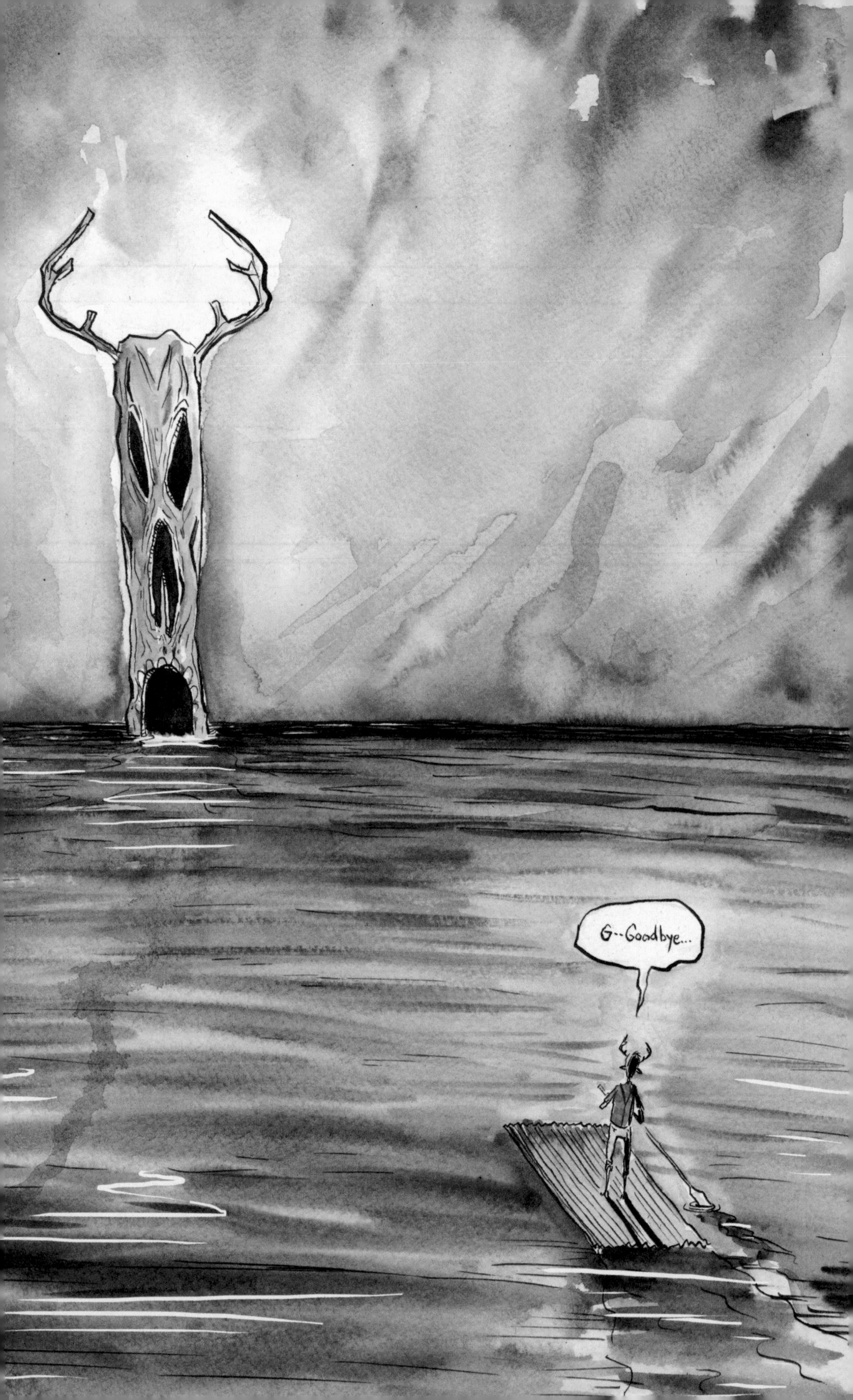
G--Goodbye...

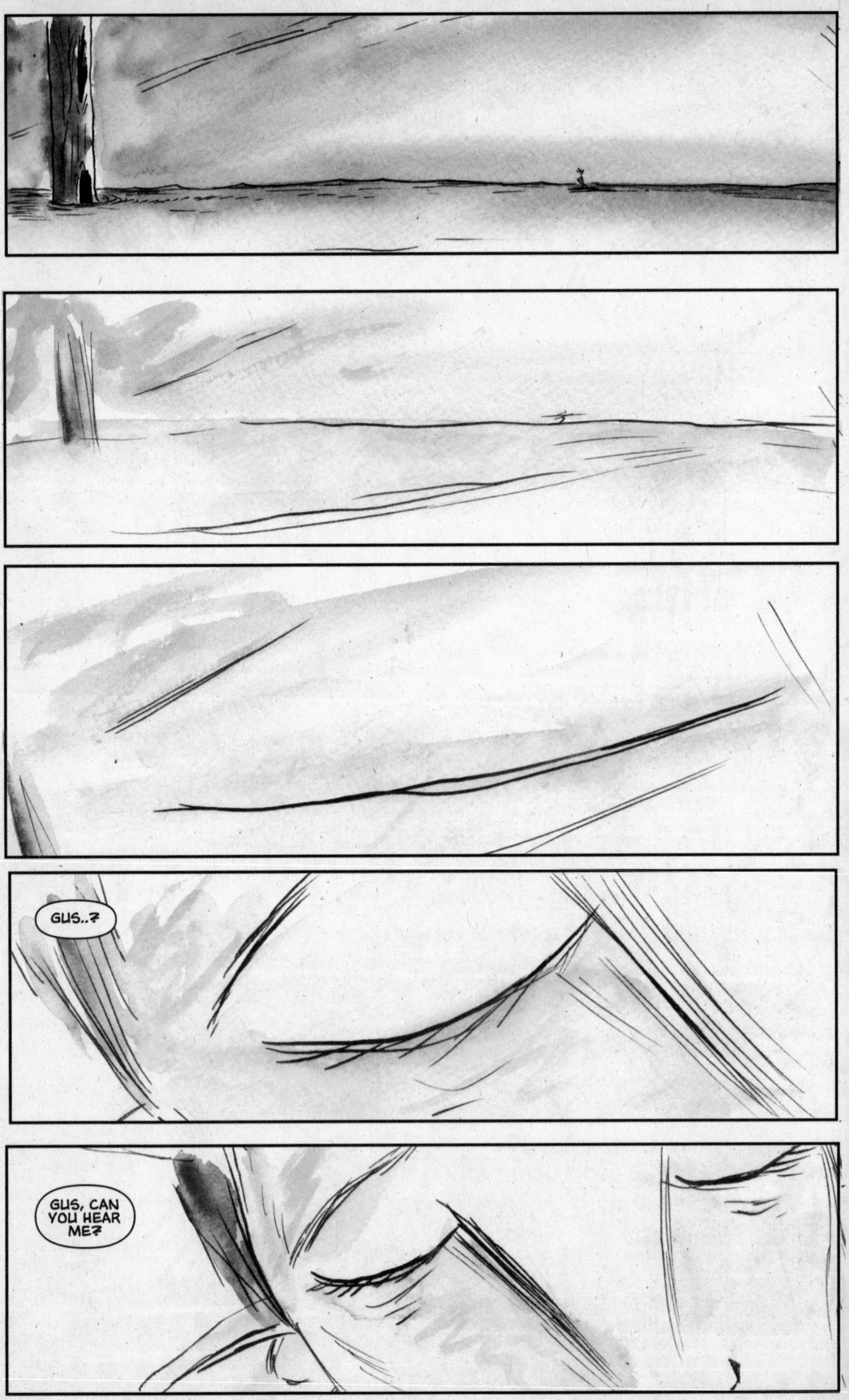
GUS..?
GUS, CAN YOU HEAR ME?

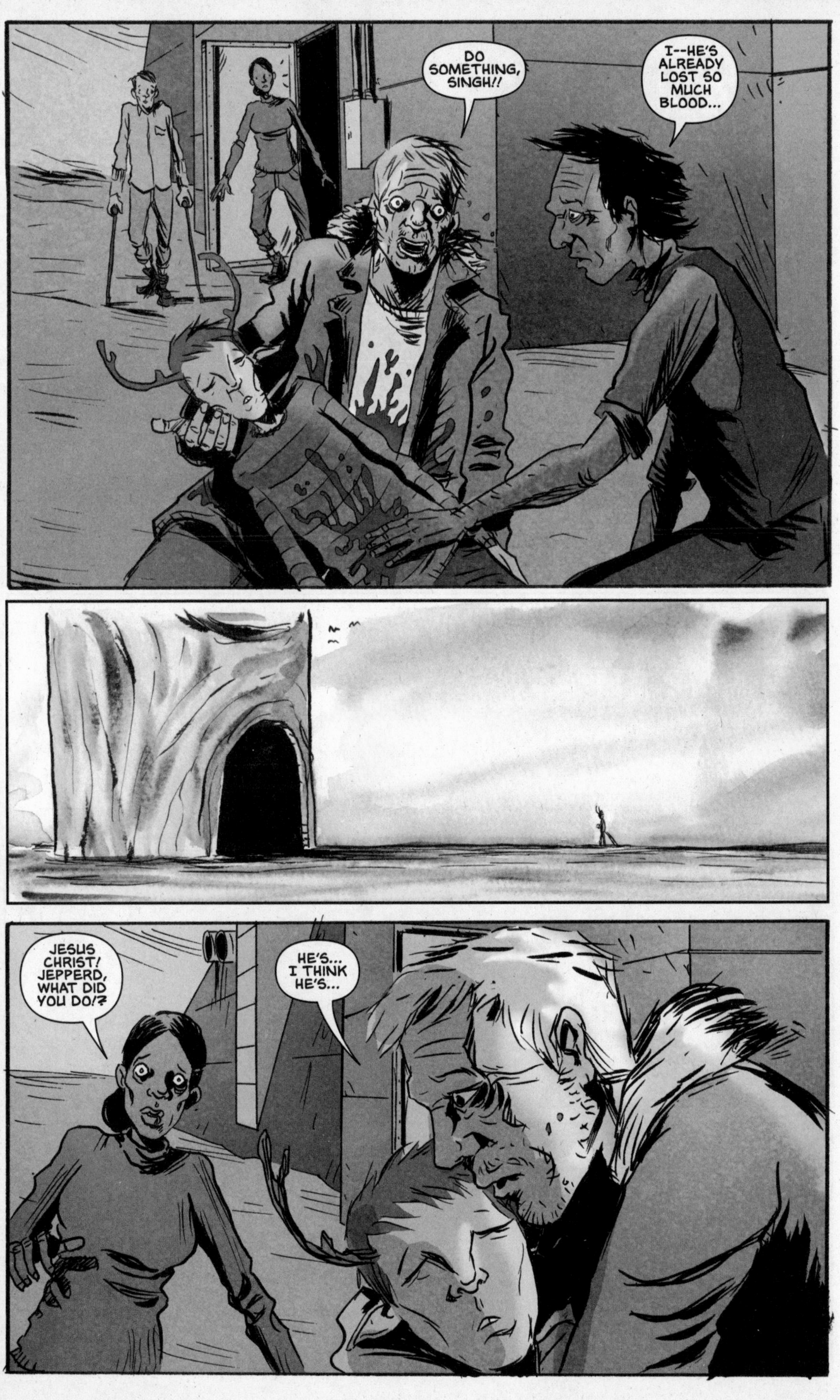
DO SOMETHING, SINGH!!
I--HE'S ALREADY LOST SO MUCH BLOOD...
JESUS CHRIST! JEPPERD, WHAT DID YOU DO!?
HE'S... I THINK HE'S...

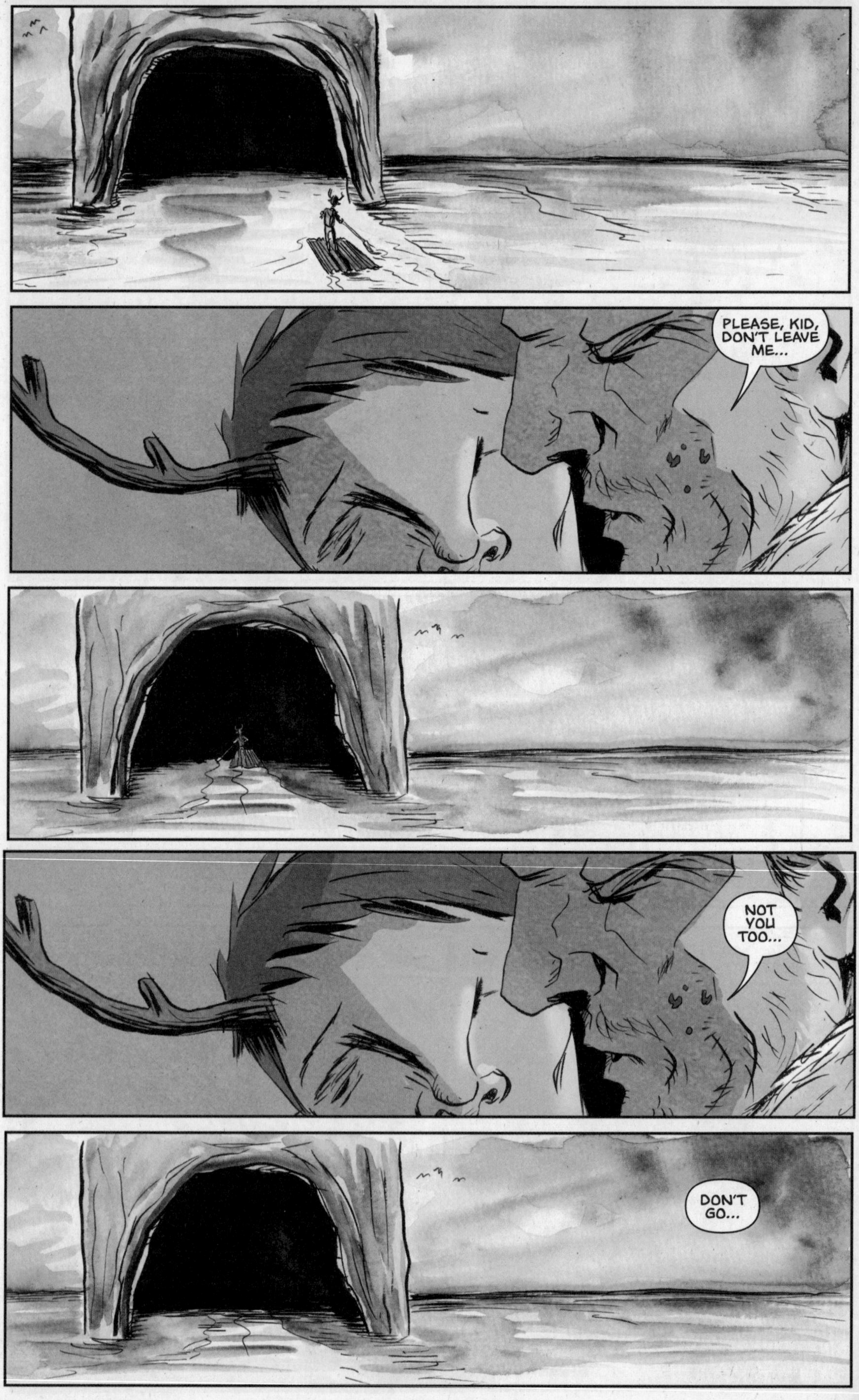
PLEASE, KID, DON'T LEAVE ME...
NOT YOU TOO...
DON'T GO...

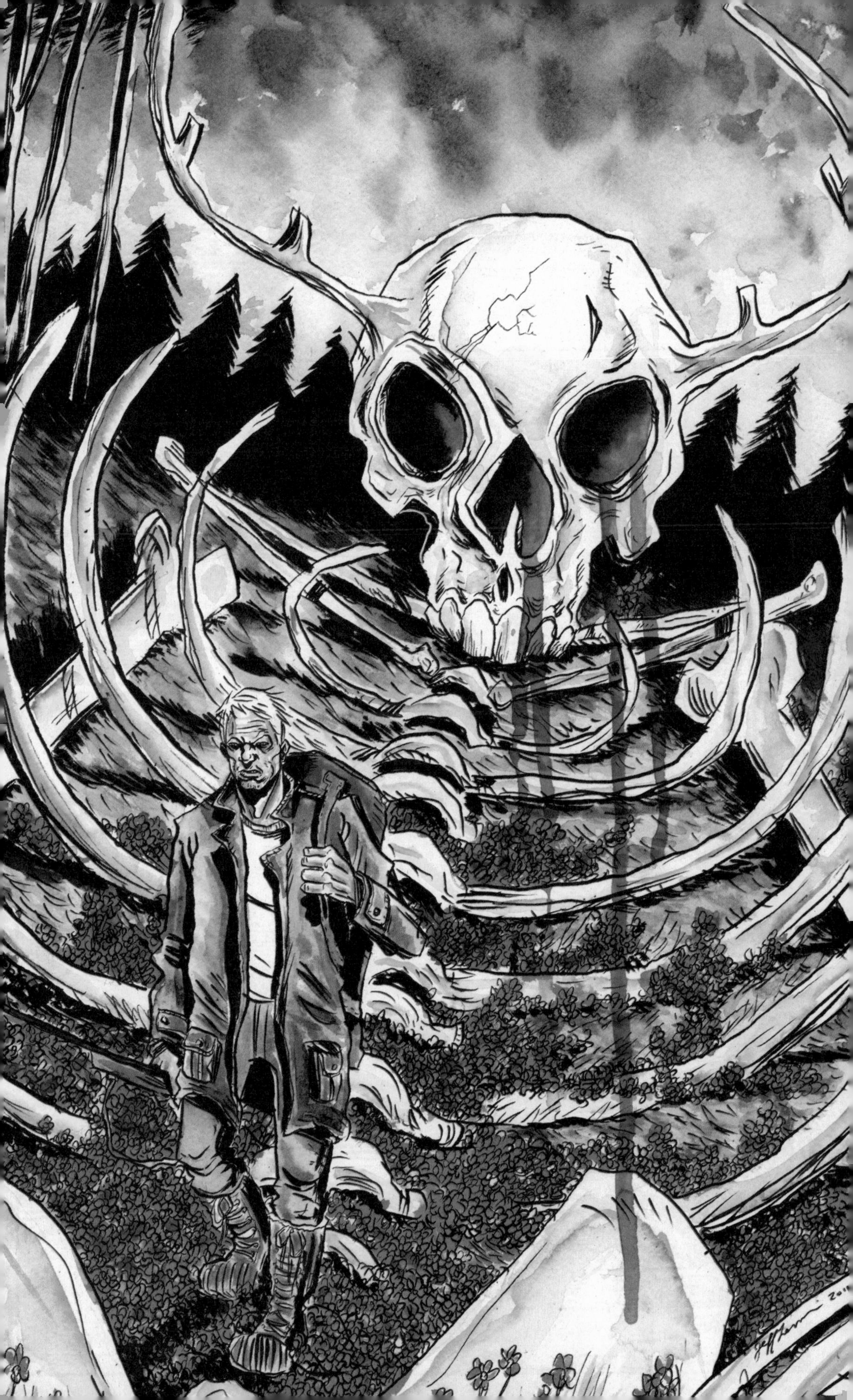

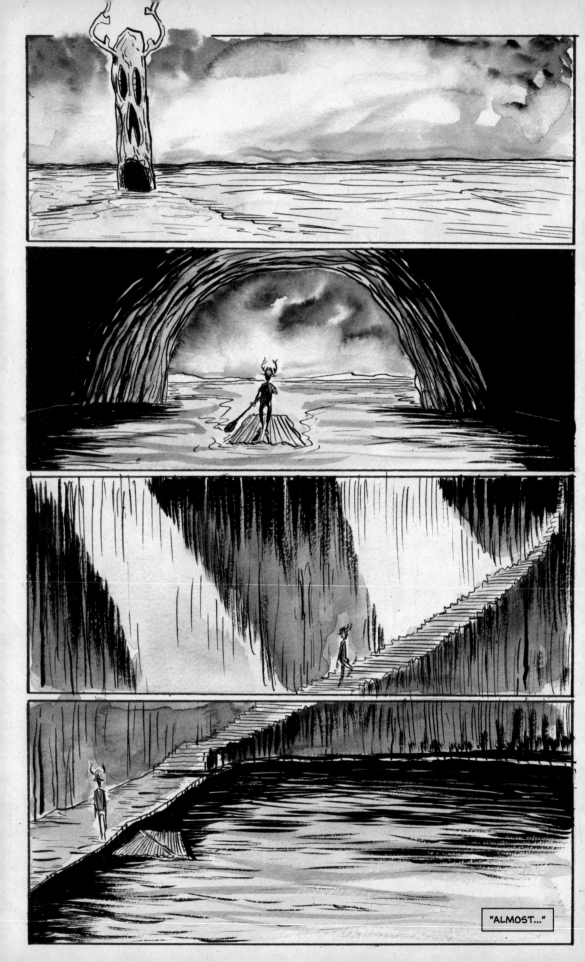

"ALMOST..."

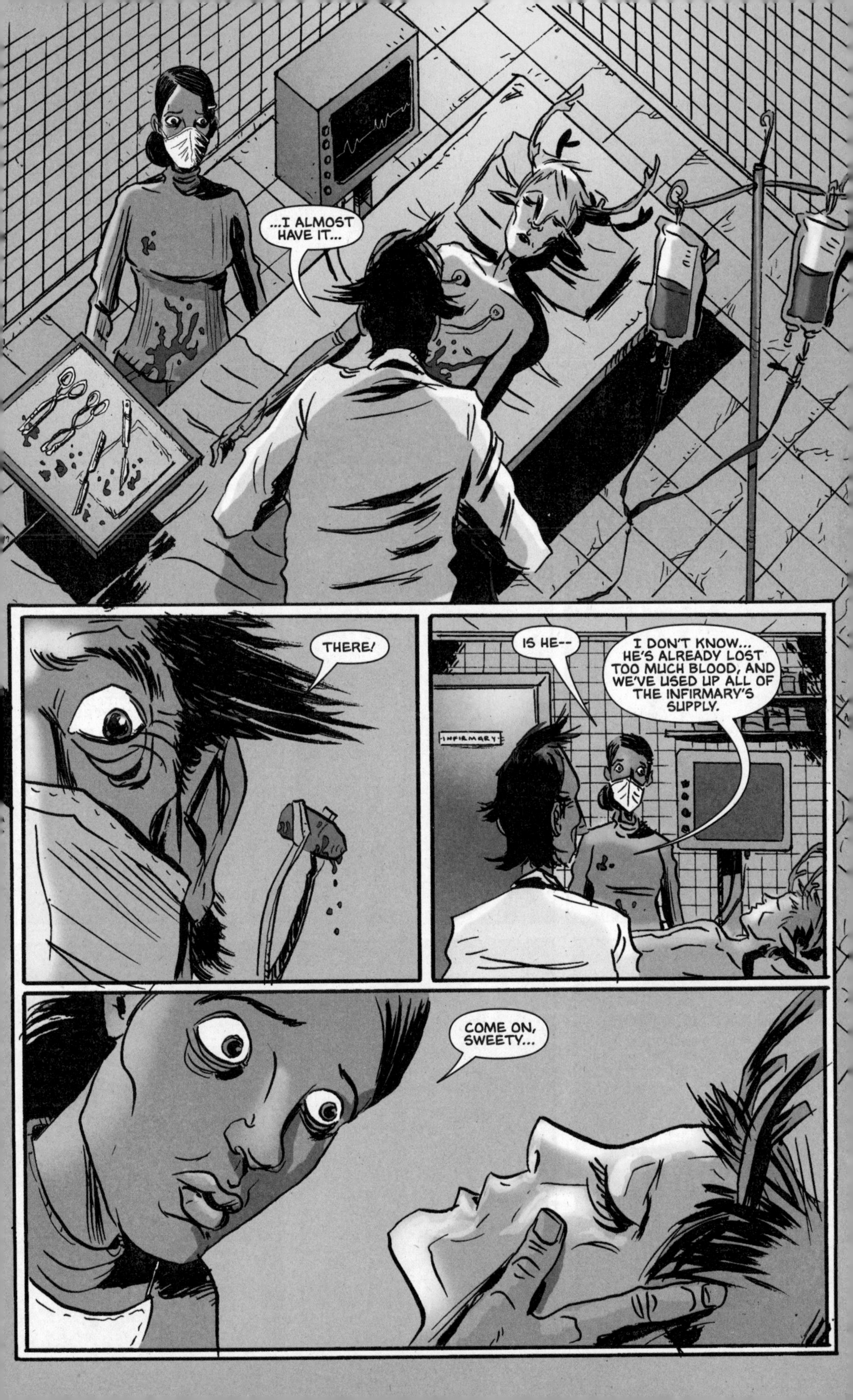
...I ALMOST HAVE IT...
THERE!
IS HE--
I DON'T KNOW... HE'S ALREADY LOST TOO MUCH BLOOD, AND WE'VE USED UP ALL OF THE INFIRMARY'S SUPPLY.
INFIRMARY
COME ON, SWEETY...

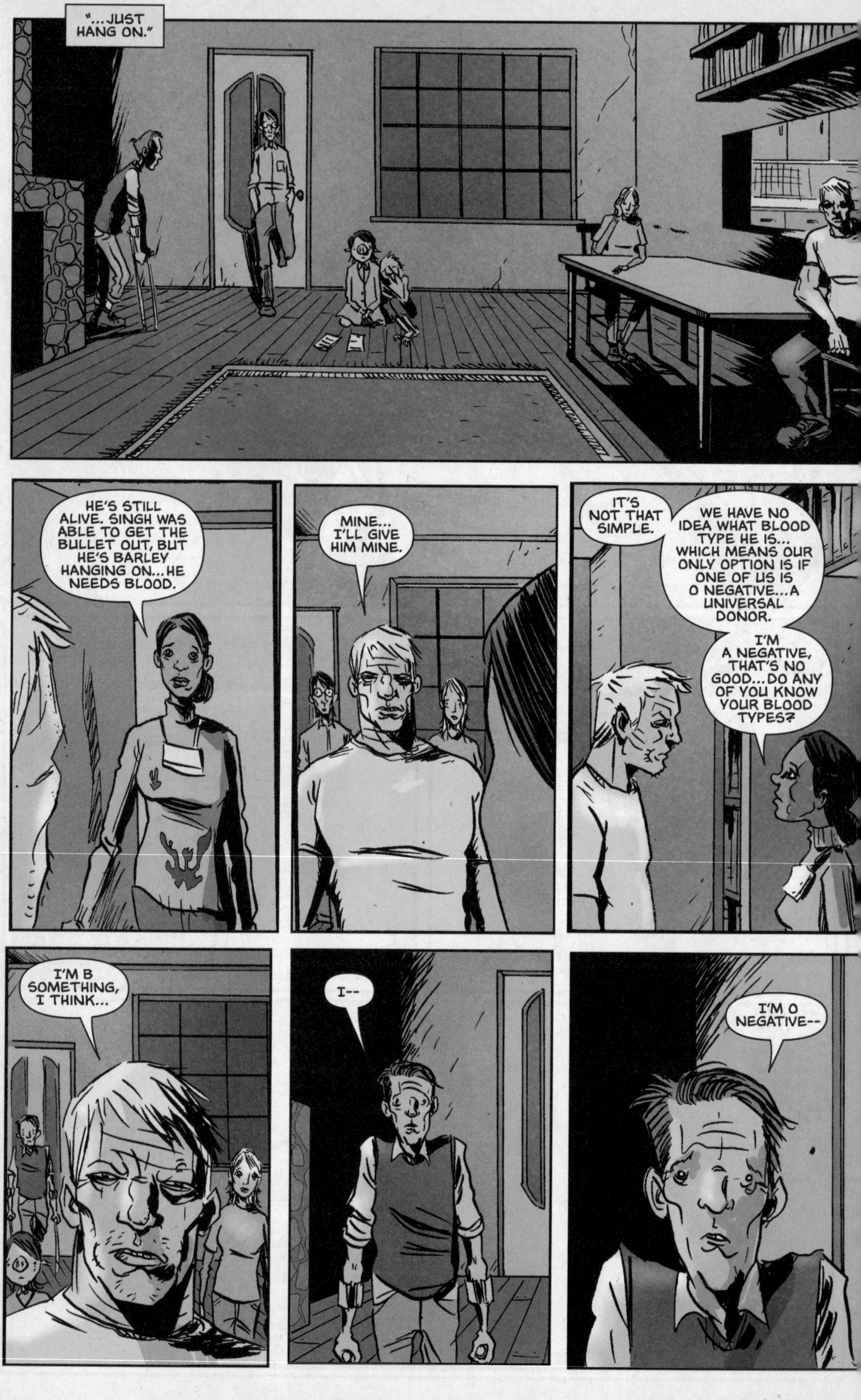
"...JUST HANG ON."
HE'S STILL ALIVE. SINGH WAS ABLE TO GET THE BULLET OUT, BUT HE'S BARLEY HANGING ON...HE NEEDS BLOOD.
MINE... I'LL GIVE HIM MINE.
IT'S NOT THAT SIMPLE.
WE HAVE NO IDEA WHAT BLOOD TYPE HE IS... WHICH MEANS OUR ONLY OPTION IS IF ONE OF US IS O NEGATIVE...A UNIVERSAL DONOR.
I'M A NEGATIVE, THAT'S NO GOOD...DO ANY OF YOU KNOW YOUR BLOOD TYPES?
I'M B SOMETHING, I THINK...
I--
I'M O NEGATIVE--

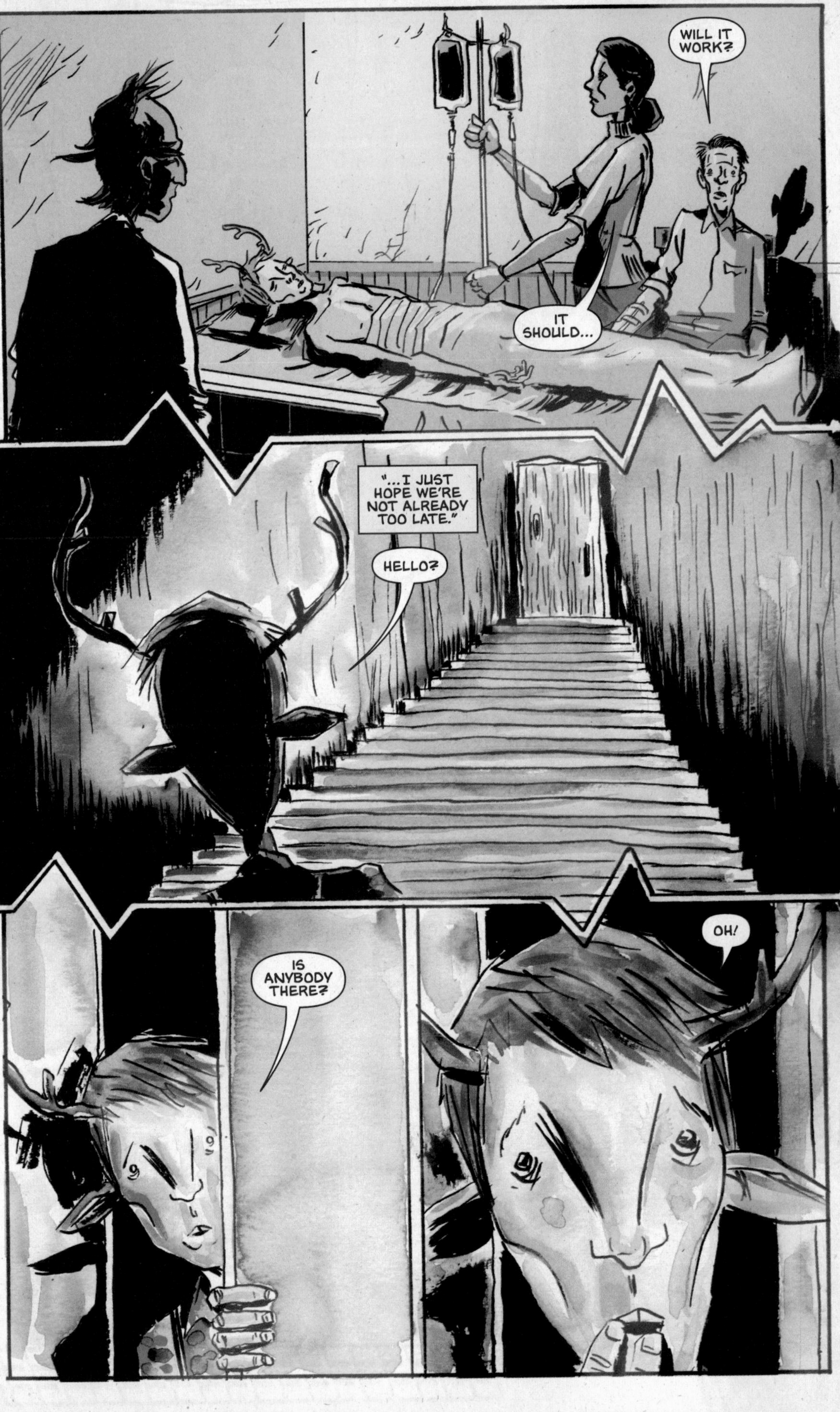
WILL IT WORK?
IT SHOULD...
"...I JUST HOPE WE'RE NOT ALREADY TOO LATE."
HELLO?
IS ANYBODY THERE?
OH!

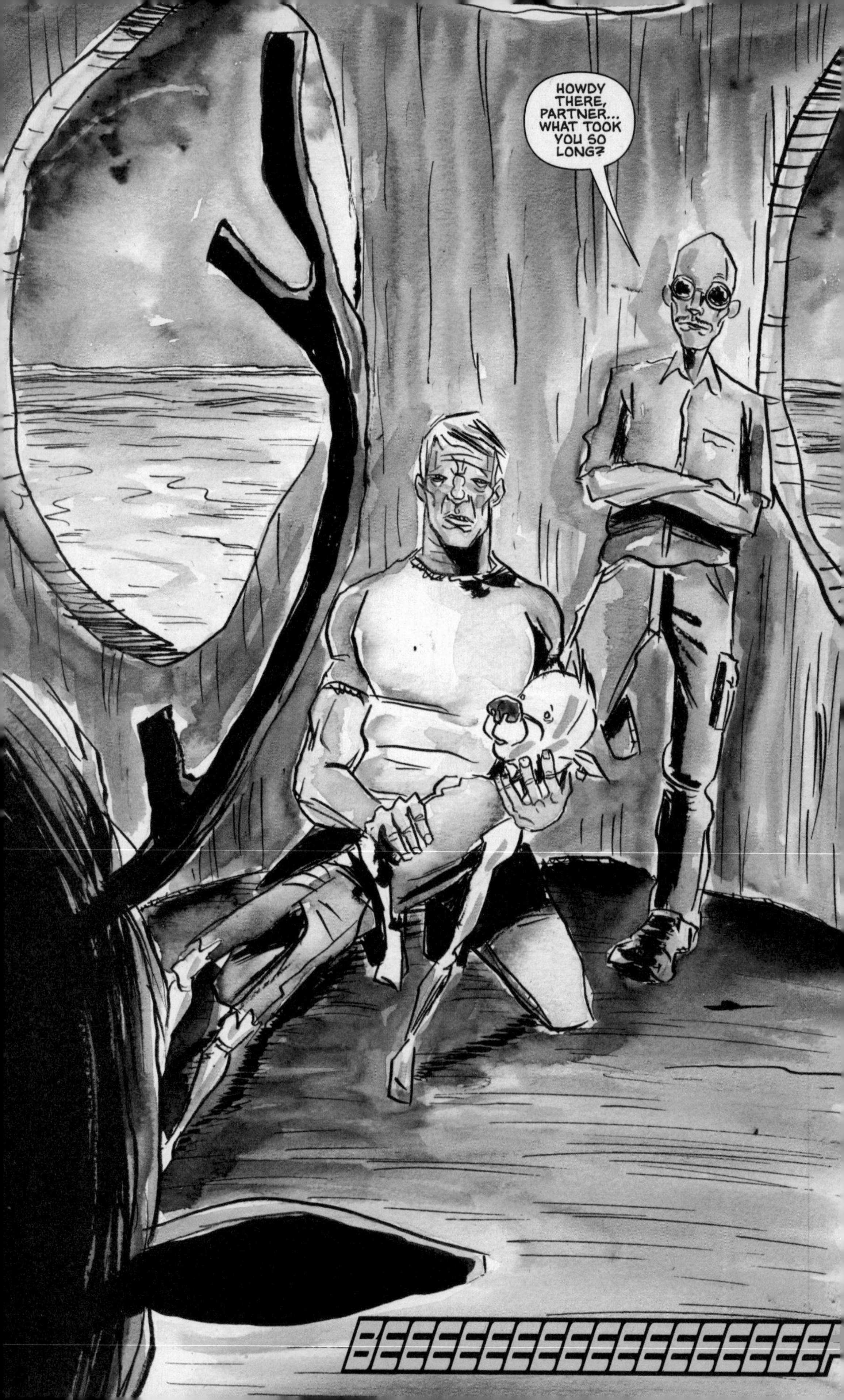
HOWDY THERE, PARTNER... WHAT TOOK YOU SO LONG?
BEEEEEEEEEEEEEEEEE

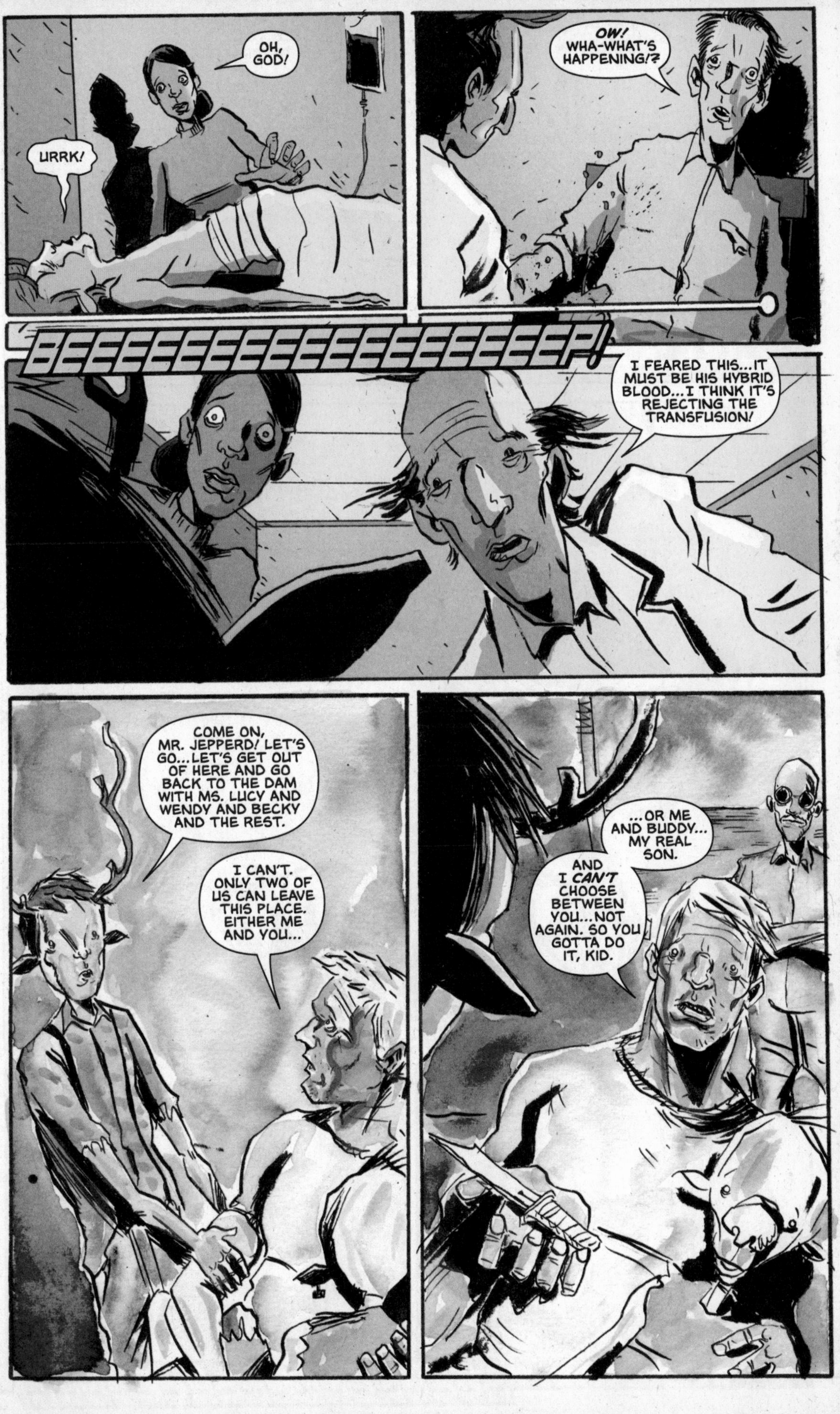
OH, GOD!
URRK!
OW! WHA-WHAT'S HAPPENING!?
BEEEEEEEEEEEEEEEEEEEEP!
I FEARED THIS...IT MUST BE HIS HYBRID BLOOD...I THINK IT'S REJECTING THE TRANSFUSION!
COME ON, MR. JEPPERD! LET'S GO...LET'S GET OUT OF HERE AND GO BACK TO THE DAM WITH MS. LUCY AND WENDY AND BECKY AND THE REST.
I CAN'T. ONLY TWO OF US CAN LEAVE THIS PLACE. EITHER ME AND YOU...
...OR ME AND BUDDY... MY REAL SON.
AND I CAN'T CHOOSE BETWEEN YOU...NOT AGAIN. SO YOU GOTTA DO IT, KID.

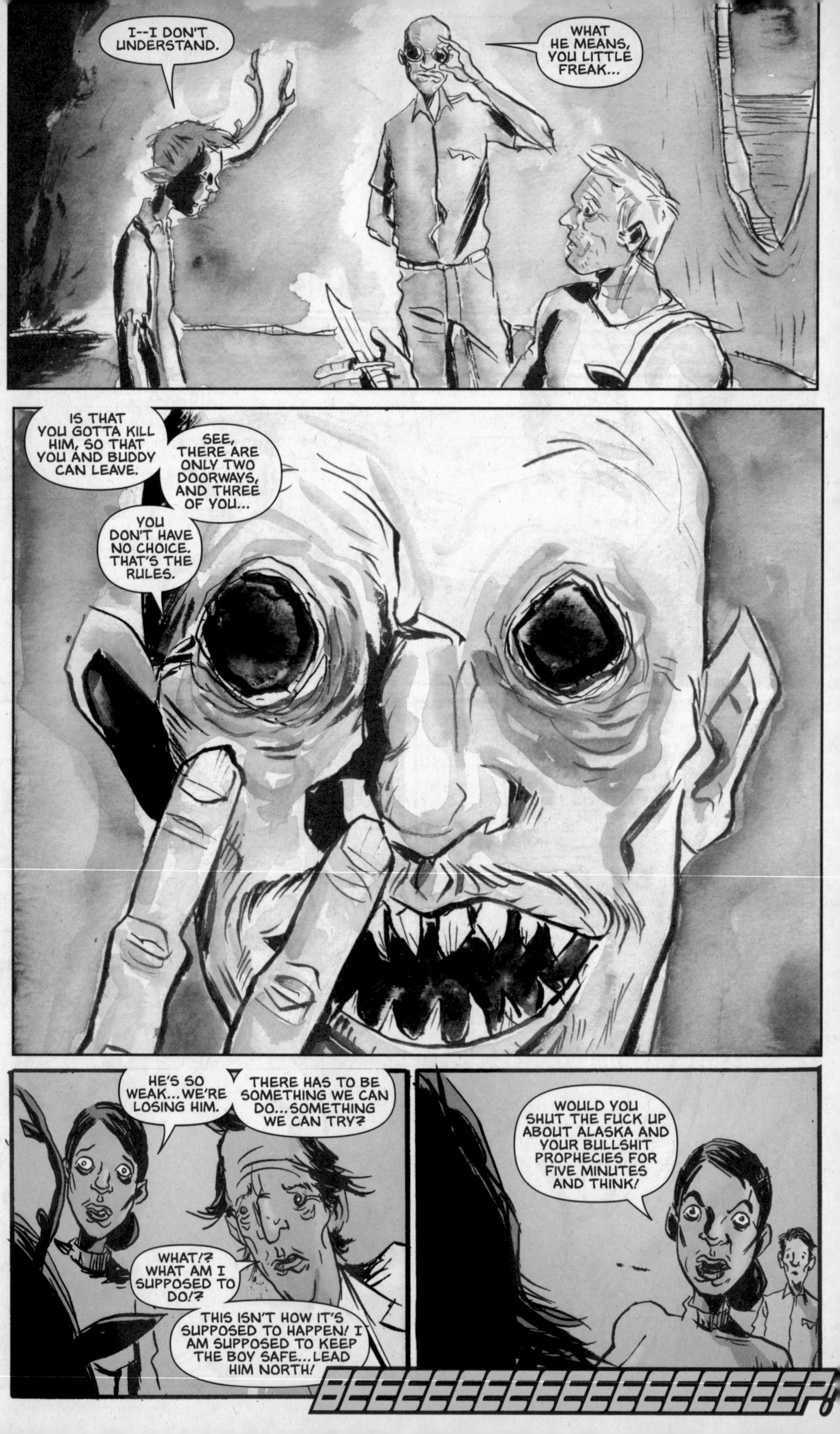

I--I DON'T UNDERSTAND.
WHAT HE MEANS, YOU LITTLE FREAK...
IS THAT YOU GOTTA KILL HIM, SO THAT YOU AND BUDDY CAN LEAVE.
SEE, THERE ARE ONLY TWO DOORWAYS, AND THREE OF YOU...
YOU DON'T HAVE NO CHOICE. THAT'S THE RULES.
HE'S SO WEAK...WE'RE LOSING HIM.
THERE HAS TO BE SOMETHING WE CAN DO...SOMETHING WE CAN TRY?
WHAT!? WHAT AM I SUPPOSED TO DO!?
THIS ISN'T HOW IT'S SUPPOSED TO HAPPEN! I AM SUPPOSED TO KEEP THE BOY SAFE...LEAD HIM NORTH!
WOULD YOU SHUT THE FUCK UP ABOUT ALASKA AND YOUR BULLSHIT PROPHECIES FOR FIVE MINUTES AND THINK!
BEEEEEEEEEEEEEEEEEEEP!

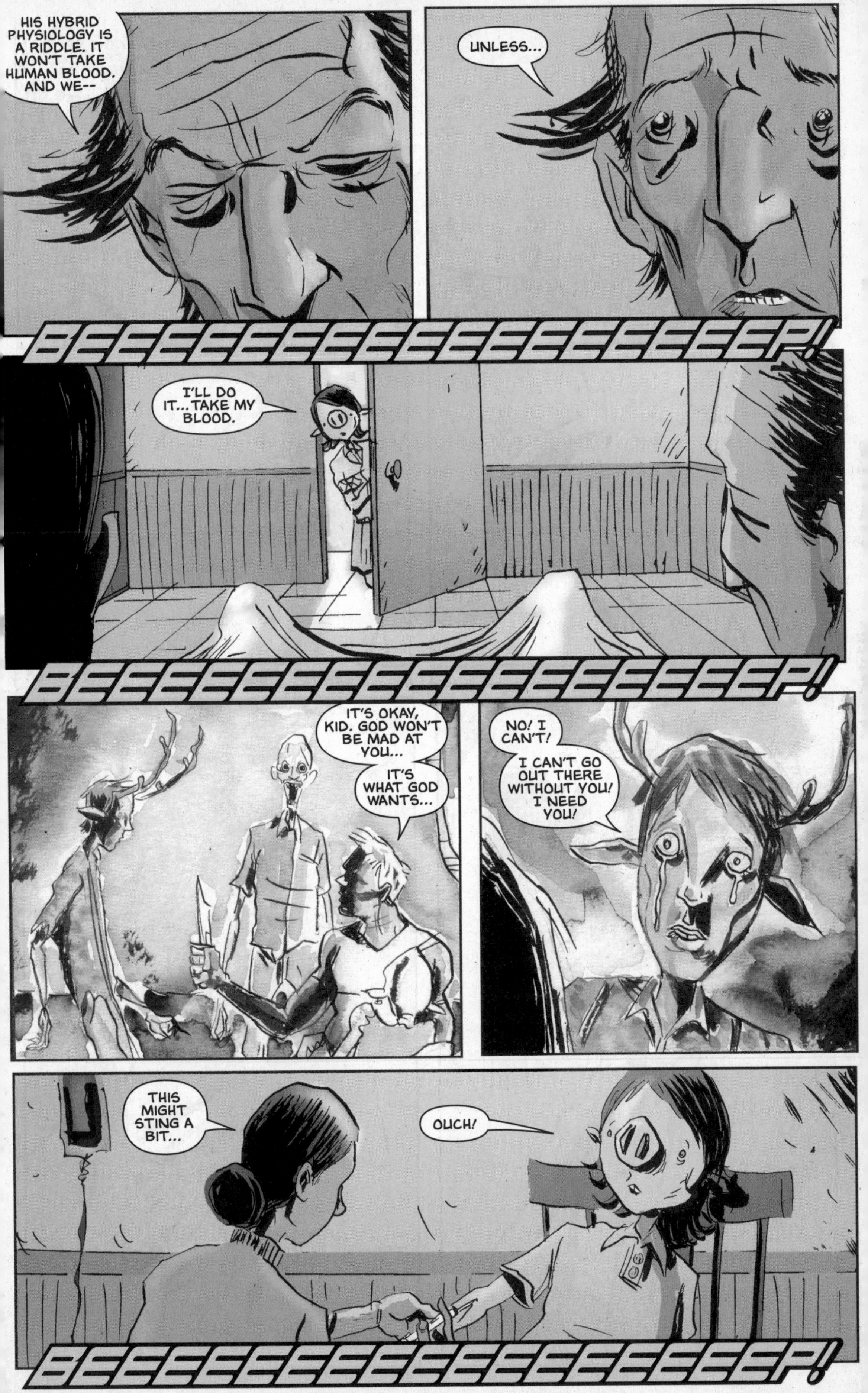
HIS HYBRID PHYSIOLOGY IS A RIDDLE. IT WON'T TAKE HUMAN BLOOD. AND WE--
UNLESS...
BEEEEEEEEEEEEEEEEEEEEP!
I'LL DO IT... TAKE MY BLOOD.
BEEEEEEEEEEEEEEEEEEEEEP!
IT'S OKAY, KID. GOD WON'T BE MAD AT YOU...
IT'S WHAT GOD WANTS...
NO! I CAN'T!
I CAN'T GO OUT THERE WITHOUT YOU! I NEED YOU!
THIS MIGHT STING A BIT...
OUCH!
BEEEEEEEEEEEEEEEEEEEEEP!

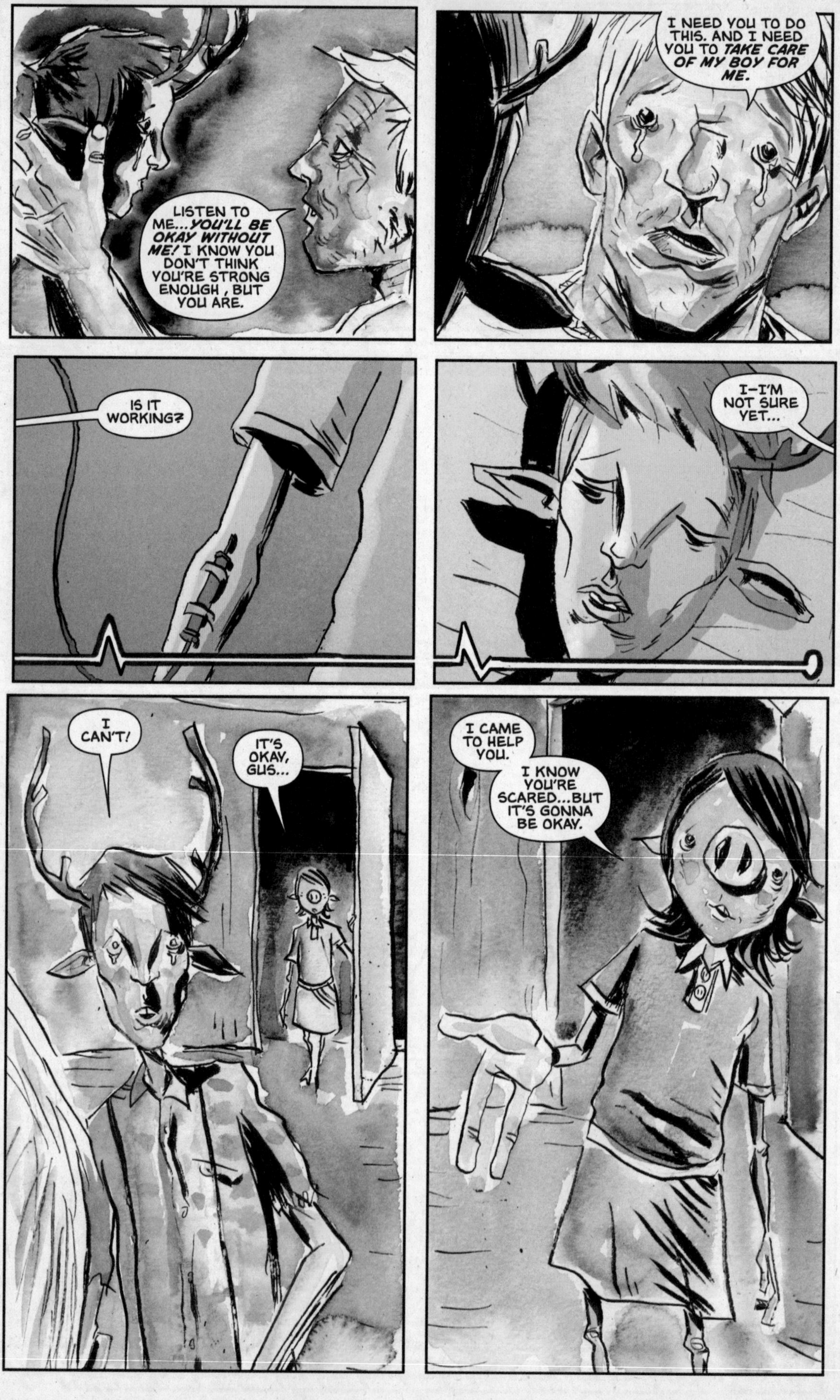
LISTEN TO ME...YOU'LL BE OKAY WITHOUT ME! I KNOW YOU DON'T THINK YOU'RE STRONG ENOUGH , BUT YOU ARE.
I NEED YOU TO DO THIS. AND I NEED YOU TO TAKE CARE OF MY BOY FOR ME.
IS IT WORKING?
I-I'M NOT SURE YET...
I CAN'T!
IT'S OKAY, GUS...
I CAME TO HELP YOU.
I KNOW YOU'RE SCARED...BUT IT'S GONNA BE OKAY.

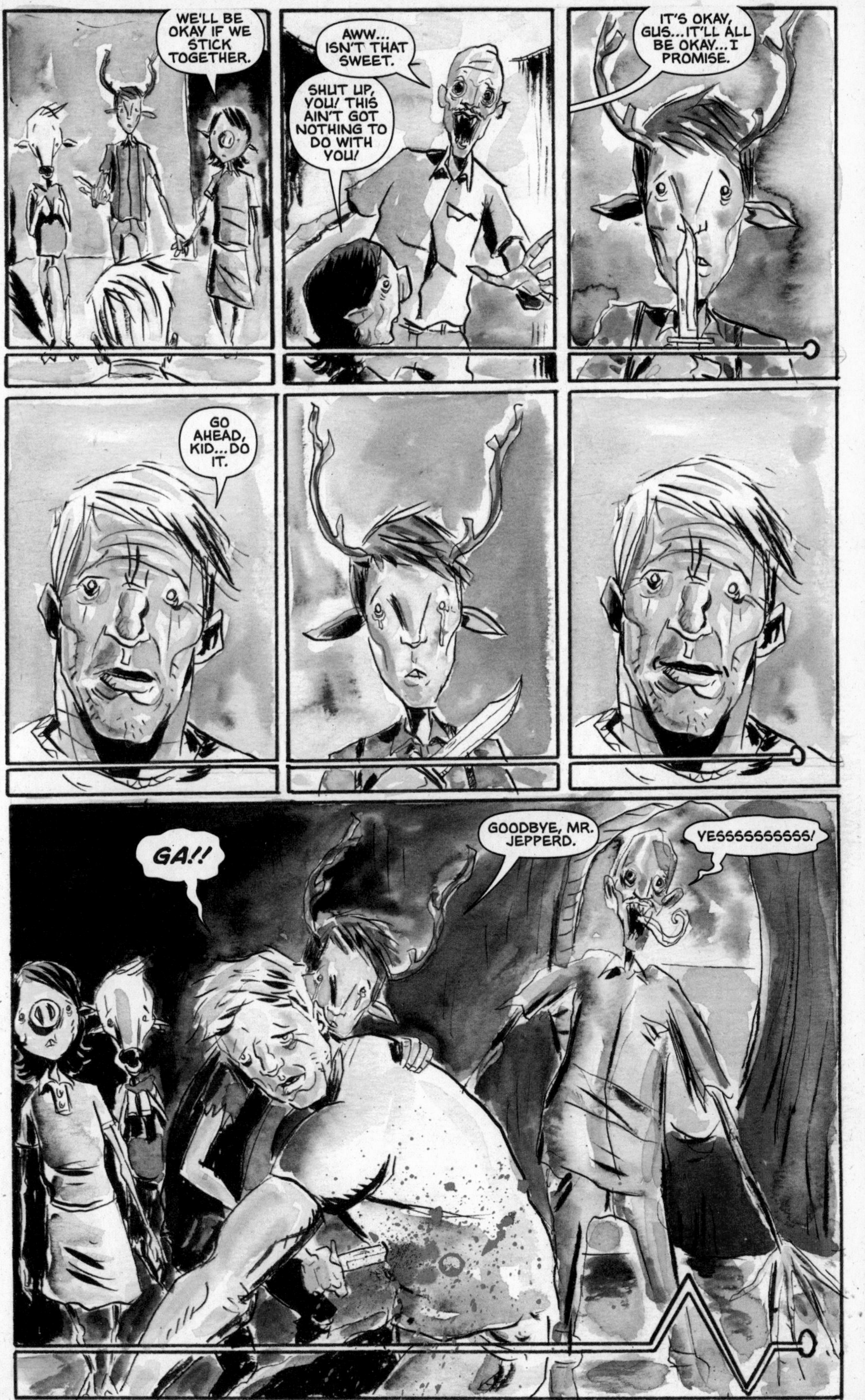
WE'LL BE OKAY IF WE STICK TOGETHER.
AWW... ISN'T THAT SWEET.
SHUT UP, YOU! THIS AIN'T GOT NOTHING TO DO WITH YOU!
IT'S OKAY, GUS...IT'LL ALL BE OKAY...I PROMISE.
GO AHEAD, KID...DO IT.
GA!!
GOODBYE, MR. JEPPERD.
YESSSSSSSSSSS!

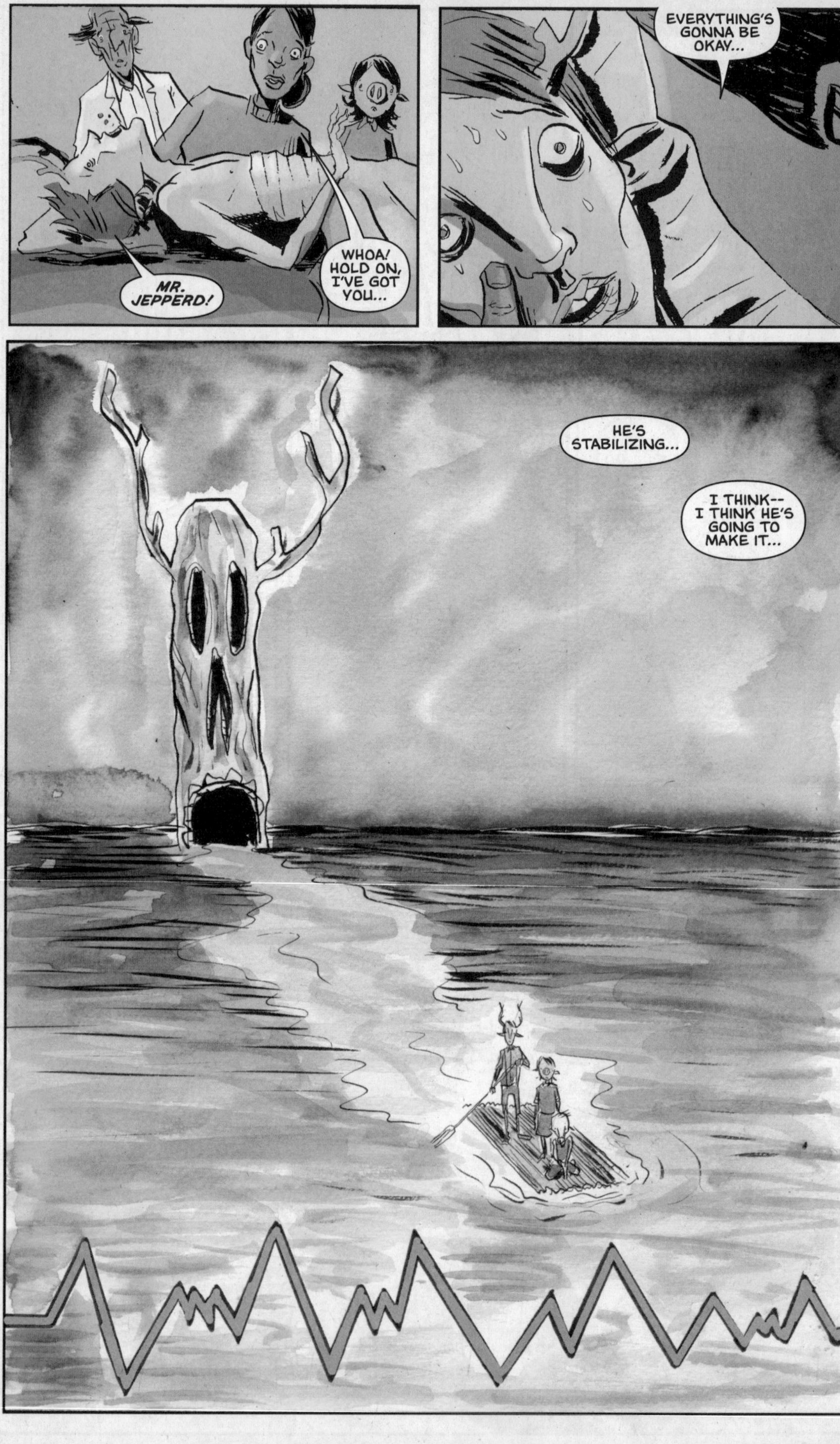
MR. JEPPERD!
WHOA! HOLD ON, I'VE GOT YOU...
EVERYTHING'S GONNA BE OKAY...
HE'S STABILIZING...
I THINK-- I THINK HE'S GOING TO MAKE IT...

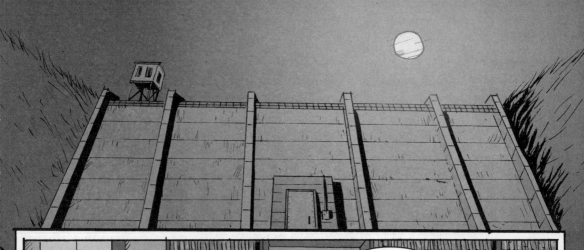

HOW IS HE?

HE'S SLEEPING. WE NEED TO LET HIM REST.

... ALL RIGHT, WHAT'S GOING ON?

WE'VE BEEN TALKING, JEPPERD...AND WE'VE ALL COME TO A DECISION.

WE WANT TO STAY.

SO, I GUESS YOU HAVE A CHOICE...EITHER YOU STOP THIS INSANE THING YOU HAVE FOR WALTER, STOP WITH THE ACCUSATIONS AND THE ATTACKS...

AND WE ALL STOP RUNNING, WE STAY HERE... OR YOU LEAVE.

YOU CAN'T TELL ME YOU ACTUALLY BELIEVE THIS LITTLE WEASEL!

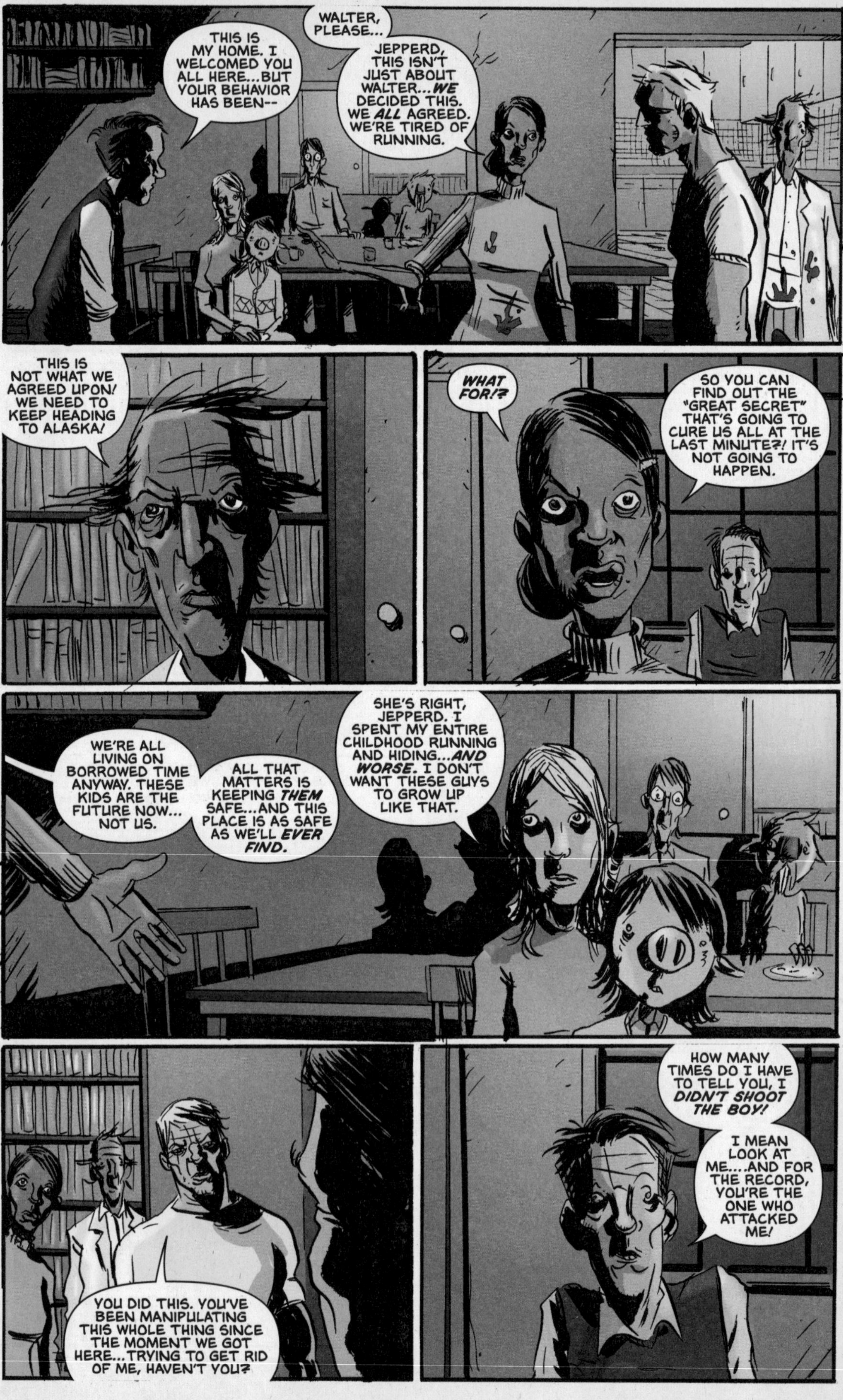
THIS IS MY HOME. I WELCOMED YOU ALL HERE...BUT YOUR BEHAVIOR HAS BEEN--
WALTER, PLEASE...
JEPPERD, THIS ISN'T JUST ABOUT WALTER...WE DECIDED THIS. WE ALL AGREED. WE'RE TIRED OF RUNNING.
THIS IS NOT WHAT WE AGREED UPON! WE NEED TO KEEP HEADING TO ALASKA!
WHAT FOR!?
SO YOU CAN FIND OUT THE "GREAT SECRET" THAT'S GOING TO CURE US ALL AT THE LAST MINUTE?! IT'S NOT GOING TO HAPPEN.
WE'RE ALL LIVING ON BORROWED TIME ANYWAY. THESE KIDS ARE THE FUTURE NOW... NOT US.
ALL THAT MATTERS IS KEEPING THEM SAFE...AND THIS PLACE IS AS SAFE AS WE'LL EVER FIND.
SHE'S RIGHT, JEPPERD. I SPENT MY ENTIRE CHILDHOOD RUNNING AND HIDING...AND WORSE. I DON'T WANT THESE GUYS TO GROW UP LIKE THAT.
YOU DID THIS. YOU'VE BEEN MANIPULATING THIS WHOLE THING SINCE THE MOMENT WE GOT HERE...TRYING TO GET RID OF ME, HAVEN'T YOU?
HOW MANY TIMES DO I HAVE TO TELL YOU, I DIDN'T SHOOT THE BOY!
I MEAN LOOK AT ME....AND FOR THE RECORD, YOU'RE THE ONE WHO ATTACKED ME!

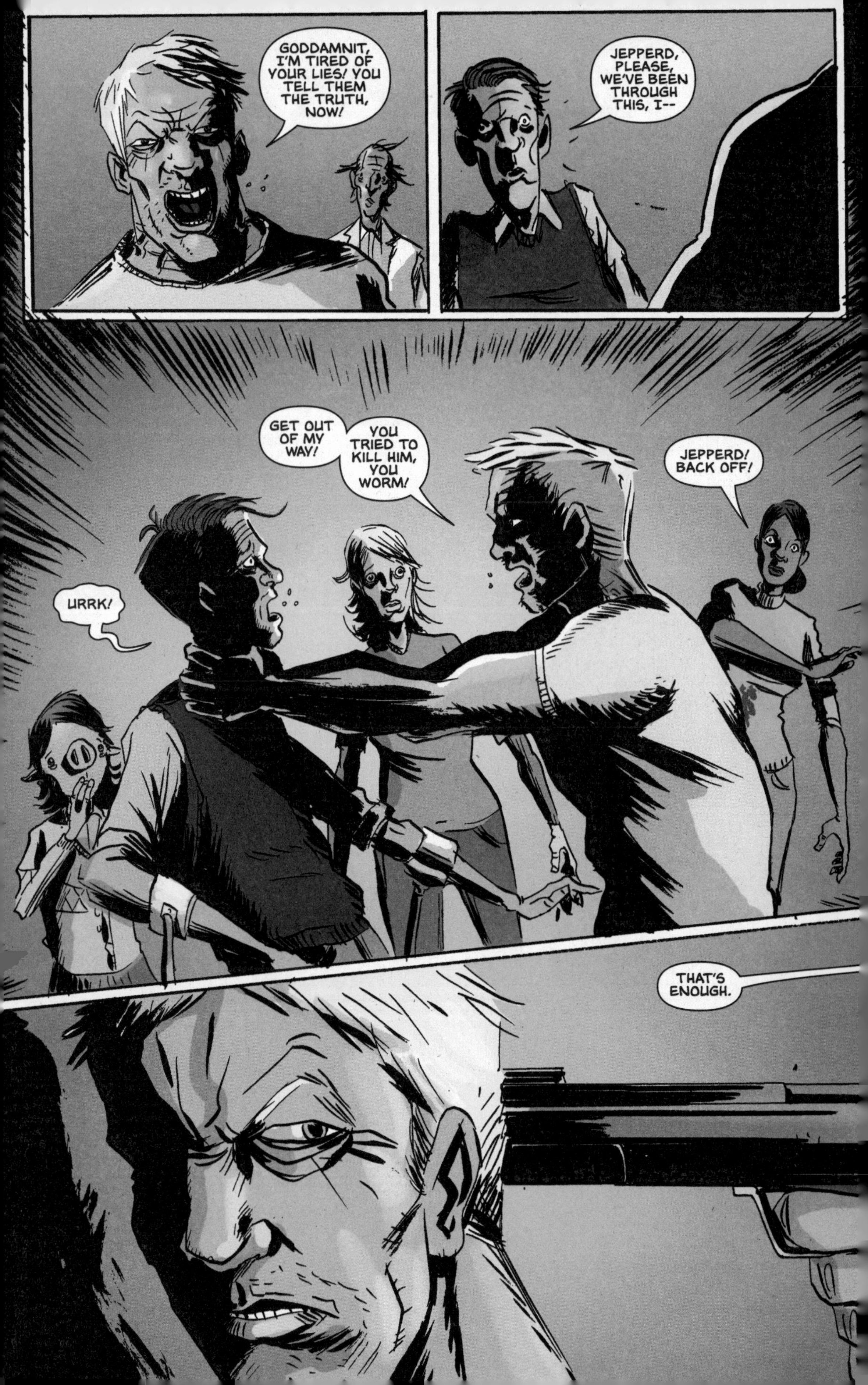
GODDAMNIT, I'M TIRED OF YOUR LIES! YOU TELL THEM THE TRUTH, NOW!
JEPPERD, PLEASE, WE'VE BEEN THROUGH THIS, I--
GET OUT OF MY WAY!
YOU TRIED TO KILL HIM, YOU WORM!
JEPPERD! BACK OFF!
URRK!
THAT'S ENOUGH.

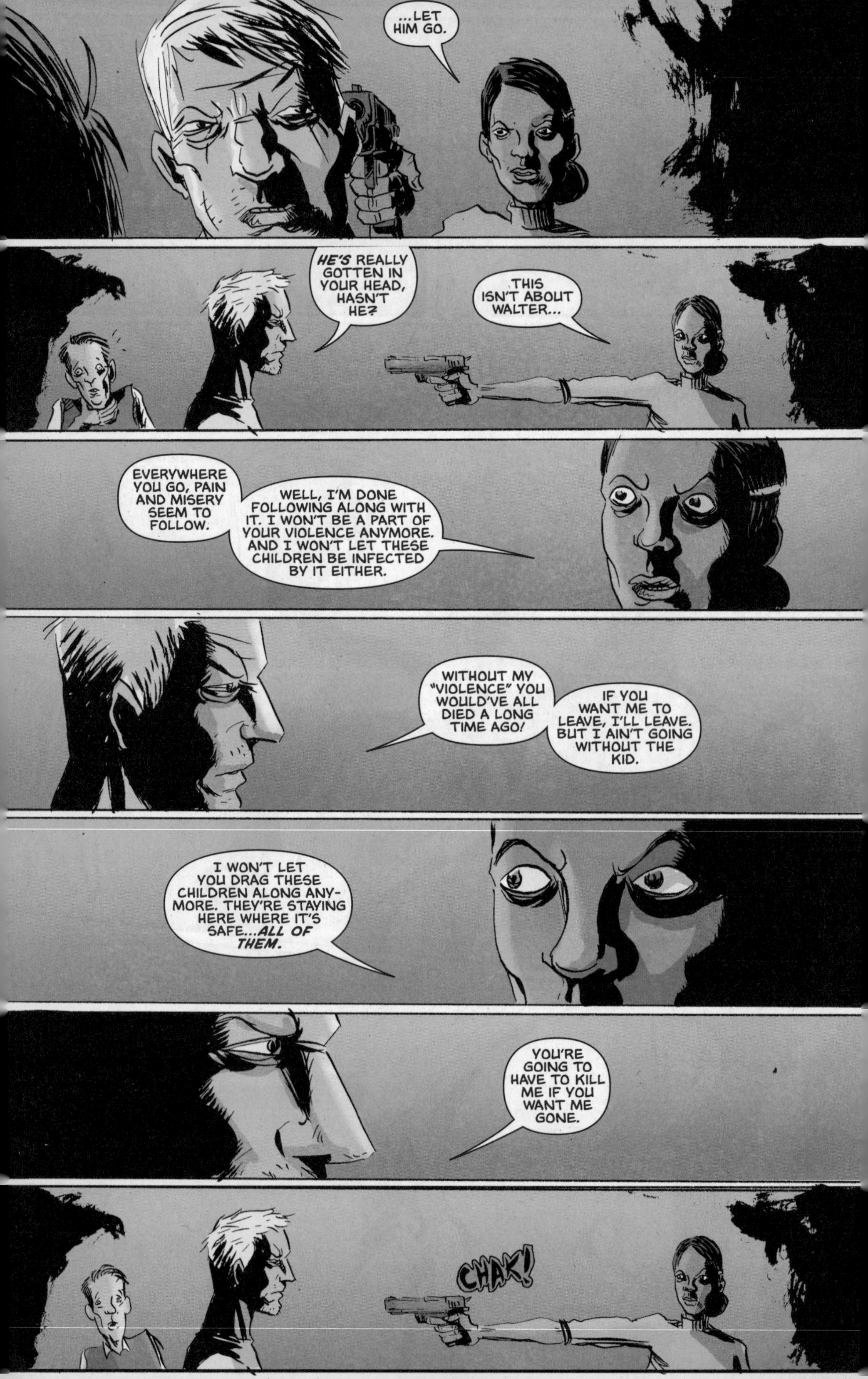
...LET HIM GO.
HE'S REALLY GOTTEN IN YOUR HEAD, HASN'T HE?
THIS ISN'T ABOUT WALTER...
EVERYWHERE YOU GO, PAIN AND MISERY SEEM TO FOLLOW.
WELL, I'M DONE FOLLOWING ALONG WITH IT. I WON'T BE A PART OF YOUR VIOLENCE ANYMORE. AND I WON'T LET THESE CHILDREN BE INFECTED BY IT EITHER.
WITHOUT MY "VIOLENCE" YOU WOULD'VE ALL DIED A LONG TIME AGO!
IF YOU WANT ME TO LEAVE, I'LL LEAVE. BUT I AIN'T GOING WITHOUT THE KID.
I WON'T LET YOU DRAG THESE CHILDREN ALONG ANY-MORE. THEY'RE STAYING HERE WHERE IT'S SAFE...ALL OF THEM.
YOU'RE GOING TO HAVE TO KILL ME IF YOU WANT ME GONE.
CHAK!

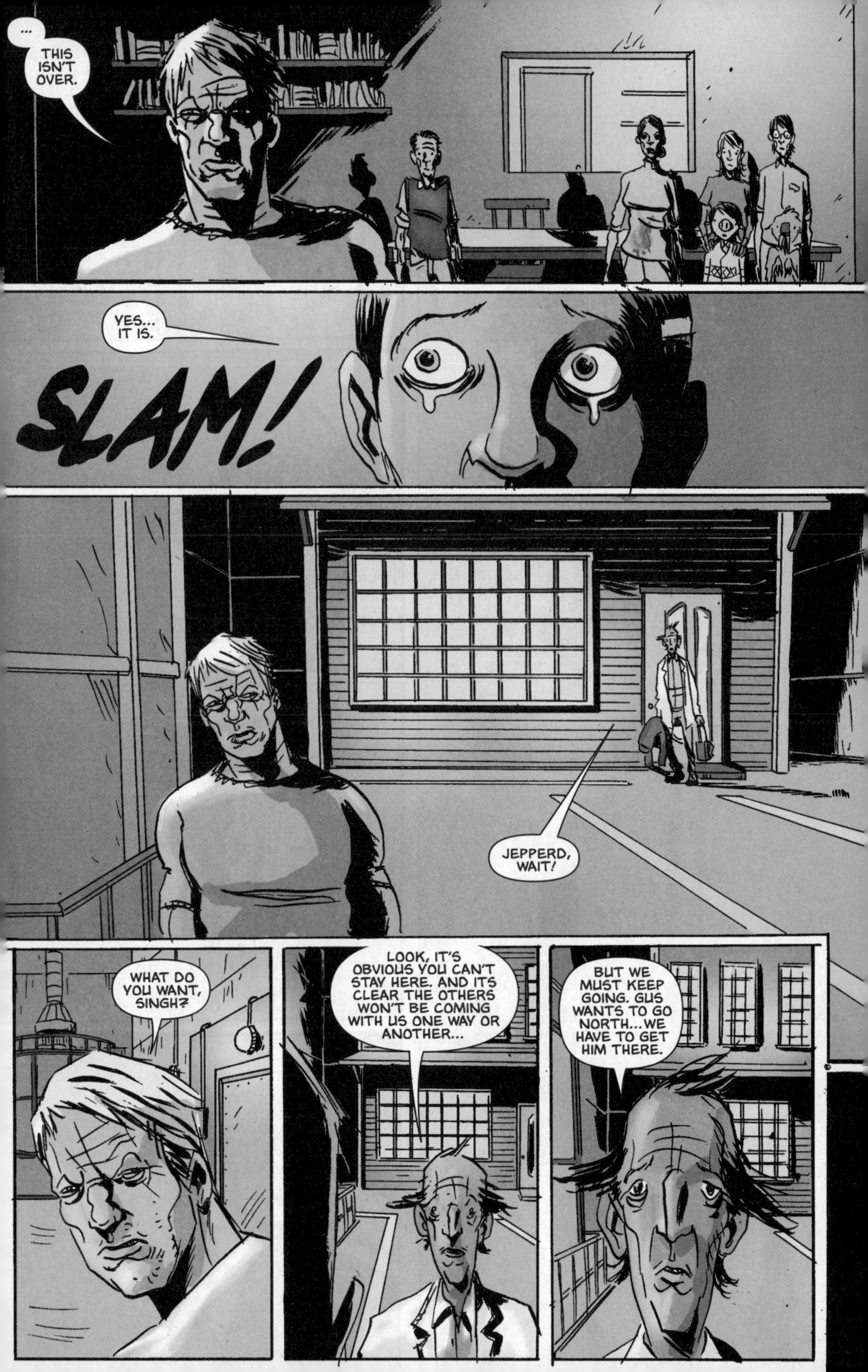
...
THIS ISN'T OVER.
YES... IT IS.
SLAM!
JEPPERD, WAIT!
WHAT DO YOU WANT, SINGH?
LOOK, IT'S OBVIOUS YOU CAN'T STAY HERE. AND ITS CLEAR THE OTHERS WON'T BE COMING WITH US ONE WAY OR ANOTHER...
BUT WE MUST KEEP GOING. GUS WANTS TO GO NORTH...WE HAVE TO GET HIM THERE.

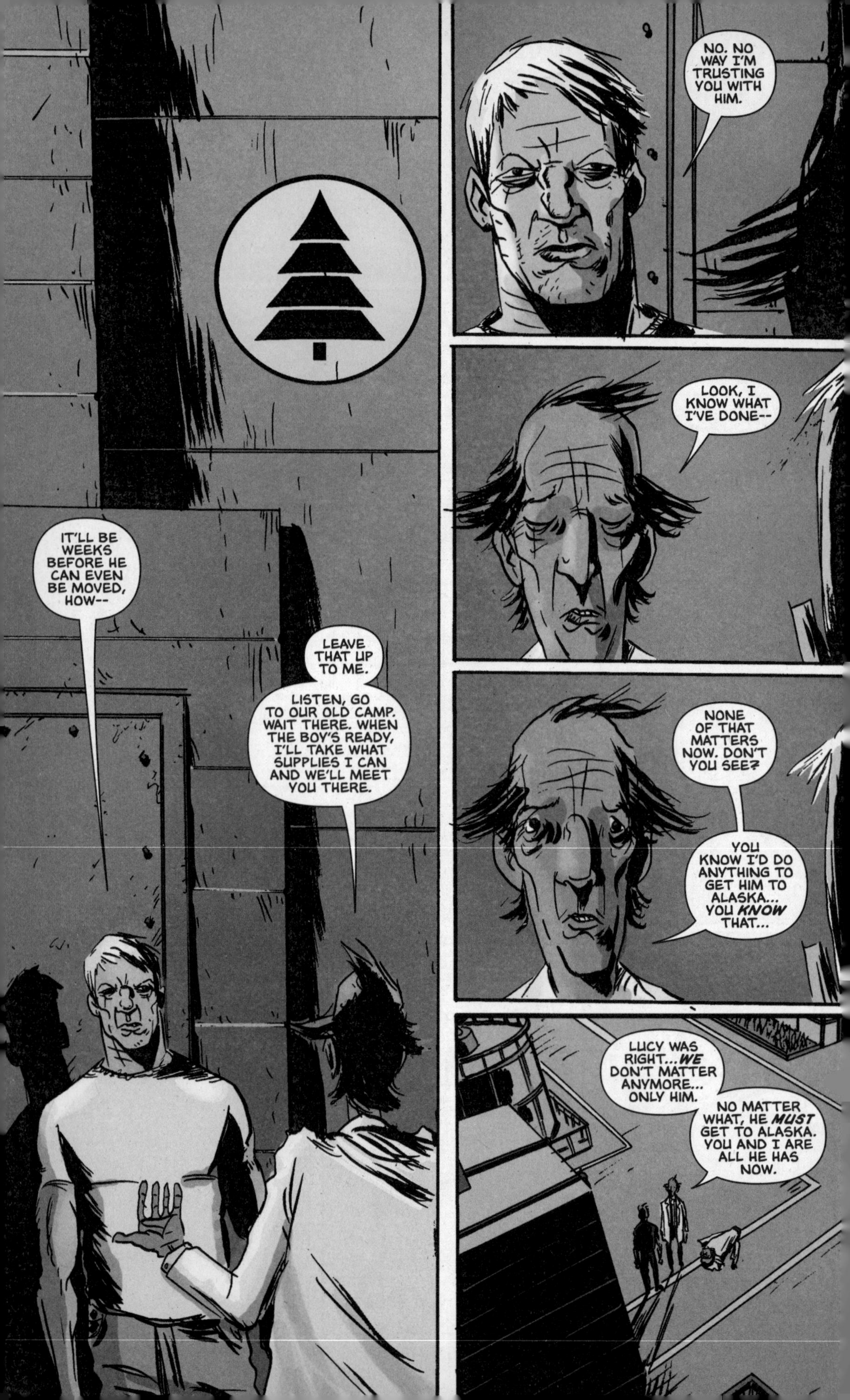
IT'LL BE WEEKS BEFORE HE CAN EVEN BE MOVED, HOW--
LEAVE THAT UP TO ME.
LISTEN, GO TO OUR OLD CAMP. WAIT THERE. WHEN THE BOY'S READY, I'LL TAKE WHAT SUPPLIES I CAN AND WE'LL MEET YOU THERE.
NO. NO WAY I'M TRUSTING YOU WITH HIM.
LOOK, I KNOW WHAT I'VE DONE--
NONE OF THAT MATTERS NOW. DON'T YOU SEE?
YOU KNOW I'D DO ANYTHING TO GET HIM TO ALASKA... YOU *KNOW* THAT...
LUCY WAS RIGHT... *WE* DON'T MATTER ANYMORE... ONLY HIM.
NO MATTER WHAT, HE *MUST* GET TO ALASKA. YOU AND I ARE ALL HE HAS NOW.

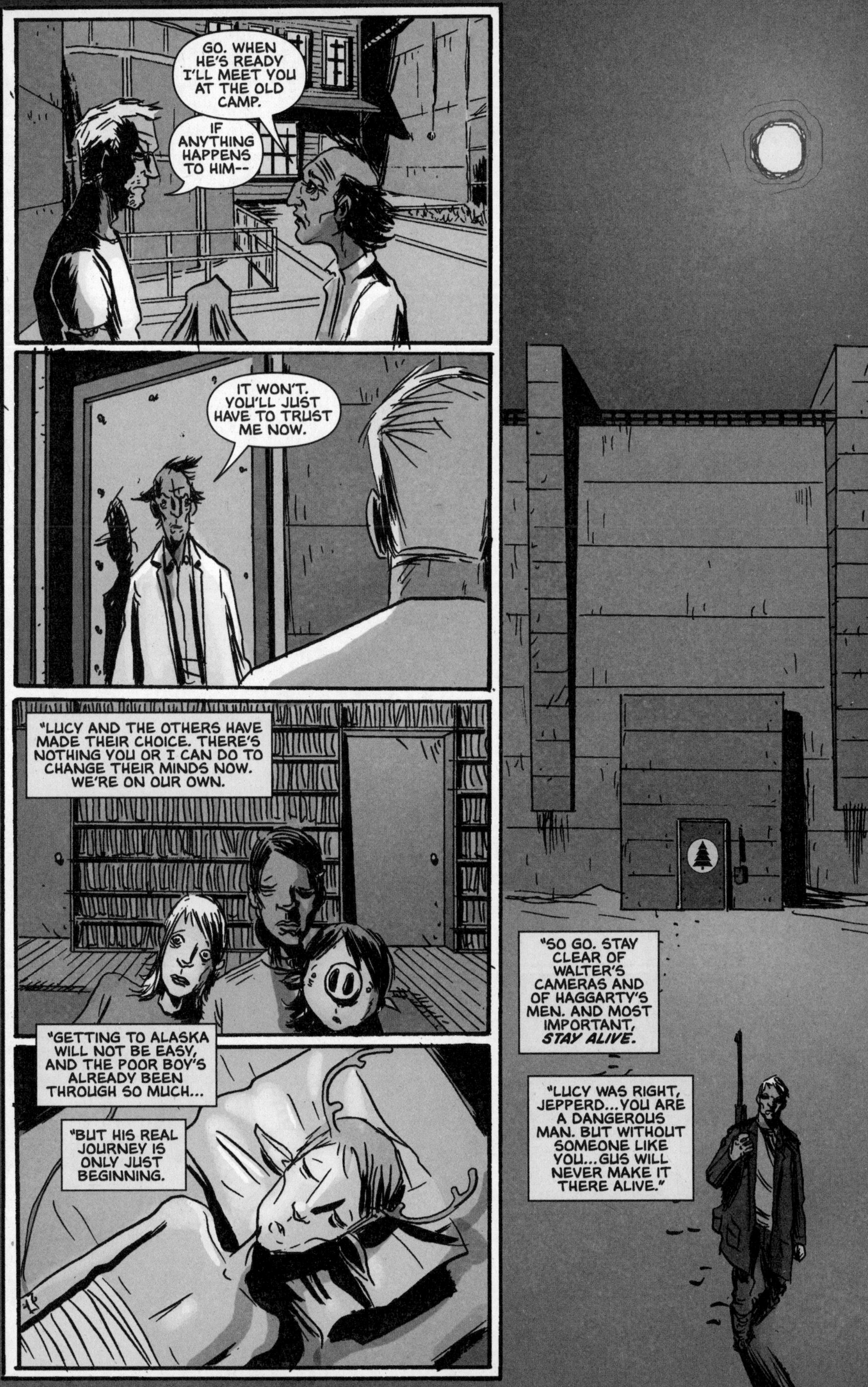
GO. WHEN HE'S READY I'LL MEET YOU AT THE OLD CAMP.
IF ANYTHING HAPPENS TO HIM--
IT WON'T. YOU'LL JUST HAVE TO TRUST ME NOW.
"LUCY AND THE OTHERS HAVE MADE THEIR CHOICE. THERE'S NOTHING YOU OR I CAN DO TO CHANGE THEIR MINDS NOW. WE'RE ON OUR OWN.
"GETTING TO ALASKA WILL NOT BE EASY, AND THE POOR BOY'S ALREADY BEEN THROUGH SO MUCH...
"BUT HIS REAL JOURNEY IS ONLY JUST BEGINNING.
"SO GO. STAY CLEAR OF WALTER'S CAMERAS AND OF HAGGARTY'S MEN. AND MOST IMPORTANT, *STAY ALIVE*.
"LUCY WAS RIGHT, JEPPERD...YOU ARE A DANGEROUS MAN. BUT WITHOUT SOMEONE LIKE YOU...GUS WILL NEVER MAKE IT THERE ALIVE."

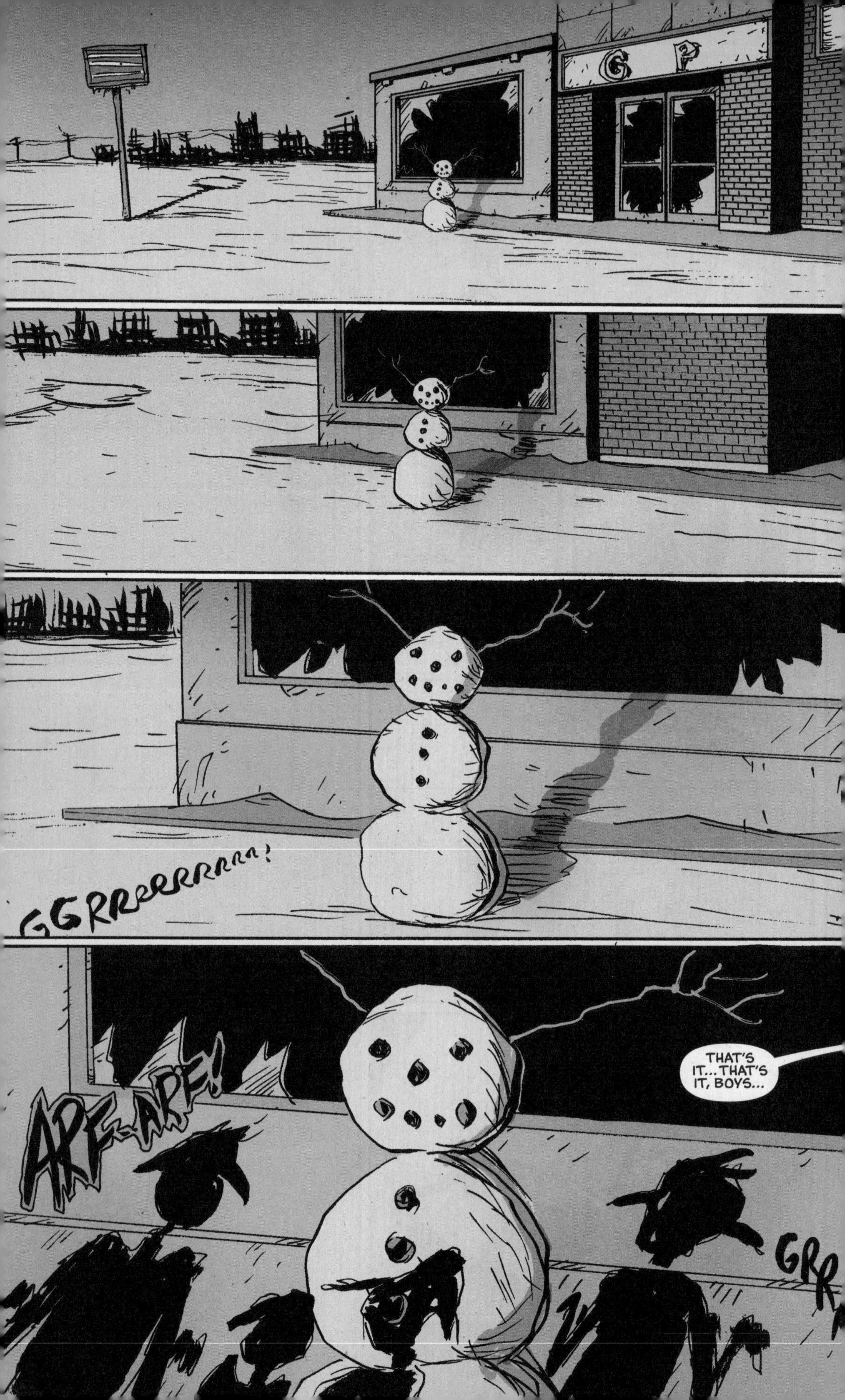
GGRRRRRRRRR!
ARF-ARF!
THAT'S IT... THAT'S IT, BOYS...
GRR

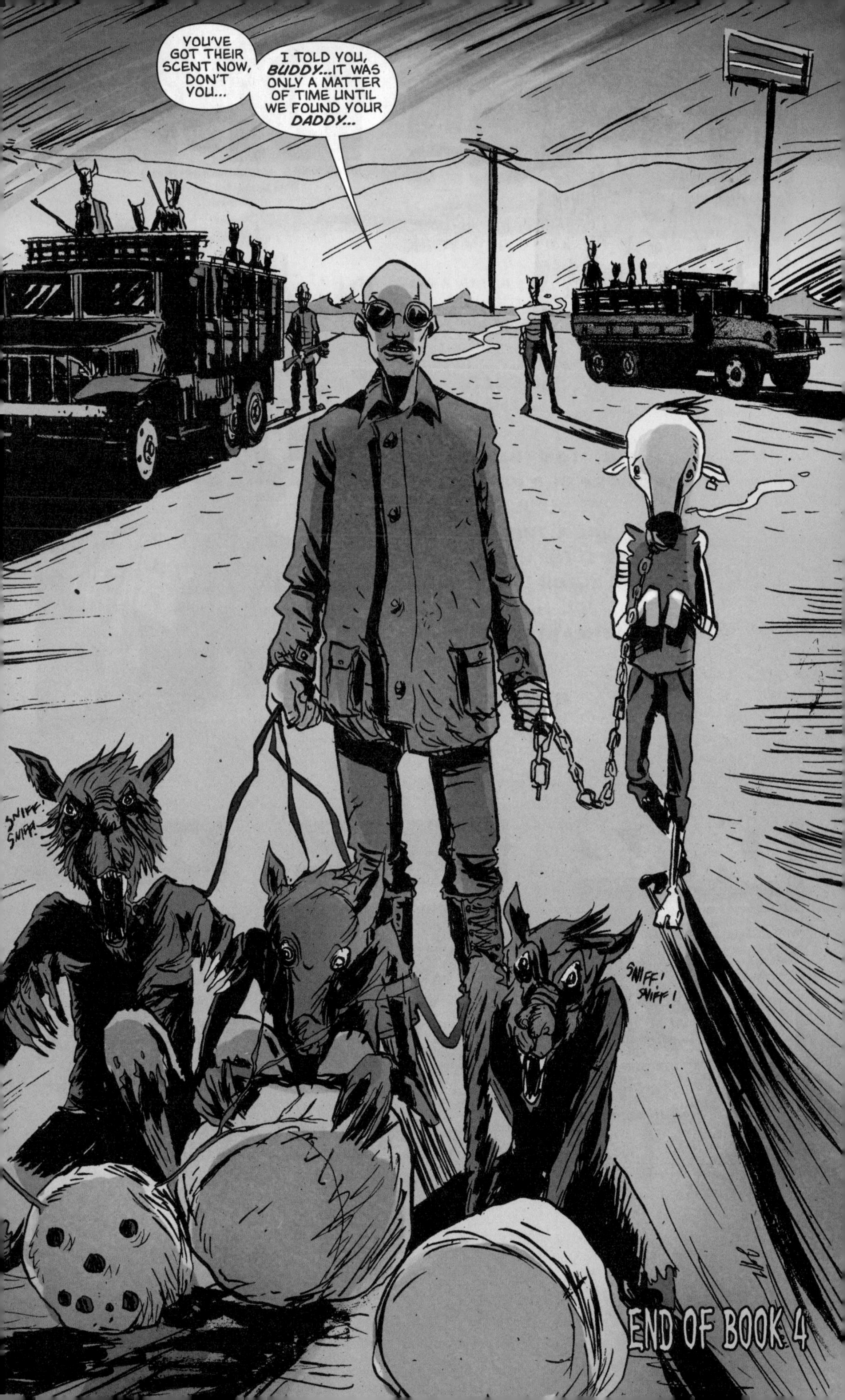
YOU'VE GOT THEIR SCENT NOW, DON'T YOU...
I TOLD YOU, *BUDDY*...IT WAS ONLY A MATTER OF TIME UNTIL WE FOUND YOUR *DADDY*...
SNIFF! SNIFF!
SNIFF! SNIFF!
END OF BOOK 4

FROM INDIE COMICS SENSATION

BRIAN WOOD

...er blockbuster."
...T NEW YORK

and ...he nightly news,
... . GRADE: A-"
– ENTERTAINMENT WEEKLY

"One of the strongest ongoing series to come
out of DC's Vertigo line in some time. GRADE: A-"
– THE ONION

VOL. 1: ON THE GROUND
VOL. 2: BODY OF A JOURNALIST
VOL. 3: PUBLIC WORKS
VOL. 4: FRIENDLY FIRE
VOL. 5: THE HIDDEN WAR
VOL. 6: BLOOD IN THE GAME
VOL. 7: WAR POWERS
VOL. 8: HEARTS AND MINDS

DMZ VOL. 2:
BODY OF A JOURNALIST

DMZ VOL. 3:
PUBLIC WORKS

DMZ VOL. 4:
FRIENDLY FIRE

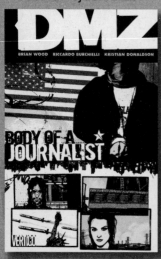

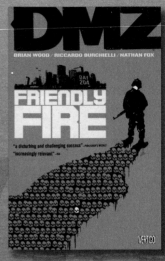

GO TO
VERTIGOBOOKS.COM
FOR FREE SAMPLES OF THE FIRST ISSUES OF OUR GRAPHIC NOVELS

Suggested for Mature Readers